Carl Zuckmayer

THE DEVIL'S GENERAL

Sebastian Haffner

GERMANY:
JEKYLL AND HYDE

The German Library: Volume 80

Volkmar Sander, General Editor

Carl Zuckmayer

THE DEVIL'S GENERAL

Sebastian Haffner

GERMANY: JEKYLL AND HYDE

Edited by Volkmar Sander

CONTINUUM

NEW YORK · LONDON

2005

The Continuum International Publishing Group Inc
15 East 26 Street, New York, NY 10010

The Continuum International Publishing Group Ltd
The Tower Building, 11 York Road, London SE1 7NX

The German Library is published in cooperation with Deutsches Haus,
New York University.

This volume has been supported by Inter Nationes,
and by a grant from the funds of
Stifterverband für die Deutsche Wissenschaft.

Printed in the United States of America

Library of Congress Cataloging-in-Publication Data

Zuckmayer, Carl, 1896–1977.
  [Des Teufels General. English.]
  The devil's general / Carl Zuckmayer. Germany—Jekyll and Hyde /
Sebastian Haffner.
    p. cm. — (The German library ; v. 80)
  The Devil's General is an abridged translation, and Germany— Jekyll and
Hyde is excerpted here.—Publisher's info.
  Includes bibliographical references and index.
  ISBN 0-8264-1719-1 (hardcover : alk. paper) — ISBN 0-8264-1720-5
(pbk. : alk. paper) 1. National socialism. 2. Germany—Politics and
government—1933–1945. 3. Europe—Politics and government—1918–
1945. 4. Hitler, Adolf, 1889–1945. 5. World War, 1939–1945. I.
Haffner, Sebastian. Germany—Jekyll and Hyde. Selections II. Komar,
Ingrid. III. Wurdak, Virginia. IV. David, Wilfrid. V. Title. VI. Series.
PT2653.U33T4213   2005
832'.912—dc22   2005010386

The publisher gratefully acknowledges permission to reprint *Des Teufels General*
(*The Devil's General*, translated by Ingrid Kolmar) by Carl Zuckmayer © Bermann
Fischer Verlag A.B. Stockholm 1946. All rights reserved by S. Fischer Verlag GmbH,
Frankfurt am Main.

Contents

Introduction

When the French speak about *La Grande Guerre* they are referring to World War I, even today. It was the first real total war in history, which more and more eliminated the boundaries between military front and peaceful homeland, a boundary which heretofore had been more or less respected. The breach of international law—the German invasion into neutral Belgium—the crimes against the civilian population, the use of poison gas, and especially the enormous loss of lives on all sides made a great impression, lasting to this day, on a population used to a long peace and great progress. The British philosopher Bertrand Russell coined at the time the cynical phrase "war aim was maximum slaughter at minimum expense." Especially at the Eastern Front—Winston Churchill had called it "the unknown war"—German troops behaved abominably. They believed themselves to be on a higher level of civilization and treated the local population with colonial condescension. In front of the eyes of the world the great German *Kulturnation*, whose professors and students had thought of themselves as the vanguard of patriotism, had thoroughly disqualified itself. Then, and not only in 1939, the basis was laid for the important changes in mentality that eventually led to the brutal policy of "Germanization," the slogan of a "necessary" crusade in which even the churches joined. The constellation of 1918–19—the Russian Revolution in the east and the Treaty of Versailles in the west, already provided the groundwork for the later inflamation. Serious historians, not only de Gaulle, look upon the period that started with 1914 therefore as a second Thirty Years' War. In the life of all participating nations, World War I had wrought a deeper change than any other major event since 1789, perhaps even since the radical changes following the Protestant reforms of the sixteenth and seventeenth centuries.

When mentioning the World War, people in the East on the other hand rather think of World War II, of Hitler and Ausschwitz.

A survey of German literature like The German Library would therefore be incomplete without taking note of these two important issues. Perhaps the best-known German novel to come out of World War I is Erich Maria Remarque's *All Quiet on the Western Front,* which is reprinted in volume 68 of this series. The present volume contains two pieces of literature that bear testimony to the disturbing events that were to change German history and have a lasting effect on its population: a play by Carl Zuckmayer and an extended essay on the Germans by Sebastian Haffner. Both were rather popular at the time and both shed some light on the major problems of the period.

Carl Zuckmayer was born in 1896 in Nackenheim near Mainz to well-to-do parents, and the sunny disposition, the close connection with the life and the feelings of the people of that Rhenish wine-producing region never left him. He participated in World War I, briefly studied Natural Science in Heidelberg, and, in 1920, went to Berlin to write for the theater. Although not very successful at first, he soon became directorial assistant at Max Rheinhardt's Deutches Theater, and one of the most sought-after playwrights of the 1920s, his fame rivaling that of his friend Bertolt Brecht at that time. In quick succession, he produced *Der Fröhliche Weinberg* (1925), *Schinderhannes* (1927), and *The Hauptman von Köpenick* (1931). *The Merry Vineyard* is a blunt, realistic comedy, full of life, depicting scenes from his native roots. *Schinderhannes* tells the romanticized adventures of a historical local thief, who took from the rich and gave to the poor, and was eventually hanged by the French. He was a sort of German Robin Hood, except flourishing around the year 1800 and with critical overtones. *The Captain of Köpenick* was perhaps Zuckmayer's greatest success, widely popular at the time, made into several movies and occasionally played even today. Its subtitle is *A German Fairy Tale* and it is the story of a poor shoemaker in Köpenick, a suburb of Berlin, who urgently needs an official stamp in his passport, which he is unable to get in the overwhelming confusion of contradictory offices. Only when he rents a captain's uniform, which he puts on to commandeer a troop of soldiers, is he successful. Of course, he is caught—but the power of imagination and the obedience to authority make him a hero in Kaiser's Germany.

From 1924 to 1928, Zuckmayer lived in Salzburg, Austria. When the Nazis came to power in 1933 his works were immediately banned. In 1939 he emigrated to the United States, became a U.S. citizen and lived on a farm in Vermont. He returned to Germany in American uniform after the War and eventually settled in Saas Fee, Switzerland, where he died in 1977. Throughout all these years he continued to write, mainly plays, but also poems, essays, some novellas and, most noteworthy, an autobiography *Als wär's ein Stück von mir* (1946), actually a line from a song of camaraderie often sung at funerals. Other better-known plays were *Katharina Knie* (1928), *Der Schelm von Bergen* (1934), *Bellmann* (1938. Later as *Ulla Windblatt*), *Der Gesang im Feuerofen* (1950), and *Das Kalte Licht* (1925).

Astonishingly enough, *The Devil's General* was written in exile (1942–48) and premiered in 1946. It soon became very popular in Germany, and was eventually made into a film with Curd Jürgens playing the lead. The figure of General Harras was based on the historic Hans Udet, one of the three so-called Flying Aces of World War I. The others were Manfred von Richthofen, the famous "Red Baron," who died, and Hermann Göring, who later became the second-in-command after Hitler and founder of the Luftwaffe. Here we have the rather straightforward story of a fundamentally decent man who follows his obsession with flying, belatedly comes to his senses, realizes what havoc his services have wrought and, old-fashioned hero that he is, takes the rather simple way out by committing suicide. As if doing the "honorable" thing were any solution for a political problem. On the one hand, to explain the great seduction in this way accounts for the enormous success of the play in postwar Germany, especially with the people who also claimed just to have been misled. On the other hand, it brings up the more universal problem of that time, that of the possibility, or perhaps necessity, of treason. For half a billion Europeans of various nations, the first half of the century posed that question of loyalty. Loyalty to whom? To oneself? To the state? Guilt by association, treason, the power and limits of government, freedom of thought, moral questions of human rights (or dropping bombs) plagued citizens of one state or another. Sheer revulsion of the baseness of Nazi ideology and action determine Zuckmayer's General Harras's decision to take his own life. Oderbruch's attitude is more complex. It, too, will cost him his life, but it shows more of the moral dilemma. The real problem was later stated in Dürrenmatt's essay on "Problems of the Theater": "The world today as it appears to us can hardly be encompassed in the form of the historical drama as Schiller wrote it, for the simple reason that we no longer have any tragic heroes, but only vast tragedies staged by world butchers and produced by slaughtering machines. Hitler and Stalin cannot be made into Wallensteins" (i.e., Schiller's tragic figure of his Thirty Years' War trilogy, cf. The German Library, volume 16 and Dürrenmatt in volume 89), and, we might add, a Harras cannot be made into a Richard III. This rupture with our old personality cult was to be depicted later on in a number of German works such as Günter Grass's *The Tin Drum* (1962), Heiner Kipphardt's *In the Case of Robert Oppenheimer* (1964), and Dürrenmatt's *The Physicists* (1963). (Cf. The German Library, volumes 89, 93, and 96.) The abridged translation used here is that done by Ingrid Komar, which was approved by Zuckmayer himself. Some of the additions that were left out of the original translations are provided by Virginia Wurdak.

The deep horror with which the world viewed Hitler and his deeds was in large part due as we know since Hannah Arendt's memorable "Banality of Evil" phrase, to the fact that the atrocities occurred not in the Gobi Desert or the reaches of the Amazon, but in Germany—a country that, until recently, had been looked upon as being at the forefront of civilization. It had, comparatively, more Nobel Prize winners, schools, theaters, libraries, and museums than any other nation. The reassuring notion that more knowledge, more "culture," more civilization was a safeguard against barbarity had obviously been proved wrong.

Sabastian Haffner's real name was Raimund Pretzel. He was born in Berlin in 1907 to well-to-do parents, went to school there, and eventually studied law. He intended to become a judge, or a higher governmental official like his father, but history intervened. He became a journalist, emigrated to Great Britain, and only returned to Berlin long after the war. It was in England that he wrote his first book: *Germany: Jekyll and Hyde*, the first one under the pen name of Sebastian Haffner, first since he wanted to protect his relatives who were still living in Hitler's Germany, and secondly because he was a music lover: Sebastian (Bach) Haffner (Mozart). In turn, he was: a subject of Kaiser Wilhelm, a citizen of the Weimar Republic, an emigrant from Hitler, a British subject, and a citizen of the Federal Republic of West Germany. As a reporter, he wrote for both right-wing and left-wing journals and remained controversial all his life. Also, his life was tightly connected with the most important events of the last century, and this fact, as well as his talent for writing, caused him to become one of the great analysts. In a way that seemed totally natural, he combined individual features with those caused by history and then provided associations that led to quite astounding and often ingenious insights. "Not everything that ever happens becomes history," he said, only what historians, those tellers of tales, think is noteworthy and thus written down. "Only the writing of history creates history." Hence, according to Haffner, history is not real and fixed for all time, but constantly needs interpretation, it is actually "a branch of literature."

In his desire to interpret history, to explain complex situations to the warring parties, and thus to reconcile them, he became something of a teacher of history. His book on Hitler, *Footnotes to Hitler*, written in 1978, is not long and scholarly, like the two biographies by Alan Bulock or Joachim Fest, but short, eminently readable, and still full of facts and persuasive insights. It was a huge success in West Germany, was a bestseller for many years, and eventually adopted in schools for classroom use. His *Germany: Jekyll and Hyde*, reprinted here was written in 1940 while he was still in a British detention camp as an enemy alien. It was the attempt to explain the two sides of a largely unknown country against which one had to fight. The *London Times* praised it as one of the "best analyses of German mentality." It was well received, so well, that Winston Churchill, as Prime Minister, made the book required reading to the members of his war cabinet.

In 1942 Lord David Astor, owner of the *Observer*, asked Haffner to join his venerable paper as coeditor-in-chief. There he remained, together with George Orwell (*Animal Farm* and *1984*) and Arthur Koestler (*Darkness at Noon, The Yogi and the Commissar*) until 1957, when he went to Berlin as correspondent for Germany. In 1948 he became a British citizen, and in 1978 he again accepted a German passport. During his lifetime he wrote some twenty books, innumerable articles, essays and series. He died in 1999, still controversial, still revered, still a representative of the enlightenment, still a learning teacher.

V.S.

Carl Zuckmayer

The Devil's General

Characters

HARRAS, General of the German Air Force, the Luftwaffe
HANSEN, his aide
KORRIANKE, his driver
FRIEDRICH EILERS, Colonel and leader of a fighter squadron
PFUNDTMAYER, pilot—same age as Harras
HARTMANN, pilot—new generation
WRITZKY ⎱ two pilots
HASTENTEUFFEL ⎰
VON MOHRUNGEN, industrialist, president of the Air Force
   Procurement Office
BARON PFLUNGK, attache of the Foreign Ministry
DR. SCHMIDT-LAUSITZ, Minister of Culture
ODERBRUCH, engineer in the Air Administration
ANNE EILERS, married to Friedrich and daughter of Von
   Mohrungen
POOTSIE VON MOHRUNGEN, her sister
OLIVIA GEISS, opera singer
DIDDO GEISS, her niece
LYRA SCHOEPPKE, another singer
OTTO, restaurant owner
FRANÇOIS ⎱ waiters
DETLEV ⎰
BUDDY LAWRENCE, an American journalist
FIRST WORKER
SECOND WORKER

A Police Detective
An SS Guard
An Air Force Guard

Place: Berlin
Time: Late 1941, shortly before America's entry into the war.

Act 1

(A PRIVATE DINING ROOM IN OTTO'S RESTAURANT. CONSERVA-
TIVE—"OLD GERMAN"—FURNISHINGS. IN THE MIDDLE, A SUMPTU-
OUS BUFFET TABLE FOR ABOUT FIFTEEN PEOPLE. WHEN THE
CURTAIN RISES, FRANÇOIS AND HERR DETLEV BEGIN TO LIGHT A
GREAT MANY CANDLES IN SILVER CANDELABRA ON THE TABLE AND
WALLS. THEY ARE ALSO PUTTING THE FINISHING TOUCHES TO THE
TABLE DECORATIONS. ALL WINDOWS ARE COVERED WITH THICK
BLACK CURTAINS)

DETLEV: What time is it?
FRANÇOIS: Quarter to midnight.
DETLEV: Gonna be a long night.
FRANÇOIS: *C'est la vie.*
DETLEV: When General Harras decides to live it up, you can count
on a few being out of the running by sunrise.
FRANÇOIS: What are you doing? No port! Harras starts off with an
Armagnac! Double!
DETLEV: How do you know, sweetheart?
FRANÇOIS: I know the General. He comes from the Reich-
schancery—a very official reception. *Donc*—he needs stronger
stuff than the port. Logical, *n'est-ce pas?*
DETLEV: It figures. When Harras has gazed his Führer in the eye, he
needs an internal wash.
FRANÇOIS: (GLANCING OVER THE PLATTERS OF FOOD) Thank God
for the occupied countries. We serve nothing but the fruits of victory. *Voilà:* the hors d'oeuvres—from Norway. The lobster—
from Ostende. The goose liver—from Poland. The cheese—from
Holland. The butter—from Denmark. And the fresh vegeta-
bles—from Italy. No caviar—from Moscow . . . yet.

DETLEV: But French champagne. Oh, la-la!

FRANÇOIS: Long live collaboration!

OTTO: (APPEARS AT THE DOOR VERY EXCITED) Herr Detlev! François! Where in Heaven are you? How do you expect me to manage with those clumsy greenhorns out there? And especially today, a Reichstag day. Every room crawling with big game.

DETLEV: Begging your pardon, Herr Otto, General Harras requisitioned us expressly for his party.

OTTO: You've got time. Herr Jannings is screaming for his pheasants!

DETLEV: Let him scream! Herr Jannings can kiss my ass!

OTTO: It's unbelievable! For the last time, are you going to help over there—or not?

FRANÇOIS: Remember your ulcer, Otto. Breathe deeply.

DETLEV: Give Auntie a little kiss, François.

OTTO: Herr Detlev—if times were different—I would throw you out on the spot. (SCREAMING AND RED AS A LOBSTER) On the spot!

DETLEV: (AMUSED) On the spot. If times were different, of course. (FRANÇOIS LAUGHS)

HARRAS: (FROM OUTSIDE) François! *'N Armagnac! Double!*

FRANÇOIS: *Voilà!* (HE HURRIES OFF WITH THE GLASS)

DETLEV: We'd better unscrew all the light bulbs.

OTTO: What for?

DETLEV: Don't you know—when Harry gets loaded he shoots them down.

OTTO: Leave two or three so he doesn't get mad; he might aim for the candles and hit my mirrors. (HURRIES OUT INTO THE CORRIDOR) A great honor, General, and a pleasure.

(DETLEV IS ALONE IN THE ROOM FOR A MOMENT. IN A FLASH HE OPENS AN INVISIBLE DOOR IN THE WALL PANELING, TURNS ON A DIAL AND CLOSES THE DOOR. HARRAS ENTERS, FOLLOWED BY OTTO. HE IS IN FULL DRESS UNIFORM, BUT HIS BEARING AND MANNER ARE CASUAL, EVEN SOMEWHAT SLOPPY. HE STILL HOLDS THE EMPTY GLASS IN HIS HAND AND A CIGARETTE DANGLES FROM THE CORNER OF HIS MOUTH. HE CAN'T BE OLDER THAN FORTY-FIVE. HIS FACE IS INTELLIGENT, YOUTHFUL, EVEN BOYISH, DESPITE HIS THINNING HAIR. BY NATURE IT IS A GAY FACE, CAREFREE, PLEASANT, AND

A LITTLE MISCHIEVOUS. NOW IT SEEMS TO BE SUFFUSED WITH A PERCEPTIBLE NERVOUS TENSION. HE LOOKS AROUND PROBINGLY)

HARRAS: Well, looks pretty decent. Almost like the good old times.

OTTO: Always good times with us, General. We do the best we can. Except for the mayonnaise.

HARRAS: Don't worry, Otto, anything will taste good to us. We have just come from a beer party with the Führer. Besides, every man in the Luftwaffe has been issued synthetic taste buds.

OTTO: (LAUGHS) Your sense of humor's as sharp as ever.

HARRAS: Ersatz humor, my friend, thistles, chicory and oak leaves. (HOLDS OUT HIS GLASS. FRANÇOIS FILLS IT) Listen, there's something ticking in here.

OTTO: Ticking? Where, General?

HARRAS: Keep quiet . . . There.

OTTO: I can't hear anything—but, then, maybe—a little hum—

DETLEV: Must be the fan, General, or the heat. You save on coal: then your pipes drip.

OTTO: Well now—there has never been any dripping in the pipes, if you please, Herr Detlev.

HARRAS: Seems to come from somewhere in this wall. Could be the pipes after all. Unless, of course, it's a time bomb.

DETLEV: That's it! A time bomb. (LAUGHS)

(DURING THE LAST FEW PHRASES SEVERAL GENTLEMEN HAVE APPEARED AT THE DOOR IN THE BACKGROUND. AT FIRST THEY'RE ONLY HALF VISIBLE. THEN THERE IS GREAT ACTIVITY IN THE ENTRANCE; EACH WANTS TO CONCEDE TO THE OTHER. THEY ARE: MOHRUNGEN, COLONEL EILERS, BARON PFLUNGK, DOCTOR SCHMIDT-LAUSITZ, HANSEN. THEY PRESS AROUND THE DOORWAY MURMURING COURTESIES SUCH AS:

"After you, Mohrungen,"
"But my dear Eilers, you, the guest of honor."
"Please, Doctor."
"Out of the question, the military first."
"Come, Baron."
"No, no. I'm at home here.")

HARRAS: (HAS WATCHED THE SCENE WITH A BIG GRIN) Who said there are no manners left in Germany. Hansen! Doff that helmet in reverence! There are lobsters present!

HANSEN: (A SMALL JOVIAL, POODLELIKE RUBBER BALL OF A MAN IN
THE UNIFORM OF A CAPTAIN BREAKS THROUGH THE GROUP AND
STORMS THE TABLE) Well then—to hell with formalities. To the
attack! Le'me at them red devils! (HE BEGINS TO EAT WITHOUT
FURTHER ADO)

(THE OTHER GENTLEMEN ENTER WITHOUT FURTHER COMPLICA-
TIONS: VON MOHRUNGEN AND BARON PFLUNGK IN TAILS, DOCTOR
SCHMIDT-LAUSITZ IN PARTY UNIFORM, COLONEL EILERS IN FANCY
DRESS UNIFORM WITH MANY IMPRESSIVE MEDALS. MOHRUNGEN, A
GOOD-LOOKING MAN OF ABOUT FIFTY WITH GREY TEMPLES, REPRE-
SENTATIVE OF THE UPPER CLASS OF HEAVY INDUSTRY. HIS JUNKER-
LIKE CONSERVATIVE OUTLOOK IS SUBDUED BY A SOUTHERN GER-
MAN NATURALNESS . . . BARON PFLUNGK, AN ELEGANT GREYHOUND
WITH SMOOTH MANNERS, COMPLETELY WITHOUT CHARACTER . . .
DOCTOR SCHMIDT-LAUSITZ, A NARROW FOREHEAD WITH FLASHING
EYE GLASSES, BEHIND THEM CLOSE-SET EYES, BARELY VISIBLE, THIN
BLOND HAIR, IN "REGULATION" OUTFIT, TIGHT-LIPPED, HIS POS-
TURE AND BEARING STIFF TO THE POINT OF EXAGGERATION . . .
COLONEL EILERS, NOT OLDER THAN THIRTY-FIVE. DARK HAIR, TALL,
WEATHER-TANNED FEATURES, AVERAGE EXCEPT FOR AN UNUSUAL
SERIOUSNESS WHICH GIVES HIM SOMETIMES AN ABSENT, ALMOST
SAD EXPRESSION)

OTTO: (SOMEWHAT UNCERTAIN) Heil Hit—Good evening, von
Mohrungen. Good eve—Heil Hitler, Doctor.

HARRAS: Just say, "Good Adolf" or "Heil Evening." That will suit
everybody. (TO THE OTHERS) I think we all know each other. This
is our Minister of Culture, Doctor Schmidt-Lausitz, from the
Propaganda Ministry.

LAUSITZ: I do not wish to intrude, General. I see—this is a private
gathering. I only came along because I have to talk over a few
details with Baron Pflungk and Colonel Eilers concerning the
foreign press conference tomorrow and the shortwave broadcast
to America.

HARRAS: Stay, relax, Doctor. You've heard about my bad jokes already, I am sure. They are all entered in my personal file at Gestapo Headquarters.

LAUSITZ: (WITH A SOUR SMILE) A joke's permissible, General, if it
doesn't go too far.

HARRAS: Let Himmler be our judge. Fortify yourselves, gentlemen! You need it after you have nipped from the Holy Grail at the Reichschancery.

MOHRUNGEN: My Lord, this almost looks like peacetime. Why it warms my heart.

HANSEN: (EATING) And the pit of the stomach. Very much to your health, von Mohrungen.

HARRAS: Well, it isn't every day we can have a feast. But when Friedrich Eilers has his big night then it must rain manna in the desert—excuse the non-Aryan comparison, Dr. Lausitz. Help yourself, Eilers.

EILERS: (SMILING, A LITTLE EMBARRASSED) You do me too much honor, General.

OTTO: All ration-free goods, gentlemen, reserved for young heroes and old fighters.

MOHRUNGEN: Now I see how provincial I have become. Lobsters. Midnight supper. At home in Mannheim, everyone is in bed by eleven.

HARRAS: Fill'em up, François. Here come the ladies.

(MRS. ANNE EILERS AND HER SISTER, MISS VON MOHRUNGEN, CALLED "POOTSIE," COME FRESHLY MADE-UP FROM THE POWDER ROOM. BOTH ARE IN EVENING GOWNS: ANNE EILERS ELEGANT BUT SIMPLE, "POOTSIE" VERY ELEGANT BUT SOMEWHAT SHRILL. ANNE IS A BEAUTIFUL TALL WOMAN IN HER MIDDLE TWENTIES WITH A QUIET, SOMEWHAT DISINTERESTED EXPRESSION WHICH ONLY TAKES ON LIFE AND WARMTH WHEN IT FALLS ON HER HUSBAND. "POOTSIE," A FEW YEARS YOUNGER, HAS A PROVOCATIVELY GOOD FIGURE AND AN ALMOST TOO PRETTY DOLL-LIKE FACE WITH A TOUCH OF VULGARITY AND RESTLESS, INSATIABLE EYES)

HARRAS: (INTRODUCING) Minister of Culture, Dr. Schmidt-Lausitz—Mrs. Colonel Eilers—Miss von Mohrungen. Baron Pflungk, you know.

POOTSIE: Miss von Mohrungen—that sounds so madly formal—downright reactionary. Why don't you call me Pootsie, like everyone else?

HARRAS: I don't dare, Pootsie. We just met a couple of hours ago.

POOTSIE: Bottoms up, Harry!

MOHRUNGEN: Pootsie!

HARRAS: Stop, young lady! Don't drink yet! François, a refill. (STEPS INTO THE MIDDLE AND A LOOSE CIRCLE FORMS AROUND HIM) So—without further schmaltz, but from the heart, I drink to Friedrich Eilers, to his fiftieth air victory which we are celebrating today. To a hundred, and to his safe return home. Your health, Friedrich.

ALL: To your health, Friedrich.

EILERS: (GAYLY FENDING THEM OFF) Thanks, thanks, I feel like a war memorial.

HARRAS: Just what y'are. (THEY DRINK AND SHAKE HANDS)

THE OTHERS: (CHIMING IN) To General Harras! (THEY DRINK)

LAUSITZ: (ALONE) To the Führer!

HARRAS: Cheers, with an empty glass. The Führer doesn't drink.

MOHRUNGEN: (HAS PUT HIS ARM AROUND EILERS'S SHOULDER) I can really be proud of my son-in-law.

ANNE: We can all be proud, Poppa, the whole German nation.

HARRAS: Best man in the Luftwaffe—or in the whole army.

EILERS: If there is anything to be proud of, then it's my squadron. Four of my officers were awarded the Iron Cross First Class today.

PFLUNGK: (SLIGHTLY PERSONAL, TO POOTSIE) Wasn't Lieutenant Hartmann among those decorated?

POOTSIE: (CASUALLY) Do you know little Hartmann? Nice boy.

ANNE: Why don't you admit you're engaged to him.

POOTSIE: Engaged. Such a ghastly word. I don't like anything that sounds so middle-class.

HARRAS: Of course, in the Hitler Youth no one gets engaged any more. That holds you up too long; you might grow up in the meantime.

HANSEN: You don't even bother getting married—just start right in and give a boost to the birth rate. Excuse me, General.

POOTSIE: (ALSO A LITTLE TIPSY ALREADY, WITH A CERTAIN PROVOCATIVE MANNER WHICH AS YET DOES NOT DIFFERENTIATE BETWEEN HARRAS AND BARON PFLUNGK) We modern girls have nothing against marriage if it's the right man. But all the rigmarole we have to go through; the proofs of Aryan blood, health certificate, proof of fertility, semen count, and so forth. Yes, it's all necessary on account of race—but who wants to wait around for all that?

MOHRUNGEN: What a way to talk, Pootsie!

POOTSIE: We all talk like that in the Hitler Youth. That is the privilege of youth.

EILERS: And what about the duties of youth.

POOTSIE: My dear Mister Brother-in-law, above all, no gloom and doom this evening. Little Hartmann has already drearified me enough. He doesn't dance, imagine!

PFLUNGK: That is a great mistake. You love to dance, I imagine, Miss von Mohrungen?

POOTSIE: I'm mad about it. But it's Pootsie, please. When I was little I couldn't pronounce my real name so I named myself Pootsie and it stuck. (SHE LAUGHS, INTOXICATED WITH HERSELF)

PFLUNGK: Very sweet. May I take you dancing sometime, Pootsie?

POOTSIE: You bet you may. Did you know I am staying in Berlin? I've been accepted for training in the Party Women's Corps. (THEY WITHDRAW EXCITEDLY INTO ONE OF THE NICHES)

MOHRUNGEN: (HAS TAKEN HARRAS ASIDE FOR A MOMENT) Tell me, General, have you discovered anything new about the situation? It's going to come up in the meeting tomorrow. I don't want to take a stand before I know your opinion.

HARRAS: To be frank—I haven't any opinion at all so far—only suspicions. Fresh reports came in this afternoon. Between us, von Mohrungen—a failure of wing structure on a dozen brand new planes. I'm having the metal checked. But the whole thing's got me completely baffled—Careful—We will talk later.

LAUSITZ: (HAS COME CLOSE TO THEM) Am I intruding? Or don't you discuss professional secrets on a social occasion? Of course, I don't know anything about technical matters, but I find the whole aircraft industry very fascinating . . .

HARRAS: No professional secrets, Dr. Lausitz. Von Mohrungen controls procurements of raw materials, I control production.

LAUSITZ: Divided responsibility. Highly interesting. As I said, I don't understand anything about it. My province is Culture. Total mobilization of the German soul, you know. And enlightenment of the neutral foreign countries. That, too, is battle— even if not with weapons.

HARRAS: I know. You use your mouth instead. That probably calls for a special kind of courage. I could never do it.

LAUSITZ: You flatter me, General. (TURNS AWAY)

HANSEN: (WHO HAD STEPPED UP PREVIOUSLY, SOFTLY) Blockhead.

HARRAS: (BETWEEN HIS TEETH) Watch your step, small fry. Don't get plastered tonight.

HANSEN: Don't worry. I only make as if. Am sharp as a tack. (HARRAS NODS TO HIM AND DRINKS HASTILY. EILERS AND ANNE HAVE STEPPED UP TO HIM)

ANNE: I just want to tell you, General Harras—I'll never forget this evening. You should hear how Friedrich talks about you. It is enough to make a woman jealous. Harras comes first—after the Führer, naturally, and then nobody else for a long time.

HARRAS: And now you've met the old Harry in the flesh. Disappointing isn't he? Not a bit of that fourstar dignity and not even a party member.

EILERS: Well, yes—in that respect—maybe we think a little differently. But in the air it makes no difference.

ANNE: Isn't it also a question of generation? We grew up with it. To us it is holy. The party gave us that little bit of meaning to life.

HARRAS: The meaning of my life was always flying. I started out in 1914. And now I can't stop anymore. It's like liquor. (HE DRINKS) Here's to you. You know, I'm so happy that we're together tonight. (SLAPS EILERS ON THE SHOULDER) How are the children?

EILERS: Haven't seen them yet—just got back from the front today. But you can imagine how I am looking forward to next week!

HARRAS: Must be nice—to come home—to have children . . .

EILERS: (SOMEWHAT ABSENTLY) Yes—to come home—(HE BECOMES SILENT, STARES AT THE GLASS THAT HE HOLDS IN HIS HAND)

ANNE: What's the matter with you, Friedrich?

EILERS: (AS THOUGH WAKING UP) Oh—nothing. Excuse me, please. It was just funny—

HARRAS: What was?

EILERS: I saw myself suddenly—there, in the glass. A little distorted—but perfectly clear. My own face. Funny. You never really know what you look like. (HE STARES ALMOST FRIGHTENED IN FRONT OF HIMSELF)

ANNE: (WITH A SOMEWHAT FORCED LAUGH) You know—you're tipsy, Friedrich.

EILERS: (AGREEING, CHANGED AND UNAFFECTED) It's true. I really can't take a drop.

HARRAS: Well, go and eat something. A lobster will do you more good than army pep pills.

EILERS: (SHAKING HIS HEAD, SMILING) Yes, I think I'll try that. (HE GOES TO THE BUFFET)

ANNE: What happened to him? Was it really that little glass of wine?

HARRAS: He should sleep it off for twenty-four hours. And when he wakes up—then he should—the first thing—look into your eyes, Anne.

ANNE: (PRESSES HIS HAND HASTILY) Thanks, Harry. You are—you are wonderful. (SHE GOES QUICKLY TO EILERS)

HARRAS: (TO HIMSELF) Damn it all. Damn it all. (HE DRINKS)

OTTO: (COMES IN BEAMING) A real big night, General. Reichsmarshal Göring himself is coming. He will be right next door. We've had to clear away the lower ranks. By the way, four junior officers are outside—from Colonel Eilers' squadron. Should I let them in?

HARRAS: (WHO AT FIRST BARELY LISTENED, ELECTRIFIED) Why sure! Hurry up! Let 'em in!

OTTO: As you order, General. (OTTO EXITS)

HARRAS: Pootsie! Hands off that diplomatic vest! Surprise coming up.

POOTSIE: Another toast?

HARRAS: Something like that. François, more glasses!

(ENTER CAPTAIN PFUNDTMAYER, 1ST LT. HASTENTEUFFEL, 2ND LTS. WRITZKY AND HARTMANN: PFUNDTMAYER ABOUT AS OLD AS HARRAS, A BAVARIAN POWERHOUSE; HASTENTEUFFEL MORE WESTPHALIAN, SHARP-EYED WITH BIG HANDS AND A HEAVY TONGUE; WRITZKY A "SHARP BOY" FROM BERLIN, SLIGHTLY EFFEMINATE BUT DASHING AND ELEGANT; HARTMANN VERY YOUNG, SLENDER, PALE, WITH AN ATTRACTIVE, SMART, BOYISH FACE)

PFUNDTMAYER: (REPORTING IN MILITARY FASHION) Captain Pfundtmayer and three officers from Colonel Eilers' Fighter Squadron reporting, sir!

HARRAS: (OFFICIAL BUT BARELY ABLE TO HOLD BACK HIS LAUGHTER) Thank you, Captain. Gentlemen, I have the honor to congratulate you on your decorations and bid you welcome to our little gathering.

PFUNDTMAYER: (SALUTES) The honor's all ours, General.

HARRAS: (BURSTING OUT) Pfundy! Y'old stud mule! You haven't grown any younger!

PFUNDTMAYER: Harry, y'old struttin' rooster! Can a body still call you that, such a powerful big critter as you've turned out to be.

HARRAS: (TO HIS OTHER GUESTS) We were front line buddies—1914 to '18.

PFUNDTMAYER: No, to '17—winter of '17, when they ketched me in the arse. My pig-luck!

MOHRUNGEN: And the gentlemen have never met since?

HARRAS: Just so happened we never did.

PFUNDTMAYER: You still able t'shoot a glass off my dome, Harry? Or don't ya dare n'more? (HE PUTS HIS GLASS ON HIS BROAD SKULL)

HARRAS: Hansen, my Luger!

PFUNDTMAYER: (TAKES THE GLASS DOWN QUICKLY AND DRINKS) Naw, naw! I guess I can't afford to risk this set of brains. They're still prewar quality, you know. (HE SHAKES WITH LAUGHTER)

HASTENTEUFFEL: (WITH A HOARSE BASS VOICE) If the General would like to shoot—at your service, sir. (HE PUTS A SMALL GLASS ON HIS HEAD AND STANDS AT ATTENTION)

HARRAS: Later, my friend, after the next bottle. Haven't got my famous steady hand yet.

WRITZKY: May I present target with a cigarette? I have a long brand. (HE STANDS IN PROFILE WITH AN EXTRA LONG CIGARETTE IN HIS MOUTH)

HARRAS: You're all right, boys. Come, I'll introduce you around. You don't need any introduction, Lieutenant Hartmann. Go ahead, make yourself at home.

HARTMANN: (SOMEWHAT EMBARRASSED) Yes, indeed, General. Thank you, General. (HE STANDS IN THE FOREGROUND WITH POOTSIE WHILE HARRAS LEADS THE OTHERS AROUND AND LOOSE GROUPS ARE FORMED)

POOTSIE: (CASUAL BUT FRIENDLY AND NOT WITHOUT PRIDE) Well, little man, how does it feel? All that laurel around so young a brow?

HARTMANN: I don't know—I'm not all here, yet. Last night over Leningrad and now—it's all so fast.

POOTSIE: Well, don't brood over it, young poet. Save the war experiences for your memoirs. You're in Berlin, boy, at Otto's, the only place in the German Reich where there's still anything cooking.

HARTMANN: I—I really wanted to spend my furlough in the country. I thought—perhaps on the Rhine—

POOTSIE: Who's stopping you?

HARTMANN: I didn't know you wanted to stay in Berlin. I thought—

POOTSIE: Look, you won't catch me in the country. I never went much for that nature stuff. Naw, the only place you can live a little these days is Berlin.

PFLUNGK: And that only on occasion.

POOTSIE: We'll have to get Harry to throw us a party in that apartment of his with the propeller bar. The goings-on there! Wow, the stories I've heard. (SHE TURNS TO HARRAS WHO IS COMING UP WITH PFUNDTMAYER AND ANOTHER GROUP)

HARRAS: That really fascinates you, doesn't it, little bride?

POOTSIE: I'd like to be at an affair like that just once. Is it true that the serving girls only wear fig leaves at your festivities? I'll come as a servant girl, I warn you.

PFUNDTMAYER: That would be a real thrill on a meatless day. (TO HARRAS) Here's to ya, old sojur! Important thing is we're still with it. I al'ays wish'd, m'self, it'uld start up ag'in. Now I just says to m'self, "If it only don't all fizzle out before I makes Lieutenant Colonel."

HARRAS: Never mind, Pfundy, mebbe you'll still make "Ginrul!"

PFUNDTMAYER: (SLIGHTLY DRUNK) Genurrull! Genurrull! You made it, Harry! But if ya really think about it—Well, I won't say nothing—

HARRAS: Go ahead, say it, Pfundy! Get it off your chest!

PFUNDTMAYER: We old party men, we didn't have no time for careers. We was obliged first to "liquidate the enemy within." After that come business and family—I married into the hops business, ya know. But it didn't pay off—Jews was in the competition and squeezed us out. Good buddy, that's when ya learn ta hate. When the party come to power I made out a little better. I did business with the Aryanization Program, cleaning out Jews. And now, in uniform, what am I now? A poor old Captain—me, with my low party number and all. And you—you're the Genurrull! Ya call that justice?

HARRAS: Well, now, listen here, ma friend. I have never been a Nazi. You're right. I'm a flier. I've risked my neck and earned my keep. I never married into nothing. I've never dipped into the party treasury, never stole anything from a Jew nor built myself villas from the proceeds. (STUBBORN—ALREADY SLIGHTLY DRUNK) General or clown. I'm a flier and that's all. And who ever don't like it, he can—(AN ABASHED SILENCE)

PFUNDTMAYER: Well, what do ya know! (WITH MOUTH OPEN)

LAUSITZ: What the General means to say is the Führer has given his life, which was passionately dedicated to aviation and to the Luftwaffe, a goal and an opportunity to serve the Fatherland from a leading position.

HARRAS: Ya see—there you have, presto, the official translation. Thanks, Doctor—That's exactly what I meant.

LAUSITZ: I don't doubt it.

HARRAS: Why should you? You know my innermost thoughts.

LAUSITZ: I believe I do, General.

HARRAS: Well then—cheers! (HE EMPTIES A GLASS OF ARMAGNAC)

(DURING THE LAST FEW SENTENCES THERE HAS BEEN NOISE AND COMMOTION IN THE BACKGROUND AND NOW THREE LADIES FROM THE THEATRE SWEEP IN, LED BY OTTO. OLIVIA GEISS, OPERETTA DIVA, HAS THE FULL BUST OF THE PROFESSIONAL SINGER BUT SLIM, ALMOST DELICATE LEGS. SHE IS ALMOST FORTY, DRESSED TOO YOUNG FOR HER AGE, VERY BLONDE, AND STILL PRETTY. HER SYMPATHETIC FACE, ALREADY A LITTLE SPONGY, IS SLIGHTLY RED FROM JUST HAVING MAKE-UP REMOVED. SHE'S NOT VERY MUCH MADE UP NOW. LYRA SCHOEPPKE IS RED-HAIRED AND WEARS A MONOCLE. SHE'S POWDERED ABSOLUTELY WHITE SO THAT IT IS HARD TO JUDGE HER AGE. SHE'S WEARING AN EXCESSIVELY TIGHT BLACK SILK DRESS WHICH SHARPLY ACCENTUATES HER GOOD FIGURE. DIDDO GEISS IS A VERY YOUNG BLONDE GIRL WITH AN UNUSUALLY FRESH, NATURAL FACE AND LARGE DARK BLUE EYES. SHE SEEMS MORE LIKE A SCHOOL-GIRL WHO IS GOING TO HER FIRST BALL. SHE WEARS A BUNCH OF FRESH VIOLETS AT HER BOSOM)

OLIVIA: Harry! When I heard you were here—nobody could hold me back! We just rolled up—the opening night party of Reichs-marshal Göring. Are you sober enough to meet my little niece? Because this child simply idolizes you!

HARRAS: (DIDDO, WHO HAS LOOKED AT HIM WITH BARELY CON-CEALED CURIOSITY, LAUGHS A LITTLE. HARRAS BENDS BRIEFLY OVER HER HAND. TO OLIVIA) And you've kept her hidden from me for nineteen years. I thought you were a friend. (HE HOLDS ON TO DIDDO'S HAND WHILE SHE BLUSHES MORE AND MORE UNDER HIS INTERESTED, PROBING GLANCE)

PFLUNGK: May I do the honors? (HE BEGINS TO INTRODUCE) Mr. von Mohrungen, Colonel Eilers and Mrs. Eilers—(HE MUMBLES THE OTHER NAMES WHILE THE GENTLEMEN BOW BEFORE OLIVIA AND LYRA, THEN THE LADIES SHAKE HANDS WITH THEM)

POOTSIE: Be daring, Hartmann! Step right up! Now's your chance to meet the famous Geiss who captivated our fathers and uncles when they were in puberty!

MOHRUNGEN: (PAINFULLY EMBARRASSED, APOLOGIZING TO OLIVIA) Don't take her seriously, dear lady. My daughter has a peculiar sense of humor.

OLIVIA: Know all about it. Today's youth.

MOHRUNGEN: What was the musical that opened this evening?

OLIVIA: *The Merry Widow* for a change. That's the only thing the Führer wants to hear besides Wagner. The whole thing was one of those gala occasions. Sort of an anniversary for me—twenty-five years ago I sang it for the first time—exactly to the day.

MOHRUNGEN: (FASCINATED) Wasn't that at Heidelberg? I saw you in that performance!

POOTSIE: What did I tell you!

OLIVIA: You remember it, Mr. von Mohrungen? Have I changed a little since then?

MOHRUNGEN: If I may be privileged to witness one of your per-formances again, then I will permit myself an opinion. But for me you'll always be the best Merry Widow. Unsurpassed.

OLIVIA: If only once they would give me something new. But it'll never come to that anymore—not in my lifetime.

LYRA: Don't make yourself out older than you are, Ollie.

OLIVIA: Why? Youth must have a chance too. My niece had her first part tonight.

HARRAS: (TO DIDDO) If I had known—we all would have come to see you. Well, what were you like on stage?

DIDDO: I haven't the faintest idea, General. I was—in a trance.

OLIVIA: She played like a young goddess. And in the intermission she was supposed to have been introduced to the good Lord himself, but after the curtain our director said to me, "No soap. Called away to the Eastern Front."

EILERS: Called away to the front! The Führer?

OLIVIA: Well, instead you're meeting our Harry. (SHE PATS HARRAS'S CHEEK)

DIDDO: I really almost wished for that more— (LAUGHTER)— When I was little I used to look at your picture secretly—the one that sits on Aunt Ollie's bedside table.

LYRA: Tut. Tut.

OLIVIA: That's right. That's exactly where it stands. With flowers. It's a little yellow and faded.

HARRAS: (PASSES HIS HAND OVER HIS HAIR—TO DIDDO) You should have met me twenty years ago. I was young once too.

DIDDO: Twenty years?—I wasn't in this world then!

OLIVIA: But I was! Cheers, Harry! (SHE DRINKS FROM HIS GLASS)

PFUNDTMAYER: (WHO IS DEVOURING LYRA WITH HIS EYES) Yes sir, let's all have a drink! Swill 'er down, everybody! This we gotta celebrate. What a sow!

LYRA: To whom are you referring, Captain?

PFUNDTMAYER: Beg pardon, Ma'am. What I mean—I'm just plain lucky. Ma first night in Berlin and lo and behold, ladies from the theater. Ma sow-luck, I call it. (THEY LAUGH)

HARRAS: (SOFTLY TO HANSEN) Call the ministry—see what's cooking.

HANSEN: Orders! (HE GOES OUT)

LYRA: Did you come here straight from the front, Captain?

PFUNDTMAYER: You know it! Yesterday we still had dead Russians for evening chow. Ya know, I never really sniffed a lady from the theater before up close over Kümmel and corn, as they say.

POOTSIE: Well go ahead and take a bite, Captain. You must have good teeth.

LYRA: (IGNORING POOTSIE POINTEDLY) You must tell me about your experiences, Captain. Madly exciting, I imagine—these duels in the air—man against man—like the tournaments of knights in days of old.

PFUNDTMAYER: Exactly! Just exactly! Ya hear that, Hastenteiffie? We're knights in days of old, you and me! (HE LAUGHS A BOOMING LAUGH)

LYRA: (LAUGHING WITH HIM) I know I must sound terribly silly—

PFUNDTMAYER: Not at all, Ma'am! Ma'am! (HE KISSES HER HAND AND PATS IT)

OTTO: (RE-ENTERS) The Reichsmarshal takes the liberty to invite the ladies and the gentlemen of the Eilers Squadron to join him for a glass of champagne—He expects the gentlemen post-haste.

HARRAS: Well, off you go, boys. Fat Hermann isn't on display every day. You can all cut yourselves a slice.

OTTO: Not coming, General?

HARRAS: Little later. Eilers, will you fly lead?

LAUSITZ: (TO EILERS) Might I speak with you beforehand—about our broadcast?—

EILERS: Of course, Doctor. (TO PFUNDTMAYER) Pfundtmayer, please take my place? Introduce the men.

POOTSIE: The gentlemen and ladies, if you please. That means us. (SHE HOOKS ARMS WITH HARTMANN AND ANNE. ALL EXIT EXCEPT HARRAS, EILERS, LAUSITZ, PFLUNGK, AND MOHRUNGEN)

OLIVIA: (WHILE GOING OFF—SOFTLY TO HARRAS) Harry. I have to speak to you alone for a moment.

HARRAS: Not easy tonight. Urgent?

OLIVIA: S.O.S.

HARRAS: Well—maybe later. Otherwise—you have my private number.

OLIVIA: I don't trust the phone. (SHE GOES OFF. HANSEN ENTERS IN THE MEANTIME, GOES QUICKLY TO HARRAS AND WHISPERS SOMETHING TO HIM)

MOHRUNGEN: (WATCHING POOTSIE GO OFF, WHO IS LAUGHING AND JABBERING LOUDLY) These two girls of mine—what a difference!—It's hard to believe they're sisters.

EILERS: Doctor, you'll have to tell me exactly what to do.

LAUSITZ: All you have to do is to speak quite naturally—from your own true experiences. The script has been prepared. All you have to do is read it.

EILERS: The most important thing to me is to catch the noon train. You understand, the children. I haven't been home for a year.

LAUSITZ: That can be easily arranged. (HE TAKES THE SCRIPT FROM HIS BRIEFCASE) Perhaps we could go into another room. You will excuse us, General?

HARRAS: Please; gladly. (AFTER LAUSITZ AND EILERS HAVE GONE OUT, SPEAKING TO HANSEN, WHO REMAINS WITH MOHRUNGEN AND PFLUNGK) All right, let's have the latest. Tomorrow, these gentlemen will hear all about it anyhow.

HANSEN: As far as they can tell at the Ministry, everything's freezing up in Russia. Way below zero. Von Bock got cold feet. They say he hollered into the phone, "Retreat immediately, or I'll not be responsible." Whereupon the great Führer swung himself into the saddle of his warhorse and headed East to see for himself. I'll call them again; they expect fresh reports any minute. (HE GOES OFF)

MOHRUNGEN: General—do you believe anything can go wrong—I mean, anything decisive?

HARRAS: It's done gone already, von Mohrungen.

MOHRUNGEN: You mean—the increased demand for raw material—

HARRAS: I mean: Russia.

MOHRUNGEN: And how do you think the whole thing can be saved?

HARRAS: (SHRUGS HIS SHOULDERS) Ask the Foreign Ministry. (MOTIONS WITH HIS HEAD TOWARD PFLUNGK. FILLS HIS GLASS)

PFLUNGK: In my opinion there is still a way out in case we can't attain a complete military victory. Keep America out of it. Cool down Japan. Negotiate peace in the Far East. Then, somehow, a separate peace with Russia even at the price of some zones of influence in the Balkans and the Near East; gentle pressure on London and a compromise between us and the British Empire. Then we'll see.

HARRAS: (LAUGHS) Ribbentrop Brand Champagne, 1914—late harvest. If he knows England, then I know the moon.

(FROM THE OTHER SIDE OF THE RESTAURANT WHERE GÖRING'S PARTY IS GOING ON, THE SOFT MUSIC OF A RECORD PLAYER HAS BEGUN A WALTZ FROM *THE MERRY WIDOW*. POOTSIE APPEARS AT THE DOOR, EXCITED)

POOTSIE: Baron Pflungk! They're dancing over there. He's madly nice—and not as fat as I thought, rather imposing, in fact. Coming, Baron?

PFLUNGK: I love waltzes.

POOTSIE: If the man can lead—(WHILE PFLUNGK DANCES OUT WITH HER) You can lead—I knew it immediately.

MOHRUNGEN: (NERVOUSLY FUSSING WITH HIS CIGARETTE—TO HARRAS WITH WHOM HE IS NOW ALONE) Tell me, General, do you trust this Pflungk?

HARRAS: Not as far as I can spit.

MOHRUNGEN: Aren't you a little careless?

HARRAS: Sure. That's my method. (HE LIGHTS CIGARETTE) They know what I think. So why not say it out loud. The minute I start being careful they'll think my pants are full and they can spit on my head.

MOHRUNGEN: You think they can't touch you—that you're indispensable . . .

HARRAS: That gang wants to win the war—There's only a handful of people who can push the right button. Too bad I'm one of them. Anyway, I don't give one whoop in hell. (HE LEANS BACK IN AN EASY CHAIR AND SUDDENLY LOOKS VERY TIRED)

MOHRUNGEN: (LOOKS AT HIM WORRIEDLY) Are you really so pessimistic?

HARRAS: Of course, I know—they can liquidate me any day despite my indispensability. (STANDS UP AND BEGINS TO WALK UP AND DOWN) We're in one hell of a mess, you know, you and I!

MOHRUNGEN: (EXPECTANTLY) You mean—the matter of the faulty materials?

HARRAS: (NODS) As far as we can tell, there is something wrong with the alloys that is throwing off the weight calculation. An error, carelessness can always occur once—but it repeated itself with a certain regularity. Three times, in three different deliveries of new fighter planes in one week.

MOHRUNGEN: Do you think it's sabotage?

HARRAS: Possible. But not very probable. The very regularity makes me think it's an organization led according to a plan. That doesn't check out with what we know about the underground.

MOHRUNGEN: Who else could have such an organization? (PERPLEXED, AS HARRAS GRINS) You mean—really? But—what possible motive could they have there—

HARRAS: (SHRUGS HIS SHOULDERS) It's all guesswork. I have no proof. But it looks as though they were stoking a furnace in hell just for me. Me—personally.

MOHRUNGEN: All you need is a handful of men on whom you can rely absolutely. Do you have them?

HARRAS: I have them. Oderbruch, for example.

MOHRUNGEN: Oderbruch—that's your chief engineer.

HARRAS: I created the position just for him. He is tireless, works night and day—and . . . he misses nothing. You know, I don't trust anyone so easily. But the few people you've been together with once—in a real jam—you know them. There are damned few. Hansen and Korrianke, my old chauffeur, and Oderbruch are the only ones I can rely on—but those, all the way.

MOHRUNGEN: It can't possibly be the fault of the raw materials.

HARRAS: That much is certain. You're not liable, Mohrungen.

MOHRUNGEN: That's not necessarily true. (INTERRUPTS, TOUCHES HIS ARM) Shhhh. I believe someone is listening!

HARRAS: (INDIFFERENT) Really? Who? Heh! Is anybody there?

FRANÇOIS: (APPEARS AT THE DOOR) You called, General? More Armagnac?

HARRAS: (LAUGHS) You're getting nervous, Mohrungen. Thank you, François—there's a full bottle here. But bring me the wine card later on—We'll need a change soon.

FRANÇOIS: Of course, General. (GOES OFF)

MOHRUNGEN: Don't you think that Frenchman is snooping around?

HARRAS: Naw, naw—the boys here are OK. And what if he is? I don't know anything myself.

MOHRUNGEN: A Gestapo plot—to sabotage its own armaments—I can hardly believe that, General.

HARRAS: You mean, they could have my scalp cheaper? Possible. I don't know. It's only a suspicion. But you see, it is not just that the Heil-boys don't like my nose . . .

MOHRUNGEN: I know, the Luftwaffe is at stake.

HARRAS: Naturally. Whoever controls the air force has the balance of power in case of a fight between the army and the party—that is why the party, that is, the SS, is trying so hard to get all the key positions in its claws. If they succeed, then they will have won the smoldering German civil war for the second time. And there are only a few heads that still stand in the way.

MOHRUNGEN: The best, however.

HARRAS: Or the thickest. However that may be, this business has to be stopped. Because it happens to be a real danger—I'm not talking about the politics now, but about our boys at the front. When they can't depend on their planes any more—

MOHRUNGEN: What sort of man is this Oderbruch? Where does he come from?

HARRAS: (LAUGHTS. TURNS TO EILERS WHO HAS JUST COME IN WITH ANNE ON HIS ARM) Friedrich! What sort of a man is Oderbruch?

EILERS: (HIS FACE LIGHTS UP) Oderbruch? Well, how should I say it? You can trust him with your fortune without receipt. Even your wife and children.

HARRAS: Bravo, Fred! (TO MOHRUNGEN) He comes from a good home. Silesian Catholics, as far as I know. Old family of government officials. He began as a mechanic, and flew with me, then with Eilers. He has the kind of technical fingertip sensitivity and knowledge of the field that you only find once in a lifetime.

MOHRUNGEN: Then you must be very happy to have him.

HARRAS: You bet. (TO EILERS) It got too wild for you two over there, eh?

EILERS: (LAUGHING) Yes. A little wild. Pootsie is dancing polkas with the Reichsmarshal.

HARRAS: Come, Mohrungen, let's have a look. (WHILE GOING OFF) I put Oderbruch on the scent. I bet he'll find out where the dog is buried— (HE AND MOHRUNGEN DISAPPEAR)

ANNE: (PUTS HER ARM AROUND EILERS) Tired, darling?

EILERS: (DRAWS HER CLOSE TO HIM) A little—worn out.

ANNE: (TENDERLY) You should be in bed.

EILERS: When I'm with you—then I'm not tired any more. That's— better than sleep. (HE KISSES HER) I missed you so.

ANNE: (SOFTLY) Don't you know—that I'm always with you? Day and night?

EILERS: (NODS) I know. That's what keeps me going. Without that—it would be hard to take.

ANNE: Is it that rough?

EILERS: (SITS DOWN AND LEANS BACK) Yes. Being separated. Being away from home. As for the service routine—war, planes, com-

bat—you get used to all that. And yet—it isn't right in the long
run. I mean—killing people.

ANNE: (STROKES HIS HAND) It has to be. For the Fatherland. For the
future. For a better world.

EILERS: Yes, it's all necessary.

ANNE: (INTENSE, BESEECHING) Don't question, darling. Believe.

EILERS: I will—to the end.

ANNE: Till victory.

EILERS: Till victory—and peace.

ANNE: (ALMOST SHY, WHISPERING) I love you. (THEY SIT SILENT FOR
A MOMENT, HAND IN HAND)

(MUSIC AND THE NOISE OF VOICES HAVE BECOME LOUDER IN THE
BACKGROUND. HARRAS ENTERS ARM IN ARM WITH OLIVIA AND
DIDDO. ALL THREE COME INTO THE ROOM WITH A SORT OF DANCE-
STEP, SOFTLY HUMMING THE MELODY OF A WALTZ. HARRAS IS
QUITE DRUNK BUT STILL IN GOOD FORM)

HARRAS: Look a' that, children. Look what's become of my party.
Empty glasses, empty plates—and one lone pair of lovers. Whose
party was this anyway? Reichsmarshal Fat Back's or mine?

EILERS: (HAS GOTTEN UP SMILING) We'll round them up over there,
eh Anne?

HARRAS: You're a good guy, Freddie. Bring the others back. It's
high time we all had another drink.

EILERS: Come, Anne. We'll be right back with the others. (HE AND
ANNE GO OFF ARM IN ARM)

HARRAS: (HAS MIXED SOMETHING IN A GLASS AND GIVES IT TO
DIDDO) Here, my child—try this. That's no cocktail. That is a
Christian-Catholic Judo-Germanic Atheistic mixture. When
you've downed that you'll believe in God again.

OLIVIA: For Heaven's sake, Harry! Please don't get the child tipsy.
Put it down, Diddo.

DIDDO: Let me be. I know how much I can take. Your health, General.

HARRAS: General. From your sweet lips. Can't stand to bear it.
Makes me—downright melancholy, is what it makes me. Call me
Harry. Would you like to?

DIDDO: On one condition.

HARRAS: Fulfilled, my child. What is it?

DIDDO: That you don't call me "my child" anymore, because that makes me melancholy too.

HARRAS: Agreed. Let's drink to it. You call me Harry and I call you Monkeywrench.

DIDDO: Monkeywrench—OK by me.

HARRAS: There, you see. From now on the two of us will never be melancholy again. (HE STANDS VERY CLOSE TO HER AND BENDS A LITTLE OVER HER DRESS) Fresh violets. Who gave you these?

DIDDO: Aunt Ollie . . .

HARRAS: Then it's all right. Now I'll have to kiss you. (HE COMES CLOSER)

DIDDO: No—please—General!

HARRAS: General—That'll cost you two kisses.

OLIVIA: Say now, aren't you two even ashamed to carry on right here in the presence of an old lady? Diddo . . . dear, could you leave us alone for a moment? I have something to tell him. Something serious. (SHE TAKES HIS ARM)

DIDDO: (SAVED) Of course, Aunt Ollie.

HARRAS: But—come back! Please!

DIDDO: Maybe— (SHE RUNS OUT)

HARRAS: (STARING AFTER HER) Absolutely—absolutely bewitching.

OLIVIA: She's already lost her head over you. You're very impressive with your fame and your personality—and you use it shamelessly.

HARRAS: (SUDDENLY QUITE SOBER) Yes, you're right, Ollie. It's unfair. Damned unfair. I'm going to be good; you can depend on it. Well now, let's have it. Whatsa matter?

OLIVIA: Is your head halfway clear now?

HARRAS: Clear as pure alcohol. Hurry up, they're coming back in a minute.

OLIVIA: (CLOSE TO HIM, SOFTLY, DESPERATE) Bergmann got out of Buchenwald. He was there for six months and they've messed him up so badly that he's in the hospital. Police hospital, naturally. But Jenny knows a doctor there who gives people death certificates. Then they can be smuggled out at night. Costs ten thousand. She's scrounged it up somehow and decided to escape with him. She says, if they ship him to Poland, he'll kill himself. Harry, you're the only one who can help . . .

HARRAS: Just a minute. (HE TAKES A PIECE OF ICE OUT OF THE CHAMPAGNE COOLER, POURS A LITTLE COGNAC OVER IT AND BEGINS TO CHEW IT) He can't get out legally? Can't get a visa to someplace? Can't even buy one?

OLIVIA: Not a chance. They're out to get him.

HARRAS: Yes, I know. Those fellows will never forgive him his Aryan wife. Not only did she marry a Jew, she's beautiful to boot and ran away from a Nazi on his account. No, he's not going to get an exit visa—unless it's to a camp.

OLIVIA: I wouldn't come to you if there were any other way. But— (TEARS CHOKE HER VOICE)

HARRAS: (HIS HAND GLIDES QUICKLY OVER HER HAIR) We'll figure out something. Is Jenny in good form? I mean, as a pilot? After all, she learned with me.

OLIVIA: I don't know. But there is nothing she wouldn't do for him—nothing she couldn't do.

HARRAS: Sure—a matter of life and death.

OLIVIA: But for God's sake, Harry, I don't want you to get yourself—

HARRAS: (CUTS HER OFF WITH A GESTURE, GOES TO THE DOOR, WHISTLES A CAVALRY SIGNAL AND CALLS) Korrianke! (GRINNING TO OLIVIA) The likes of us have their bodyguard too, just like the other gangsters.

(KORRIANKE ENTERS AT A TROT. HE IS AN OLDER MAN, SQUARE BUILT AND SLIGHTLY FAT, WITH A RED FACE AND A DOUBLE CHIN. EVEN THOUGH HE WEARS THE UNIFORM OF THE LUFTWAFFE, THE CHAUFFEUR IN HIM IS IMMEDIATELY APPARENT TOO. HE HAS A THIN, SOMEWHAT HUSKY VOICE AND LISPS A LITTLE)

KORRIANKE: Ready for action, Herr General!

HARRAS: Pay attention, Korriandoli. If someone comes in now, we are planning a trip to Kohlhasenbruck with Mrs. Geiss and her niece. Get it?

KORRIANKE: I'm with it . . . Herr General. Kohlhasenbruck.

HARRAS: (IN A LOWERED VOICE) Do you remember Professor Bergmann? Samuel Bergmann, the surgeon?

KORRIANKE: (LIGHTING UP) The one who patched us up when we had that tough break with a curve at 120 m.p.h.?

HARRAS: Right. The magician who takes people's hearts out like a pocket watch, repairs them and puts them back again.

KORRIANKE: Easy as pie.

HARRAS: Cut it! They stuck him in a concentration camp for miscegenation and mauled him for six months.

KORRIANKE: Sons of bitches, Herr General.

HARRAS: Cut it! Remember his wife? I taught her to fly.

KORRIANKE: A blonde! Hard to forget, Herr General. (SMACKS HIS LIPS)

HARRAS: Cut it!—Here's the pitch!—You will meet said doctor and the blonde in the apartment of Mrs. Geiss here—(TO OLIVIA) When?

OLIVIA: (PALE, ALMOST TREMBLING) Day after tomorrow, at night.

HARRAS: Day after tomorrow, at night. The exact time I will tell you later. You will take along: for the professor, an old military coat and a cap of mine; for the lady—pilot's overalls, helmet and goggles. Do you think you can drive my car through to hangar 35 without being stopped for inspection?

KORRIANKE: For certain, Herr General. Hangar 35. Easy as pie.

HARRAS: All right Korrianke. (VOICES BECOME AUDIBLE OUTSIDE. IT IS PFUNDTMAYER AND LYRA, WHO ARE FOOLING AROUND IN THE HALL. SPEAKING LOUDLY) Well then, Kohlhasenbruck—next Sunday.

KORRIANKE: (LOUDLY) Kohlhasenbruck, Herr General. (GOES OFF)

OLIVIA: (QUICKLY) Harry—what is hangar 35?

HARRAS: (SOFTLY) There's a little sports plane there, always ready for flight with an exact map and directions for a fast, safe air route to Switzerland. For all emergencies.

OLIVIA: And—Korrianke?

HARRAS: Where do you think that guy left his front teeth? I fished him out of a concentration camp myself in '34.

OLIVIA: Harry—you are—(REACHES FOR HIS HAND)

HARRAS: (HE EMPTIES A BIG GLASS) So, on Sunday, not too early though! Say around noon.

OLIVIA: I'd love to.

HARRAS: It's a deal . . . if "little violets" comes along.

OLIVIA: You hen-happy old rooster! (BOTH LAUGH, FROM OUTSIDE VOICES, CALLS, AND LAUGHING COME CLOSER. PFUNDTMAYER

COMES IN, LYRA, THEN IN SHORT SUCCESSION WRITZKY, HAS-
TENTEUFFEL, HARTMANN, EILERS, LAUSITZ)

LYRA: They're adjourning over there. Excuse us, Ollie, for breaking
up your *tête-à-tête,* but you've flirted enough with your old
flame. Are you coming up to my place now? Our director is there
with half the company.

OLIVIA: Heavens, yes, our colleagues. I don't know—Actually, I'm
a little tired. And that child has to go to bed.

LYRA: (LAUGHS) "That child" has already said she'd come, Ollie.
You can't send her home right after her first performance.

PFUNDTMAYER: Couldn't you manage to stay a little longer,
Ma'am? Such a broken-off evening. Downright unhealthy, it is.
I mean—we understand each other, Ma'am.

LYRA: (FORMALLY) Sorry, Captain. Why don't you come up to my
place with your friends when you finish off here? You too, of
course, Harry. We're sure to be up until the morning papers
come out.

PFUNDTMAYER: Accepted, Ma'am, accepted. Gonna come.

LYRA: It isn't far, Motzstrasse 3, corner of Nollendorf. Hurry up,
Ollie, the Reichsmarshal is going to take us in his car—

OLIVIA: Goodbye, Harry. (SHE BRUSHES HIS CHEEK WITH A KISS)

HARRAS: (HAS GLANCED NERVOUSLY THROUGH THE DOOR) See you
soon. But where is Diddo?

LYRA: The Junior Miss, went on ahead with a couple of Lieutenants. (SHE DISAPPEARS WITH OLIVIA)

WRITZKY: (LAUGHING AS HE ENTERS) Now, if that doesn't beat everything! The way he tells it himself, I think that's downright big
of him.

LAUSITZ: The Reichsmarshal has a profound feeling for the German
sense of humor.

PFUNDTMAYER: That Lyra—she's really put together.

HARRAS: The epitome of modern technology. You keep after, her,
old man!—We used to call her the service station.

PFUNDTMAYER: The what? Boy, that's a pisser. (LAUGHS, SOME-
WHAT DUMBFOUNDED)

EILERS: Harry, why don't you sing something?

HARRAS: (PULLS HIMSELF TOGETHER) Why sure, Freddie. But first,
let's take in some high octane. Waiter! (DETLEV ENTERS)

DETLEV: The General wishes. . . ?

HARRAS: Let's have the dream catalogue.

DETLEV: The wine card, General? (HANDS IT TO HIM)

HARRAS: We'll need something special now—something noble, something festive, an augmentation of our existence. (LEAFS THROUGH THE WINE LIST) There are eternal values involved here. Here it is!—I think this is your best and just right for tonight. (HE READS) Lieserer Niederberg.

DETLEV: Beg pardon, General, but that one has a little cross.

HARRAS: A little cross? What does that mean?

DETLEV: Reserved. There may be only a few bottles left in the cellar.

HARRAS: Reserved? For whom?

DETLEV: I'll check the reservation list. 96. (TAKING THE NOTEBOOK FROM FRANÇOIS HE LEAFS QUICKLY THROUGH IT) 96. Here it is. Reserved for—(HE BITES HIS LIP)

HARRAS: Well, out with it.

DETLEV: For Mr. Remarque, General.

HARRAS: For Mr. . . . ! (HE SLAPS HIS THIGHS AND LAUGHS UPROARIOUSLY) Now there is true German loyalty. That's tradition. I suppose you are reserving it for a happy reunion. (HE LAUGHS UNTIL HE CRIES)

DETLEV: (EMBARRASSED) Of course, the reservation is no longer valid, General. I'll bring it at once. (HE GOES)

LAUSITZ: (HAS COME CLOSER) For Erich Maria Remarque? The emigrant?

HARRAS: (STILL MORE AMUSED) Imagine!—The poor man is stuck . . . in America with nothing to slurp but whiskey!

LAUSITZ: (LIVID WITH RAGE) Fifty marks a bottle! You see how these Jewish swine carried on before we cleaned out the barn.

HARRAS: You know, I am sure, that Remarque is not a Jew.

LAUSITZ: With riffraff like that there is no difference. (FULL OF HATE) Whoever associates with Jews is himself a Jew.

HARRAS: And whoever eats with pigs out of a trough is himself a pig.

LAUSITZ: (CUTTING) What do you mean by that, General?

HARRAS: Just talking to myself.

PFUNDTMAYER: (WHO HASN'T UNDERSTOOD ANYTHING) You mean whoever picks other people's noses is himself a pig. That's a joke—ha, ha, ha! (HE LAUGHS)

WRITZKY: Do you remember the joke from the Röhm period: "Whoever puts his hand in other people's pants is one of the Storm Troopers." (HE SIGHS) Those times are over. (HE AND PFUNDTMAYER LAUGH)

LAUSITZ: (AFTER A SUDDEN SILENCE) May I excuse myself? I am on duty early, General. (HE BOWS TO HARRAS) Gentlemen. (HE SALUTES) Heil Hitler!

HARRAS: Doctor. (HE BOWS SLIGHTLY, DOCTOR SCHMIDT-LAUSITZ EXITS. HARRAS TAKES A VERY DEEP BREATH) Thank God! Now, now I can sing, Freddie. But I just couldn't with that Super-Aryan Siegfried in the room. (BEAMING WITH GOOD HUMOR) Detlev! Where's that wine? (HE POURS HIMSELF A DRINK— CLEARS HIS THROAT) Let's start off with a prehistoric pilot song. You'll all have to chime in, let's say—according to rank. Eilers first.

EILERS: God forbd, I'm completely unmusical.

HARRAS: Doesn't matter.

(HE HAS TAKEN A GUITAR HANGING ON THE WALL, STRIKES A FEW CHORDS, AND BEGINS TALKING TO THE SONG)

To the tune of "Mademoiselle from Armentieres"
We fly up in our aeroplanes
   Way up high.
We fly up in our aeroplanes
   Way up high.
We fly up in our aeroplanes
Looking down for Frenchy dames,
Walking on the earth below.
The dames we spied there from the air,
At closer look they had gray hair.
To hell with all the earth below.

We shoot our guns and drop our bombs
   Ack, ack, ack.
We shoot our guns and drop our bombs
   Ack, ack, ack.
We shoot our guns and drop our bombs
The S.O.B.'s are shooting back.
Mama, I am flying home!

(ALL CHIME IN WITH SHOUTS AND HAND CLAPPING, AND THE REFRAIN IS REPEATED AT A FASTER TEMPO)

EILERS: (SMILING) That's good!

HARRAS: Damn stupid, but beautiful—Children, all I say is, prosit. (DETLEV HAS POURED AND PASSED THE GLASSES) You take a glass too, Hartmann. This is liquid sunlight. Just smell it. (ALL HAVE LIFTED THEIR GLASSES AND ARE SNIFFING THE WINE— HARRAS, ALMOST SOLEMN) Mosel wine! From the valley where the vine trees grip the slate slopes. Been growing for a thousand years—a thousand years of life and work and people—completely without propaganda.

EILERS: (SOFTLY, RAISING HIS GLASS) To Germany.

HARRAS: (HIS GLASS TREMBLING) To the Germany in which it grew. The true, the immortal Germany.

(ANNE, EILERS, POOTSIE, MOHRUNGEN, AND BARON PFLUNGK AP-PEAR IN THE DOOR)

POOTSIE: Well, what happened here—somebody die? Sounds like a funeral oration.

EILERS: You missed something. Harry sang.

HARRAS: Let's go, children—, Let's boom once more for the ladies.

PFUNDTMAYER: (CALLS OUT) Harry, let's sing one from the last war! (HE STARTS IT)

I think—I think a pigeon flies
up there . . .

(HARRAS PLAYS AND SINGS. POOTSIE AND PFLUNGK DANCE. PFUNDT-MAYER IS WALTZING WITH HASTENTEUFFEL. WRITZKY SQUEAKS IN A HIGH VOICE IN THE MANNER OF A FEMALE IMPERSONATOR. EILERS HAS PUT HIS ARM AROUND ANNE AND NOW THEY TOO BEGIN TO DANCE. MOHRUNGEN LOOKS ON SMILING. HARTMANN, ALONE, SUDDENLY EMPTIES THE GLASS THAT HE IS STILL HOLDING IN HIS HAND, FILLS IT AND EMPTIES IT AGAIN. HARRAS IS NOW STARTING IN ON POPULAR SONGS OF THE LAST WAR WHICH HE COMBINES AND MIXES UP WHILE THE MOOD AND THE NOISE MOUNT)

(HANSEN HAS ENTERED FROM THE CORRIDOR. HE HAS REMAINED STANDING IN THE DOOR. HIS FACE IS SERIOUS. HE SIGNALS TO HAR-RAS WITH HIS EYES. HARRAS, THE GUITAR ON HIS ARM AND STILL PLAYING, SAUNTERS OVER TO HIM WITHOUT ATTRACTING ANY AT-TENTION WHILE THE OTHERS CONTINUE SINGING AND DANCING. THEN THE GUITAR PLAYING BREAKS OFF)

POOTSIE: (SINGING THE LAST PHRASE OF A SONG ALONE)

—They don't take love so tragically.
(IT BECOMES STILL)

HARRAS: (SLOWLY WALKS THROUGH THE ROOM, PUTS THE GUITAR
DOWN BETWEEN THE EMPTY PLATES AND GLASSES ON THE TABLE,
TURNS AROUND AND LOOKS AT EILERS. IT HAS BECOME VERY
QUIET. EVEN POOTSIE, LEANING AGAINST PFLUNGK, IS SILENT.
AFTER A FEW SECONDS HARRAS, IN A VERY CALM AND SOBER
VOICE SAYS:) Gentlemen! The Eilers Squadron is ordered back to
the front. You will report to the Air Ministry Transport Division
at 8:30 A.M. and will take off in new planes for Army Headquar-
ters at Smolensk. (HE IS QUIET FOR A MOMENT AND LIGHTS A
CIGARETTE) Well, that's that! And not the first time either.

EILERS: ! (PALE, RESOLUTE) Gentlemen, I repeat: 8:30 A.M., Air
Ministry, Transport Division. Heil Hitler!

(THE OFFICERS STAND AT ATTENTION)

HARTMANN: (HIS EYES FLAMING, LIFTS HIS HAND) Heil Hitler!

THE OTHERS: (REPEAT FORMALLY) Heil Hitler!

MOHRUNGEN: (HAS TAKEN ANNE'S HAND AND IS STROKING IT)
That's war, my dear: when duty calls there is no private life.

EILERS: (smiling) There might be a bright side to this thing! If they
cash in on a week with us now, then they will have to give us
Christmas leave this year. And what could be better than Christmas at home? Last year we spent the holiday on the North Sea
patrol. (HIS CALM, MEASURED THOUGHTFULNESS IS GENUINE
AND BEGINS TO AFFECT THE OTHERS. THE SHOCK IS WEARING
OFF. EVERYBODY'S TALKING)

PFUNDTMAYER: And I thought I had pig's luck. What a double cross
jus' now, when I've gone an' met the woman of ma life! Aw,
what the hell—there's still gonna be some roaring tonight.

EILERS: I know you'll excuse us, Harry. I think it only sensible to
get some sleep.

HARRAS: Why sure. Go on home, children.

POOTSIE: (HAS STPPED UP TO HARTMANN) You seem to be downright happy, little man. First time you've put on a human face all
night! (HARTMANN DOESN'T ANSWER)

PFUNDTMAYER: Whoever goes home is a dog. 'Cept, of course, the married couples.

POOTSIE: I like that. You're a real fighter—a real hero. (SHE PUTS HER ARM AROUND HARTMANN. WITHOUT ANSWERING HARTMANN QUIETLY BUT VERY DEFINITELY FREES HIMSELF) Well, pardon me, then don't. I won't throw myself at you.

HARRAS: Ladies and gentlemen, you are at liberty. I suppose you're still going up to Lyra's?

PFUNDTMAYER: And how! We're going to hold out till eight, and then a cold rubdown. Brrrr.

HARRAS: Perhaps, I'll follow you—after I settle up here. (HE SAYS GOOD-BYE TO PFUNDTMAYER AND HASTENTEUFFEL WITH A HANDSHAKE AND THE THREE EXIT)

POOTSIE: Shouldn't we go up for a little while too, Baron?

PFLUNGK: To Lyra's? I don't think that would be altogether proper.

MOHRUNGEN: Quite improper. You will now come up to the hotel, Pootsie.

POOTSIE: My God—paternal authority. Isn't it lucky you have to go back to Mannheim.

MOHRUNGEN: Pootsie—

POOTSIE: All right, all right, little old man. I'm coming. (SHE KISSES HIM LIGHTLY ON THE FOREHEAD)

PFLUNGK: I can take all of you. My car is outside.

HARRAS: (WITH ANNE AND EILERS AT THE DOOR) Good night, Anne.

ANNE: Many, many thanks. It was a beautiful evening. (SHE PRESSES HIS HAND WARMLY) Good-bye.

EILERS: How about visiting us for Christmas, Harry, if I get leave?

HARRAS: It's a promise.

(DURING THE LAST SENTENCES HARRAS AND HANSEN HAVE ACCOMPANIED THE GUESTS OUTSIDE AND NOW THEY DISAPPEAR WITH THEM TO THE CLOAK ROOM AND FROM THERE WE CAN STILL HEAR VOICES AND GOODBYES)

POOTSIE: (HAS REMAINED STANDING WITH HARTMANN WHO HASN'T GONE OUT YET) You mad at me? (HARTMANN, WITHOUT LOOKING AT HER, SHAKES HIS HEAD) We can still be good friends.

HARTMANN: (STIFF) Of course.

POOTSIE: Well then—good-bye. And lots of luck. (WITH AS MUCH WARMTH AS SHE CAN MUSTER) Keep well, dear. I'll think of you.

HARTMANN: Thanks.

(SHE BRINGS HER FACE CLOSE TO HIS AND OFFERS HIM HER LIPS, BUT HE ONLY BENDS BRIEFLY OVER HER HEAD; SHE SHRUGS HER SHOULDERS AND EXITS. HE STRAIGHTENS HIMSELF UP, TURNS ON HIS HEELS, GOES SLOWLY TO THE TABLE, STANDS WITH HIS BACK TO THE AUDIENCE AND EMPTIES A GLASS)

HARRAS: (COMES BACK WITH HANSEN) Well, bud, now the two of us . . . (HE NOTICES HARTMANN AND STOPS. BOTH LOOK AT HIM FOR A MOMENT)

HARTMANN: (TURNS, HESITATES, SNAPS TO ATTENTION, THEN SOMEWHAT HELPLESS) May I take my leave, General?

HARRAS: Why don't you help me finish this bottle, Lieutenant Hartmann?

HARTMANN: (UNSURE) I don't want to disturb you, General.

HARRAS: I'd be glad to have you stay—

HANSEN: (EMPTIES HIS GLASS) Has the General any other orders?

HARRAS: Tell them outside to get my bill ready.

HANSEN: Anytime, General. (HE EXITS)

HARRAS: (FILLS HIS AND HARTMANN'S GLASSES, TAKES A CIGARETTE OUT OF THE CASE, AND OFFERS ONE TO HARTMANN WHO DECLINES. HARRAS, TOO, DOESN'T LIGHT HIS CIGARETTE, JUST PLAYS WITH IT. SPEAKING ALMOST TO HIMSELF) No—not with this wine, no smoking. Prosit, Hartmann.

HARTMANN: Thanks, General. (HE DOESN'T DRINK, LOOKS DOWN ON THE FLOOR)

HARRAS: (PUTS HIS GLASS DOWN, PULLS UP A CHAIR CLOSE TO HIS AND LEANS TOWARD HIM) Well, Hartmann, I want you to open up once. Go ahead, burst, man! Explode! Say after me: "Damn it all to hell!" And when you say it, think about whomever or whatever you please. Come on, we'll do it together. One—two—three.

BOTH: Damn it all to hell!

HARRAS: Louder!

BOTH: Damn it all to hell!!

HARRAS: Still louder!

BOTH: Damn it all to hell!!! (HARTMANN, AFTER THE LAST TIME, EMPTIES HIS GLASS)

HARRAS: Bravo! You feel better now?

HARTMANN: (BREATHING HEAVILY AND QUITE FRIGHTENED BY HIMSELF) A little, General.

HARRAS: Well, that's pretty good for a start. Did you damn me along with the rest of 'em?

HARTMANN: I don't understand, General.

HARRAS: You think my jokes outrageous, and my political position scandalous. Right?

HARTMANN: I don't permit myself a judgment, General.

HARRAS: You're a tough nut to crack. What's the score with you and little Miss Pootsie?

HARTMANN: (UNMOVED, WITH AN ALMOST MASKLIKE FIXEDNESS) It's all over, General. Miss von Mohrungen has broken off the engagement.

HARRAS: So—hmmm. And why would that be?

HARTMANN: (HALTING BUT ALWAYS IN THE TONE OF A MILITARY RE-PORT) Because of the confusion in my family tree, General. You see, my family comes from the Rhineland. My father and grand-father were regular officers—there is no ground for suspicion of Jewish blood mixture. But—it appears that one of my great-grandmothers came from a foreign country. That happened fre-quently in old Rhineland families. She cannot be traced. The pa-pers are simply not to be found.

HARRAS: (HAS BITTEN HIS LIP AND IS MUMBLING TO HIMSELF) So that's the problem! A poor boy running around with an unde-finable grandmother. (IN GROWING ANGER) Oh, come on! Who knows anything about the Lady great-grandmother's capers! I bet no-one ever asked for an Aryan Pass! Or are you one of the descendants of the Crusading Hartmanns who married into that wine firm in Jerusalem?

HARTMANN: (FACTUALLY) Investigation into racial purity doesn't go that far back, General.

HARRAS: It should, though. It must! If, then properly. Just think . . . all the things that can have happened in a family that old. And from the Rhine, as well. From the Rhine . . . that mill of the peo-ples of Europe. That great European wine-press. (MORE QUI-ETLY) And just think about your own ancestors . . . just since the time of Christ. There you have a Roman Centurion. A dark man. Brown as a ripe olive. He teaches a blonde girl a little Latin. And then there's a Jewish spice handler in the family. He was a serious man who converted to Catholicism before he married, and so started the family tradition. Then there was a Greek doctor, a Celtic legionnaire, a Swiss mercenary, a Swedish rider, one of Napoleon's soldiers, a Cossack deserter, a raftsman from the Black Forest, a journeyman miller from the Elsass, a fat Dutch bargee, an Hungarian, a Pandur, a Viennese officer, a French actor, a Czech musician . . . and all of them lived, fought, drank, sang and produced children . . . and . . . and Goethe! He was of the same clay, and so was Beethoven, and Gutenberg and Matthias Grünewald and . . . ah, go look it up in the encyclopedia. They were the best, my friend. The best in the world! And why? Because that's where the races mingled. Mingled as the water from spring and stream and river combine to form a great living torrent. From the Rhine—that means from the Occident. That's nature's nobility. There's breeding for you. Be proud of it Hartmann and hang you grandmother's papers in the toilet. Cheers.

HARTMANN: (UNCHANGED, ONLY SOMEWHAT SADDER) Miss von Mohrungen has papers covering four generations. That is enough for a marriage contract with an SS man and for any party career. She will not settle for less than that. She is ambitious. She does not want to . . . take second best.

HARRAS: (BURSTING OUT WITH A RED FACE) Then for Pete and Joe's sake be glad you're rid of the bitch! Damn it all! (HE POUNDS ON THE TABLE UNCONTROLLED) She's cheap like a half-eaten apple. Fun for a week's leave at best. (HARTMANN HAS LET HIS HEAD SINK ON HIS CHEST. HARRAS FALLS SILENT—LOOKS AT HARTMANN, QUITE FRIGHTENED, STANDS UP—STEPS UP TO HIM, VERY TENDERLY) My God, boy, did I hurt you? I—didn't mean it like that.

HARTMANN: (LOOKS UP, LOOKS AT HARRAS) You meant it, General. (SOFTLY) You were right.

HARRAS: Don't even think about it anymore. There are better things in this world. Bigger ones.

HARTMANN: Yes indeed, General. Death on the battlefield is big. And pure. And eternal.

HARRAS: Come on, man! Didn't you see the gory mess of bodies lying around? What's great about it? And eternal? Look, I'm an old soldier myself. I know something about this business. And I tell you, if you wanna win, ya gotta survive first. Whoever fights without hope is half a casualty before he starts. And *hope* means you look forward to something, to living. With or without Pootsie. Don't you look forward to coming home when the war is over?

HARTMANN: I don't know, General. (SINCE HARRAS IS LOOKING AT HIM QUESTIONINGLY—AFTER A PAUSE) I don't have a real home that I can look forward to. My father fell in the last war. I never knew him. My mother married again—I never had a home, General, until—

HARRAS: Hmm?

HARTMANN: —Until I joined the Hitler Youth. My home was the training camp. The Officers' School. And then—the Eilers Squadron. (HIS FACE, WHICH FOR A MOMENT HAD GROWN SOFTER, HAS LOCKED ITSELF AGAIN. HE LOOKS DOWN)

HARRAS: (LOOKS AT HIM SILENTLY, FILLING THE GLASSES. THEN HE BEGINS TO WALK UP AND DOWN, SPEAKING SLOWLY, SOFTLY, ALMOST AS IF TALKING TO HIMSELF) Listen to me, Hartmann: Life is in front of you—but you don't know what life is. You're stuck in an oyster's shell. You think your shell is the world, but you don't feel how all around you outside the enormous ocean roars. Take it from me, life is beautiful. The world is wonderful. We human beings try like hell to louse it up but we are no match for it—for the original concept. I don't know who thought the whole thing up. I am no philosopher, but I know—the concept is good. The plan is right. The design is magnificent. And the meaning of it is—not: Power. Not: Luck. Not: Gratification. But—"Beauty." Or—"joy." Or both. I don't care what you call it—maybe there's no word for it. It's something we feel and possess in our best moments. And that's the only reason we are alive. Are you listening, Hartmann, to what the old man is babbling?

HARTMANN: (QUIET, SIMPLY) Yes.

HARRAS: Do you have an idea what I'm talking about?

HARTMANN: Yes.

HARRAS: I'm talking about you, my boy, about you and about me.
Men are a funny species of animal. From time to time a great
frenzy seizes them and they go berserk till they get it out of their
systems. War is our oldest excuse for running riot. Of course
men are never completely normal. There's always a screw loose
somewhere—we build up a world and then we destroy it, but the
original design, the one that always continues to attract us—that
is beautiful even if we don't understand the formula. Why are
rocks beautiful? And the Northern Lights? Or the grain in a
piece of wood? And even some of our own creations motivated
by viciousness—if they work, they're beautiful. A tank is beautiful. And a heavy bomber—a fighter plane—as beautiful as a
horse taking a jump. And a curved steel bridge over a river. And
an old worm-eaten hope chest. A tree in autumn. A thunder-
storm. A sunflower. And sometimes even a human face—Lord
God Almighty, Hartmann! Don't you think it's worth it to live?
To live a long, long time? To grow very old? (HE EMPTIES HIS
GLASS. HARTMANN LIFTS HIS GLASS TO HIS LIPS WITHOUT DRINK-
ING. HE SITS MOTIONLESS AND TEARS RUN DOWN HIS FACE)

DELTEV: (LOOKS IN HOLDING A PLUG-IN TELEPHONE) Sorry to dis-
turb you, General. A call for you. (HE PLUGS IN THE TELEPHONE
AND AT THE SAME TIME PUTS THE FOLDED BILL ON THE TABLE
AND SLOWLY GOES BACK TO THE DOOR)

HARRAS: (HE PICKS UP THE TELEPHONE) Hello, Lyra! Come over? I
don't know. Tell me, is the little one still there? Yes, please—like
to talk to her. (HE WAITS FOR A MINUTE WITH THE TELEPHONE AT
HIS EAR AND WITH HIS FREE HAND LIGHTS A CIGARETTE AND
HUMS NERVOUSLY TO HIMSELF) Good morning, Monkeywrench.
I keep thinking about those violets you wore. Put them in water,
will you? OK. That's a promise. What? Going to press them and
keep them in my scrapbook like a little girl. Oh, yes, I'm serious.
No—I'm coming over. You'll have to stay now. (HE HANGS UP—
PICKS UP THE RECEIVER AGAIN FOR A SECOND, LISTENS, AND PUTS
IT BACK AGAIN. HIS GLANCE GLIDES OVER TO HARTMANN, WHOSE
HEAD HAS SUNK ONTO THE BACK OF THE CHAIR. HE LOOKS MORE
DEAD THAN ASLEEP. HARRAS GOES QUICKLY TO THE DOOR,
WHISTLES AND CALLS) Korrianke!

(KORRIANKE APPEARS, BEHIND HIM DETLEV AND FRANÇOIS. HAR-
RAS POINTS WITH HIS HEAD TO THE SLEEPING—OR EXHAUSTED
HARTMANN.)

KORRIANKE: Champagne corpse, General?

HARRAS: Naw—combat fatigue. Take him home, Korrianke—put him to bed. When I get home we'll make him a good breakfast. He has to take off for the front at 8:30.

KORRIANKE: The young man ought to report for sick call, General.

HARRAS: He wouldn't do it. Well—let's move. Can you make it alone?

KORRIANKE: Easy as pie. (HE LIFTS HARTMANN UP WITH BEARLIKE ARMS BUT WITH AN ALMOST MATERNAL CARE AND CARRIES HIM OUT)

HARRAS: Take my car, it has better springs, and call me a taxi. (HE TAKES THE CHECK, LOOKS IT OVER HASTILY, TAKES A BIG BILL OUT OF HIS WALLET AND GIVES IT TO DETLEV)

DETLEV: I'll be right back with the change, sir.

HARRAS: Nonsense. Split the difference between you.

DETLEV: It's too much, General—

HARRAS: You won't reform me any more, Detlev. He who is born a spendthrift, dies a—oh well, I'm too tired to be funny. Good night.

DETLEV *and* FRANCOIS: Good night, General. Many thanks. *Merci. Merci.*

HARRAS: (PICKS UP THE TELEPHONE RECEIVER ONCE MORE AND LISTENS) Funny noise in there. (PUTS THE RECEIVER BACK AND LISTENS TOWARD THE WALL AS HE STARTS OUT) Still ticking, too. So—tick! Who cares? (HE EXITS)

(DETLEV AND FRANÇOIS REMAIN ALONE. FRANÇOIS BEGINS TO PUT OUT THE CANDLES AND IS WHISTLING SOFTLY TO HIMSELF. DETLEV GOES TO THE TELEPHONE—DIALS A NUMBER, WAITS. FRANÇOIS STOPS WHISTLING—WATCHES HIM, SIPPING FROM A GLASS OF WINE SOMEONE HAS LEFT)

DETLEV: Hello? Detlev, here. Secret Office C, Captain Degenhardt—Yes, indeed, Captain. Everything went smoothly. But there was a slight ticking that almost gave it away. Beg your pardon? Only partly intelligible? That wasn't my fault, Captain. The noise here, you know—yes, indeed. At your service. (HANGS UP) Only worked part of the time. Something new . . . a radio dictaphone with telephonic recording device. There's a few wrinkles like that ticking they've still got to iron out.

FRANÇOIS: (UNDER HIS BREATH) It's disgusting.

DETLEV: (WHEELS AROUND AND STARES AT HIM) You keep your trap shut. If that Otto finds out, you'll see something.

FRANÇOIS: It's disgusting.

DETLEV: (CLOSER TO HIM, MENACINGLY) I've got you in my hand—my barbed wire sweetheart. You want to land in a camp! Maybe ya like forced labor? (CALMER) Think I like to do it? Makes me puke. Show me a guy who isn't a son of a bitch around here. What are you supposed to do if one of them comes along and gives you a speech: "Well now, listen to me, Herr Detlev. You, as a waiter, have a special opportunity to serve the state." And all the time he gives you one of those ice cold stares—You don't say no, mister. Besides, I got a family.

FRANÇOIS: Shit.

CURTAIN

Act 2

(GENERAL HARRAS'S APARTMENT IN A NEW WESTERN SUBURB OF BERLIN. A ROOMY STUDIO APARTMENT ON THE TOP FLOOR OF A MODERN BUILDING. IT IS FURNISHED IN MODERN STYLE, SOLID AND FUNCTIONAL, BUT IN A SOMEWHAT ADVENTUROUS WAY. A FEW WELL MADE PIECES OF FURNITURE: A LONG, NARROW DRAWING TABLE COVERED WITH ALL KINDS OF TECHNICAL MATERIALS; A DESK WITH PAMPHLETS, DOCUMENTS, AND A TELEPHONE. AN OPEN RED BRICK FIREPLACE, A FEW COMFORTABLE CHAIRS, AND A FEW WOODEN ONES, A LOT OF SMOKING EQUIPMENT, A COUCH COVERED WITH A CAMEL'S HAIR COVER, AND A RADIO PHONOGRAPH. THE WALLS ARE PAINTED IN A LIGHT COLOR AND HALF COVERED WITH BOOKCASES. ABOVE THESE, A FEW OLD LUTES, A COLLECTION OF EXOTIC BUTTER-FLIES, AND A TARGET WITH A LOT OF HOLES IN IT. A FEW WOODCUTS AND PICTURES OF ANIMALS BY FRANZ MARC. HERE AND THERE THE WILD GRIMACE OF AN AFRICAN DANCING MASK. IN A CORNER A BOW AND ARROW, AN ARABIAN SADDLE, AND AN AFRICAN DRUM.

IN A SIDE ROOM A SORT OF DRESSING ROOM WHICH JOINS ONTO THE STUDIO, HALF HIDDEN BY A BAMBOO SCREEN, A BAR HAS BEEN BUILT. ITS FRAME IS MADE OF SPLINTERED PROPELLORS AND ALL

KINDS OF BROKEN AND SHOT-UP PARTS OF PLANES. INSIDE, THE BAR IS FULL OF FANTASTIC STUFF, TROPHIES OF WAR AND TRAVEL, PHOTOGRAPHS OF FLIERS, GIRLS AND WILD ANIMALS.

AT LEFT AND RIGHT DOORS LEAD TO THE KITCHEN AND THE HALL. IT IS LATE AFTERNOON BUT STILL LIGHT, SHORTLY BEFORE DUSK. THROUGH THE HIGH STUDIO WINDOW ON THE BACK WALL ONE CAN SEE THE WINTRY GLARING-WHITE SKY OVER THE CITY OF BERLIN. THE BLACKOUT CURTAINS ARE PULLED BACK.

KORRIANKE STANDS MOTIONLESS AT THE WINDOW AND WATCHES THE STREET BELOW WITH BINOCULARS. HANSEN, SMOKING, WALKS BACK AND FORTH WITH HEAVY, HASTY STEPS, ALWAYS COMING BACK TO THE SAME SPOT)

HANSEN: (AFTER A WHILE, REMAINS STANDING, LOOKS AT HIS WATCH) Damn it. (HE STAMPS HIS FOOT, GOES TO THE TELEPHONE AND DIALS A NUMBER) Hello, Air Ministry? Captain Hansen speaking. Give me extension 1296—Oderbruch?—Anything new? No. Not here either—I told you already, at ten o'clock I got orders: "Be ready at his apartment." Now it's five. . . . Naturally. As soon as I know anything. (HANGS UP) Damn it all. (BEGINS WALKING UP AND DOWN AGAIN. KORRIANKE HAS PUT DOWN THE BINOCULARS AND LISTENED TO THE CONVERSATION. NOW HE PICKS UP THE BINOCULARS AGAIN AND LOOKS DOWN IN THE STREET) Stop that, man. This is not a regatta!

KORRIANKE: (GRIMLY) Please, Captain. You've been waiting seven hours—me, I bin· waiting two weeks. So the word is: Calm down!

HANSEN: Calm down!

KORRIANKE: (ALMOST SCREAMING) For two weeks! An' it come like a bolt from the blue! We'd cooked up a little trip to Kohlhasen, car full of gas an' all—all of a sudden, he come up all alone an' says: "Korriandoli, step lively 'n get my small bag, toothbrush, 'n pajamas enough—I've got to go traveling f'r a few days! And out he goes! I give a look down the stairs—Mercedes-Benz, Model '41, black limousine, flag up front, party emblem and a big red G—Gestapo!

HANSEN: You have told me that story exactly eighteen times. (RUMMAGES AROUND IN HIS POCKETS AND BRINGS FORTH AN EMPTY

CIGARETTE BOX) The devil. That was the last one. (HE THROWS THE BOX AWAY)

KORRIANKE: Captain, hand on your heart, do you believe the rumors?

HANSEN: I believe nothing! Officially, the word is he's at the Eastern Front and there isn't nobody believes that! And today. Why would they have ordered me to report here? To receive his ashes? They send those through the mail. (BEGINS TO PACE BACK AND FORTH)

KORRIANKE: The elevator! Pssst! The elevator is coming up! (THROUGH THE OPEN HALL DOOR WE HEAR THE WHIRRING NOISE OF AN ELEVATOR. BOTH LISTEN)

HANSEN: He's coming! (KORRIANKE RUNS OUT. A MAN IN CIVILIAN CLOTHES COMES IN HASTILY. HE HAS HIS HAT PRESSED DOWN OVER HIS FACE. KORRIANKE IS CLOSE BEHIND HIM)

KORRIANKE: Stop! Stop! Who are you anyway?

HANSEN: (HAND ON HIS GUN) Halt! Stand still! What do you want here?

LAWRENCE: (PUSHES BACK THE BRIM OF HIS HAT) Hello, Captain! How are you?

HANSEN: Buddy, it's you!

LAWRENCE: Yes, it's me—they had a guy shadowing me but I shook him. (HE THROWS HIMSELF INTO A CHAIR, EXHAUSTED, AND BEGINS TO SMOKE. HE IS IN HIS MIDDLE TWENTIES WITH INTELLIGENT, SOMEWHAT SAD EYES. HIS FACE CREATES A CLEAN-CUT EFFECT EVEN THOUGH HE IS UNSHAVED AND DUSTY)

HANSEN: Unwind, Korrianke. You know Buddy Lawrence, don't you—Our friend from the decadent American press.

LAWRENCE: Was, Captain, was! My press card was cancelled yesterday. Waiting for an exit permit. Hope I get it in time.

HANSEN: Because you stuck your nose in this Harras affair?

LAWRENCE: That was just foam on the beer. My stein was running over. (HE LAUGHS)

KORRIANKE: Where is General Harras?

LAWRENCE: That's what I'm asking you. The afternoon editions say: "General Harras just returned from an inspection of the Eastern Front." Seen, he wasn't, by nobody. And the story that he'd been liquidated we got from the front.

HANSEN: From the front? They've got too much time at the front. They eat too many beans and they squat around for hours in the latrine squeezing out rumors.

(LAWRENCE SHRUGS HIS SHOULDERS. HE PUTS OUT A HALF-SMOKED CIGARETTE)

HANSEN: How about a little business deal, sir? Two cigarettes for a cognac.

LAWRENCE: Thanks. (DRINKS) Just in time. On Kaiserstrasse I jumped off the bus and zigzagged for ten blocks. They're already in my apartment. But I was tipped off.

HANSEN: Why don't you go to your Embassy?

LAWRENCE: Stuffed shirts. Only in an emergency. I spent the night in the waiting rooms of assorted Berlin railroad stations. It was very educational. (HE YAWNS)

KORRIANKE: Pssst!! The elevator. (THEY LISTEN. IMMEDIATELY AFTER THAT, THE DOORBELL RINGS)

HANSEN: Run, man.

KORRIANKE: That isn't him. He's got a key.

HANSEN: Ya damn fool. He could have lost it.

KORRIANKE: Not him. Never. (THE DOORBELL RINGS AGAIN. KORRIANKE GOES)

HANSEN: (TO LAWRENCE) Wouldn't it be smarter if you made yourself scarce? (POINTS TO THE KITCHEN DOOR) You never know.

LAWRENCE: Not on a bet. Too nosey.

(BOTH STARE AT THE DOOR. IN WALKS DR. SCHMIDT-LAUSITZ IN HIS BLACK PARTY UNIFORM. HE STANDS IN THE DOORWAY FOR A MOMENT AND INSPECTS THE TWO WITHOUT GREETING, KORRIANKE RIGHT BEHIND HIM)

LAUSITZ: (TAKES HIS HAT OFF, SUDDENLY TURNS AROUND WITH A SHORT JERK TO KORRIANKE, HANDS HIM HIS HAT) Hang it up!

KORRIANKE: (MURMURS) Delighted. Easy as pie.

LAUSITZ: (STEPS FORWARD, LIFTS HIS HAND QUICKLY) Heil Hitler. (HANSEN GIVES A MILITARY SALUTE)

LAWRENCE: Howdy.

LAUSITZ: You should be more careful. About jumping off moving vehicles, I mean. Something could easily happen to you.

LAWRENCE: Don't worry. I can take care of myself.

LAUSITZ: Good for you. I trust that you have already applied for your exit visa?

LAWRENCE: As you see, I am making my farewell calls. But I'm having trouble finding my friends at home. Alive, I mean.

LAUSITZ: If you would like to say goodbye to General Harras why don't you try the Adlon Bar. He stopped off there to report to the foreign press on his inspection trip to the Eastern Front. The truly neutral foreign press, of course.

LAWRENCE: I no longer have the honor to belong to that select group.

LAUSITZ: I'm pleased to hear that you consider it an honor—

KORRIANKE: (WHO, STANDING BY THE DOOR, HAS EXCITED SIGNS) Elevator! Elevator! (SHORT SILENCE. THEN THE DOORBELL RINGS—KORRIANKE GOES, DISAPPOINTED. IMMEDIATELY AFTERWARD WE HEAR HIM LET OUT A SORT OF YODEL THAT COULD ALSO BE A CRY OF PAIN OR FRIGHT. EVERYBODY IS STARTLED. THEN WE HEAR HIM YELLING) Captain, on the double. It's him!

HANSEN: (WIPES HIS BROW) Lord Almighty, ma legs won't work. (HE STUMBLES OUT)

LAUSITZ: (WITH MOCKING GLANCE TO LAWRENCE) The dead rise up.

LAWRENCE: Perhaps only a "corpse on furlough."

LAUSITZ: That is what we all are.

(LAUSITZ GIVES A BRIEF HITLER SALUTE AS HARRAS ENTERS WITH THE BEAMING KORRIANKE WHO CARRIES COAT, CAP, AND BAG, AND POURS A LARGE GLASS OF KIRSCH WITH HIS FREE HAND. HARRAS IS DRESSED IN A GRAY FIELD UNIFORM, SEEMS UNCHANGED, ONLY SOMEWHAT PALE, WITH RED-RIMMED EYES)

HARRAS: (WHILE ENTERING) Naw, naw, children—I never lose keys or cigarette lighters or corkscrews. I only lose money. As for the key, it seems to have fascinated somebody else. (LOOKS AT SCHMIDT-LAUSITZ) If, by any chance, you have any idea who might be bent on secret visits to my apartment, then tell them that the lock will be changed today.

LAUSITZ: I don't know what you're talking about.

HARRAS: Not important, I got it from a detective story. Hey, Buddy! What are you doing here?

LAWRENCE: Looking for trouble, I guess. Sorry to see you're still alive. I bet two years' poker winnings that the rumors were true.

HARRAS: Double your bet and wait a few weeks. How about a drink, Buddy, you look worn out.

LAWRENCE: What I need is a shave. May I use your shaving equipment?

HARRAS: Of course. Courtesy of the Luftwaffe. (TO KORRIANKE) Unpack my stuff and show him the bathroom.

KORRIANKE: (WHILE GOING OFF WITH LAWRENCE) Come along, old fellow.

HARRAS: (CHANGED, REMAINS STANDING IN FRONT OF LAUSITZ, STARES AT HIM, SPEAKING SOFTLY WITH AN EFFORT AT SELF-CONTROL) I do not recall giving you permission to come here.

LAUSITZ: I did not ask for permission, General. I have an official message for you.

HARRAS: An order?

LAUSITZ: That is a matter of—interpretation.

HARRAS: I can tell you right off, I don't take orders from you.

LAUSITZ: Too bad. You don't seem to grasp the seriousness of your situation.

HARRAS: You think I don't know the stakes in this game after two weeks in Hotel Gestapo. Your threats are nothing compared to the service I had there.

LAUSITZ: Your bearing and physical condition prove that you cannot complain about your treatment.

HARRAS: Maybe I'm supposed to thank you because they did not fracture my nose-bone? They'd have broken my eggs with rap-· ture if I didn't have a few friends in the General Staff who could raise a rumpus.

LAUSITZ: In your position I would not rely too heavily on the friends in the General Staff. And even less on the friends in foreign countries and public opinion. We take care of public opinion. You owe your temporary freedom to purely practical considerations.

HARRAS: I have taken cognizance of the word "temporary." (SITS DOWN IN A CHAIR WITH HIS BACK TO LAUSITZ)

LAUSITZ: You are being given an opportunity for complete rehabilitation, General. However, there is a time limit, non-extendable. As director of the department you are responsible for the recurrent sabotage in airplane production. This problem must be conclusively explained and removed within ten days.

HARRAS: (WITHOUT TURNING AROUND) Otherwise?

LAUSITZ: There is no otherwise. You have ten days to disprove this suspicion by clearing up the problem completely.

HARRAS: That means ten days "stay of execution."

LAUSITZ: "Stay" is correct. I hope that now you know where you stand. (HARRAS DOESN'T ANSWER, JUST SMOKES) Personally, I would like to add—

HARRAS: Thanks. I know.

LAUSITZ: You will hear it just the same. Personally, I wouldn't delay ten days—not even ten minutes, to render a person like you harmless.

HARRAS: Likewise.

LAUSITZ: I know. In me you see a mortal enemy. You are quite correct. There is no room for us both in this world.

HARRAS: Not under my roof either. Should I go?

LAUSITZ: Your arrogance is misplaced here. Your sarcasm is inappropriate. The game is up. You won't cheat us out of the results of our fight. You believed you could take the cream of it and grow fat on the proceeds. That you could pour us into the pigs' trough with the slops. You are mistaken. It is quite the reverse.

HARRAS: (INDIFFERENTLY) Possibly. Things can always change. The wheel turns for just as long as it spins.

LAUSITZ: The wheel won't be turning for you anymore. Never again on high. You and your kind have looked down on us for long enough. We don't look down on people, we tread on them.

HARRAS: Yes, in the guts. And only ever the defenseless. As a mob, in closed ranks. With the approval of the authorities. (HE GAZES AT HIM, WITH AN ALMOST ASTONISHED LOOK OF DISGUST) And such types want to rule the world. You're in for a surprise.

LAUSITZ: For the present, it's the others who are surprised. You, however, General Harras, don't need to take pride in your personal courage. Anyone can have that. And we decide what constitutes honor. Despise us for as long as you can. We'll pay you back.

(HARRAS TAKES A GUN OUT OF HIS POCKET AND UNLOCKS THE SAFETY CATCH. LAUSITZ HASTILY GOES TO THE DOOR)

LAUSITZ: For God's sake, General Harras, you are taking the road to ruin.

HARRAS: Don't worry. I'm just trying to steady my aim. (HE AIMS FOR THE TARGET ON THE WALL AND FIRES FROM A SITTING POSITION. KORRIANKE AND HANSEN RUN IN) The gentleman wishes to leave. Elevator.

HANSEN: (LOOKING AT THE TARGET) 23. Not bad.

HARRAS: Not good enough. (SHOOTS AGAIN)

HANSEN: Bull's eye.

HARRAS: All right. (LAUSITZ GOES OFF QUICKLY WITHOUT A GOODBYE. KORRIANKE FOLLOWS. WE HEAR THE NOISE OF THE ELEVATOR. HARRAS PUTS THE REVOLVER AWAY, TAKES THE FULL GLASS. HIS HAND TREMBLES A LITTLE. HE SHAKES HIS HEAD, EMPTIES HIS GLASS AND LEANS BACK. HANSEN AND KORRIANKE RETURN) Open a window. Let some fresh air in here.

KORRIANKE: Maybe I can still hit him! (HE RUNS TO THE WINDOW, OPENS IT AND SPITS DOWN) Tough luck, too much wind.

HARRAS: (TIRED) There, you see. Even the weather is against us.

KORRIANKE: (CHANGED—WHITE-FACED—WITH CLENCHED FISTS) If something had happened to you, Herr General. I—I don't know what I—

HARRAS: S'all right, Korriandoli. (GOES TO HIM AND PUTS A CIGARETTE IN HIS MOUTH) Go ahead and smoke one. Be calm and breathe deeply the doctor said as he turned on the gas. (TURNS TO HANSEN) The shit is up to our chins and seems to be in the process of rising.

KORRIANKE: Looks like we have to grow a little.

HARRAS: I sort of have the feeling I'm growing shorter. What did the commentors say at the Ministry?

HANSEN: Icy silence over a foggy ocean. Everyone looked in the other direction except Oderbruch.

HARRAS: Any results up to now?

HANSEN: Nothing tangible—as far as the wing covering is concerned.

HARRAS: New accidents occurred?

KORRIANKE: No more reports came in. Stopped suddenly about two weeks ago.

HARRAS: Two weeks ago. That's weird. That smells like a sinister systematic plan. But where—where is the root?

HANSEN: The important thing is—you'll fly lead again. Now we're certain to catch the fox.

HARRAS: (SOFTLY TO HIMSELF) I think—there's no longer any point in it. I think—there's no point in it. No point at all.

(HANSEN LOOKS AT HARRAS AND BITES HIS LIP. KORRIANKE HAS BROUGHT IN A LOOSE, SOFT SUEDE JACKET, WHICH HARRAS CHANGES FOR THE COAT OF HIS UNIFORM)

KORRIANKE: Mufti, mufti. Jus' like at Mother's.

HARRAS: Thanks. How's our Yank?

KORRIANKE: He's rolled himself up on the couch pounding his ear like a bear in winter. Didn't even hear the shooting.

HARRAS: Let him sleep. We have to find a way to spirit him off to the Embassy. (THE TELEPHONE RINGS. KORRIANKE TAKES IT OFF QUICKLY BEFORE HARRAS CAN REACH FOR IT)

KORRIANKE: We're here, who's there? Sure, sure, but sure. Arrived promptly. What did the ole Easter Bunny tell you? Fresh as a daisy. Washed and shaved— What, sleep? Out of the question. Clear—understood, hup, hup—click, click. (HE HANGS UP)

HARRAS: Who was that?

KORRIANKE: (BEAMING) Wouldn't Herr General like to know!

HARRAS: Well, what's going on?

KORRIANKE: Regrettable lapse in your powers of observation, Herr General.

HARRAS: What is this?

KORRIANKE: (DISGUSTED) I do believe you've lost your nose for fine detail. (PUTS A VASE OF FLOWERS IN FRONT OF HARRAS'S FACE)

HARRAS: (OPENS HIS EYES) Hmmmm. Violets. Was she here?

KORRIANKE: Every day, five o'clock on the dot after rehearsal. Have I heard anything? Is there any news? Do I know where you are and when you are coming back? I didn't. Sometimes I fibbed a little. So I told her stories about Herr General's childhood.

HARRAS: Childhood! But I only met you in '17!

KORRIANKE: 'S all the same. Every grown-up had a beautiful child-hood. I know what a young lady like that wants to hear. (CLICKS HIS TONGUE) Class, Herr General.

HARRAS: Korrianke, you're turning into a matchmaker.

KORRIANKE: There wasn't much matching to do, Herr General. An affair like that just matches itself. (BELL RINGS) But if you please, go easy at first. The little Miss was terrible upset. (HE RUNS OUT)

HARRAS: Let's go, let's go! (QUICKLY DRINKS A KIRSCH)

HANSEN: Mouthwash would be more advisable.

HARRAS: Out!

(HANSEN DISAPPEARS THROUGH THE OTHER DOOR WHILE KORRI-
ANKE LETS DIDDO IN FROM THE HALL AND WANTS TO LEAVE AGAIN,
BUT DIDDO HANGS ON TO HIS HAND, THROWS HER ARMS AROUND
HIS NECK AND KISSES HIM ON THE CHEEK)

KORRIANKE: (SPEAKING OVER HER HEAD) Blank cartridge, Herr
General. Not meant for me personally.

HARRAS: Cut—

KORRIANKE: —it. Easy as pie. (QUICKLY GOES OFF)

DIDDO: (HALF LAUGHING, WIPES HER EYES) I don't want to cry.
Isn't it disgusting that you have to cry when you're happy.

HARRAS: (COMES UP TO HER) I don't call that crying, those few
drops of holy water. That's family tradition. I know all about
that from Aunt Ollie.

DIDDO: (LAUGHS, RELIEVED) I was supposed to meet her at the Wit-
tenberg subway station but I stood her up. I hope she waits a
long time before she follows. She—she was terribly worried.

HARRAS: Nonsense. No reason to get upset just because I fly to the
front.

DIDDO: (SOFTLY) We were afraid it was true—what was being
whispered.

HARRAS: And if it had been true—would that have been so bad for
you?

DIDDO: (LOWERS HER HEAD) Yes, or I wouldn't be here.

HARRAS: (VERY SERIOUS) Will you believe me if I tell you that nothing better ever happened to me? Please believe it.

DIDDO: I believe it. I want to believe it. I can't really imagine what
it would mean to you. But to me you are everything.

HARRAS: And when you say that you don't even look at me.

DIDDO: No—that is asking too much. But I would like to look at
you. After all, I hardly know you! Couldn't you look somewhere
else for a minute? Maybe out the window?

HARRAS: (TURNS HIS FACE TO THE WINDOW) Sunset—made to
order.

DIDDO: Now I'm looked at you.

HARRAS: Still?

DIDDO: Still.

HARRAS: Can I look at you now?

DIDDO: Yes, you can turn around now.

HARRAS: (LOOKS INTO HER FACE) You—changed. You're older. More beautiful.

DIDDO: Do you know why? (HARRAS NODS, TAKES A STEP TOWARD HER. DIDDO DRAWS BACK SOMEWHAT)

HARRAS: Come. (ALMOST WITHOUT TOUCHING HER, HE LEADS HER TO AN EASY CHAIR AND SITS DOWN NEXT TO HER ON THE ARM) I have to confess something to you. I didn't know this. I didn't expect it at all. I've had bad dreams recently— You didn't go with them. And ten minutes ago—or is it only five?—I had a moment there when everything was all the same to me—It may come back. Worse than Ash Wednesday. But now—do you know how I feel now?

DIDDO: (TAKES HIS HAND) Tell me.

HARRAS: Playing hookey from school! Mardi Gras! Long vacations!

DIDDO: (LAUGHS) You must have been quite a pest at home in school! Korrianke was telling me!

HARRAS: Yes—he was always around!

DIDDO: And at thirteen already after the girls!

HARRAS: Told you that too? I'll have to button his lip.

DIDDO: I don't really care. I like it.

HARRAS: (BENDS DOWN TO HER) Damn it—I should have guzzled mouthwash. Reeking of alcohol again.

DIDDO: That goes with you. That's how I got to know you. Come— (TAKES HIS FACE IN HER HANDS AND PULLS IT ALL THE WAY OVER TO HER FACE. KISSES HIM ON THE LIPS AND FREES HERSELF AGAIN IMMEDIATELY) Oh, I'm almost not scared of you anymore. But please, give me something to drink. Anything. I think I feel very weak.

HARRAS: (POURING A DRINK) And now just let someone come along and tell me that life isn't beautiful. A long time ago I tried to tell a young man that life was worth living if only you can look forward to something. I had almost forgotten it myself these last few days.

DIDDO: (DRINKS WITH HIM) There must have been a time when you could simply be happy to be young? Weren't you?

HARRAS: I don't remember now. I don't think it is easy to be young any time.

DIDDO: No. I think it's a sort of sickness. (SHE SHUDDERS A LITTLE) Sometimes I am only a feather in the wind that has no weight at all. Sometimes I'm as heavy as a stone at the bottom of a well. But—now I want to be happy! Quite madly happy. Isn't it all right?

HARRAS: It's more than all right. Your whole lifetime you're supposed to love and be happy. We need a whole world of joy—to outweigh all the misery—or else the world would get so heavy it wouldn't be able to turn anymore.— Do you know we're both already a little drunk?

DIDDO: Oh, it's wonderful. It's wonderful to be a little drunk— Aunt Ollie, you know, always takes everything so terribly tragically—it is really tragic too, of course. But after all, I can't help it that I'm not Jewish. She worries about the poor Jews day and night—believe the men she loved the most were all Jews— outside of—of course—

HARRAS: (LAUGHS) You mean: present company excepted. You don't have to blush.

DIDDO: I'm not blushing. Look . . . I . . . often I don't know where I'm at anymore. I only know one thing. I would like to get out, out! Sometimes I think if I were Jewish and had to emigrate— maybe it wouldn't be so bad. To see the world—my God! New York! Just once, to be all the way to the top of a skyscraper and let your handkerchief fall down, and watch it get smaller like a snowflake over all the traffic! And the ocean—and the harbors— maybe China—or Rio de Janeiro. Sometimes I envy the Jews madly. I mean the ones outside.

HARRAS: (TAKES HER IN HIS ARMS) Maybe we'll be honorary Jews, us two. Maybe we'll wander through the world sometime. Maybe they'll throw us out at the right time because we're so illegally happy.

DIDDO: I don't need the world when I'm with you. I want to stay with you today. Always. Come—take off my jacket for me now. (THROWS IT BEHIND HER) After all, I'm at home here.

HARRAS: You are wonderful.

DIDDO: You are wonderful.

HARRAS: Gee, we are stupid.

DIDDO: Gee, we are stupid.

HARRAS: (BENDS HER HEAD BACK) Come—kiss me—like that.

DIDDO: Easy as pie—

HARRAS: Cut—

DIDDO: —it. (KISSES HIM)

HARRAS: (AFTER A LITTLE WHILE) In a British play the maid would come in now to serve tea or the telephone would ring.

DIDDO: Telephone!—God. It's getting dark already— Yes, I have to call somebody.

HARRAS: No, I don't like that.

DIDDO: But I promised—to make up my mind by tonight. I've been holding him off for two weeks—

HARRAS: Him? Who?

DIDDO: Roisterer—our new director— He made me a proposition—real wild—a lead!

HARRAS: (GRUMBLING) Don't like it. Don't like it.

DIDDO: I demanded a shameless salary and they said yes. But I would have to go to Vienna for six months, because it opens there first. Because, I think, he is from Vienna or from Linz. I don't know exactly.

HARRAS: Oh, isn't this wonderful! Oh, isn't this marvelous! I'm already jealous!

DIDDO: Of Roisterer? (SHE LAUGHS) You should see him! He looks like a rabbit!

HARRAS: For God's sake not that! Rabbits are terribly sexy.

DIDDO: Will you stop! Roisterer—it's just silly!

HARRAS: Please, don't wreck my beautiful jealousy! Nothing like this has happened to me for such a long time—to be so magnificently, so stupidly, in love.

DIDDO: But I can't imagine me with Roisterer!

HARRAS: You're not supposed to, you rascal!

DIDDO: Besides, I'm turning it down. (RUNS TO THE TELEPHONE) You don't really believe I'm going to leave now?

HARRAS: (FOLLOWS HER QUICKLY AND PUTS HIS HAND ON THE PHONE. CHANGED) Wait a minute. Is there such a big hurry?

DIDDO: I want to get it over with. It's only fair to let him know.

HARRAS: You will have to think it over some more.

DIDDO: (LEANS AGAINST HIM) Please, please don't say I should think of my career. Let me stay here.

HARRAS: (HOLDS HER CLOSE, BREATHES INTO HER HAIR SOFTLY) It isn't because of your career. Let me have a little time. When does he have to know?

DIDDO: Before tonight's curtain—

HARRAS: (LOOKS AT HIS WATCH) We still have an hour. Will you give me an hour? No questions asked? And will you leave—the decision to me? Just this once?

DIDDO: (LOOKS AT HIM) Yes.

HARRAS: Thanks. (STROKES HER ARM AND HER HAND)

DIDDO: (TOUCHES HIS HAND, IN WHICH HE IS STILL HOLDING THE WATCH, TOUCHES HIS WATCH JUST AS HE IS STARTING TO PUT IT AWAY) What a funny kind of watch you have—

HARRAS: That's no watch. That's my time-grinder.

DIDDO: It must be terribly old. Does it work?

HARRAS: It runs so fast you have to chain it down. That is, if it doesn't stop. And then all ya have to do is this—(HE KNOCKS THE WATCH AGAINST THE BACK OF HIS HEAD)—Did you hear it ring? Genuine nickel plate.

DIDDO: Where did you get it?

HARRAS: Someone gave it to me. (HE PUTS THE WATCH AWAY)

DIDDO: You don't have to talk about it if you don't want to.

HARRAS: He was the first pilot I shot down. I was there when he died. He said: "Souvenir"—and gave me the watch. And grinned and smoked a cigarette. Suddenly I knew I would stay alive as long—as long as I had the watch. Of course, that's silly. Superstition. But when he grinned at me so calmly and a little sly, it suddenly struck me: "He knows." Dying people see more than the rest of us. Whoever has the watch stays alive so the other one isn't forgotten. You shouldn't really talk about things like that. I've never done it. Never before . . .

DIDDO: Don't you think you could talk about everything with me?

HARRAS: (WALKS UP AND DOWN, REMAINS STANDING IN FRONT OF HER, SPEAKS RAPIDLY, SOFTLY) You should know how things stand with me. Right now my life is worth less than the old watch. They're after me—I'm trying to beat my way through—but the chances are slim. And if I make it, it'll be because of you.

DIDDO: Now I know you love me. (EMBRACES HIM)

HARRAS: (ALMOST WITHOUT TONE) For now and always. (COMMOTION OUTSIDE—STEPS, LOWERED VOICES. THE DOOR IS PUSHED OPEN. KORRIANKE APPEARS CARRYING OLIVIA)

DIDDO: (CLINGING TO HARRAS) Is she—is she—

KORRIANKE: (QUICKLY) Don't worry. Fade out, technically speaking—she grabbed on ta ma sleeve and then she went, "Ugh," and then she was gone. (HE PUTS OLIVIA ON THE COUCH)

HARRAS: I lived through it a hundred times about twenty years ago. She'll still be fainting when she's ninety.

(KORRIANKE IS WORKING OVER OLIVIA, PUTS A PILLOW UNDER HER HEAD AND IS RUBBING HER JOINTS)

KORRIANKE: Should I call a doctor?

HARRAS: No. (TO DIDDO) You'd better go out. She doesn't have to see you the minute she comes to. I'll call you.

KORRIANKE: (GOING OFF) A little cologne—or better yet, a few drops of Schnapps—

HARRAS: I know something better. (AS SOON AS THEY ARE OUTSIDE HE WINDS HIS WATCH AND HOLDS IT UP TO OLIVIA'S EAR, LETS THE ALARM RING AND CALLS OUT IN A CHANGED VOICE) Mrs. Geiss! Your cue! You're on!

(OLIVIA OPENS HER EYES, SITS UP AND LOOKS AROUND ABSENTLY. HARRAS PUTS HIS WATCH BACK IN HIS POCKET AND GETS A BOTTLE OF RED WINE FROM THE BAR)

OLIVIA: I smell violets. Is my little girl here?

HARRAS: (WORKING ON THE BOTTLE) Came just a minute ago. You must have been at the wrong exit. She waited for you for an hour.

OLIVIA: Tell me no stories. I'm very happy for her.

HARRAS: Ping! (HE PULLS THE CORK)

OLIVIA: I feel better already. I guess I made a fool of myself again—

HARRAS: (GIVES HER THE CORK) First Aid. Ersatz smelling salts. (GETS THE GLASSES)

OLIVIA: The subway was jammed—I had to stand up the whole trip.—, And oh, the air!—Nobody has any soap these days.

HARRAS: Yes. The heroic age stinks of dirty laundry. Have a drink.

OLIVIA: And then all the worry about you—the strain—you don't even know yet what happened!

HARRAS: Bergmann? I haven't had time to ask Korrianke—

OLIVIA: Go and make sure no one comes in—(STARTING) My God—where's my pocketbook. Oh, here—thank the Lord. (SHE RUMMAGES AROUND IN IT)

HARRAS: (AT THE DOOR) Yes, she's chirping again. How about fixing up a little supper? Anything at all—a few hot sausages or something like that. I think we are going to have company. (WE HEAR DIDDO OUTSIDE LAUGHING WITH KORRIANKE. HARRAS CLOSES THE DOOR. OLIVIA HAS TAKEN AN UNOPENED LETTER OUT OF HER POCKETBOOK, TURNS IT NERVOUSLY BACK AND FORTH) I couldn't get this Bergmann business out of my mind—just didn't have a chance to do anything. But now we'll certainly rock the baby. What's that?

OLIVIA: Too late.

HARRAS: (TAKES THE LETTER, HOLDS IT UNOPENED IN HIS HAND) Did they escape?

OLIVIA: Poison.

HARRAS: And—Jenny?

OLIVIA: Both of them—together. She didn't want to be without him. The doctor brought this to me. It's his good-bye to you.

HARRAS: (SITS DOWN NEXT TO HER ON THE COUCH) Damn it all. Damn it all. Why couldn't they . . . a day later—I could have worked it—

OLIVIA: It was too late anyway. He didn't care anymore.

HARRAS: Damn it all. (TURNS ON A READING LAMP, OPENS THE LETTER, READS IT QUICKLY, HANDS IT TO OLIVIA)

OLIVIA: (WITH TEARS IN HER EYES) I can't—I don't have my glasses. — Do you mind?

HARRAS: (WITHOUT HUMOR) Cry-baby. (READS IN A MONOTONE VOICE) "My Dear Friend—This is the only way to freedom possible for us. We are calm. I haven't the strength for what people call a 'new life' and I can't buy it with the sacrifices of my friends. I know what you were ready to do for us. You did it for others. Our blessings will forever—the thought that there are still human beings like you"—I can't go on. Thanks, etc. (HE HAS BECOME QUITE PALE)

OLIVIA: (WEEPING) You deserve it even if you didn't succeed this time. You can be proud of that letter.

HARRAS: Proud? Of all things! (THROWS THE LETTER ON THE DESK) We're guilty for what's happening to thousands of people we don't know and can never help. Guilty and damned for all eternity. Permitting viciousness is worse than doing it.

OLIVIA: But what in Heaven's name are we supposed to do? Are we supposed to take poison too?

HARRAS: That isn't necessary. We'll all have our turn in due time. One after the other. It's already rising up out of their graves— high as the sky. Don't you see it? Didn't you ever see it?

OLIVIA: What—who?

HARRAS: (GOES TO THE WINDOW) Look out there. When I'm alone and it gets dark in the evening, it grows over there above the rooftops. Like this—(HE LIFTS HIS CLOSED FIST AND SLOWLY UN-FOLDS ALL HIS FINGERS UPWARD) Only one hand. Five fingers. But—gigantic. Monstrous. Big enough to take hold of a city and lift it up and smash it to the ground. (HE LETS HIS ARM DROP) Then it shrivels up again. Then, it grows again. I know it's only the searchlights from the flak station radio tower, five searching pillars of light. That's all. But to me it's a hand. And I know whose hand it is. (FOR A MOMENT HE STARES INTO THE TWI-LIGHT, THEN TURNS AROUND) And now you're going to say: "overstrained nerves." No. I don't have nerves! Never had any!

OLIVIA: (SOBBING) My God, Harry! What did they do to you? If you give up, what's to become of us?

HARRAS: (PUTS AN ARM AROUND HER SHOULDERS) But I'm not giv-ing up. Quite the contrary. I'm just beginning all over again.

OLIVIA: Listen, Harry. You should take off. Anywhere, any coun-try. It doesn't matter if they lock you up till the war is over. There's no point in staying here anymore.

HARRAS: Maybe you're right. But I've still got things to do around here.

OLIVIA: And besides, you had too much success with women. That's the worst of it. With our Nazis everything is really jeal-ousy, bed-jealousy above all. But on that point they're way below zero—almost the whole bunch of them. That's why they're always wanting to go to war and make out like great men—it's all a fake. Either you've got it or you haven't got it. But those boys. First great sounds—then it's all over before it really began and off they run, back to duty. Nebbish!

HARRAS: For you the value of any man is completely fixed by a sin-gle definition. (HE SMILES)

OLIVIA: But it is, isn't it? Except for geniuses, perhaps. Goethe is supposed to have been very superior in that department. About

Napoleon you hear less that's good. But with your Adolf—there's nothing there at all—God, I hope the little one isn't listening.

HARRAS: (QUITE GAY, KISSES HER ON THE EAR) She can't learn anything wrong from you. You have a completely healthy viewpoint. (TURNS ON THE RADIO) Come, let's let it tinkle a bit so that Diddo knows it's all right to come in here again. (ON THE RADIO, "SIEGFRIED'S DEATH" FROM GOTTERDAMMERUNG)—Thank you, no. (TURNS IT OFF) Hitlerian destiny music. Brmmm, brmmm, brmmm—Siegfried's death.

OLIVIA: Maybe somebody's been killed—a general or something.

HARRAS: Just wait—I've got something here. (PUTS A RECORD ON THE PHONOGRAPH WHICH PLAYS AN OLD POPULAR SONG HOARSELY AND DRAGGING A BIT)

OLIVIA: God, our old song!— (SHE TRILLS ALONG A BIT, PUTS HER HAND LIGHTLY ON HIS SHOULDER. HE HOLDS HER AROUND HER WAIST AND ROCKS HER A FEW STEPS IN THE RHYTHM OF THE MELODY)

HARRAS: Do you still remember? Russian Tea Room? Pigeon Casino?

OLIVIA: God, Harry, why were we so cynical? I mean, so frivolous?

HARRAS: Were we?

OLIVIA: We loved each other. Why didn't we take it seriously? And build something together? We'd be so much better off now.

HARRAS: We weren't the right people for that, neither of us.

OLIVIA: Why not? I think it was a sin—or cowardice.

HARRAS: But you were just going to play Joan of Arc.

OLIVIA: Yes, that's the way it always was.

HARRAS: (LETS GO OF HER. PLAYS THE RECORD AGAIN) Listen, Ollie—maybe I'll try it yet. Or do you think it's too late? Am I too old for her?

OLIVIA: There's no such thing. If it's really serious—

HARRAS: I've never been more serious. Perhaps I'll pull my neck out of the noose yet. And if I get out of it, you'll get to be my mother-in-law.

OLIVIA: Better'n nothing. Let's drink to it.

HARRAS: (POURING) Let's drink to it. (CALLS) Hey, you in the kitchen, don't be so discreet!

HANSEN: (POKES HIS HEAD IN) Light music and heavy red wine! In matters of good taste we can always rely on the older generation.

HARRAS: Don't brag, you bum. You're getting bald already.

HANSEN: And you, General, haven't got any hair on your chest yet. (BOWS TO OLIVIA) Madam . . .

OLIVIA: Therein lies the secret of his charm. I never cared much for woolly bears. (SHE PUTS THE NEEDLE BACK AND BEGINS TO DANCE WITH HANSEN)

DIDDO: (HAS COME IN) Well, you seem to have recovered completely—Aunt Ollie. Who's taking who to the theater tonight? (DRINKS FROM HARRAS'S GLASS)

KORRIANKE: In an emergency that'll be accomplished with a wheelbarrow. (SPEAKS FROM THE DOOR. THE DOORBELL RINGS) We seem to be getting an addition. (GOING OFF) Supper's served, Herr General. The little Miss has a positive genius for making sandwiches. (HE GOES OFF TO THE CORRIDOR)

HARRAS: You can found a household on that.

DIDDO: Did she notice anything?

HARRAS: Everything. The science of wave transmission.

DIDDO: So much the better. Then we don't have to watch out for our waves anymore.

HARRAS: It's impossible anyway. They twitter like squirrels. (HE HAS PUT HIS ARMS AROUND HER WITHOUT DANCING)

DIDDO: (ALMOST AT HIS MOUTH COMPLETELY ENTRANCED) Since when do squirrels twitter—(SHE BREATHES A KISS ON HIS MOUTH)

HARRAS: (JUST LIKE HER) Yes—since when do squirrels twitter—

DIDDO: If you say they twitter, then they twitter.

HARRAS: They twitter, you can depend on it. (THEY DISAPPEAR BEHIND THE BAMBOO SCREEN. IN THE MEANTIME KORRIANKE HAS APPEARED AT THE DOOR AND GIVEN SIGNALS TO HANSEN. HANSEN EXCUSES HIMSELF QUIETLY FROM OLIVIA—GOES TO KORRIANKE, AND LEAVES THE ROOM AFTER A FEW WHISPERED DIRECTIONS. THE RECORD IS OVER, BUT STILL RUNNING. OLIVIA GOES QUICKLY TO THE PLAYER AND TURNS IT OFF) What's the matter? Where's Hansen?

KORRIANKE: Someone asked for him, Herr General.

(HARRAS LETS GO OF DIDDO AND STANDS IMMOBILE FOR A MOMENT. HE IS ABOUT TO GO TO THE DOOR WHEN HANSEN COMES

BACK. HE IS SLIGHTLY FLUSHED AND TRYING TO APPEAR UNAF-
FECTED)

HANSEN: Sorry to have to say good-bye, General. Two gentlemen
with stiff hats and shiny boots. Rather plebeian—but irresistible.

HARRAS: Did they say what they wanted from you?

HANSEN: Only answer a few questions—to relieve an urgent need.
I've always wanted to see the Gestapo from the inside. It will be
a completely one-sided pleasure. My name is Bunny and I don't
know nuttin' about it. (HE LAUGHS, EMBARRASSED, FALLS SILENT
AND MAKES A SIGNAL TO HARRAS WHICH IS PROOF OF HONOR.
HARRAS RESPONDS AND RETURNS IT, THEN GIVES HIM HIS HAND.
HANSEN PRESSES HIS HAND SILENTLY, LOOKS BRIEFLY INTO HAR-
RAS'S EYES AND LEAVES. SILENCE. HARRAS GOES TO THE TELE-
PHONE, HESITATES. MUMBLES)

HARRAS: There's no point in it. (KORRIANKE BRINGS IN A FULL
GLASS) Thanks. (PUTS IT UNTOUCHED ON THE TABLE)

DIDDO: Can they really—can they do anything to him?

HARRAS: (SHRUGS HIS SHOULDERS) They know how to strike.

(HE STANDS WITH CLENCHED FISTS. OLIVIA IS HOLDING DIDDO'S
HAND—VOICES AND LAUGHTER COME FROM THE HALL OUTSIDE. IN
WALK BARON PFLUNGK, MOHRUNGEN, AND POOTSIE. POOTSIE IS
WEARING A PARTY UNIFORM, ELEGANTLY TAILORED, WITH A SHORT
SKIRT, LONG STOCKINGS AND A TIGHT BLOUSE. IN HER GARISH MAN-
NER SHE CREATES A RATHER EXAGGERATED EFFECT. THE TWO GEN-
TLEMEN, ON THE OTHER HAND, ARE ALMOST DISTURBED AND
BREATHLESS, NOT JUST FROM CLIMBING THE STAIRS)

POOTSIE: Please, let's close the elevator door for future generations.
We thought the thing was out of order. Just when we had
climbed the last summit—zoom, it whizzed off. (LOOKS
AROUND) Well, so this is the ill-famed robber's cave. Not as bar-
baric as I thought.

MOHRUNGEN: Pardon the invasion, General, but the hall door was
open.

PFLUNGK: I trust we are not barging in at the wrong moment.

HARRAS: You're just in time. At the stroke of twelve, spirits appear.

MOHRUNGEN: (LAUGHS, SOMEWHAT UNCERTAIN. NOTICES OLIVIA)
If I had known you were going to be here, Madam . . .

OLIVIA: Then you would have shot up the stairs like a sky-rocket.

MOHRUNGEN: Like Cupid's arrow, Madam.

OLIVIA: The fastest method of travel. Why didn't you come to the theater?

MOHRUNGEN: But I came! Didn't you get my flowers?

OLIVIA: Why didn't you come back to my dressing room?

MOHRUNGEN: Uninvited? Wouldn't that have been somewhat forward?

OLIVIA: So I've got a new admirer and already he doesn't dare.

MOHRUNGEN: What is not may yet be. (KISSES HER HAND. THEY WITHDRAW TO THE BAR)

POOTSIE: (SHE GOES UP TO HARRAS) How do you like my new uniform? (SHE SALUTES HIM)

HARRAS: Too brown.

POOTSIE: You old tease. Maybe you prefer flesh color?

PFLUNGK: (TURNS TO DIDDO) I hope we're not intruding. Bachelor quarters always have a certain fascination for young ladies.

DIDDO: (GLANCING AT POOTSIE) That depends on the young ladies.

HARRAS: Would you like something to drink?

POOTSIE: Yes—a little fuel won't hurt. Who's that young man? (LAWRENCE HAS COME BACK IN. HE IS WASHED AND SHAVED AND LOOKS TEN YEARS YOUNGER)

HARRAS: That's my friend, Buddy Lawrence. Miss von Mohrungen.

POOTSIE: American. Broad shoulders, narrow hips, long skull, but nothing in it. No enlightenment, I mean. In your country they claim every "man is born equal," even if he is a Jew.

LAWRENCE: That's what we say. Were you ever there?

POOTSIE: No, but we get all that in the course.

LAWRENCE: What course?

POOTSIE: NSRFF—Special School for Advanced Reichswomen Leadership Candidates.

LAWRENCE: (PULLS OUT HIS NOTEBOOK) You'll have to repeat that slowly.

POOTSIE: In case I decide to grant you an interview, do you have a clean bill of health?

LAWRENCE: You mean—am I kosher? Not in the full sense of the word.

POOTSIE: It's not my worry. The censor will rap your knuckles. What do you want to know? Shoot.

LAWRENCE: What do you learn in your course?

POOTSIE: World outlook, of course, from the woman's point of view. We hear top authorities on the subject of race politics, breeding selection, sex hygiene, body culture. Right now the lecture series is based on Nietzsche's philosophy: The value of suffering in the Life of the Nation.

LAWRENCE: (WRITING) Is that of concern to women?

POOTSIE: And how! The strength of the emotional life begins with the mother. When I have a baby there won't be any anesthesia. It's going to be a matter of suffering wide awake and screaming till the seams burst.

HARRAS: I'd like to midwife that. (DOWNS A SCHNAPPS)

POOTSIE: I bet that would suit you. (SHE TALKS MORE TO HIM) You should watch us do our exercises. Your tongue would hang out. Strapping girls, all of them, wearing nothing but panties.

HARRAS: That would cure me.

POOTSIE: Well, your big mouth impresses me. I suppose you're never afraid?

HARRAS: Oh yes, Pootsie, I could be, of you.

POOTSIE: Is that supposed to be a compliment?

HARRAS: No—flattery.

POOTSIE: Funny. All my affairs begin with a fight. (IRRITATED, TO LAWRENCE) Now you can put a period. You won't get any more out of me. I have to undertake an inspection here. (SHE TURNS AWAY AND WALKS AROUND IN THE ROOM)

LAWRENCE: (TO HARRAS, WHO IS HANDING HIM A GLASS) Ghastly. I'm going to take her apart—if only she didn't have such a pretty rear. It's time I got out of here.

HARRAS: (SOFTLY) Impossible. The house is being watched.— Are you all right?

LAWRENCE: Perfect.

HARRAS: I want you to meet a young lady who—to me—that is, I'm going to marry her.

LAWRENCE: Congratulations. But isn't this quite sudden?

HARRAS: Not at all. It was settled five minutes ago.

LAWRENCE: Then what about my bet?

HARRAS: Better write it off. I intend to live—now. I care.

LAWRENCE: Do you think you can last? It's all got to blow up sometime.

HARRAS: I'm going to try one way or another. (TAKES LAWRENCE TO DIDDO WHO IS STANDING AT THE WINDOW WITH PFLUNGK)

POOTSIE: (HAS LOOKED AROUND IN THE ROOM) The famous propeller bar? Sharp! (POINTING TO THE JUNK) He shot these down himself and reworked them. (SHE SCRATCHES ON A PIECE OF METAL) Is that blood or rust?

MOHRUNGEN: (WHO HAS COME OUT OF THE BAR WITH OLIVIA, SOMEWHAT EMBARRASSED) Really very interesting.

HARRAS: The seat is from my old Rumpler-pigeon, 1915.

PFLUNGK: Original decor.

POOTSIE: Well, I like it. (SHE ROCKS ON THE PLANE SEAT)

HARRAS: You would. I call it my reservoir of barbarism.

POOTSIE: And who is the faded beau in the middle? (SHE POINTS TO A WREATHED PHOTOGRAPH OF A PILOT)

HARRAS: (SPEAKING MORE TO DIDDO) My best enemy from the last World War. His mother gave me the picture. I visited her afterward.

POOTSIE: The famous chivalric gesture. Good for the historic reputation but antiquated. (DIDDO TURNS SHARPLY AND GOES OUT) What's the matter with the little blonde—jealous already?

HARRAS: Not at all. She's helping Korrianke so we can have a bite of something.

(HARRAS WITH A NERVOUS MOTION HAS ALMOST AUTOMATICALLY TURNED ON THE RADIO. A VOICE IS SNARLING)

VOICE: . . . are standing their ground everywhere, despite premature snow-storms and unbearable cold, which is costing our troops the heaviest . . . (HARRAS TURNS OFF THE RADIO)

OLIVIA: Brrr. I thought I heard something about hot sausages before. That would be a positive salvation.

HARRAS: Excuse me, please, I'm a bad host. May I trouble you to come to the kitchen? I have sort of a Tyrolean corner there instead of a dining room.— No, Baron, no trouble at all—just a bite so we can go on drinking. (TO OLIVIA) Can I leave K.P. to you and Diddo? We will come along in a minute.

(HE REMAINS BEHIND WITH MOHRUNGEN, WHO HAS MADE A SIGN TO HIM, WHILE THE OTHERS DISAPPEAR INTO THE KITCHEN FROM WHICH WE HEAR NOISES AND VOICES)

MOHRUNGEN: Tell me— (LOWERS HIS VOICE) —can one be over-heard here?

HARRAS: Only by your conscience, Mohrungen.

MOHRUNGEN: I cannot talk with you in that tone—

HARRAS: Then let's go eat something.

MOHRUNGEN: (HOLDING HIM BY HIS ARM) Why don't you listen to reason—your very life is at stake!

HARRAS: That is my affair!

MOHRUNGEN: Listen to me for a minute—without prejudice. There is only one way for you and I want to help you.

HARRAS: Yes?

MOHRUNGEN: You have got to join the Party, take a completely different position, make peace with Himmler—

HARRAS: And deliver the Luftwaffe into the arms of the SS.

MOHRUNGEN: But you can't prevent it anyway. It is the command of the hour. We are in a war and unity must come first, before—we must save Germany from Bolshevism.—Not only Germany. The world.

HARRAS: Go ahead and save, Mohrungen. Save away. Save your executive board position and your dividends. But do me a favor, don't try and save me.

MOHRUNGEN: Harras, you must realize your ideals too are at stake. The whole of Christian civilization is at stake!

HARRAS: Then save that too. After all, everybody is saving something these days. Religion, culture, democracy, the West—in every direction you blow your nose—a crusade for a big thing you can't even prove exists. I'd like to meet just one guy honest enough to admit that all he wants to save is his own skin. I sure would like to hang on to mine. My ideal is quite modest: Not to have to spit in my face. Not even in a crosswind.

MOHRUNGEN: (HIS ANGER RISING) Do you mean to say— (AFTER A PAUSE—SOFTLY) That I have given up my honor?

HARRAS: Yes.

MOHRUNGEN: (TURNS AWAY) We don't live just to be happy. After all, we do have to make sacrifices.

HARRAS: I'm thirsty. There's beer in the kitchen.

MOHRUNGEN: Can't you understand me at all?

HARRAS: Oh, yes, Mohrungen, I understand completely. (GOES TO THE KITCHEN DOOR)

POOTSIE: (ENTERING WITH A HALF-EATEN FRANKFURTER IN HER HAND, FOLLOWED BY PFLUNGK) Peace-time goods, completely free of horse-shoe nails. Momma Geiss is keeping it hot for you! (TO HARRAS) May I use your telephone? Official business, of course.

HARRAS: Certainly. Even if it's official love. Come, Mohrungen. (HARRAS GOES WITH MOHRUNGEN OFF TO THE KITCHEN)

PFLUNGK: Now, Pootsie, you don't want to telephone at all. Why did you step on my foot?

POOTSIE: I discovered something here. Might interest you, too. I just got a quick look at it before. (SHE GOES TO THE DESK WHERE BERGMANN'S LETTER WAS LEFT AND PICKS IT UP) Somebody must have just brought it to him or he would have hidden it. Maybe that Geiss woman. I've been suspicious of her for a long time! (SHE READS, PFLUNGK READING OVER HER SHOULDER)

PFLUNGK: From one of his Jew-friends, naturally. He's supposed to have smuggled a couple of them over the border already.

POOTSIE: But these are anti-state activities! This is high treason!

PFLUNGK: Give me the letter.

POOTSIE: Wouldn't think of it.

PFLUNGK: Give me the letter.

POOTSIE: What do you want it for?

PFLUNGK: You'll see. (TEARS THE LETTER OUT OF HER HAND AND STARTS TO THROW IT INTO THE FIREPLACE IN WHICH KORRIANKE HAS MADE A FIRE. HOWEVER, HE THROWS TOO SHORT AND POOTSIE CATCHES IT IN MIDAIR BEFORE IT CAN FALL)

POOTSIE: Idiot. Can't even throw. What's the big idea anyway?

PFLUNGK: Because I don't want you to do anything foolish.

POOTSIE: Foolish?

PFLUNGK: With this letter you can destroy Harras—

POOTSIE: So what.

PFLUNGK: It would be foolish, even dangerous. Pootsie, you are too young to understand that. We are not unconquerable. In war there is fortune and misfortune. Things could be different sometime. Then you will need people like Harras.

POOTSIE: You are thinking a little too far, Baron.

PFLUNGK: Better than too short.

POOTSIE: Aw, go take your shakes somewhere else! You make me puke.

PFLUNGK: What are you going to do with the letter?

POOTSIE: That depends on him. Maybe—maybe I'll make him real big. Maybe I'll let him fall. (PUTS THE LETTER INSIDE HER BLOUSE. VOICES GROW LOUDER, COME NEARER FROM THE KITCHEN. POOTSIE QUICKLY TAKES UP THE TELEPHONE RECEIVER AND PRETENDS TO TALK) Well then, shall we meet at the juice bar? On a bombless night, of course. (HANGS UP) —Well, how was that for an act?

PFLUNGK: (HASTILY) I tell you you're playing with dynamite. You don't know what you are stirring up—

POOTSIE: Tell it to your maiden aunt! (SHE LOOKS IN THE BAR FOR CIGARETTES. BARON PFLUNGK, STILL WHISPERING TO HER, FOLLOWS HER INTO THE BAR. THE OTHERS HAVE COME BACK FROM THE KITCHEN, SOME OF THEM WITH GLASSES, SOME OF THEM SMOKING. MOHRUNGEN AND OLIVIA IN A SUBDUED CONVERSATION COME UP TO THE DOOR AND DISAPPEAR AGAIN. HARRAS COMES IN WITH DIDDO AND LAWRENCE. TURNS TO THE WINDOW AND STARTS TO PULL THE DRAPES)

HARRAS: Time to put the blackout drapes between us and the enemy fliers.

DIDDO: What a shame! The twilight is so lovely.

HARRAS: *L'heure macabre.* Deep sea station.

LAWRENCE: Yes, there's something of the aquarium about it.

HARRAS: When it gets dark the house sinks like a diving bell.

DIDDO: (HAS PUT HER ARM IN HIS) I've always wanted to play a madwoman. I don't know why. Perhaps to get rid of something that's trapped inside me, that might not come out otherwise. Is that mad? (HARRAS DRAWS HER CLOSE TO HIM BUT DOES NOT ANSWER)

LAWRENCE: I envy you Germans your word "Wahnsinn"—the mad sense. It's a poet's word, almost a holy word. Also "Leidenschaft"—the pain of passion. Also "Ehrfurcht"—the spirit of honor. "Sehnsucht"—the sickness of longing. "Begeisterung"—fullness of spirit.

HARRAS: You know our language.

LAWRENCE: (SADLY) I love Germany.

HARRAS: Is it still worth being loved? In spite of everything?

LAWRENCE: Yeah, or I wouldn't have hung around this long with my head in the lion's mouth. Tomorrow I may be rotting in a camp. On account of just that German mad sense—your madness.

HARRASS: I'm sick of it. It's laid too many rotten eggs for us—the house of mad Siegfried, the insane delusions of grandeur. Oh, Buddy, how I long sometimes for a simple nation—for football players, mechanics, gum chewers.

LAWRENCE: I love the Germans.

HARRAS: Me too. To the point of hate. (HE PULLS THE BLACKOUT CURTAINS AND TURNS ON THE LIGHTS)

OLIVIA: (IN THE KITCHEN DOOR) Diddo, for Heaven's sake, I must get to the theater. In one hour the curtain goes up.

HARRAS: You can still make it in a taxi.

OLIVIA: But you can't get one.

HARRAS: (HE CALLS) Korrianke!—Korrianke, Mrs. Geiss needs the wheelbarrow and I need the evening paper. I'm dying to find out what experiences I had at the Eastern Front.

OLIVIA: Korrianke is an archangel. Get ready, little one, so we don't get into a mess. I'm sorry, Mr. von Mohrungen—it's time for the show. (TURNS BACK INTO THE NEXT ROOM)

HARRAS: (TO LAWRENCE) Do me a favor and leave Diddo and me alone for a minute. Hold the others off. Thanks. (LAWRENCE NODS, TURNS TO POOTSIE AND PFLUNGK WHO ARE COMING OUT OF THE BAR, ARGUING SOFTLY. HARRAS TAKES HIS WATCH OUT OF HIS POCKET) Now pretend I'm showing you something. Don't answer. Pay attention: I'm thinking of clearing out—via air, with no ticket. (DIDDO NODS EMPHATICALLY AND PRETENDS TO BE LISTENING TO THE WATCH. HARRAS GOES ON) When and how I don't know yet. If it works— (HE INTERRUPTS HIMSELF) —careful, they're coming back.

DIDDO: (ALMOST WITHOUT TONE, UNDER HER BREATH) It must work. It must.

HARRAS: You hear? It's ticking again. It isn't wrecked, not by a long shot. (PUTS THE WATCH BACK)

DIDDO: It'll last a hundred years in your pocket.

HARRAS: (LAUGHING) If the seam doesn't burst.

(KORRIANKE HAS APPEARED IN THE HALL DOOR HOLDING NEWSPAPERS IN HIS HAND. AT THE SAME TIME OLIVIA RUSHES IN, FOLLOWED BY MOHRUNGEN)

OLIVIA: Taxi? That's what I call blitz-service.

KORRIANKE: General—

HARRAS: (LOOKS AT HIM) What's the matter?

KORRIANKE: Something's happened.

MOHRUNGEN: (HAS STEPPED UP TO KORRIANKE) Special edition? Black border? Did somebody— (HAS TAKEN ONE OF THE PAPERS AND TURNS PALE) Dear God— (DROPS THE PAPER)

HARRAS: (WITHOUT MOVING—ALMOST WITH CERTAINTY) Eilers?

POOTSIE: (HAS RUN UP TO MOHRUNGEN, PICKS UP THE PAPER, READS) "—fatal accident—crash over the field—unexplained mechanical defect—in the plane of Colonel Friedrich Eilers . . . (MOHRUNGEN TAKES HER ARM) It isn't possible . . . (SHE IS SILENT, LOOKS AT HARRAS)

HARRAS: (THROUGH HIS TEETH) From the paper—no telephone call—no telegram.

POOTSIE: (SOFTLY, AFFECTED) Anne—could she know?

MOHRUNGEN: (COMPLETELY BROKEN) We must try to call. I will go there on the next train—

PFLUNGK: (READING) "The Führer has ordered a State funeral." That will console her a little.

MOHRUNGEN: I hardly think so. (POOTSIE STROKES HIS HAND. HE NODS WRETCHEDLY)

OLIVIA: And now you are supposed to sing. I don't want to go on at all any more . . .

HARRAS: (CHANGED, WITH COLD VOICE) Korrianke, take the big car. Make it fast. Drive to Oderbruch— Bring him here. I don't want to use the phone. Tell him to bring all the records he has on hand. (KORRIANKE STANDS AT ATTENTION, THEN GOES)

MOHRUNGEN: (TO PFLUNGK) Can you take us to the hotel, Baron? I must pack. Where's Pootsie?

PFLUNGK: I don't know. She must have gone ahead.

MOHRUNGEN: (CALLS) Pootsie—Why does she run away now?

PFLUNGK: (SHRUGS HIS SHOULDERS) She has her moods.

MOHRUNGEN: (HIS EYES MEET HARRAS, GROW HARD) This won't end here. This case is going to be cleared up conclusively. (HARRAS RETURNS HIS LOOK—BOWS SILENTLY)

PFLUNGK: (EMBARRASSED) Goodbye, General.— Thanks for the hospitality.

HARRAS: Oh, please, would you drop Mr. Lawrence off—at the American Embassy. It's on your way.

PFLUNGK: Gladly, with pleasure.

LAWRENCE: Good luck, Harry. (PUTS OUT HIS HAND)

HARRAS: Good luck to you. Your bet is getting hotter. Put a month's salary on it. (BRIEFLY PRESSES HIS HAND. MOHRUNGEN, PFLUNGK, AND LAWRENCE GO OFF. OLIVIA HESITATES AT THE DOOR. WE HEAR THE ELEVATOR. HARRAS TO DIDDO—CALMLY AND FIRMLY) Go to Vienna. Everything's changed now.

DIDDO: Not for me. I won't leave you—not now.

HARRAS: (TAKES HER HANDS) You are always with me.

DIDDO: How can I be—when I'm far away?

HARRAS: Much more so than here. What's coming now I have to do alone.

DIDDO: How will I hear from you?

HARRAS: I can reach you more easily there. Here you would be watched. Or—worse. Will you promise me that you will go?

DIDDO: I'll go.

OLIVIA: (SOFTLY) Come now, Diddo.

(DIDDO TEARS HERSELF LOOSE, GOES QUICKLY WITH OLIVIA. HARRAS ALONE IN THE BRIGHTLY LIT ROOM GRABS THE BACK OF A CHAIR WITH AN UNCONSCIOUS MOVEMENT, GRIPS IT WITH HIS HANDS, CLOSES HIS EYES. WHEN HE OPENS THEM POOTSIE IS IN THE DOOR. HE STARES AT HER, LOOSENS THE GRIP OF HIS HANDS)

HARRAS: Who let you in?

POOTSIE: (WITHOUT SHYNESS, BUT NOT FRIVOLOUS) Nobody. I hid in the closet till they were gone. I must speak with you, Harras.

HARRAS: I have work to do.

POOTSIE: Harry, things can't go on like this with you.

HARRAS: What do you mean?

POOTSIE: Why do you insist on smashing yourself up? It doesn't add up!

HARRAS: Maybe it does to me. And anyway, Pootsie, what business is it of yours?

POOTSIE: I can't stand watching it. There aren't that many real men in the world. You could make it, Harry.

HARRAS: Make what?

POOTSIE: You're no Jew and no Communist. Don't be a fool! You have blood, race, spirit. You were born to rule, to grasp, to possess. You didn't seem to mind becoming a Nazi General. The glamour, the power, that suited you, didn't it? So why quit now? Well why don't you aim a little higher?

HARRAS: Thanks.

POOTSIE: Haven't you any "instinct" any more? In one year you could be the greatest of 'em all—the power behind the Führer. Power is life. Power is pleasure. Harry, just say the word. I'll make you real big!

HARRAS: And why, if I may ask? What do you get out of it?

POOTSIE: I liked you right off. And Pootsie gets what she wants. You need me, Harry.

HARRAS: (WITH A TOUCH OF SYMPATHY) I'm the wrong man. Look for another. There are so many.

POOTSIE: The Good Shepherd with the little lamb in his arms—it doesn't suit you. You've got eyes like a hawk and fangs like a wolf. What do you want with the green lamb's lettuce?

HARRAS: Run along now, Pootsie. I've warned you enough.

POOTSIE: Let yourself be warned, Harras. Don't push me too far. You don't smuggle old Jews over the border unpunished just to play the Good Samaritan. No one has the right to do that, not even you.

HARRAS: (HAS LOOKED AT THE DESK, STARES AT HER) What's this? Stealing, blackmail, extortion?

POOTSIE: I'm through talking.

HARRAS: (JUMPING TO THE WALL, TEARS A HEAVY AFRICAN WHIP DOWN AND STARTS TOWARD HER) If you don't get out I'm going to pull this thing across your face, so you'll be marked as long as you vegetate. (RAISES HIS ARM)

POOTSIE: (RAISING HER ARMS, BACKS QUICKLY TO THE DOOR AND STANDS THERE) You coward. I'll teach you. You traitor. (SHE BACKS OUT AND SLAMS THE DOOR)

(HARRAS STANDS FOR A MOMENT BREATHING HEAVILY, THEN THROWS THE WHIP AWAY. CLUTCHES HIS THROAT AS THOUGH HE COULDN'T BREATHE. QUICKLY GOES THROUGH THE ROOM TO A LIGHT SWITCH AND TURNS OFF ALL THE LIGHTS UNTIL IT'S COMPLETELY DARK. THEN TO THE WINDOW, PULLS BACK THE DRAPES,

OPENS THE WINDOW WIDE. LOOKS OUT, BREATHING DEEPLY. THE
ROOM IS FILLED FROM OUTSIDE WITH A WEAK SHIMMER OF LIGHT
THAT BECOMES STRONGER. IN THE MIDDLE OF THE BLACK WINDOW
FIVE FANNED BEAMS GROW SLOWLY IN HEIGHT AND STAND IN THE
FRAME OF THE WINDOW LIKE THE FINGERS OF A GIANT OUT-
STRETCHED HAND. HARRAS STANDS FOR A MINUTE MOTIONLESS,
THEN PULLS THE DRAPES VIOLENTLY AND REELS DRUNKENLY BACK
INTO THE ROOM. WE CAN'T SEE HIM. HE SEEMS TO HAVE SUNK INTO
A CHAIR OR TO THE FLOOR. HIS VOICE COMES OUT OF THE DEPTHS)

HARRAS: Lord in Heaven. I am afraid. I am afraid. I am afraid—
(FALLS SILENT. A DOOR OPENS. HARRAS IN THE DARKNESS JUMPS
UP, SCREAMS) Halt! Don't move! Who's there? (THE LIGHT GOES
ON, HARRAS AT THE SWITCH, A GUN IN HIS HAND)

(ODERBRUCH STANDS IN THE DOOR WITH A BRIEFCASE UNDER HIS
ARM. HE'S A MAN IN HIS FORTIES, SLIM, ASH BLOND, WITH SIMPLE,
CLEAR FEATURES AND NOTHING PARTICULARLY REMARKABLE ABOUT
HIM. HE IS WEARING THE UNORNAMENTED UNIFORM OF THE SPE-
CIAL TECHNICAL TROOPS, WITH NO DECORATIONS. AS HE COMES
NEARER WE NOTICE THAT HE LIMPS A LITTLE, ALMOST IMPERCEPTI-
BLY. HIS SPEECH IS BRIEF, MEASURED, SOMETIMES A LITTLE HALT-
ING—CONTROLLED AND THOUGHTFUL)

ODERBRUCH: Did I frighten you? Korrianke gave me the key. (GOES
TO THE DESK AND PUTS DOWN THE BRIEFCASE AND THE KEYS)
HARRAS: Oderbruch! Thank God you're here. (HE LAUGHS BRIEFLY)
I always thought I had no nerves.
ODERBRUCH: You get to feel that way if you have to sit on them
day and night.
HARRAS: You know about Eilers? (ODERBRUCH NODS) Since when?
ODERBRUCH: Korrianke just told me.
HARRAS: Lucky you were home. Did I disturb you?
ODERBRUCH: (SMILING) It's my Thursday.
HARRAS: Oh, that's right. I'm sorry. What was it this evening?
ODERBRUCH: Schubert—C Major Quintet, with two cellos. It
wasn't easy to dig up the second cello. There aren't that many
cellists.
HARRAS: Isn't it horrible about Eilers?
ODERBRUCH: He was my friend too.

HARRAS: Do you have any explanation? A clue?

ODERBRUCH: It could just as well have been anybody else. The Squadron had a delivery of new planes, all tested, all inspected.

HARRAS: We'll have to order all of them back.

ODERBRUCH: I have already issued the order, on my own, from home.

HARRAS: Good. You don't really believe it was an accident?

ODERBRUCH: Accidents do happen.

HARRAS: Yes—and a life is wrecked. Not only that, also a home, also a family. If you had seen those two together! I was planning to spend Christmas with them. Do you want a drink? (FILLS TWO GLASSES)

ODERBRUCH: Thanks. After work.

HARRAS: Didn't you ever think of getting married?

ODERBRUCH: At first it wasn't possible financially. Later no longer the right time.

HARRAS: Those aren't real reasons. Not if you really wanted to.

ODERBRUCH: You know, I was supposed to be a priest once. (SMILING) Maybe that stuck to me.

HARRAS: I didn't want to miss anything—and now it seems to me I missed the best. You shouldn't leave love for nice weather. For me a sport plane would be enough for a beginning, or a trailer. Gypsy wedding. Migratory bird *ménage*. If only the world weren't blocked with barbed wire—

ODERBRUCH: You can fly over it.

HARRAS: (LOWERS HIS VOICE) I must confess something to you, Oderbruch. I have thought of flight, for good reasons. Now Eilers holds me back. Do you know where I've been these last two weeks?

ODERBRUCH: I can imagine.

HARRAS: Then you know what the stakes are. Eilers is dead. They've come for Hansen. I have to get to the bottom of this. You are the only man who can help me. Do you think we can find it. The truth?

ODERBRUCH: It will come to light one day.

HARRAS: One day!—I have only ten left. (ODERBRUCH TAKES THE GLASS THAT HARRAS FILLED BEFORE AND EMPTIES IT. HARRAS IS WATCHING HIM. HARRAS GOES UP TO HIM) Oderbruch—do you know something you're keeping from me? Are you hiding something? Don't spare me, for Heaven's sake! For truth's sake!

ODERBRUCH: It will come to light.

HARRAS: And if it's too late?

ODERBRUCH: It's never too late for the truth.

HARRAS: Your calmness, man—I wish it would grow on me like a beard. Sometimes I wonder why you don't wear one.

ODERBRUCH: (LAUGHS A LITTLE) That would be too much mask.

HARRAS: Yes—it's better to hide yourself behind a naked fence.

ODERBRUCH: (STARTS TO OPEN HIS BRIEFCASE, LETTING THE LOCK CLICK) Here are the results of our investigations to date. Of course, without the latest incident.

HARRAS: (SLAPS HIM ON THE SHOULDER) Let's get at it. (HE TURNS ON THE WORKING LIGHT) Is that the analysis of the tests on materials?

ODERBRUCH: (NODS) Here are tests number one: Normal aluminum weights. Messerschmidt—alloy percentage. Tests number two: Variations . . . Slide rule calculations. Decreased angle of incline. Tests number three: (HARRAS IS BENT OVER THE TABLE, MUMBLING. SIRENS WAIL OUTSIDE AND GET LOUDER. DISTANT FLAK FIRE, COMING NEARER WITH THE SOUND OF BOMBERS)

HARRAS: (LIFTS HIS HEAD) The gentlemen from the River Thames. Do you want to go to the cellar, Oderbruch?

ODERBRUCH: Why? What for?

HARRAS: You're right. The enemy is here. (BOTH BEND OVER THEIR WORK)

CURTAIN

Act 3

(TECHNICAL OFFICE AT A MILITARY AIRFIELD OUTSIDE BERLIN. COLD, SQUARE CONSTRUCTION OF STEEL, CEMENT, AND GLASS. WORKTABLE WITH METAL EDGES AND CORNERS. SKETCHES OF PLANE MODELS AND WEATHER MAPS ON THE WALLS. NO PICTURES OR ANY KIND OF ORNAMENTATION. A SMALL VASE WITH A FADED BUNCH OF VIOLETS IS STANDING ON THE LEDGE OF AN ELECTRICAL SWITCH-BOARD. IN THE CORNER, A SMALL SOFA MADE UP AS A BED BUT NOT SLEPT IN. NEXT TO IT A SMALL OPEN SUITCASE. IN THE BACK-

GROUND, HIGH WINDOWS WITH A VIEW OF HANGARS, SHEDS, RUN-
WAYS, AND THE STARTING APRON. THE REDDISH LIGHT OF AN EARLY
WINTER MORNING FALLS INTO THE ROOM. THE LIGHTS ARE STILL
BURNING. HARRAS IS AT THE WORKTABLE IN AN UNBUTTONED MILI-
TARY JACKET. NEXT TO HIM IS A BREAKFAST TRAY WITH A THERMOS
BOTTLE. THE WORKTABLE IS COVERED WITH RECORDS, PAPERS, TEST
MATERIALS, AND MEASURING INSTRUMENTS. KORRIANKE, AT THE
SOFA, IS TAKING THE BEDDING OFF AND PUTTING IT IN THE SUIT-
CASE)

HARRAS: (PICKING UP A PIECE OF PAPER AND TOYING WITH THE
PEN) What's the date, Korrianke?
KORRIANKE: Saturday, December 6, 1941.
HARRAS: December 6—St. Nicholas Day. Apples and nuts for all
the good children. Whips for the bad ones. (HE YAWNS, PUTS
DOWN THE PEN AND LIGHTS A CIGARETTE)
KORRIANKE: You didn't sleep again, General.
HARRAS: No time. I wasn't tired. Say, when did Eilers go down?
KORRIANKE: Thursday of last week. Ten days ago.
HARRAS: Hmmmm! Then today is the delivery date. What's the sit-
uation like out there?
KORRIANKE: Two Panzers 'n front the main portals. SS Guard,
Shock Troops. Exit and entrance by special pass only.
HARRAS: Then we're as good as prisoners.
KORRIANKE: Not quite, General.
HARRAS: No, not quite. (TAKES UP THE PEN) December 6. Apples
and nuts. Stupid. I can't write letters. (GETS UP, STRETCHES)
KORRIANKE: (GOES TO THE TABLE, TAKES THE THERMOS BOTTLE) All
gone?
HARRAS: All gone.— Listen, Korriandoli; quick, before somebody
comes! In case anything goes wrong—stop shaking your head.
Of course it can go wrong. You know that . . . in case something
happens to me, you leave immediately for Vienna. I'll leave you
enough money. So—she doesn't do anything foolish! You're such
a good storyteller. Damn it, you know what I mean.
KORRIANKE: I know, General. Easy as pie! (STARES AT HARRAS,
FRIGHTENED. REPEATS SLOWLY) Easy as pie, General.
HARRAS: (AT THE TELEPHONE) Well, what is it?
KORRIANKE: You forgot "Cut it!"

HARRAS: Excuse me. (ROARS) Cut it!

KORRIANKE: (AT ATTENTION—SWALLOWING) Thanks, General. (GOES OFF QUICKLY)

HARRAS: (AT HIS DESK, CRUMPLES THE PAPER HE WAS GOING TO WRITE ON, THROWS IT IN THE WASTEBASKET. THE TELEPHONE RINGS. HE PICKS UP THE RECEIVER) Oderbruch? Yes, interrogation of the two workmen. Send the detective in here—or—no, you come with them and stay. (HE BUTTONS HIS JACKET, LOOKS AT THE DOOR. IN WALK ODERBRUCH AND A MAN IN CIVILIAN CLOTHES)

DETECTIVE: Morning, General. I brought the two birds over as you ordered. But you won't get nothin' out of them. Cross-examination, spotlights, intimate approach—nothing works with them.

HARRAS: It's possible they are innocent and really don't know anything.

DETECTIVE: Then God have mercy on them. Have you read my report?

HARRAS: Yes. (TO ODERBRUCH) These men are on the suspected list, aren't they?

ODERBRUCH: Yes, whatever that means. They worked on a shift that handled the faulty planes. That's all we know.

HARRAS: And why were these two fished out?

DETECTIVE: One is an old Social Democrat, unpopular in the Worker's Front, a grumbler. The other is suspected of sympathizing with a secret Communist Youth Organization.

HARRAS: Do me a favor, Detective. Let us talk to them alone. We might just possibly get more results that way.

DETECTIVE: (SHRUGS HIS SHOULDERS) I doubt it. But—as you wish, General. (TURNS TO THE DOOR AND GIVES AN ORDER)

(A GUARD BRINGS THE TWO WORKMEN IN AND GOES OFF WITH THE DETECTIVE. THE TWO MEN ARE NOT HANDCUFFED AND ARE WEARING THEIR WORK CLOTHES. THE OLDER ONE, AROUND FIFTY, HAS A BONY WEATHERED FACE AND GRAYING HAIR. THE YOUNGER IS THIN AND VERY PALE. BOTH SEEM CALM AND LOOK AT THE FLOOR)

HARRAS: (OBSERVES THEM FOR A MOMENT) Would you like to sit down?

THE OLDER: (WITHOUT LOOKING UP) Thanks. We would rather stand.

HARRAS: Yes, I imagine you're tired of sitting. Walk up and down if you like. I'm going to refrain from offering you a cigarette. That's an old bully's trick to get a man to talk. But it would be easier to get started if you looked at me.

THE OLDER: (WITH A SUGGESTION OF A SMILE) That can be arranged.

HARRAS: Well now! I'm not your enemy. I don't consider you guilty until you have been proven guilty.

(THE WORKMEN LOOK AT HIM UNMOVED)

HARRAS: To begin with I don't give a damn about your private political opinions. I carry the responsibility for our planes and the security of our pilots, that's all. Sabotage occurred and I want to see to it that it stops—nothing else.

(THE WORKMEN LOOK AT HIM, SILENT)

HARRAS: I'm sure you know you're up the proverbial creek. (THE WORKMEN ARE SILENT) I don't want to rush you. Take your time. Think it over.

THE OLDER: There is nothing to think over. We have nothing to say.

HARRAS: Have you made any kind of—observations? (THE WORKERS REMAIN UNCHANGED)

HARRAS: (EVEN MORE SLOWLY) If you would like to tell me anything confidentially I will give you my word that I will not betray it. That goes for my chief engineer, too. Isn't my word good enough?

(THE OLDER WORKMAN SHRUGS HIS SHOULDERS ALMOST UNNOTICEABLY)

HARRAS: (CLOSE TO THEM) Whatever you say can be between us. We could decide together what we put down on the record. Fix it up for you the best we can. Do you have anything to say to me?

THE OLDER: No.

HARRAS: (LOOKS AT THE YOUNGER ONE. THE YOUNGER ONE BITES HIS LIPS AND SHAKES HIS HEAD. HARRAS LOOKS AT ODERBRUCH) Do you want to add anything? Any questions? (ODERBRUCH, WHO HAS STOOD MOTIONLESS IN THE BACKGROUND, MOTIONS

HIM OFF) Then I'm afraid we have to give up. (HESITATES A MO-
MENT) I'm sorry. For you, too. (THE WORKMEN REMAIN UN-
CHANGED. HARRAS GOES TO THE TABLE AND PUSHES A BUZZER.
TAKES OUT HIS CIGARETTE CASE) Now, at least, I can offer you a
cigarette.

THE OLDER: Thanks. I don't smoke.

(THE YOUNGER ONE TAKES A CIGARETTE WITHOUT A WORD. HARRAS
GIVES HIM A LIGHT. HE SMOKES GREEDILY. THERE IS A KNOCK. HAR-
RAS OPENS THE DOOR. THE DETECTIVE COMES IN. BEHIND HIM DR.
SCHMIDT-LAUSITZ AND AN SS GUARD. THE GUARD REMAINS STAND-
ING IN THE DOOR)

DETECTIVE: What did I tell you, General? A waste of time. Or am I
wrong?

LAUSITZ: (TO HARRAS) Did you take down a statement, General?

HARRAS: No. Nothing was said to warrant a statement.

LAUSITZ: And what is your personal impression of these suspects?

HARRAS: I'd say these people have nothing to do with the matter.

LAUSITZ: Possible. We shall see. (TO THE DETECTIVE) You can issue
the release papers.

DETECTIVE: You mean I'm no longer responsible for these men?

LUUSITZ: No. We have other plans for them. (HE LOOKS AT THE
WORKERS, WAITS A WHILE. THE WORKERS LOOK DOWN. THE
YOUNGER ONE SMOKES. LAUSITZ SIGNALS TO THE SS GUARD) You
will take charge of the prisoners. Prepare them for deportation!
(THE SS GUARD TAKES A STEP FORWARD. THE YOUNGER WORKER
LETS HIS CIGARETTE DROP, STEPS ON IT. HE SWAYS A LITTLE. HIS
HEAD DROPS TO HIS CHEST. THE OLDER ONE LOOKS AT HIM. LAU-
SITZ HAS WATCHED THEM. HE STEPS UP TO THE YOUNGER ONE)
Perhaps you wish to make a statement? (THE YOUNGER ONE
LIFTS UP HIS HEAD. HE IS VERY PALE. HE MEETS THE GLANCE OF
THE OLDER ONE, STRAIGHTENS UP, STANDS MOTIONLESS—LONG
SILENCE) Take them away! (THE SS GUARD GOES OFF WITH THE
TWO WORKERS. THE DETECTIVE FOLLOWS. LAUSITZ CLOSES THE
DOOR BEHIND THEM. HARRAS HAS TURNED AWAY, STEPPED UP
TO THE WINDOW AND LOOKS OUT. ODERBRUCH REMAINS UN-
CHANGED AT THE DESK) Well, that ends that—at least as far as
you're concerned, General. Unless—you have some other solu-
tion to the problem—through your material tests?

HARRAS: (OVER HIS SHOULDER) I'm still working on them.

LAUSITZ: Not indefinitely. I am commissioned to deliver this official order to you.

HARRAS: (PUTS OUT HIS HAND WITHOUT LEAVING THE WINDOW. LAUSITZ GOES UP TO HIM SLOWLY AND HANDS HIM A PAPER. HARRAS LOOKS AT IT BRIEFLY, TURNS TO ODERBRUCH) The investigation committee expects a final report—by seven o'clock tonight. (HE PUTS THE PAPER IN HIS POCKET AND LOOKS OUT THE WINDOW AGAIN)

LAUSITZ: I will appear at the appointed hour to receive it. In the meantime, I do not wish to disturb you in your work—

HARRAS: (LOOKING OUT AT THE AIRFIELD WITH TENSION— WITHOUT PAYING ANY ATTENTION TO LAUSITZ) There she is. M41-1304. (ODERBRUCH STEPS UP TO HIM. BOTH LOOK OUT)

LAUSITZ: (FOLLOWING THEIR GLANCE) What sort of plane is that— that's being rolled down the runway?

ODERBRUCH: A Messerschmidt—the sister-ship of the plane in which Eilers crashed. That was M41-1303.

LAUSITZ: And is the plane—defective?

ODERBRUCH: We don't know yet. We can't find anything wrong with it on the ground. We want to try it out in the air. Perhaps it is all right.

LAUSITZ: Can that be tried out—without danger?

ODERBRUCH: No, not quite, but with a parachute.

HARRAS: (TO LAUSITZ, SARCASTICALLY) Would you like to risk a little test flight with me?

LAUSITZ: Thank you, no.

HARRAS: Afraid I might fly to hell with you?

LAUSITZ: It might appeal to you to challenge the devil in hope of out-bluffing him. What is it? (A GUARD HAS COME IN, GOES TO LAUSITZ AND WHISPERS) No objections. (TO HARRAS) A Lieutenant Hartmann from the Eilers Squadron would like to see you. He's on sick leave—wounded. Would you care to see him?

HARRAS: Hartmann— Oh, yes, Hartmann! Naturally—gladly. (TO ODERBRUCH) We can't do very much right now anyway. I will call you up when I've drafted the report. (LAUSITZ AND ODERBRUCH GO OFF. ALMOST AT THE SAME TIME HARTMANN COMES IN, REMAINS STANDING AT THE DOOR AND SALUTES WITH HIS LEFT HAND. HIS RIGHT ARM IS IN A BLACK SLING. HARRAS IS

CHANGED, REFRESHED) Hartmann, come on in. I'm really happy to see you—and on your feet already—I hear they got you—Where, exactly?

HARTMANN: Over the north sector, between Schluesselburg and the north coast. But I brought back the plane.

HARRAS: Bravo. But I meant your wound.

HARTMANN: That's not important, although I don't know if I'll be able to fly again. Mig fire—in the elbow joint.

HARRAS: Why don't you sit down!

HARTMANN: I hope I'm not disturbing the General—

HARRAS: For Pete's sake, drop that "General" stuff. You make me feel like a war memorial!

HARTMANN: I thought I could ask the General—could ask you for—something to do, General. I feel strong enough for light duty. I'm left-handed, you know, General.

HARRAS: (LAUGHS) Untamable. I'll bet you'd go on duty with your toes. (LOOKS AT HARTMANN) You should give yourself a little time. A few weeks' relaxation.

HARTMANN: I think I would recover faster if I had something to do.

HARRAS: Still the sorrows of love?

HARTMANN: (SMILES UNMOVED) No, General.— It's funny, I'd almost forgotten that.

HARRAS: Now I could say, "What did I tell you"—but I won't.

HARTMANN: (SERIOUS AGAIN) I didn't know how much you can learn in a few weeks—even in one hour. May I ask you a question, General?

HARRAS: Sure. Go ahead.

HARTMANN: First, I must explain— Have you really time for me, General?

HARRAS: At the moment I wouldn't know of anything better to do with my time.

HARTMANN: Maybe—it's always been like this—and I just didn't see it. Didn't want to see it. (HE SPEAKS RAPIDLY, HASTILY, LIKE SOMEONE WHO WANTS TO GET RID OF SOMETHING THAT HE DOESN'T WANT TO ADMIT TO HIMSELF) The atrocity stories you hear about—they are all true. I saw it with my own eyes. And they are the same—the same boys who lived with me in the Hitler Youth. I had a school friend—he wouldn't have hurt a fly—he was shy, sensitive. I met him again in Lodz—I didn't know he was with the Extermination Commandos. He took me along. "It's going to be quite a show," he said. They shot at defenseless people as a joke, they laughed when the victims whimpered with fear—they—I can't say it, General. There is no justification for what they did. General, I am asking you, will we all get to be like that? Could I get to be like that? Is there no defense against it?

HARRAS: Civilization has tried for thousands of years to build a protective wall against inhumanity. But it can be demolished in less than one man's lifetime—I know that's no answer. You haven't asked me yet what you really want to know.

HARTMANN: In the Hitler Youth they told us we were the crusading knights of a new age. The old Christian time was supposed to have had its two thousand years. The new one was to be constructed from our plan, an empire of strength and magnificence in this world. I believed all that. But how can a new thing become strong and good if it begins by unleashing the lowest and meanest in human beings?

HARRAS: There is no such thing as a "new age." Time—is always the same—without beginning or end. And yet, whenever a human being makes a fresh start in life then the world is created anew.

HARTMANN: Do you believe in God?

HARRAS: (AFTER A LONG PAUSE) I don't know. I never met Him. But that was my fault—I didn't want to meet Him. He would have made me face decisions that I would rather avoid. I believed in the "thinkable" and the "knowable"—in what you can test, discover, and find. But the greatest invention of all time, I did not recognize. Its name is God, in many forms—always God. It is an invention of the human soul or rather a discovery, a revealed knowledge. That's why it is true. Man doesn't dream anything that isn't true or that won't come true. If he dreams God, then God exists. I don't know Him but I have looked the devil in the eye. That's how I know that there must be a God. He hid his face from me. You will meet Him.

HARTMANN: Did you ever pray?

HARRAS: Yes, I think so. When I was very happy.

HARTMANN: Then you must have met Him. Most people only pray when they're afraid.

HARRAS: I don't know.

HARTMANN: It is very hard to have faith.

HARRAS: It has always been hard—for everybody who questioned. For your generation it is probably the hardest. You were born the day justice fell apart. But believe me—there is a justice. Believe, Hartmann—go ahead and believe confidently in divine justice! It will not betray you.

HARTMANN: I would like to work near you, General. I've had a little technical training.

HARRAS: Near me—that—will not be so easy. But we'll see what we can do. (GOES TO THE TELEPHONE, PUSHES A BUZZER) Chief Engineer!—Oderbruch? You've been looking for a reliable co-worker, right? There is a young officer who is no longer on flight duty. Yes, he has some technical background. Sound him out. I'll send him over. (HANGS UP) You can report to the Chief Engineer! Room 9.

HARTMANN: I thank you, General. For everything.

HARRAS: Thanks for stopping in, Hartmann. You told me more than I told you. Now I must work. (GIVES HIM HIS HAND. HARTMANN EXITS)

(HARRAS STEPS UP TO THE WINDOW AND LOOKS OUT. MUMBLES "M 41-1304." IN THE CORRIDOR OUTSIDE WE HEAR LOUD VOICES, STEPS, AND CALLS. HARRAS TURNS AROUND AND LOOKS AT THE DOOR. THE DOOR OPENS. A WOMAN STANDS IN THE DOORWAY. SHE IS DRESSED ALL IN BLACK AND WEARS A BLACK VEIL OVER HER FACE. A GUARD IS TRYING TO STAND IN HER WAY)

GUARD: Halt! Stand back! I must insist on seeing your pass—(THE WOMAN LIFTS HER VEIL)

ANNE: I am Mrs. Eilers.

GUARD: Oh—I beg your pardon. (HE EXITS)

HARRAS: (GOES TOWARD HER WITH HIS HANDS OUTSTRETCHED) Anne. How good of you to come.

ANNE: I don't want your hand. (SHE STANDS MOTIONLESS, WITH HER HEAD HIGH AND A FIXED, ALMOST BLANK FACE)

(HARRAS LOOKS AT HER. LETS HIS HANDS DROP)

ANNE: (HARD, TONELESS) I demand an accounting.

HARRAS: From me?

ANNE: Eilers did not die in combat. He was murdered. You are his murderer.

HARRAS: (WITH DIFFICULTY, SEARCHING FOR THE WORDS) Anne—do you really believe that I failed him or worse? What have they been telling you? Yes, I carry the technical responsibility. But I don't know, even now, whether it was really a crime—or a vicious, murderous accident.

ANNE: An accident does not murder. I don't know what you're talking about. (SHE LOOKS AT HIM WITH LARGE BURNING EYES)

HARRAS: What do you accuse me of, Anne. What did I do?

ANNE: Nothing, that's what you've done. You didn't believe in what Eilers believed. But you let him die for it, die senselessly. You stood by and never did a thing to save him.

HARRAS: Could I have saved him by believing in what was false? Could you save him? Did you try? Or even—think of it?

ANNE: I didn't think—as long as Freddie was alive. I had to believe with him. Now I know that he died for nothing. But you, Harras, you always knew. You knew that you were sending him to a senseless death. You are still doing it with thousands of others every day. Your war is murder. His was sacrifice.

HARRAS: It was the same war. (TO HIMSELF) It will be the same death.

ANNE: You have nothing in common with him, in life or death. Friedrich Eilers would never have gone into a war he didn't believe was just. He would never have killed a man without believing that he was doing it for a just cause. You kill without justice or belief for a cause that you hate and despise. You are a murderer. Eilers was a hero.

HARRAS: Then everyone is a hero who doesn't know what he is dying for. Then everyone is a murderer who can't change the world, every ordinary mortal on this earth.

ANNE: Only he who knows and doesn't acknowledge it.

HARRAS: What does a man know? What can a man know? (HE TURNS AWAY)

ANNE: (STEPS UP BEHIND HIM. SPEAKS ALMOST IN HIS EAR) Do you believe this war is just? Then why do you let it happen? Do you believe our leadership is good? You know it is ruinous. Why do you watch it? You put on a great show of courage with your sarcasm and luke-warm doubt. What good is that to anybody? You are a part of the rottenness. You are guilty of every murder committed in the name of Germany. You stink of death!

HARRAS: (TURNS AROUND TO HER) Why did you come?

ANNE: (ALMOST WHISPERING) Because he loved you. His blood screams for yours.

HARRAS: But that is madness, Anne. Don't you see what is happening in the world? Who am I to change it? (ANNE IS SILENT. HARRAS ALMOST CRYING OUT) I'm no God. (HE STARES UP. IT SEEMS AS THOUGH HE WOULD COLLAPSE)

ANNE: (UNMOVED) A God became a man to be able to suffer like a man, to comfort and console all who mourn and suffer. But you, you are not fit to utter His name.

HARRAS: (AGAIN CONTROLLED, CLOSE TO HER) and who are you, Anne? You come like the black angel from the kingdom of death and demand reckoning. You accuse and you judge. You have known grief that can't be relieved, felt a tragedy for which there is no consolation. But don't you know that everyone builds his own fate? How could you ever have believed in a cause whose stinking rottenness burned your nose every day? Everybody knows what's going on in this country!

ANNE: (CALMLY, SADLY) We knew what was happening. But we had to take it in the bargain. Eilers strugged hard with it. We thought that everything new had to be born in pain and blood. We had examples—we looked for parallels in history. There were other times when men were sacrificed—heretics burned—innocent children killed—horrors committed in times of upheaval, great revolutions when new worlds opened.

HARRAS: All those you looked to as examples, Anne, believed in human beings and a way of life which could exist better than anything they destroyed. But the men who are blowing up our world despise human beings. So they treat them accordingly. Beat them, burn them, and slaughter them! That's what they believe in. And they are right. We are hopeless, depraved, pitiful, wretched tramps.

ANNE: Eilers wasn't wretched. Eilers is dead.

HARRAS: What are you going to say about me when I'm dead?

ANNE: Nothing. (PULLS DOWN HER VEIL AND EXITS)

HARRAS: Nothing. It checks. (SLOWLY GOES TO THE WINDOW AND LOOKS OUT)

SHORT BLACKOUT

(DISTANT DRUM MUSIC UNTIL THE STAGE LIGHTS UP FOR THE LAST SCENE. THE SAME ROOM, REDDISH LIGHT FROM OUTSIDE AS AT THE BEGINNING OF THE ACT, ONLY DEEPER, WARMER, AS IN THE EVENING. THE DRUMS GO ON FOR A MINUTE, THEN FANFARES OF A MARCH FOR PRESENTING ARMS. HARRAS IS AT THE WINDOW AS BEFORE. ODERBRUCH STANDS AT THE TABLE READING A PAPER)

HARRAS: Why the big blow?

ODERBRUCH: Replacements moving out. Fresh young troops.

HARRAS: At least this mess lets me out of having to give them a pep-talk. I can't tear myself away from this window. (OPENS ONE SECTION OF THE WINDOW) Frost on the hangars. Clear sky. A cold landscape. That's how I picture hell: steel, cement, aluminum, rubber—durable materials, solid construction. (CLOSES THE WINDOW) Now it's getting cold. (ODERBRUCH STANDS IN THE SAME SPOT AND LOOKS AT HARRAS. HARRAS GOES TO THE TABLE) Should I sign it now? It won't change a thing. The one thing that now seems fairly certain to me isn't in there.

ODERBRUCH: (WITH CONTROLLED SUSPENSE) What "one thing"?

HARRAS: (LOOKS AT HIM, HESITATES A MOMENT) I'm almost certain that our friends, the Gestapo, don't know anything. On that point I was on the wrong track. They are hunting in the dark just like we are, hoping I'd turn up something. (HESITATES AGAIN WITH A SEARCHING GLANCE AT ODERBRUCH) Otherwise, why should they wait? The case against me is ready. Some dame who "loves me" has supplied them with plenty of material. But they're holding out, hoping to learn something they don't know. Look in here. (WITH A QUICK MOVEMENT HE OPENS A DRAWER AND TAKES OUT A PISTOL. GRINS) Schmidt-Lausitz must have slipped it in here. It's my own. I had to hand it in. Tactful invitation to the dance. Gentleman's exit. But I'm not going to do them that favor. (HARRAS POCKETS THE REVOLVER. ODERBRUCH LOOKS AT HIM AND MOISTENS HIS LIPS) I'm not quite ready. It's a disgusting feeling to move out of a room without cleaning up. Oderbruch, I know I'm very close to the solution. Skin-close. Arm's length. I feel it—I sense it—with every nerve. It is only a thought—that stands in the way.

ODERBRUCH: (WITH EMPHASIS) Why don't you think it, General Harras.

HARRAS: (LOOKS AT HIM A LONG TIME. BOTH ARE VERY PALE. HE SPEAKS SOFTLY, DELIBERATELY) Oderbruch. If I swear by a sacred oath, not by my honor, not as a general, officer, soldier, but as the man you know, the man with whom you flew for twelve years and as a man in his last hour, I swear to you that nothing you say will ever seep out of these four walls, nothing will ever cross this threshold that either of us may say now. Oderbruch, do you want to talk? (ODERBRUCH IS SILENT. HARRAS CLOSE TO HIM) The truth, Oderbruch! The truth! (STARES INTO HIS EYES, ODERBRUCH RETURNS HIS LOOK AND NODS) You, Oderbruch?

ODERBRUCH: (ALMOST TONELESS) We.

(HARRAS TAKES A DEEP BREATH AND WIPES THE PERSPIRATION FROM HIS FACE. AFTER A PAUSE, SPEAKS QUIETLY)

HARRAS: Who is "we?" Who are the others?

ODERBRUCH: We have no names.

HARRAS: Who are you?

ODERBRUCH: We fight, unknown, unnamed. We know about each other, but we hardly know each other. We have no names, only—a goal! And an enemy.

HARRAS: Was Eilers the enemy? I thought—he was your friend?

ODERBRUCH: I had none better. Outside of you, General.

HARRAS: Why do you strike us out of the dark? Why do you hit us—instead of the enemy?

ODERBRUCH: You are Hitler's weapon with which he can win. And if he wins, Harras—if Germany wins this war—then Germany is lost. Then the world is lost.

HARRAS: Have you thought what defeat means? Foreign domination? New subjugations?

ODERBRUCH: There is no subjugation that would not be liberation—for our people.

HARRAS: Is there really no other way to free Germany?

ODERBRUCH: There is no other way. We need the defeat—we must help it with our own hands. Only then can we rise up again, cleansed.

HARRAS: Defeat—that is certain. Resurrection—is a dream.

ODERBRUCH: No, it's a law of life, the one like the other. Both equally hard. Both written in blood.

HARRAS: With the blood of friends?

ODERBRUCH: Also with our own.

HARRAS: Explain this thing to me, Oderbruch! Help me to understand it. How did you get to this point? You were non-political. You liked technology. You made music. What came over you?

OBERBRUCH: What comes over anyone? Shame.

HARRAS: Don't evade me, Oderbruch! Tell me everything!

ODERBRUCH: There isn't much to say. What came over me? Nothing that I can pinpoint—no personal reason. None of my brothers died in a concentration camp. I loved no Jewish girl. No friend of mine was hunted out of the country. But one day I was ashamed that I was German. Since then—I can't rest—till it's over.

HARRAS: And the others?

ODERBRUCH: Some came out of shame. Others were driven by anger or hate. Some because they loved their homeland—many because they loved the idea of freedom. But all—even those who hate irreconcilably—came because they loved something more than themselves.

HARRAS: How many?

ODERBRUCH: I don't know. We have no way to count. We are becoming fewer instead of more. Many disappear and never reappear. The two men today—I had never seen them before. They didn't know me. But I knew they belonged to us. (HARRAS LISTENS QUIETLY, HIS FACE FROZEN)

HARRAS: What is your goal?

ODERBRUCH: Destruction, a bitter solution, but the only one left us. We cannot stop for our friends. We can't stop to ask where a man's heart is, Harras, only where he stands. Gregory the Great said: "The martyr alone is nothing, but he who knows why he suffers, his testimony is stronger than death." We know why.

HARRAS: (LURKING, DANGEROUS) And you believe—I'm going to let myself be slaughtered with the others? Am I supposed to fold my hands and say, "Amen," when my life is at stake— (TURNS AWAY AND GOES TO THE WINDOW)

ODERBRUCH: (SOFTLY) Your soul is at stake.

HARRAS: (WHEELS AROUND) And what if I don't have a soul? Who told you that I won't betray you to save my own skin?

ODERBRUCH: You swore by an oath, General Harras.

HARRAS: (STARTS TOWARD HIM) This is the hour of the broken word, the day of perjury, the day of false oaths. Perhaps I have a great need to go on living? Perhaps someone needs me? Who are you to think I will accept your verdict without defending myself? How dare you put your life in my hands? And the lives of all your friends too?!

ODERBRUCH: Because in this hour you are one of us. You do not betray what you believe.

HARRAS: (AFTER A PAUSE—SIMPLY) That was the signature. I accept. Too bad. My physical heart would have made it for a couple of decades more. (HE GOES TO THE TELEPHONE AND PUSHES A BUZZER. ODERBRUCH LEANS AGAINST THE TABLE, PALE, AS IF EXHAUSTED) Commando guard! Dr. Schmidt-Lausitz! Harras speaking! Your case will be settled in ten minutes. Then you can come down for my reports. (PUTS THE TELEPHONE DOWN, TAKES IT UP AGAIN) Chief Engineer's office. Ask Lieutenant Hartmann to come in please. (HANGS UP, TURNS TO ODERBRUCH, SPEAKS MEASUREDLY, ALMOST DREAMILY) Tell me one more thing, Oderbruch. What is it that you love more than yourselves? Is it Heaven's mercy? Is it justice on earth?

ODERBRUCH: Both in one. It is eternal justice.

HARRAS: What is eternal justice?

ODERBRUCH: Justice is the uncompromising ruling law to which spirit, nature, and life are subservient. When it is fulfilled—it is called freedom.

HARRAS: (LOOKS AT HIM, NODS) One more thing, Oderbruch. What kind of songs do you people sing?

ODERBRUCH: One doesn't sing in the catacombs.

HARRAS: There is no victory without a song.

ODERBRUCH: We know we won't see the victory. But those who follow us, they will have their own songs.

HARRAS: Thank you. I know enough now. (HE TAKES THE PEN AND SIGNS THE REPORT. HANDS IT TO ODERBRUCH) Here. You'd better sign. I'd rather have everything in order. That's better for you, too. Now I feel better. (BRIEFLY PRESSES ODERBRUCH'S

HAND, GOES TO THE WALL, TAKES DOWN HIS FLYING JACKET AND HIS OLD HELMET AND PUTS THEM ON)

ODERBRUCH: What do you plan to do?

HARRAS: (GRINS) Exit. My own way.

ODERBRUCH: What are you going to do, General Harras?

HARRAS: An experiment. I have always liked to experiment.

ODERBRUCH: All the exits are guarded.

HARRAS: Except one. (HE POINTS TO THE WINDOW)

ODERBRUCH: Yes, the direct one from this room to the airfield. But the guards are there.

HARRAS: They don't scare me.

ODERBRUCH: What are you going to do, Harras? (HARRAS SMILES, ALMOST GAILY, LIGHTS A CIGARETTE. ODERBRUCH IN A SUDDEN WAVE OF EMOTION:) General Harras—if you wait another ten minutes—until it's dark—we could get to hangar 35 without being seen. I'll help you start the engine. I'll get out of it somehow afterward. If we make it quick we can get through.

HARRAS: (CASUALLY, A LITTLE IRONIC) I think the verdict is written in blood. (TURNS TO A SMALL DOOR NEXT TO THE WINDOW)

ODERBRUCH: (STEPS BETWEEN HIM AND THE DOOR) I always hoped it would come to this talk. It's changed a lot of things. It isn't your death we need, Harras. You could do a lot of good abroad, in another country. You could be of more use alive, General Harras, if you only wanted to. I have an address in Switzerland—

HARRAS: (SHAKES HIS HEAD, UNPERTURBED) Too late, my friend. I've been the Devil's General on earth too long. I'm going to fly an advance mission for him in hell too—in preparation for his imminent arrival. Don't give up now, Oderbruch. (BENDS OVER TO HIM, SOFTLY, WITH ALMOST A SMILE) Besides, Korrianke is waiting in hangar 35, ready to go. I can still take that way out in case— (THERE IS A KNOCK AT THE DOOR) Who's there?

HARTMANN: You called for me, General?

HARRAS: Yes, Hartmann, my boy. I have to rush off for an indefinite period. I want you to stay with Oderbruch. He will explain all the details to you. All of them, Oderbruch! (HESITATES A MOMENT, AS IF SOMETHING OCCURRED TO HIM). Tell me, Hartmann, do you have a watch?

HARTMANN: Yes—a wrist watch with a luminous dial.

HARRAS: Let's trade! Take mine for yours. (TAKES THE WRIST WATCH FROM HARTMANN'S LEFT WRIST AND GIVES THE OLD WATCH FROM HIS POCKET TO HARTMANN) It isn't a very good deal for you, but it's durable. If it stops you hit it against the back of your head! See, like this. Then it'll run again. Don't lose it. (PRESSES IT INTO HARTMANN'S HAND. TURNS, GOES TO THE SMALL SIDE DOOR, OPENS IT A LITTLE AND LOOKS OUT) Hmmmm! Light north wind. Smells of the sea. Good take off weather . . . (HE GOES QUICKLY, ODERBRUCH RUNS TO THE WINDOW, STARES OUT)

HARTMANN: (FOLLOWS TO THE WINDOW) Is he flying to the front?

ODERBRUCH: (PALE, ALMOST ENTREATING) Hangar 35—

HARTMANN: Where is hangar 35?

ODERBRUCH: (TEARS OPEN THE WINDOW, LEANS OUT) He isn't going there—he—he's going the other way.

HARTMANN: What kind of plane is that he's going to?

ODERBRUCH: (ALMOST WHISPERING) M 41–1304.

(OUTSIDE LOUD SHOUTS OF "STOP." HARRAS'S VOICE, A SHORT, DISPARATE LAUGH. THE ROAR OF AN ENGINE)

ODERBRUCH: He's climbing . . . higher . . .

(THE NOISE OF THE ENGINE INCREASES, DROWNING OUT OTHER SOUNDS AND A FEW SINGLE SHOTS)

ODERBRUCH: They're trying to get him . . . they can't . . . he's climbing higher . . . he'll make it.

(HE AND HARTMANN ARE STANDING CLOSE TOGETHER, LEANING FORWARD, LOOKING UP)

HARTMANN: Look—(HE CLUTCHES ODERBRUCH'S ARM. THEN HE COVERS HIS FACE WITH HIS HANDS. THE SOUND OF THE ENGINE STOPS ABRUPTLY. SILENCE)

ODERBRUCH: (AFTER A PAUSE—SAYS QUIETLY) Our Father, who art in Heaven . . .

HARTMANN: (JOINS IN, WHISPERING)

(THE DOOR OPENS—LAUSITZ ENTERS SILENTLY, GOES QUICKLY TO THE TELEPHONE)

LAUSITZ: Headquarters? Mission accomplished, without a hitch. In the line of duty, General Harras has just had a fatal accident. Yes, testing one of his aeroplanes. Yes, of course. State funeral.

CURTAIN

Translated by Ingrid Komar;
additions by Virginia Wurdak

Sebastian Haffner

Germany: Jekyll and Hyde

Contents

Publisher's Note (1941): Sebastian Haffner

The author is an "Aryan" German under forty years of age, who has lived all his life in Germany. He was trained as a lawyer and worked for six years under the Nazi regime. Having been brought up in the Liberal tradition he determined to leave the land of his birth. His escape was exciting. To give further biographical details might well endanger his family.

1

Hitler

"Hitler" is Germany, Germany is Hitler," Nazi propaganda has proclaimed with trumpet-blasts for the least seven years, and the impeachers and foes of Germany all over the world readily agree.

This assertion cannot be disposed of with a shrug of the shoulders, as the German opposition, German emigrants and pro–German Left circles everywhere are apt to do. No matter how many and how eminent are the Germans who shudder at the thought of being identified with Hitler, the fact remains that Hitler at the moment can speak and act for Germany to an extent rare in the history of the world. It is no less true that, in spite of the treachery, deceit, and foul play that accompanied the seizure and maintenance of power, Hitler by more or less normal means of persuasion and attraction has gained more adherents in Germany and come nearer to absolute power than anyone before him. It is also clear that after seven years of terrible atrocities Hitler has a large enough following in Germany to secure for his regime at least the appearance of popularity and real authority. All that is no small achievement. For though it is true that Hitler has always used a generous measure of lies, tricks, and threats, and that some or perhaps many of his followers were deceived as to his real aims, they could never have been deceived as to one thing—the specific odor of his personality. He was never able, and seldom tried, to disguise this with fragrant perfumes. To many Germans, therefore, this smell must have been agreeable, or at least not too revolting. And while it is true that since his rise to power Hitler has compelled obedience and apparent enthusiasm, love, and adoration by threats of torture and death, there is a degree of hate and aversion that cannot be overcome by such menaces. At least Hitler has not become loathsome and horrible to this extent to the majority of his German opponents.

Thus there are weighty reasons enough to warrant a discussion of the dictum "Hitler is Germany." Inquiry will fix the limits of its accuracy. But before we can ascertain the extent to which Hitler is a specifically German phenomenon we must explore the phenomenon's peculiarities.

Clarity on this point is singularly wanting. Though endless reams of paper have been covered with ink concerning Hitler, he is still able to "surprise" the world, a proof that the key to his personality and his behavior has not yet been found. Yet this key is within easy reach. Its whereabouts are so obvious that no one suspects it—a kind of hiding-place familiar to every reader of detective novels.

Nearly all biographers of Hitler have made the mistake of trying to connect Hitler with the spiritual history of his times and explain him in terms of it. They have sought to stamp him as the "product" and "exponent" of something or other. This approach accords, firstly, with the leading scientific fashion—introduced by the Marx–Engels materialistic theory of history—of dethroning man from his position as the protagonist of history and of subordinating his role as far as possible to semimythical abstractions such as "economic conditions," "ideas," "cultures," "nations," and "dynamics." Secondly, it panders to the natural desire of Hitler's opponents to make his personality appear as puny and contemptible as possible, deny him historical magnitude and paint a picture wherein Hitler is likened to a cork borne up on a wave. Doubt prevails as to the nature of the wave. According to the most naïve interpretation, Hitler is only the pawn of German militarist and capitalist cliques who use his demagogy as a cloak for their wars and business deals. Other theories are forthcoming to account for the fact that Hitler has risen, so to speak, automatically, without merit or worth, to his present position: among these are the resentment of the German middle class, impoverished by the inflation of 1923; the despair of German patriots at the Treaty of Versailles, and its too slow revision; the fear of Bolshevism.

All this is most unconvincing. Every attempt to regard Hitler as a tender hitched onto the locomotive of an idea or a movement leaves men gasping with surprise when the apparent tender, obviously on its own power and taking with it the entire train of Germany, suddenly strikes off on a new line. Thus people were bewildered when the "patriot," "nationalist," and "racialist" Hitler suddenly uprooted the South Tryolean Germans and acquired millions of Czechs and Poles; or when the "arch anti-bolshevist" concluded the Soviet Pact and sold large portions of Eastern Europe to bolshevism. People will be similarly taken aback when the imperialist Hitler, at a tactically favorable moment, turns out to be a federalist and pacifist. It has dawned on the world—slowly enough in all conscience—that Hitler does not keep his word. Many do not yet realize that he is not bound by his proclaimed objects, program, and ideas. For this reason they achieve so little who wish to fight Hitler by combating his *immediate* "program" and "philosophy." Just when they have succeeded in establishing the fact that he is an extreme nationalist, Hitler will step forward as the pioneer of the "United States of Europe"; when they have proved him to be the murderer of the workers he will show him that he is just as good at murdering capitalists. In fact, to tabulate Hitler, as it were, in the History of Ideas and degrade him to an historical episode is a hopeless undertaking, and can only lead to perilous miscaculations. Much more progress toward an accurate estimate of the man can be made if one takes exactly the opposite course and considers German and European history as a part of Hitler's private life. Let us not feel humiliated by this way of looking at things. It is no more than one among a large number of alternatives, and it will be a happy coincidence if it helps to solve the riddle of Hitler. (If anything is humiliating, it is that we have allowed this man to grow to such menacing proportions that we must exert our minds to understand him.)

The historical events of the last twenty years—first in Germany, then in Europe—have not only altered the map of Europe and shattered its spiritual and moral foundations; not only cost nations their freedom, their honor, and their civilization, and hundreds of thousands of men their lives; not only placed the Christian tradition of Europe in deadly peril; not only wrecked the League of Nations and those unspoken customs and agreements based on good faith and trust which, in the pre–League era, enabled European nations to live side by side on terms of mutual respect; not only brought the leading culture of the world into immediate danger of dissolution. They have, above all, permitted a certain Hitler to rise from that social underworld where the casual laborer jostles the professional criminal to the sphere of crowned heads and prime ministers; to rise from starveling to multi-millionaire, from military police spy of the lowest grade to supreme War Lord of the German Reich, from an habitué of a Viennese doss-house to despot of the lives of eighty million people, from one despised and shunned to the idol of a great nation. It would be surprising if, for the man who has achieved it, this career were not by far the more important of the two inseparable series of events. We get much nearer to an understanding of Hitler's actions if we realize clearly that the Nazification of Germany with all its consequences signifies for Hitler a social career—the means by which a life, that had gravitated from the petty bourgeoisie to the rabble, suddenly ranked as an equal with the King of England and the President of the United States of America.

It is a completely unique case, in no way comparable with the harmless and frequent occasions when men of the working class or the petty bourgeoisie have "risen" to eminence. In all these cases the story is one of personal ascent: accomplishment, success, service, first in small then in larger spheres; finally, as the crowning achievement, power—legitimately conferred power. There is nothing more superficial than to set Hitler's beside such familiar figures. Hitler's life-curve starts downward, and continues downward. The son of the small Customs official fails in his artistic ambitions—life's first blow! Instead of an artist he becomes a house-painter, immediately sinking from the bourgeoisie to the proletariat. There, too, he cannot keep his place. He is a bad workman and a worse comrade. He sinks from the proletariat to the rabble, to the under-world of the men's doss-house in Vienna where the denizens give him the nickname "Oom Kruger." It is his second rebuff. Then the war: the salvation and last refuge of so many ruined lives—but it does not save Hitler. Four years' service at the front and he is still only a corporal. This is his third defeat. His superiors do not think fit to promote him; his character makes it impossible to entrust him with the leadership of the smallest unit of troops. After the war he remains, since there is no place for him in the civil world, in the army—in the lowest and most humiliating position: as a petty, despised, political police spy, employed to pry and denounce, and poorly paid for the job.

Let us take a good look at Hitler at this stage. It is the decisive turning-point, the hour when that immense evil force within him is unleased; it is the start of an unexampled personal career for which Germany, Europe, the world must pay an unexampled price. It is, at the same time, the lowest point to which men can fall: the position of professional spy and professional traitor as a social step below that of professional criminal. Hitler has again and again been rejected by life and society. First the bourgeoisie cast him forth, then the proletariat, and finally, out of their underworld, the rabble spued him out into the unmentionable Acheron. This thrice-repeated judgment of society is annihilating proof of the man's true worth. For it is much rarer than novelists concede that noble, sensitive, and fine characters are wrecked by life. It is almost always bad, rotten, ugly, impossible characters, the moral cripples and the misbegotten, whom life rejects. They are ignorant of the very elements of life. They cannot work, cannot better themselves, cannot inspire or, needless to say, bestow love. Together with Hitler's social bankruptcy, the fact of this total erotic bankruptcy must be taken into account if we are rightly to assess the figure, who in a Munich attic makes mice jump for crumbs and accompanies this amusement with wild and bloodthirsty fantasies of power, revenge, and annihilation. It is a frightening picture, and one may well shudder at the thought that from the rejected of the great cities, from the rag-pickers, thieves, and police spies, from the street beggars and pimps a second Hitler may emerge, a supreme resentment and will-to-power driven to extremes, a motor of immense drawing power, who will immolate the whole world in a final gesture to the individual, a-social "I," as did Herostratus at Ephesus.

Here lies Hitler's undoubted greatness. Supreme is the outlaw's resolve to affirm, out of perversity, all the bad and unsocial qualities for which he has been outlawed by the world, and to make himself the world's master; greater, of course, than to go under and be submerged; greater than to reform and "begin a new life"; greater even than to turn revolutionary and to raise on high that lowest place where he stands; greater, but how evil and how loathsome! It is typical of the discouraging superficiality of modern thought that the word "greatness" denoting quantity not quality, is used as a term of appraisal, such as "beauty," "goodness," "wisdom." That which is great today is almost automatically regarded as beautiful and good. But it need not be so. For example, the stadiums and congress halls built by the Nazis are unusually great and unusually hideous. Similarly, Hitler is unusually "great" and unusually base. It is time we assessed these expressions anew and did not gape in veneration of greatness, as if it were the be-all and end-all, as if a greater criminal did not deserve ten times greater punishment than a lesser.

Behold, then, the police spy, Hitler! The man without family or friend or calling, without upbringing or education, the adult spiteful child, the man whom no one loves or respects, and with whom no one has anything to do, the man about whom there is a vague noisome odor, but who still clings, embittered and mulish, to his stagey egotistic "lonely" images out of the worlds of Makart and Wagner and, despite everything, yearns for the life of a hero out of opera. He is full of a secret cowardly consciousness of inferiority that only serves to nourish a wild love of himself and a wild hatred of the world that has not allowed him to have his own way and does not love and honor his unpleasing person; a wild hatred of the artists who did not approve his pictures; of the trade unionist builders who would not listen to his political sermon; of the entire Austrian State, in which he, Adolf Hitler, had to frequent a doss-house; of the Jews who had pretty mistresses while he was loved by no one; of the influential lords and high-born officers who despised him. One day he will pay them all out, all—the organized workers and the Jews, the artists and the Austrian State. And then he will have not only automobiles and villas, private airplanes and special trains; then he will not only exchange congratulatory telegrams with kings—but far more than that. That would be small beer. He will hold jousts and tourneys like the heroes of his boyhood books, speak to acclaiming crowds and jubilant devotees, as one did on the stage, march into conquered towns like the emperors and queens in Makart's pictures, play today with bricks and tomorrow with soldiers like an almighty spoilt child, and let off wars like fireworks. . . . Scorned by life, the thirty-year-old ne'er-do-well paints the life of a great man in extravagant childlike daydreams. *At forty, head of the State, called by the people in extremity to be dictator; at fifty, a victorious war.* Much later, these speculations and his habit of regarding the events of European history as decorative episodes of his private life, are expressed in significant declarations. For instance, in 1932, he says to Papen, with a look of angry impatience: "I am now over forty, I must now rule." Again, in August 1939, to the British Ambassador, with an air of one who looks at life with philosophical detachment: "I am now fifty. I would rather have the war now, than when I am fifty-five or sixty."

Here we have the key to Hitler's politics. Not anti-Bolshevism, not service to the State, not zeal for the "German Race," not German concern about *lebensraum,* not an obsessing theory about the organization of Europe, nor whatever else it is he wishes to trick us into believing is his guiding star. How easily he has given up every one of these advertised principles, betrayed and distorted them! But there was no need to wait until he abandoned or revised them to realize he was not serious. Already the incredible hollowness and inconsistency, the ill-digested knowledge of all the utterances of Hitler prove that everything he teaches and preaches is no more than a mask and a curtain. He never even takes the trouble to understand, or to think things out. How different is his tone when he shifts his ground and tells you frankly how he looks at things—as ingredients of his own biography. "When I marched out with seven men. . . ." That is a leitmotiv. And one of the most curious images of self-encouragement and intimidation recurring at least twenty or thirty times in his speeches, often at decisive crises, runs like this: "The task 'I' have today"—such as to defy the League of Nations as Dictator of Germany, to challenge Russia or to lay siege to the Western Democracies—"is much easier than my former ascent out of nothing to the German dictatorship. If 'I' succeeded them, why should 'I' worry now?" He himself is scarcely conscious of the naïve self-revelation implicit in these pronouncements. All the more is it evident that the only stable element in Hitler's politics, bound as they are by no ties, is their devotion to his own person. Resentment, career, and satisfaction of a theatrical urge to see his own ego in many banal radiant roles of doubtful taste, these are the three positive aims to which Hitler, without a thought, sacrifices civilizations, nations, and men's lives.

Anyone who does not accept this truth because it sounds too crude and simple, and who seeks to ascribe to Hitler some kind of statesmanlike motive, only exposes himself to new and repeated disappointments and deceptions. No such motive exists. Hitler is no statesman, but a swindler in a statesman's mask. Though he has done all in his power to efface his past and have it forgotten, he himself has not effaced or forgotten it. Just as he still wears the pimp's curl of his Viennese doss-house years, and speaks the Viennese suburban dialect of that period of his life; just as he still relapses into the manners of the underworld and the professional criminal—indeed not always by accident; one often feels that it must appease one of his resentment when he, say, in the scene with Schuschnigg at Berchtesgaden or with Hacha in Berlin, lets fall the mask and openly introduces the social deportment of the underworld into the diplomatic world; just as in outward appearance he goes among the heads of states and ministers as a badly disguised rascal, within himself he is still the same despised and half-starved "Oom Kruger," who each day enjoys afresh his role, his revenge, his power; who knows well that the day the spell breaks, his life ends, and clings to power with the very instinct of self-preservation. For no pension awaits Hitler, no dignified retirement. He justly feels that the instant he loses the supreme power which today protects and renders him invulnerable, he will sink back again where he belongs—into the abyss, which, as he secretly knows, is always yawning for him.

It is, however, improbable that he will let himself come to that. Hitler's end is not a matter for speculation. There is, reported by Goebbels, a most genuine-sounding declaration dating back to the Strasser crisis of December, 1932. After walking up and down gloomily brooding, Hitler burst out: "When the Party falls to pieces"—the Party was at that time the only basis of his power—"I shall end it all in five minutes with a pistol." It is conceivable that he will do that when the game is up. He has the exact kind of courage and cowardice for suicide in despair. Moreover, this solves another riddle, for it provides the key to his almost unbelievable love of a gamble, with high stakes at that. Hitler is the potential suicide par excellence. He owns no ties outside his own "ego," and with its extinction he is released and absolved from all cares, responsibilities, and burdens. He is in the privileged position of one who loves nothing and no one but himself. He is completely indifferent to the fate of States, men, commonwealths, whose existence he stakes at play. As far as his own person is concerned, it is an object upon which is lavished an asocial degree of solicitude and responsibility. Behind him extends the retrospect of an Inferno, the milieu, as he is well aware, to which he rightly belongs in normal times; and before him lies the prospect of immediate painless death at a chosen moment—and since he is an atheist there is for him no world beyond. So he can dare all to preserve or magnify his power, that power to which he owes the present, and which alone stands between him and speedy death.

This is sufficient reason to destroy the man as a mad dog. With the destiny of a great nation in the hands of a swindler, a gambler, a potential suicide, we face a constellation that, if any can, portends the fall of mankind. Man, we know, survives in a physically hostile and overwhelming environment by means of civilization, and the distinguishing mark of civilization is the elimination of force. It is the old threat of death hanging over mankind, for force cannot be eliminated without leaving a residue; so that the most complete eradication of force leaves behind an inevitable and, in its way, deadly power-center; the State. (If, as Left publicists counsel, states should delegate this power to a super-state there would arise a still more dangerous ultimate concentration and monopoly of force. One can imagine what would happen if the super-state should one day fall into the hands of a Hitler.) The menace of this highly charged power-center will manifest itself again and again in the form of warlike explosion or political oppression. But mankind, unable logically to solve the problem of eliminating force, has discovered means which ensure survival, "as if" there were no force. These are to be found in the social sphere, such as the rearing of certain classes to the rulers of the state, as well as the formation of political constitutions that link exercise of power with control, responsibility, and duty. But—it is impossible here to go into details—it must be admitted that these are temporary expedients and not solutions. If they fail, and if the criminal, in this most dangerous power-center where every switch releases untold consequences, takes the place of the responsible, benevolent statesman, universal catastrophe is inevitable. It is tragic that the statesmen did not instinctively grasp this in time in Hitler's case. This man, from the first day of his advent to power, has had full diplomatic recognition de jure and de facto, and has negotiated as an equal at the conference table with people whose first duty it was to have him locked up. Now we are in the midst of the catastrophe. The one way of saving ourselves is the immediate riddance of Hitler, dead or alive. But this is by the way.

We have seen the only stable idea behind Hitler's policy. It is, in a word, Hitler. However, we have not fully probed into his method, the method that made possible the stupendous rise of a down-and-out, first to civic reputation and finally to the highest rank, and that is still employed by the "statesman" with obstinate monotony.

This method is again so immensely simple and obvious, that in their search for Hitler's secret of success men have almost always overlooked it. It is called "Force."

Everything else plays a subordinate role. Of course, lies, demagogy, calumnies, and promises are also used. Hitler himself is particularly proud of certain rules of propaganda that he has regularly applied. These are expounded as an immense stroke of genius in *Mein Kampf:* only big lies, no small ones; no proofs, but perpetual repetition; exclusive concentration on the most stupid, and so on. Probably Hitler over-estimates both the originality and the effectiveness of this recipe. The ingenious and special feature that explains the extraordinary effect of his very crude propaganda lies rather in the fact that Hitler from the first has continually coupled propaganda, persuasion, and negotiation with force and terrorism. Force, the constant, direct, unconcealed use and exploitation of naked force to back up every assertion and demand—that is Hitler's method by which he stands or falls. In its discovery lies no less of what might be called his genius than in his resolve, sworn in the profoundest depth of despair, to impinge sedulously and unscrupulously upon the world.

Hitler vaulted from his post of military police spy and denizen of the underworld straight into a position of absolute power which he has never since surrendered. It was methodically extended. At first, it was not absolute power over the German Reich, but only over a club composed of two or three dozen political backwoodsmen. But it was absolute power from the very first moment. The first thing that Hitler did in the "German Workers' Party," which he entered as member Number 7, was to intrigue the committee out of office and replace it, not with another committee, but with a dictator, exacting the oath of allegiance and unconditional obedience from the other members. Here he realized for the first time that power attracts and protects. The possessor of power is irresponsible, he is respectable, he is protected. He possesses in the bodies ruled by him something that the Jewish legend calls a *Golem,* a mechanical contrivance that performs the deed or which its creator lacks the strength or courage.

(It is, in passing, interesting to note that Hitler's "rise" begins with a "seizure of power" without any service rendered, and, as we shall soon see, consists simply in the gradual extension of this initially grasped power; whereas hitherto in the "rise" from the social depths, power has been the final reward of manifold services and successes. In Hitler's case, it is not the result but the means of personal advancement.)

There has been no change in this power and its exercise from 1919 to 1940. Hitler today has exactly the same kind of position as in his mouse-haunted attic in 1919, just as he is today the same asocial person burdened with the same resentments as of old. What has altered is the compass of his power, and with it the social sphere in which his life and his resolves have play. The small obscure group grew into a Party; the Party into a State within a State; the State within the State into the State itself, and today the State into an Empire. Instead of pub scraps Hitler now orders real battles; and business is transacted not with beer-cellar hosts and printing press proprietors, but with Finance Ministers and People's Commissars for Petroleum. The nature of the business, the manner of waging war, and the exercise of power have remained the same. The discovery of this technique of exercising power is Hitler's second stroke of genius.

There are in fact two kinds of power: passive imposed power or Lordship and active motor power or Leadership. The first demands of its subjects only obedience and docility; the second exacts discipleship and action. Hitler has found that Leadership conduces to an almost automatic expansion of power and binds the "disciples" more helplessly to the "Leader," since it uproots and forces them into constant action and unforseen situations. The creation of an "action" and the forcible conversion of the ruled into disciples corresponds roughly to the transformation of a standing peacetime army into a mobile wartime field force. Although subjection and servitude for those led are far more complete, and for the rest of the world far more dangerous than for those ruled, they are less, or differently, conscious of their state. Hourly surprises and their consequences—the whirling changes of the conditions of life, or of words, of enemies, of aims—constant action, in brief, does not allow the sense of oppression and criticism and the will to freedom to develop as it does under a static burden of Lordship. Hence the complete fruitlessness of all psychological conceptions that merely look on the German people as being "oppressed" and "enslaved" in the classical sense, and that count on reactions similar to those of the Dutch under Philip II or of the Poles and Hungarians in the nineteenth century. The situation is completely different, and so are its psychological potentialities. The German nation is not enslaved, but by forcible persuasion pressed into the service of a robber band in which they find life more soldierly than servile, unforeseen and not particularly desirable, but gay and adventurous and, above all, rewarded to date with tremendous and almost alarming triumphs and captures of booty. It is clear that a revolt of these willy-nilly robbers against their leader must depend on other psychological causes and be inspired by other catchwords than the rising of oppressed and enslaved helots against their tyrant. The old slogans are therefore useless.

Meanwhile, to reurn to Hitler, we have now a fairly clear picture of his historical appearance, his motives, his aims, his methods. Once more the *essential* points: Hitler serves no idea, no nation, no statesmanship conception, but exclusively the propulsion of his ego. His motives are mulish self-love, resentment, and a corrupt imagination. His aims, pursued in the following sequence and only so far as each does not endanger its predecessor, are: (1) Maintenance and extension of his personal power. (2) Revenge on all groups of persons and institutions against whom he feels resentment, and they are many. (3) The staging of scenes out of Wagner's operas and the posing of pictures after Makart with Adolf Hitler as chief protagonist. All else is pretence and tactic. There is greatness in the immense tenacity and the lack of scruple of his self-love, and genius in the instinctive realization and exploitation of certain forms of power. As a whole his character, of which the basic traits are resentment and conspicuous bad taste, is uncommonly revolting, ugly, and vile. Benevolence, generosity, chivalry, humor, and even courage are completely lacking. With no dignity, he is a poor specimen of manly bearing. True grandeur is beyond him. He is, moreover, a hypochondriac.

Having analyzed the personality, policy, and methods of Hitler, we may turn back to our initial query: is Hitler Germany? Those who glibly deny it do not for the most part rightly understand the question. They read it to mean: is Hitler a typical German? This is quite another and far more superficial question. Let us at once assure the friends of Germany that it may be answered in the negative. Hitler is no typical German.

There is no lack of good nature and generosity in the normal German, no lack of physical courage, and certainly no lack of humor; qualities of which Hitler is totally innocent. As a type, he represents nothing in which the German can willingly recognize his own nature. The German is expansive, fond of eating, drinking, and making a noise; hearty, pleasant, phlegmatic, extravagant, tirelessly thorough in work and play, quick-tempered but easily appeased. The suppressed, flaring, profoundly unpleasant Hitler, with his sustained hatred, his vegetarianism, his dread of alcohol, tobacco, and women, his stony stare and his repugnant convex mouth—the German mouth, as a rule, is thick-lipped and harmless—this figure is an anomaly in Germany and to the average German instinctively appears queer. If one wants to know what a typical four-square German dictator would have to look like one need only turn to Göring. Göring enjoys genuine popularity in Germany: even his opponents and victims rarely succeed in hating him. His bouncing brutality is German. Hitler's suppressed sadism is not German. The overfed gourmet evokes amusement among Germans; the puffy carrot-eater arouses uneasiness.

Hitler then is not popular. He is God or Satan. A human attachment to his person or even to the legend of his person does not exist. There are no good-natured witticisms about him, no human anecdotes. There is no warm personal love and devotion inspired in his followers to weigh against the immense unsleeping disgust and loathing felt by his enemies. For the former, his image floats on a dizzily high pedestal of power and success, among the clouds. (Some intellectual Nazis actually play with the idea of deifying Hitler after his death and preparations to this end are already being made.) He is nowhere loved as a man is loved. If the pillar of power and success crumbles under him nothing will prevent his disillusioned worshippers from quartering and roasting him as all primitive people do with their fallen idols. Certainly a close scrutiny of his person will not help to prevent this fate.

But all this is not particularly important, because Hitler's power over the German people rests on quite other foundations than popularity. Hitler the person may be un-German and unpopular but not the institution of "Leader" which he incarnates. Hitler may be no typical German but as the Führer he may still be Germany. Let us recall that even before his advent to power he had immense legions of Germans behind him. And even today, exposed in all his subhumanity, he has many genuine adherents. He is, to most of them, strange. Such an effect must have certain deep-lying causes which justify the phrase "Hitler is Germany"—at least to a certain extent.

They are to be found precisely in what we recognized as the only constant, and, as it were, bona fide cardinal points in Hitler's policy: his will to power, his resentment, and his lust for display. Just those three things make an appeal that is certain to evoke fervid response in Germany, even when they proceed from a Hitler.

Everyone who is able and willing to seize power, to rule and to lead, will find in Germany an immense crowd to obey and follow him with joy and relief. That is something the Western countries do not understand, often do not believe, and, if they believe, despise. They love freedom and self-determination above all things, and cannot visualize a mentality that sees in them a burden to be cast off with delight. But such is the German mind. And, let me add, that it is not for this reason to be despised any more than the freedom-loving nations. German history reveals no example of successful and glorious revolution, and scarcely one of notable and effective self-government.

On the other hand, it has known long periods of splendid rule: the Emperors of the Middle Ages, the wise and mild regime of many Princes of the Church, the successful patriarchal conduct of many famous dynasties, the stylish and large-minded government of the Hanseatic merchant oligarchy, and others. In the course of many centuries the German has learned that to renounce political self-determination, for which his talent is small, does not mean to surrender human dignity, though, for other nations, it may have that meaning; further, that it does not even rob him of that freedom which he really desires, the freedom of an extensive private zone; and, finally, that in this way he generally fares well.

Indeed, during the last century this outlook, like everything else in Germany, has degenerated. We cannot here go into details as to how and why. Suffice it to say that the justified wish for authority and good government has, with many Germans, turned into a cheap and vulgar worship of naked brute force. Sheer power empty of content is exercising an ever-increasing magic spell on the present generation of Germans. A sultry and oppressive mass-masochism is widespread. The "strong man" rouses their enthusiasm, the government that "strikes hard." That is the state of mind which Hitler found and fostered. The muzzling of the press, the abolition of free speech and free thought, the Gestapo, the concentration camp, all this not only intimidates but, compared with the "sloppy" and "weak-kneed" rule of liberal democracy, bewitches. (And, incidentally, for this very reason, nothing would help the Allied cause in Germany as much as a brutal and forceful military coup; and nothing has done their prestige more harm than the policy of patience and appeasement that was blind to this psychological disposition of a great number of present-day Germans.)

The psychological advantage to Hitler of this mass-inclination to submit to power has been partly lost by the dynamic nature of his "Leadership." We have seen that he has won other advantages in exchange. The power that the majority of Germans respect is static power, conservative vigorous rule that establishes peace and order and guarantees private spheres of homely comfort. But dynamic leadership which transforms everyone into disciples, which is total, and knows no private zones and no easy-going comfort, but demands and compels perpetual action, is only desired by a youthful minority—by the real Nazis—and is displeasing and burdensome to the majority. We shall return to these matters in greater detail when we analyze the state of mind of the Nazis and of the loyal population. These are weaknesses which anti-Hitler propaganda can effectively exploit. They cannot, however, prove mortal. For Hitler is able, thanks to his complete freedom from shackling program, aim, or person, to drop dynamics and totality and even his own followers for a while and become conservative and static, if this should appear necessary for the maintenance of power. He has already done so with success, on June 30, 1934. Besides, his will to power is not the only psychological pillar of his regime. Still more fateful is his league with Germany in the name of resentment.

It was a disastrous coincidence for the whole world that Hitler's personal plight so well matched Germany's plight in 1919. Like Hitler, Germany had suffered a terrible defeat in life—defeat not only military but of the whole German conception of life, which is also like Hitler's, a Wagner-Makart conception. Like Hitler, Germany reacted to this defeat, not with an honorable resolve to look it in the face, to seek her faults and change her ways, but with resentment, defiance, and spite. This inclination to resentment is a most profound danger and pathological weakness of the German character. The German—the individual no less than the nation—is always inclined to feel himself persecuted, slighted, and ill-treated. He always likes to see himself as the "honest, good, stupid German

Michel," to whom the wicked, false, envious world grudges every-thing and whose good-nature is continually exploited and duped. This, however, is not the place to pursue this calamitous German idiosyncrasy to its historical origins. It is no more than about a hun-dred and fifty years old, yet seems ineradicable. It is the result, as we know, of a pathological self-confidence. This affection is of a complicated kind. It is not that the German lacks self-confidence; in many respects his self-confidence is even hypertrophic. He has immense confidence in his own strength and ability, and is always confident that if he "only turns up his sleeves" he can take on the whole world. Of course, this is a delusion. On the other hand, he feels himself—and that is probably another delusion—to be help-less as a child in all peaceful and civil activities: he is in constant dread that he is being cheated, and only feels safe when he can strike a blow. His is not a peaceable but a warlike self-confidence, a dangerous mixture.

The result is terrifying when, as in the World War, this military self-confidence is broken. The defeat can never, in any way, be rec-ognized. A dagger in the back, Jews, Freemasons, they must all be used to conjure it away. If anyone tells the unpleasant truth he must be struck dead forthwith. The snarling, blood-thirsty resentment that spread throughout Germany after 1918 is identical with the state of mind with which Hitler, rejected by life and doomed to his doss-house attic, reacted to defeat. Hitler had only to substitute "Germany" for "Hitler" to arouse in thousands and millions of Germans the terrible, envenomed resentment of which he was pos-sessed.

Let us scan the passages in Hitler's speeches which evoke the most spontaneous and heated applause. They are always the ones in which he invites resentment, such as: "Here the World Press found no cause for excitement—it was only Germans who were being tortured," and similar remarks. As for the themes in his pro-paganda which have real box-office appeal, they are always those which awaken a sense of inferiority and thirst for revenge, such as "encirclement," "the infamy of Versailles," "the Jewish world con-spiracy against Germany," "English plutocracy." One must listen to the tone of venomous delight with which even his German critics refer to his speeches on foreign policy ("This time he let them have it.") to realize to what degree Hitler is Germany.

It must be admitted that there are exceptions to this widespread resentment in Germany, and that Hitler's own venom has largely contributed to their increase. This does not alter the fact that he found a universal inclination to this attitude. In fact, it is not far wrong to say that Hitler's hate, born of a sense of inferiority, and his frantically defiant assertion of all the worst qualities of his ego are German, and not solely Hitlerian phenomena. It is quite impossible to cure them by "meeting Germany half-way" or by "removing grounds for complaint." This is only suggested by people ignorant of German psychology. Inherent in diseased conditions of the mind is their faculty for creating the reality-substance that they need. Proof of this is the recent genuine encirclement hysteria during Poland's own active encirclement by Germany. If and how this German mental affection is to be cured cannot be discussed here. It is certainly impossible so long as Hitler systematically and daily encourages it. It can be attempted only after his removal. Meanwhile, all propaganda is doomed to failure which ignores it and tries to discuss subjects—distorted by their resentment for their own ends—with the Germans, as with reasonable people. It is today impossible to talk to them about all those matters which in Germany come under the heading of "Germany's rights which are wrongfully withheld from her and which she must seize for herself." To this the only effective answer, for the present, is a cudgelling. This is not to say that there are not many other matters which one may well discuss with them. We shall encounter many in the course of our survey.

One may be brief about the third characteristic that Hitler has in common with Germany: the lust for display. It is one that at the moment plays no important part in politics. It may, however, be noted here that the Wagnerian Hitler—Wagnerian in more than a musical and aesthetic sense—met with a ready response from the German Wagnerians. In fact, in the conflict round Wagner that has never abated during the last hundred years, we see before our eyes no other than the struggle between the Nazis and their opponents. The Hitlerian school of thought and life was fully anticipated by Wagner and his followers. Those who would delve deeper can establish the fact that as early as the nineties the first model of Hitler's Third Reich, accurately shaped to its smallest detail, had already sprung out of the Bayreuth circle: the colony founded by Bernhard

Foerster in Paraguay and called "New Germany." We cannot stop to ponder over this subject however great and melancholy its attraction and academic interest. Hitler's wanton political exhibitionism, however, his preference for theatrical coups, cheap startling effects, imposing parades and celebrations, and would-be grandiose buildings are antipathetic and repellant to the anti-Wagnerian minority, but exercises a definite lure for the Wagnerian majority in Germany. It cannot be turned into a means of propaganda against Hitler as easily as some socialist propagandists would have us believe.

Let us briefly recapitulate the results of our investigations: (1) Hitler is bound by no political idea or conception. He can let any such drop when it is no longer tenable. To put an end to the danger Hitler it is necessary to put an end to the man Hitler. (2) Hitler is Germany inasmuch as he corresponds to the German idea of a wielder of power, flatters German resentment against "the world," and satisfies a certain German lust for display. It is misjudging German psychology to believe that by dilating on these points, obnoxious as they may appear to other nations, Hitler could be made to appear obnoxious to the Germans. (3) Hitler becomes insecure and vulnerable the moment his disguise is torn away. His disguise consists of the facile, ever-shifting gay banners of ideas and political conceptions, and the heavy armor-plate of power. The formula "War against Hitler" must, therefore, be taken quite literally. It must, from the outset, be made clear that this war cannot be concluded by negotiations *with* Hitler but *about* Hitler. As far as the German people are concerned, they must be told, firstly, that we are quarrelling with them because they are fighting for Hitler; and, secondly, that Hitler has a good reason in making them fight, since only the bodies of his soldiers stand between his head and the halter. The spell of Hitler will be broken the moment he is no longer treated as a statesman and ruler, but as the swindler that he is— whose removal is the preliminary basis of any negotiations for peace.

But let us understand the word "removal" in its true sense. Merely political removal, perhaps in the form of voluntary abdication in favor of Göring or Hess, carried out with theatrical pomp and represented as a "sacrifice," would be quite useless. It would only mean a strategic withdrawal to a better protected position. It would not destroy Hitler's power, and might possibly increase his prestige. Translated into the Grand Old Man of Ober-Salzberg, basking in the old glory of his former successes and the new sanctity of his abnegation, he would continue to rule from his apparent retreat through the person of his deputy, styled successor. If Nazi leadership and Hitler survive, then Hitler remains in power. For, in spite of all the personal rivalries and ambitions, the Görings, Hess's and their like, know that Hitler is the pivot of the whole Nazi system, and that if they give him up the whole edifice will collapse.

Nor would suffice the elimination of his person, by means, for instance, of a successful attempt on his life. It is an old error, repeatedly refuted but always revived, to think that the power of a personality can be broken by his physical removal. It may sound like an empty phrase but is an actual fact that, in such cases, "the spirit lives on." Hitler would live on, no longer the power in the background, but as a martyr, a saint, as God. It is possible that, if this happened, the struggles of rivals for the succession—which in the event of his "abdication" would probably be prevented by his authority—would for a time disrupt and cripple the regime. But after this transitional period, it would stand all the more firmly, for it would then possess what it now lacks: an indestructible myth. Hitler would simply return in the role that Lenin is playing in Stalin's Russia and Dollfuss played in Schuschnigg's Austria.

The removal of Hitler must be total to be effective: political, moral, physical. Whether the physical removal should take the form of execution or permanent exile, such as at St. Helena, is of secondary importance. What is important is that it should have the character of an execution of judgment, and that the judgment should leave no doubt that a continuation of the Hitler regime is impossible, that rule can no longer be carried on in Germany in his name. Only in this way can we oust the firmly entrenched Nazi leadership which would otherwise keep Hitler alive beyond his death. It is true that the Nazi leaders have no firm hold on the nation, not even on the Nazi rank and file, but depend on Hitler. Failing his power and his person, the Hitler myth would suffice to maintain them in their position. If we are to be rid of him, Hitler would have to be three times done to death—as institution, man, legend. The institution, the "Führer," must be abolished, the man removed and the spurious glory of his successes obliterated.

If Hitler be thus thrice exterminated, the Nazi regime will automatically come to an end.

2
The Nazi Leaders

It is with deliberate intention that Hitler and the Nazi Leadership are dealt with in two separate chapters. Nothing is more misleading than to speak of Hitler, as is sometimes done, in the same breath as of the Nazi bigwigs, such as Goebbels, Göring, Ribbentrop, and Himmler, to look upon him as a *primus inter pares.* He is a completely self-sufficient phenomenon; a force working independently of the stratum of leaders put into position and used by him, while they are in no way able to act independently of him. Hitler and the Nazi leadership are two different forces in Germany today, forces of entirely different caliber. It would be naïve to think that Hitler might one day be replaced by one of his lieutenants such, for example, as Göring, so that "Heil Göring" would be said instead of "Heil Hitler." Göring could only rule by making people continue to say "Heil Hitler." The Nazi leadership, including its most prominent representatives, will only be able to rule in the name of Hitler, living or dead. Once Hitler is uprooted, all the Görings and Goebbels will fall like leaves from a dead tree. Not one of them has Hitler's power of identifying Germany with himself. One or the other of them may have a superficial popularity, like Göring. But that is relatively unimportant, just as Hitler's superficial unpopularity is unimportant. A benevolent static monarchy might possibly be founded on mere popularity, but never a dominion such as Hitler's. That needs to penetrate much more deeply into the unconscious, as when the mystic marriage was consummated between the defiant resentment of the scoundrel Hitler and the defiant resentment of the German people.

Hitler, whatever else may be said about him, is undoubtedly an unusual phenomenon. Not one of the approximately 10,000 more or less well-known Nazi notables who form under him the Nazi leadership, whether as personnel of the higher Party organizations, the Gestapo, the Food-growing Front and Labor Front staffs, or the Government of the Reich, is personally anything but an ordinary fortune-hunter and careerist blessed with more or less technical qualifications and more or less personal unscrupulousness. Hitler was the horse that won the race. They were all only the lucky punters who had backed the right horse. Hitler alone discovered the secret of how to climb from nothing to absolute power, and how, regardless of everything, to extend that power at an unexampled pace. The others only had the instinct to hang on to his triumphal chariot at some more or less advanced stage of its journey. They may have made themselves useful in the movement, but it was none of them who *fathered* the movement. That was Hitler's role. And none of them added anything whatever to Hitler's strategic and tactical methods, or altered them in any way. In every sphere they have been and are only executants and imitators—even in oratory and gesture, in which they represent copies, for the most part shockingly bad, of Hitler. And as, in contrast to Hitler, they have had no creative part in establishing Nazism in Germany, but only "leapt on" when the train was moving, likewise, in contrast to Hitler the potential suicide, they are quite ready and on the qui vive to "leap off" again before the train hurtles into the abyss. The prominent among them have, as we know, already made preparations against this event by transferring large sums abroad to neutral countries. The lesser lights, unable to do this, will turn traitor at the eleventh hour and deny they ever had a finger in the pie.

One cannot be sufficiently warned of the extent to which Göring is over-estimated among foreign politicians of the Right, Goebbels by intellectual emigrants, Himmler by a certain circle of second generation Nazis, and Ribbentrop by himself. None of them, without or against Hitler, could continue to weave the Hitlerian spells. None of them has, like Hitler, a single creative (in its bad sense) political contribution to offer; none of them, apart from self-advertisement, has shown more than a furiously exaggerated departmental activity, the highly questionable character of which will presently be laid bare. None of them is more than a finger of Hitler's hand, and of his left hand at that. None of them merits, as a personality, any such interest as Hitler undoubtedly deserves as a phenomenon. None of them, considered for himself alone, is a political force or even potentiality of the least importance.

But what unfortunately is a political force and potentiality is the Nazi leadership as a whole, from the aforementioned unduly famous four persons, the more shadowy figures of Hess, Ley, and Bürckel, and the Nazi provincial and local bosses unknown to the outside world, to the quite anonymous men in the Gestapo offices, a body of about 10,000 persons, who together make up the apparatus that today rules, organizes, and moves Germany. They are just as interesting as a group as they are uninteresting as individuals. They constitute throughout a homogeneous ruling class with persistent qualities. In contrast to the one and only sans pareil Hitler, this stratum represents an impersonal, limitlessly self-generating mass. It could survive the death and replacement of its most prominent members without noticeable alteration in its effectiveness or character; and it could, so long as circumstances allowed, continue to rule in the same manner. It is just because of its relative mediocrity that it is the most stable element in Nazism; at the same time it is the element that gives Nazi rule its unmistakable stamp down to the smallest detail—a thing impossible to the man Hitler. This class finds and shapes its personnel with an instinctive sureness of touch. All play their roles in the same style and have the same personal bearing. It is, in fact, no exaggeration to say that most of them have certain unmistakable facial resemblances. Anyone who has sufficiently observed them can recognize at once the Nazi-leader visage despite all individual differences. This is seen in its truest form (among the best known of them) in Darré, Minister for Agriculture, in Frank, now Governor of Poland, in Ley, and in Kerrl, Minister for Ecclesiastical Affairs. But one only needs to look at a group photograph of the "Reich Governors" to discover this mysterious uniformity.

That such a homogeneous ruling class could be formed in Germany in so short a time and without any perceptible tradition or common schooling is a remarkable phenomenon. We should be grossly overestimating Hitler's capacities if we think he could have created this mass out of nothing in the course of twenty years. He must have found it ready-made. Outwardly almost unnoticed, the raw materials of Nazi leadership must have lain ready to be dug out of the amorphous German masses, the bourgeoisie, but also the commercial classes, head masters, minor pedagogues, the universities, the middle grades of the bureaucracy and the old reserve officer class. Drawn by the magnet of Hitler's personality and certain hollow sentimental sonorous phrases known as the "National Socialist

World-Conception," they suddenly banded together to form an aggressive, shock-troop elite, instinctively united in purpose.

It is not difficult today, after the event, to follow their tracks back into the past and trace the personal factual evidence concerning the present Nazi leaders deeply embedded in Imperial and even pre-Imperial Germany. It is to be found, for example, in the middle-class sections of the former student clubs (*Burschenschaften*), the German Gymnastic Association (*Turnerschaft*), among the school-masters of Wilhelm II's Germany and in other more obscure parts of the social organism. That does not alter the fact that the sudden mushroom growth and ready-made existence of this class is something most astonishing and terrifying. At least for a moment one is tempted to believe the Nazi leaders when they say of themselves that they are the natural ruling class sprung from the soil of Germany, and to deduce from this phenomenon consequences that leave no hope for Germany. For it is indeed a rare experience in the history of a people that a class so unified and uniform, willing and partially equipped to rule, has risen without tradition and upbringing out of the midst of a nation. Nevertheless, it is probably a mistake to give up all hope for Germany because of these observed facts. In the teeth of present appearances I dare to maintain that Germany possesses the capacity to repeat yet another six times at least the miracle of birth of an elite out of apparent nothing, and to show the astonished world each time quite a different face that passes for her true and integral face. Just as the Nazi leaders lay for a long time hidden in obscure parts of the social texture and trained themselves secretly and modestly to rule, similarly today in Germany there lie hidden in many parts potential forces of leadership. When their hour strikes they will be ready to reveal themselves and assume power. In Western Europe people have scarcely any idea of the chaotic fertility of this land called Germany, ready every day to start life afresh, to deny yesterday's ego and put its whole being into a new experiment—for good or evil.

This must be borne in mind when we ascertain the essential characteristics of Nazi leadership and investigate how such a body of men came to power. Nothing that we may say precludes the possibility that fundamentally different groups in Germany might also happen upon just such an opportunity, assuming they find the moment, the man and the slogan.

The essential characteristics of the Nazi leaders are boundless corruption, boundless efficiency, and boundless cynicism. Let us make this perfectly clear.

The corruption of the ruling class is without parallel in measure and extent. Not a crass exception, but an example of a widespread state of affairs is the fact that in six years seven of its prominent men between them have stolen 142 million marks in mobile capital and transferred them abroad in spite of the laws which they themselves enacted, imposing the death penalty for such offenses. Alone, these seven men, who came to office as bankrupt debtors, possess today, apart from these 142 millions of foreign capital, castles, country and town houses, and hunting-boxes in Germany, the value of which is at least equal to their fortunes abroad, as well as an equivalent sum of mobile capital at home. But it is not only these seven prominent leaders who have stolen large fortunes from the State, Party, and other public coffers. The upkeep of all the Reich Governors, *Gauleiters,* high SS and SA leaders, reaches a financial peak only possible on the basis of the freest disposal of public money. Almost all these men come from the petty bourgeoisie and almost all lead the life of magnates.

Frequently enough this embezzlement serves as pretext when one of them has to be removed: in the cases, for example, of the two *Gauleiters* Kube and Koch (the last-named has been pardoned), and of the unfortunate Röhm and his subordinates, corruption was one of the pretexts for their dismissal and execution. But since the style of living and scale of expenditure of all the higher Party officials are exactly the same, it is evident that those whom it is expedient to pick for punishment form no exception.

Moreover, corruption is spread far beyond the financial sphere. For example, Göring's habit of commandeering pictures for his various houses and shooting-boxes from the public museums, while Goebbels claims a monopoly of film actresses as of a harem. Almost all higher Nazi leaders employ SA or SS men as servants and orderlies for their banquets and receptions. For alcoholic exploits Ley, for erotic excesses Streicher, have a special fame, though neither of them in this respect is more than *primus inter pares*. In a word, in the spheres of money and morals every Nazi leader feels himself above the law; everyone feels that up to a certain point the moneys and goods administered by him are his personal property and the men governed by him his personal slaves. Everyone feels he ought to cut as large a slice of the German cake as he can guzzle.

What is interesting about these goings-on is their potential prevalence, by which, paradoxically, they are shielded. The Nazi leaders have instinctively transferred to the field of corruption Hitler's doctrine that only the biggest lies have any chance of being believed—because it seems impossible that anyone can have the courage to tell them—whilst the small shy liar is found out. The Nazi leaders have thus successfully speculated on the incapacity of the German public to recognize corruption on such a scale as corruption—while modest forms of corruption are seen through and accordingly damned. For example, it was formerly held to be highly discreditable to the republican ruling class in Germany that some social democratic magistrates of Berlin, petty bourgeois fathers of families anxious, with their modest means, to present an appearance of respectability—had accepted from a textile firm seeking municipal orders some gifts of wearing apparel and silk shirts. Every middle-class father in Germany would have been tempted to accept such presents, and punished the impulse by severely judging those who had indulged it. That anyone should simply transfer a couple of millions of tax-money to his own banking account would not seem possible to the same man. Faced with such conduct, his legal sense fails him and he can only stand and gape, a gesture in which there is admiration, surprise, and, above all, incredulity. He refuses to believe it, and if it is incontestably proved, his indignation succumbs to his amazement.

Indeed, because of their immensity, the dazed German public no longer calls the peculations of the Nazi leaders by their proper name. These robbers are such great robbers that they have become great lords. Their power and audacity are so enormous that people feel more gratitude to be left with something than fury to be despoiled of such much. This feeling, moreover, is shared by the Nazi leaders themselves. They regard themselves, according to Rauschning's significant expression, as the "new high nobility." The picture that they see of themselves, and that many dazzled Germans accept, is not one of bandits who steal tax-money, but of great financial lords who magnanimously offer a part of their due tithes to the public weal. The Nazi leaders have cleverly sought to make use of ideas and associations that are venerated survivals from the feudal centuries. They have slyly wrapped themselves in the ermine mantle of the former territorial princes: which does not fit. In all the trappings of the new high nobility, they remain monstrously swollen-headed, new-rich bourgeois. But that is only perceived by the classes with more education and better taste, and does not penetrate the mind of the masses. In the long run the corruption is recognized but swallowed, and arouses no real anger. Propaganda that wishes to evoke such wrath would have a long, though perhaps not a hopeless task before it. It would have to set to work with great patience. It would probably achieve more with disclosures of small, comparatively harmless details than with the revelation of the vast scale of plunder. But in any case it would meet with the sentimental objection that is best summed up in the biblical saying: "Ye shall not muzzle the ox that treadeth out the corn." To excuse their corruption the Nazi leaders would vaunt their terrific efficiency, and that, in the eyes of the majority of Germans, would gain them absolution.

For there is no doubt about one thing—in administrative work this leader-gang reveals an efficiency and energy that breaks all records. It is their second basic trait and, at the same time, their trump-card in Germany as well as in certain circles outside Germany. Their Prussian characteristic—though it is quite wrong to look upon Nazi leadership, as is sometimes done, as a continuation or culmination of the Prussian ideal. Their corruption and love of luxury, for example, offer the greatest possible contrast to the rigid honesty and asceticism of the former Prussians. Un-Prussian, too, is their adventurism and fortune-hunting, as well as their unbounded cynicism, about which much remains to be said. But the fury of their technical efficiency is Prussian, as is their inclination to exaggerate and over-estimate it.

In fact, efficiency in many parts of Prussia and throughout Nazi Germany has become an end in itself. This lesser virtue has been allotted a role to which it is in no way suited, that of an absolute value. The result is frightful, far more frightful than that of the moral anarchy and corruption prevalent among the Nazi leaders, but scarcely recognized and understood. On the contrary.

"We must admit they have accomplished something," say the apologists of the Nazis in Germany, and their eyes light up. No one asks what this "something" is. It is considered quite unimportant beside the sublime fact of its accomplishment. "We may have erred and made mistakes," Goebbels is wont to say, with an attempt at a noble quiver in his voice, at least once in every speech, "but of one thing we cannot be accused. We have not hesitated to take hold of things. We have not shied off from difficulties and problems." These words are certain to bring down the house every time. Moreover, it is no lie. It is one of the rare occasions when Goebbels does not lie.

It is true that every political and governmental job is tackled by the Nazi leaders, so to speak, with sleeves rolled up and with a gesture that more or less signifies: "Now we'll show them!" And they do. When a Nazi leader takes charge of German foreign policy—this happened, as we know, in February 1938—it takes our breath away. Not a note of the diplomatic keyboard that is not struck! Ultimatums with a three-hour time limit; military occupation of small neighboring states; every few months the promulgation of epoch-making ideas as the basis of new European and world orders; "steel pacts" that are abandoned three months later; friendship pacts with powers against whom world coalitions were being forged the day before; a wild-goose chase that leaves the onlooker gasping; a bewildering succession of somersaults and a dumbfounding harvest of prompt and spectacular successes, of newly conquered provinces and newly subjected countries. At the same time a rapid depletion of international and diplomatic credit, complete self-outlawry, and, one day, a war against two Great Powers—but what does that matter!

When the Nazis take up rearmament—well, we have seen how they work. "In two months three thousand airplanes will be ready." And ready they are, although at the time they are ordered there are neither factories, raw materials nor money. They make their bow, and on the National Flight Day at the Tempelhof one German says to another: "This Göring certainly does not get his salary for nothing," and forgives him even what he gets beyond his salary. It is true, as the Reich Bank Vice-President, Brinckmann (declared to be insane), recently remarked, that the Germans paid for them ten times as much as other countries and have got inferior goods in return. It is true too, if the Army and Air Force *are* "ready," that the currency is undermined, industry disorganized, the people underfed, the railway system worn out, and the export trade ruined—but what does all that matter! All that is the concern of other departments, and they can see to it that similar results are obtained there with similar efficiency. The Army and Air Force are ready, and that in world-record time. Efficiency! Pluck! Achievement!

Nazi efficiency is efficiency with blinkers on. What the Nazis intend at the moment is carried out on a "gigantic," "colossal," hitherto unheard-of scale, and each time on completion it is observed to be hydrocephalous. But it imposes on the Germans. Having discovered that propaganda is a part of politics, the Nazis have organized the most powerful propaganda machine in the world: every German abroad an envoy (and spy) of his country, every newspaper an organ of the Ministry of Propaganda, films, literature, music, art, science—all branches of National Socialist propaganda. And though the result may be that every German abroad is shunned and hated, no German newspaper read, no German film imported, that literature, art, and music in Germany have gone to the dogs—yet the "most gigantic propaganda machine in the world is ours!" And the staunchest German emigrant cannot quite suppress his admiration for the "smart little fellow," for the immensely efficient Minister of Propaganda who has brought it about.

Police. Defense of the State. With us they are more efficient than with any other nation, past or present. Lock up the enemies of the State? Not nearly effective enough. Here they will be tortured, a much better deterrent, anyhow. And not only enemies of the State! No, we lock up and torture anyone who is not an enthusiastic first-class citizen. In that way the attraction of becoming one is greatly increased. And—master-stroke of energy and efficiency—how does the first-class citizen prove he is one but by informing against everyone who is not and delivering him over to torture! Every German a police spy! No, if the Reich does not last a thousand years it won't be for lack of efficiency. Is culture going to the devil? That is the affair of the Board of Education. Is the joy of life languishing in Germany? The "Strength through Joy" organization will see to it that Germany is screaming with the joy of life! And it does see to it with devastating efficiency.

That is Nazi efficiency. It is the efficiency of the old German Latin coach, cramming the prize-winning scholar, with spectacles and dwindling muscles, who mutters irregular verbs in his sleep; the efficiency of the old German gymnastic instructor who reared gymnasts with record biceps and birdlike foreheads. It is the efficiency of Schlieffen, Tirpitz, and Ludendorff who let Germany begin and lose the World War by drawing up a unique plan of campaign, building a gigantic fleet, waging "unrestricted" U-boat warfare, and organizing the most powerful offensive in the History of the World. It is the efficiency of a man who runs amok to beat the world record. It is, in a word, the most menacing form of stupidity known to man.

But this is not in the least admitted by the majority of Germans in their present state of mind and education. They do not know, for example, that they lost the World War through excess of efficiency and lack of wisdom. On the contrary, they still believe that just a trifle more efficiency would have reversed the result. Since the foundation of the German Reich they discovered that they have a greater share of efficiency—which is, within limits, a virtue, but a minor one, not unlike the similarly relative and two-edged virtue of thoroughness—than other nations. And their history since consists of a dreary attempt to prove to themselves and to the world that this efficiency is the highest good and confers the right and capacity for world domination. Let us hope they will one day realize they are wrong; perhaps after this war. At present they do not. They have completely forgotten what their philosophers once knew, that every action produces together with its one intended effect, some thousands of other far-reaching unintended effects, and that hence it is, in nine cases out of ten, cleverer and better to remain inactive and not "act with vigor." The fact does not intrigue them that large realms such as the former Habsburg monarchy, the present British Empire, and the democracies in general were and are ruled, and most successfully ruled, with a great deal of patience, toleration, discussion, consideration, deliberate non-interference, waiting, slowness, and circumspection; in short, with everything that the Nazis call a "jog-trot pace." The fact does not make them ponder. It only gives rise to contempt and boasts of superiority. Nor does the fact worry them that with all their efficiency they are no better off. At the most, it gives rise to resentment against the false and treacherous world that does not willingly hand them the proper reward for their efficiency. All the more reason to intensify this same efficiency. Efficiency has become, in the eyes of most Germans today, so completely a value and end in itself that there remains no higher standard by which to measure it. Not even tangible profit. When, in 1923, all Germans were reduced to abject poverty by the inflation of the mark, while the handful of men who brought it about and profited by it acquired fantastic fortunes, many Germans were quite seriously proud of the fact that they at last had in their midst some of the richest people in the world. On the other hand, the great successes of Stresemann and his associates in social, economic, and foreign policy, though affecting every private purse, gave no real satisfaction to most Germans because their efficiency was not sufficiently spectacular. "A slack lot" was the verdict passed on these republican statesmen whose patience ensured success in their dealings with foreign creditors. They did not even hit back when abused at home for their success. Göring and Himmler are quite different specimens! Alas, it cannot be denied that the contemporary German has come by rather less wisdom to set against his greater efficiency than most other people.

Thus it is their furious and determined efficiency, their mania for rushing about, their "dynamic," their "activism" (to use the current terms of Nazi jargon) that gives the Nazi leaders their credit with the German nation. It gives them something even more important: steadiness, self-assurance, a good conscience. Just as their corruption has to protect itself by its immeasurable extent, so too their efficiency finds its basis and motive in its raging activity. It lacks any real significance. It serves nothing. Nor are those efficient Nazi leaders quite ignorant of this fact. Their completely cynical nihilism is the third distinguishing trait of these men, the trait that gives them their typical visage, so terrifyingly repulsive.

Belloc ranks the godless among the "seven bad smells." The Nazi leaders are in the deepest and most comprehensive sense godless; hence their bad odor. These corpulent, fleshy, flabby men with clumsy gait, unwrinkled fat faces, cold fishlike eyes, and brutal shapeless mouths are a fearful living picture stalking about as a warning. That is how men look to whom nothing is sacred. That is what they come to.

It is platitudinous to remark that the Nazi leaders have no religion, no morals, no humanity, and no traditional restraints. They themselves openly boast of this, and it would be waste of time to reproach them with it. Perhaps they are not equally aware that they are completely blank and empty from the aesthetic point of view, that they are devoid of those aesthetic norms that often replace religion, such as honor, conduct, grace, taste. But everyone knows it who has seen their rowdy manners, their disgusting way of playing about with riding-whips (without ever having been astride a horse), their delight in insulting the defenseless, their sneaking personal cowardice at moments of crisis or danger, their mutual treacheries, their characterlessness, and their lack of humor. It is enough to watch a film of a Conference of Reich Leaders at the Party Congress or to listen to the radio during a speech by Hitler at the Reichstag in order to hear the bestial mooing, neighing, barking, and meowing of the assembled upper eight hundred during the duly provided pauses.

But there is little profit in talking of this. These men are innocent of religion, morals, and aesthetics. They lack even a social norm; "humanity" in their vocabulary is known as "the human whirligig." As they are absolute parvenus they have no tradition to which to turn, no ancestors of whom to prove worthy. But what is as strange and alarming as it is monstrous is that there is nothing, absolutely nothing, that they recognize as a law above them, that they can serve with their relentless efficiency. Apart from all the sacred values of Europe, which they deny, and by which all the leaders of civilized Western countries tacitly feel bound—God, honor, truth, faith, humanity, tradition—the statesmen of other countries serve king, constitution or country. The statesmen of the Soviet Union, with whom all these institutions likewise have an extremely dubious value, at least serve their Marxist substitute for religion and the cause of the Bolshevik World Revolution. The Nazi leaders have nothing; no constitution, no principle, no ideal. They do not even serve their country.

Germany has, we know, no crowned monarch. It does not possess that radiant center of all the forces encircling the principles of "highness," hierarchy, nobility, and the dignity of service. But it also possesses no constitution, nothing comparable to the "liberty, equality, fraternity," of the French. Perhaps the champions of the Nazis will here interpose: "What about the National Socialist world-conception?" To which we must answer that, save for the title, it does not exist. Behind the ostentatious name there is nothing; or, at most, the doctrine that it is permitted and even commanded to rob, torment, and kill Jews. Somewhat scanty contents for a world-conception!

There is contradiction and confusion galore with regard to the next generalization: the search for a "racial" interpretation of history and the theory of the supremacy of the "German master race." The "Nordic" race, according to this, is called upon to rule all other races: the right of domination must only be conferred upon the Slav-Roman-Germanic hybrids who inhabit the German Reich, but not upon the equally Nordic Scandinavians and English. Germans are a nation of masters, but they must be strictly forbidden to exercise thought, personal choice, and individual freedom: if they are not Nazis, they must be beaten in concentration camps, but if Nazis they must prove it by unlimited and slavish obedience. That is called the Leader principle. Thus, though they are a nation of masters, the Germans are a nation of slaves, and, though the Nordic race is destined to rule the world, their members must be deprived of their domains. In fact, this world-conception is rubbish if not an impudent fraud. Moreover, none of the Nazi leaders takes it seriously. The National Socialists are a reality, but their world-conception is not.

There remains a last thing the Nazi leadership could serve and believe in: Germany. Are the Nazis patriots? They claim they are. Loyal Germans believe them, though full of doubts and increasingly shaken in their faith. Some well-meaning foreigners also believe them. They are all wrong.

It is doubtless true that Nazi leadership has extended Germany's frontiers, increased its military strength and striking power, and raised its prestige abroad. There is on display a spectacular, shop-window socialism—unemployment has given place to scarcity of labor: there is a gigantic organization for compulsory entertainments and a "Winter Relief" association that makes more noise than all the public assistance organizations in the world put together. The strange thing is that in spite of all this, want in Germany has increased and not decreased, and that the greater, more powerful and superior-armed Germany is today poor, decaying, and disrupted as never before. "By their fruits ye shall know them." It is no accident and no unaccountable fate that the successful and efficient work that the Nazi leaders have done "for Germany" has in point of fact only harmed the country and made it more unhappy.

There is a reason for that. It is this. The Nazi leaders have not worked at all for Germany. They do not love Germany. They are entirely indifferent to her, and never take the trouble to know and question her. To destroy her would mean nothing to them.

The Nazi leaders love Germany in the way an inconsiderate race-horse owner "loves" his horse; he wants it to win the race, nothing more. To this end it has been trained and ridden as hard and as inconsiderately as possible. Whether the horse shares his desire for glory and wants to be a racehorse; whether it comes to grief or is henceforth lamed for life, are questions that do not concern him. The comparison is not apposite in so far as one can say of horses that they are there to race. But certainly nations and the men composing them are not there to be collective athletic teams, the fate that the Nazis have imposed on the German people. The Nazi leaders aim at converting Germany into a gigantic sports club which is always winning "victories"—and thereby losing its happiness, character, and national identity.

Nothing can be more inconsiderate than the way in which these men destroy everything German that opposes the fulfillment of their ideal, and nothing more full of hate and contempt than the manner in which they speak of those inborn German qualities that make Germany unsuited to a racehorse existence. The word "German" they use with such freedom and bombastic pathos, when it serves to adorn their rhetoric, assumes a note of loathing and objurgation in their mouths when they use it in its more precise sense, indicating certain attributes. They seem thus to wage war on "German objectivity," "German kindliness," "German overestimation of foreigners," or on particular types such as the "unworldly German professor," the "German Philistine," and the "German dreamer."

The Nazi leaders, from the outset, have ruled over Germany not as their Fatherland, feeling the beat of its pulse, and understanding its weaknesses, yearning to save the country they love. They have treated Germany like a conquered land, a colony to be used and abused without consideration, to be exploited to the full, and its national spirit, happiness, and well-being to be sedulously ignored. The image that Rilke applied to the Bolsheviks and Russia exactly fits the Nazis and Germany: they have made a penwiper out of cambric. Indeed the cambric cloth functions admirably as a penwiper.

It does not long survive such usage. And no one will say that he who has made an efficient penwiper out of it has thus proved himself to be a lover and connoisseur of cambric.

Never before has a ruling class mauled the body of a country, its landscape and its towns, with such an entire lack of feeling as the Nazi lords in cutting down German forests, setting up their fortresses and motor roads and "transforming" German towns. (It would take a whole chapter to describe these impudent constructions with which they have ruined the appearance of the noblest German towns; childish box-of-bricks erections of giant size. Their monumental vapidity matches the monumental hollowness of Hitler's speeches and the National-Socialist World-Conception. Commemorations in stone of over-compensated inferiority complexes.) Never has a ruling class so inconsiderately bossed its fellow-countrymen, so cynically ignored their wishes, their needs, their happiness. Never have rulers so flauntingly treated the ruled as mere ciphers and supers, while insisting that they expend themselves wholly in such an existence. Never have rulers been so completely indifferent to the essential character, what one might call the "spirit of the people" of Germany, their religious, spiritual, and poetic traditions, to that which used to be called "education" and is now less clearly described as "culture." (The unconscious ignorance of this class is incredible; are they not able to sit in their box quite unmoved through *Egmont, William Tell,* or *Fidelio* without, in their innocence, feeling the least concerned?) Never, in a word, has a ruling class felt so little love for their country.

They enlarge the borders of Germany but first they destroy her. What they really enlarge is not Germany but their domain, now become anonymous. We need hardly say they have "brought" nothing to the countries they have conquered and enslaved, to Austria, Czechoslovakia, and Poland. We know that where they trod nothing will grow. But it is not sufficiently clear that the first country where they have trod is Germany. Not even Germany is sufficiently aware of this. But it is probably not too much to say that there, for some time past, this knowledge has been dawning.

For this ruling class appears strange to the Germans in spite of its impressive efficiency and its glaring, placarded successes. There is a saying current even among loyal adherents of the Nazis: "We can stand Hitler but it is the little Hitlers. . . ." And this unspoken repudiation, concealed only by fear, has recently grown more vehement. While Hitler's personal prestige has soared to regions where ordinary critics can no longer aspire to reach, criticism today tends to concentrate on that which is still accessible: "the regime," "the little Hitlers," "the little gods," or whatever they are called. Naturally, this criticism is not fully rational. Every possibility is lacking to reason it out into clarity by discussion. There is a vague feeling that one does not like being governed by these people; that "it won't do" and "it can't do." Somehow people feel that something originally justifiable and popular has developed into a cancer; that the wild chase no longer has goal or end; that from success to success and from triumph to triumph things go from bad to worse. They sense without being able to name the strange nothingness behind the more and more violent "Forward." It is just this nihilism of the Nazi leaders that makes them increasingly suspect to the German people, who are themselves unable to say why. It is the emptiness behind the dynamic. People see the patriotic pretexts wearing thin. Before, for instance, they were inclined to look on the abandonment of the Southern Tyrol as a subtle move in the game of high politics, and not take offense. But now the Balts as well! And tomorrow perhaps the Saxons of Transylvania and the Swabians of the Banat? At first they put up with over-organization and compulsion. It seemed necessary to tackle unemployment and other economic problems. But now—after seven years of "ascent"—compulsion, and over-organization as never before! Forcible conversion of the small artisans and shopkeepers into workmen—just when the "dissolution of the large industries" has been promised! Transplantation of the rural population—just when "Blood and Soil" has been pronounced sacred! Encouragement of an exodus from the country to the towns just when the Germans were to be "bound to the soil" again!

All this bores into the consciousness of the German masses without, until now, being put into words, completely understood and pondered. And, moreover, were it fully realized it would not immediately provoke reaction. The pressure of established power is still far too strong. But, nevertheless, here is a weak spot in the Nazi regime, one of the spots where surprises are possible, if for one instant the pressure from above be relaxed. Hence it is one of those spots where intelligent propaganda should steadily and relentlessly seek to pierce. The ground is not unprepared for a recognition of the fact that the Nazis are *no* patriots, that they do *not* work for Germany, that they are active nihilists and are consciously leading Germany into the abyss of nothingness. However, to cultivate it, the statesmen outside Germany must themselves have perceived the fact. I am not quite sure they have everywhere done so.

Heiden tells us that Göring in the Kaiserhof on January 30, 1933, uttered this weighty observation: "Our predecessors lasted fourteen years. Now we shall see whether we can hold out as long." It is a saying that illuminates like a flash of lightning the mentality of the whole Nazi ruling clique and their attitude to their job. He that hath ears to hear, let him hear. This keyhole reveals the whole truth. This careless little remark is the original bacillus of all the gay irresponsibility, the unscrupulous exploitation of power conscious of its ephemerality, the unrestrained striving for momentary success at the expense of the future; of the belief in force, the belief in efficiency, the corrupt resolve to make hay while the sun shines and, at the same time—the only vestige of foresight—to strengthen their position against a rainy day; the complete lack of bonds, the almost naïve cynicism of men who plunge into history without thinking even fourteen years ahead. This saying is the secret motto of the Nazi regime.

For one who thinks in longer stretches of time, there might be comfort in the fact that all the characteristics of this regime point clearly to a short life. And one should not feel discouraged by the fact that the breakdown, predicted after the first year, has held off seven years, and has at one time or another been wrongly foretold during this period. The features that promise an early end have grown more marked, not less; even its many lucky accidents and successes have not made the regime more secure.

But there is another matter that must alarm even the most composed and unperturbed observer. For reasons outside our theme, the pace of world history seems temporarily to have quickened in a menacing way, so that seven years in the twentieth century have far more significance than formerly was allotted to their span. Seven years are but a second's interval in the history of the world, but there have been periods when they have sufficed to lay the foundations of an ineradicable tradition. Let us recall those seven years in France, from the First Republic to the Consulate! Likewise, for the

Nazis seven years of rule have sufficed to create something like a tradition. There is already in Germany something that can be called a Nazi second generation; a youth that has grown up entirely in the shadow of Nazi domination and is already successfully isolated from all traditional and cultural values. This youth is, perhaps, more dangerous than the present ruling elite, who, in spite of everything, cannot somehow be taken quite seriously. It is the shadow over the future of Europe.

Let us look at it—and in its proper context; in its relation to the class that actively supports and maintains the present regime in Germany. Let us scrutinize the Nazis. And let us, from the outset, make it quite clear that they are more important and more dangerous than their contemptible leaders.

3

The Nazis

To every system of government, good or bad, belongs a particular type whom it fits like a glove, who flourishes and rejoices under it. Its strength and probable duration can be judged by the extent to which those who are *not* of this type can live and be content under it; while its worth can be measured by the worth of the type favored by it and its works.

So long as everything proceeds in a natural and healthy manner, the type favored by the regime constitutes its support and defense. But it may happen that, under the pathological influence of an abdication-psychosis, such a type will itself abandon and destroy "its" rule—as the German republicans did with their republic. On the other hand, tactical considerations, lack of counsel, fear of worse times ahead, or sheer irresistible pressure may make people defenders of a regime which, at the bottom of their hearts, they long to send to the devil. This happens very often today in the Third Reich. Moreover, when we remember that the system of menace and espionage in Germany frequently compels even opponents of the regime to assume—in the form of membership of some Nazi organization—protective coloring, we get an extremely blurred and unidentifiable picture. The actual political camps, though more fiercely opposed than ever, are camouflaged. Outwardly, almost complete unity reigns. On prescribed days the swastika waves from the window of almost every dwelling. Almost every adult German with an occupation belongs to at least one of the compulsory or semi-compulsory organizations provided for him. Almost every German obeys the order to turn out, if what Goebbels has christened a "spontaneous demonstration" has been arranged. The "elections" that are held from time to time almost always produce a 100 per cent vote for the Government. The people who are beaten in concentration camps and those who beat them, all, without distinction, attend the same "spontaneous demonstrations," hang the same flag out of their window, read the same newspaper, and hang the same portrait of Hitler on their wall. A foreign interviewer is received by both with the same "Heil Hitler," and they declare with the same assurance that they are ardent followers of their Führer. So it is not easy to pierce political realities in Germany today.

However, it is no longer necessary to give many proofs to show that the vaunted "oneness" and "national unity" in Germany are mere sham, stage management, and lies; though it is not long ago that they duped shrewd foreign politicians, to say nothing of innocent tourists. But realization of the deceptive and bluffing exterior does not provide knowledge of what is concealed beneath. It would be rash to assume, as is sometimes done, that there is nothing to be found but discontent, secret opposition, and repressed decency. These can be found, but certainly not to the exclusion of all else.

In broad lines, then, such is the picture of public opinion in Germany, seen from within. An immense cleavage splits the whole nation into two irreconcilable camps; partisans and opponents of the Regime. It is impossible to overestimate this clear-cut and radical cleavage. Compared with it, political antagonism of the kind existing between left wing and right wing in other countries, or in pre-Nazi Germany is, even during the most agitated and strained times, a harmless and mild differnce of opinion between good friends. The adherents and the adversaries of the regime are more foreign to one another than different races or different species of animals. They speak different languages. Black to one is white to the other. Understanding or discussion is impossible between them. If they accidentally encounter one another, death threatens—chiefly, of course, for the opponent of the regime who must expect, without further warning, to be denounced, arrested, and tortured to death. But the opponents of the Nazis are for the most part no less convinced that Nazis cannot be parleyed with, but must be killed. This gulf runs through classes, regions, callings, levels of culture and confessional groups. It also cuts across ages, though it is true that the Nazis are chiefly enrolled from the younger, their opponents from the older generation. However, it can in no way be said to be simply a struggle between the two generations. Partisans and opponents live almost in different worlds. They avoid and ignore one another whenever they can. Almost all clubs and societies dating from before 1933 have been dissolved because their members, belonging to the two camps, could no longer put up with one another. Millions of former friendships have ended leaving their trace only in complete estrangement. In large commercial concerns, the Nazis and "the others" form separate cliques, who confine mutual intercourse to an irreducible minimum. In private life, the Nazis and their opponents associate only with their like; which often leads both to the assumption that only the like-minded exist. If, by chance, an intruder from the other world turns up at a party, it is instantly doomed and the host can scarcely reckon on any of his guests ever again accepting an invitation from him. For both sides look upon it as an insult and a serious lack of tact if they are brought into contact with their deadly enemies on a basis that calls for forbearance and politeness.

It is very difficult to assess the numerical proportion of the one camp to the other. Naturally, any objective clue is lacking, such as is provided in other countries by elections or party memberships. The only remaining method is that of making as many individual observations as possible and generalizing on their basis. The figures we thus glean differ in different regions, as well as vary from time to time. The last approximately correct election figures in Germany (March 5, 1933) still showed a proportion of 56–44 against the Nazis. But there is scarcely any doubt that in the course of the year 1933 the Nazis won over the majority of public opinion. In 1934, this majority sank low. The late summer of 1934—when the events of June 30 and July 25 horrified the conservative bourgeois friends of the Nazis and aroused confusion and panic among the Nazis themselves; when Barthou's clear and purposeful policy in France presented the Germans with the alternative of a fall of the Government or war—is the only time during which one can safely say that the Nazis had a compact majority of the nation against them.

Since then their moral prestige has continually fallen but their power prestige steadily risen. In the years 1935 to 1937 they may have had a narrow majority behind them. The year 1938 brought another low level. The Jew-baitings were for the most part unpopular and the war policy against Czechoslovakia, against whom very few Germans felt inimical sentiments, caused the numbers of Nazi supporters to fall rapidly; in September it sank from week to week, and finally from day to day. Possibilities of revolution dawned on the horizon. Then came Munich. Whatever else Munich may have been, for internal policy it was the greatest triumph that the Nazis have ever achieved, and internal opposition from that day to this has not recovered from that brutal blow. The whole mass of wavering and non-political people became once more loyal and devoted to the Führer. His foes despaired. Their hopelessness and paralysis has never left them since, not even at the outbreak of the present war, which, after all, began with a far more popular slogan than the 1938 crisis—Poland, quite unlike Czechoslovakia, is almost universally hated in Germany—and was followed by an initial triumph. All the same the number is still large of those who despair rather than make peace with the regime. Today, with due reservations, a fair estimate of the ratio of the two sides would be 60–40.

But not much has so far been gained by this crude distinction between partisans and opponents of the regime. In this demarcation the active political forces on both sides are reckoned together with those whose political attitude is only expressed in a more or less loyal or disloyal personal sentiment toward the Nazis. If we distinguish between the "active" and "inactive" on both sides, we see at once the great superiority of the Nazis over their opponents. There exist among the latter only feeble layers—or should we rather say a sediment—of organized political purpose. And this Opposition, if we may apply this term to such organized political purpose, is again split up into many groups: firstly, the Opposition at home and the Opposition abroad—the political emigrants—between which there are only few and weak ties; next, the different political alignments, the communists, social democrats, liberals, conservatives, and Catholics. New unifying ideas have not yet had time to clarify; nothing is fully debated, no new fronts are formed; 90 percent or more of the opponents of the regime do not form an "Opposition," but only the "disloyal population," unorganized, lonely souls, each of whom fights out his personal duel with the "Third Reich" in brave hopelessness and isolation. The most valuable human material in Germany is amongst them. At the moment, however, they form no active political factor.

The position of the adherents of the regime is very different. Among them, too, there is, as is only natural, a high percentage who are only the "loyal population," and perhaps not quite trustworthy, as the internal political landslides of 1934 and 1938 showed. But there exists a solid kernal of real Nazis, the type that flourishes under the regime and hence is ready to answer for it with body and soul. They are highly organized, determined, armed, unscrupulous, and morally inaccessible. They form a numerically strong and politically even stronger bodyguard of the regime. They could perhaps even maintain the regime by intensifying "frightfulness" if the whole "loyal population" became disloyal. They constitute the German peril.

They are the type of men who, already under William II, had come to the fore, brought about the World War and increasingly controlled Germany throughout its duration. They instinctively called Hitler "their man" and carried him to power. And they, and they only, will be ready after the Lost War to construct and maintain out of perversity a Soviet Germany. They are the un-European and anti-European element in Germany. They are the reason why Europe must in despair face the prospect of fighting a war to the death every twenty-five years against Germany. It is against these men that the war "against Hitlerism" must be waged if it is to succeed and bring peace, a lasting peace. Only their elimination can secure peace, freedom, and civilization in Germany and Europe. It is the chief aim of the war. Their disappearance will enable us to do without Federal Union. If they survive as a force, no organization, however well devised, will preserve Europe from new tragedies.

It is this type we mean in this book when we speak of "Nazis"— not all loyal Germans, among whom there are many deceived or misled people, personally decent; nor all those who wear the Party badge, amongst whom are many who wear it by accident or through compulsion. As to where one looks for and how one recognizes the real Nazis, we shall learn in due course. First, let us terminate this quasi-statistical demarcation of the German nation.

All experimental computations lead unanimously to the conclusion that the number of Nazis in Germany may be estimated at some 20 percent of the whole population. Some 40 percent are loyal to them, 35 percent disloyal (the figures are liable to vary, as we have seen; there have been times when the disloyal were in the majority), and, at the most, five percent constitute the Opposition. We have to consider the émigrés separately, who, like the Nazi leaders, are not of much numerical weight, but contain the nucleus of a general staff of intellectuals; among them, moreover, is the only place "in" Germany where new ideas can be conceived and debated.

Such a division, it seems to me, is the only one appropriate to the present situation. If one attempted to divide Germany according to political tendencies one would have to place giants and dwarfs on the same stage, and 75 percent of the population, who at the moment have no political convictions, would have to be overlooked. There prevails much chaos in Germany, and it would be pointless to ignore it. The mental and political chaos in the brains of the vast majority of Germans is in itself an important element in shaping present and future policy. Paradoxical though it may seem, it is waiting to be understood. We must, therefore, familiarize ourselves with the ideas of the loyal and disloyal Germans, without trying to credit them with a sense of political order and logic that is not there. But next the Nazis.

Who is a Nazi? How can he be recognized?

Certainly not by his hanging a swastika flag out of his window; everyone does that in Germany today. It means nothing. Nor by his being a member of some Nazi organization or of the Party itself. Everyone who has a family to care for and cannot afford to lose his job is in one or another Nazi organization, and if he has the bad luck to pursue a calling in which membership of the Party is demanded, he joins the Party. For a time even members of certain opposition groups deliberately entered the Party and Party associations in the naïve hope of being able to form "explosive" cells and cause confusion within them. The real Nazis, therefore, are not to be easily identified.

There exist, however, a number of signs by which a man may know, until he has proof of the contrary, that he is dealing with a

Nazi. Roughly speaking, the Nazis are found among the older SA or Storm Troop formations (with striped sleeves), the lower Party functionaries, "leaders" of the Hitler Youth, and, above all, the SS or Black Guards. In addition, there are many Nazis among the ordinary Party members and Hitler Youth. But the Party badge, as we have seen, is no sure proof—even if acquired before 1933. On the other hand, there are Nazis outside the Party and its annexes, among the apparent opposition, especially among the Black Front, a schismatic Nazi sect bitterly persecuted by the orthodox, the younger officers of the Army and Navy, and particularly of the Air Force, which is hardly less Nazi than the Party itself.

But if it is not easy to recognize the Nazis from external signs and badges there are some shibboleths, some touchstones, from which it is possible in every single case to establish whether a particular individual is a Nazi. Of these the most important and the most simple is the attitude to the policy pursued toward the Jews in Germany. Many people who are loyal adherents of the regime disapprove of the anti–Semitic excesses, others seek to ignore, to minimize or, in border cases, to excuse them. All such are not Nazis. A Nazi is one who assents unreservedly to this general and permanent sadistic orgy, and takes part in it. The chief aim of anti–Semitism is to serve, firstly, as a kind of secret sign and binding mystery among Nazis, like a continuous ritual murder; and, secondly, as the conscience-killing course in the education of the second generation of Nazis.

This purpose has long ousted the original motive, the venting of Hitler's private resentment, and has given anti–Semitism its present form. Likewise, the demagogic uses of anti–Semitism frequently exploited in earlier days, such as the maltreatment of a defenseless minority as a scapegoat, and as a safety-valve for anticapitalist sentiments, have long been abandoned. For years now the Nazis no longer take the trouble to think out pretexts for robbing, torturing, and murdering the Jews. And with calculation. The people who need such pretexts are those expected to stand aside and quail. Those who, without pretext, can torture and beat, hunt and murder, are expected to gather together and be bound by the iron chain of common crime, bound together in that Nazi Order, which, naturally selected from the most unscrupulous and the "most dynamic," is to subjugate the world.

To the Nazis this, and this alone, is the significance, all-important and fundamental, of anti–Semitism, and not the "purity of the German race," the "suppression of all un-German influence," the "defensive war against the Jewish world conspiracy" or any such nonsense. Anti–Semitism serves as a means of selection and trial, just as certain tests of courage, secrecy, and obedience used to be, and still are, imposed before initiation into the old knightly orders and the modern secret societies. Very significantly, however, the test by which one proves oneself to be a Nazi is a test not of courage but of lack of scruple. The novitiate must be able and disposed to persecute, rob, and murder the defenseless. That the object of all this training and testing in victimization happens to be the Jews is not in itself important: they happen to be a small, sufficiently rootless and able community, ready, so to speak, at hand; some other groups would have served just as well, but there had to be one and it happened to be the Jews.

To look for further reasons for anti–Semitism is rather pointless, although the loyal German bourgeois and some obliging foreigners have done the Nazis the kindness of raking up and examining by searchlight everything that could be said against the Jews. They have overlooked the essential point. The Jews obviously have faults like every other nation; but to say that because of these faults they ought to be persecuted by the Nazis is immediately to accord the Nazis the right to persecute all men and all nations, for no man and no nation is without blemish. That the Nazis should slander the Jews whom they murder is only natural, for it has always been one of the common defenses of the murderer to represent the victim in an unsympathetic light. What is serious is that so many people in Germany and elsewhere have been ready to lend an ear to the Nazis, and thus, in fact, to sanction murder. Moreover, the treatment by the Nazis of their non-Nazi fellow countrymen—of the Austrians, Czechs, and Poles—shows that they know how to apply what they learn in ill-treating the Jews to other peoples. And this is their object in learning. But the Jews remain the permanently destined victim, on whom they are to study and practice their unscrupulousness. Anti–Semitism consequently remains the great badge of the Nazis. When all those Nazis who have taken part in Jew-baiting, or have assented to it, have been removed, we shall be confronted with the startling fact that not only the Jews, but the Poles,

Czechs, Austrians, and oppressed Germans, the whole world breathes freely again; that the German menace will be dead and Germany of her own accord return to the bosom of European civilization. It is, in a sense, all to the good that the inhuman and the sub-human, which in most nations are dispersed in the blood-stream and only become occasionally perceptible in individual criminals, have in Germany found a slogan causing them to suppurate palpably in one spot and form a gigantic abscess. When the abscess has been lanced the blood will be immensely purified, and very possibly Germany will be a better country than it was before the era of the Nazis.

We have now reached the crux of the present German problem, and I must be pardoned for entering into elaborate detail. This point must be grasped because otherwise nothing can be understood. And all partial acquaintance with the facts is worthless and misleading unless it is thoroughly digested and absorbed. It is this: *Nazism is no ideology but a magic formula which attracts a definite type of men. It is a form of "characterology," not ideology. To be a Nazi means to be a definite type of human being.*

Thus, the Nazis fundamentally differ from other political parties, with which outwardly they stand on the same plane. It is true, one can jokingly depict the conservative, the liberal, the socialist as types with a predestined point of view: so one speaks of the old conservative gentleman with mustache and pipe, and the liberal university man with spectacles. But this is playful and superficial, and no one will seriously deny that one and the same man, on more comprehensive reflection, may change over from conservatism to liberalism or socialism or vice versa without in the least altering his character; and that amongst the adherents of all these political doctrines, one may find men of the most diverse nature, the circumspect and the enterprising, the sensitive and the thick-skinned, the man of honor and the intriguer, the adventurer and the respectable paterfamilias. Not so the Nazis. Nazis are a kind apart—we shall presently examine them more closely—and what is called the "National–Socialist World-Conception" has no other aim than to collect and rear this species. This explains, by the way, the fantastically low mental level of their "World-Conception," which is not to be compared with other political doctrines, and is not worth combating or discussing. Its political tenets and program are disconnected and undigested phrases, culled from third-class popular literature. But that does not prevent this "World-Conception," which is not one, from being very effective as a means of linking together a certain type of men, and as an appeal to certain instincts. We are exposed to two deceptions: firstly, because of the resounding self-advertisement of the Nazis, into thinking that such a thing as Nazi "ideology," "doctrine," or "world-conception" exists; secondly, because of the non-existence of such a doctrine, into thinking that nothing at all exists. The liquid in a bottle bearing the inscription "Best brand of wine" is not necessarily a drink. It may be a very potent rat-poison.

No one has been more outspoken about this central feature of Nazism than Hitler himself, and we may well make his utterances our starting-point, although they, as is usual, contain a veiled but clumsy lie. But this lie is easily detected.

In a triumphal speech at the "Party Victory Congress" in 1933, this is in effect what Hitler said: He, Hitler, was ready now, after the victory, to disclose its secret. It was that he had pondered over the foundations of political success; his opponents had neglected to do so. The secret lies in proclaiming a "World-Conception" and issuing a slogan that automatically lures and gathers together all the most dynamic, active, self-sacrificing, heroic, and forceful natures. To this body of the strong and energetic success cannot be long denied, because the strong always overcome the weak. Marxism or Liberalism can only attract the cowards and the weaklings, and are, therefore, vanquished by a doctrine that collects Titans round it. He, Hitler, had certainly done this. He had never promised his adherents anything but had exacted from them constant sacrifice, constant risk, and constant heroism. Thus he had collected followers with an unexampled capacity for sacrifice, risk, and heroism. Those who did not possess these qualities had stayed away. The result had been an invincible troop; "and this troop will never again be undermined and broken up. . . ." Here the speech shrills into an operatic climax that is not reducible to rational terms.

But what preceded is interesting enough, and it is a great pity that it has not been more carefully considered. It contains the perfectly true confession that the National–Socialist World-Conception was founded on the plan of enlisting a certain type of men to form an "invincible troop" capable of conquest and domination.

That applied, in the first place, to internal political warfare, but it is no longer necessary to explain that those ambitions extend far beyond Germany. In fact, the Nazi song must be literally interpreted:

> *Today all Germany is ours;*
> *Tomorrow the whole world.*

Now comes the lie. This is when Hitler maintains that the essential traits required in his followers are heroism and self-sacrifice; that these are the qualities that led the Nazis to victory. The problem is more complicated. It is well known that the Nazis did not attain power through brave deeds but through court intrigues; and that the "heroic" SA and SS men were let loose on their opponents not a moment before the latter were completely disarmed, disorganized, and helpless. Hitler has never asked anything else of them. His explanations, after 1923, always took the line that he would come to power "in a strictly legal manner," and that only then would "heads roll," etc. So it is not to heroism that Hitler appeals, though the word is constantly on his lips, but rather to sadism, to the pleasure—to use some of Hitler's favorite expressions laden with morbid appeal—in "brutal," "fanatical," "merciless" oppression and persecution of those who have already been over-powered and rendered defenseless by "strictly legal" means. The "struggle" that Hitler demanded his adherents to wage was a strictly legal but also a strictly unsportsmanlike struggle against a mild, diffident, and patient Government; a struggle without risk, in which Nazi assassins could safely count on mercy. It was only in the exploitation of victory—here he left no doubts from the outset—that he demanded of them an entire lack of restraint. It is obvious that the appeal was not exactly addressed to heroic and self-sacrificing natures.

To whom then? What kind of man was it who felt himself instinctively lured by Hitler, by his promises, his threats, his furious rage against all and sundry, his demand for unconditional obedience, and his invitations to unheard-of orgies of revenge? What kind of man was it who responded without fail to this extremely complex mixture of rigidity, roughness, discipline, self-effacement, and Spartanism, combined with heroic phrase-making, sensationalism, neverending adventure, luxury, and collective debauchery; to this strange alloy of bulldog faithfulness and corruptness, of old-fashioned German simplicity and hyper-modern organization, of "back to the soil," and streamlined cars and super-airplanes, of the "master-race" and standing to attention, of camp fires and rewards for denunciation? How was it possible that the secret unity of this whirl of apparent contradictions should be easily and instinctively grasped by such a relatively large number of men? Where lies the Archimedean point in the mass-soul of the Nazis by which Hitler directs them firmly and securely and keeps them in place behind him in all his somersaults? Whence this almost mystical under-standing that enables his followers, in their millions, to feel on hear-ing one of their Führer's lies that he is only lying to "the others"? What unites the Nazis since it cannot be the fraudulent collection of contradictions that constitutes their "world-conception"?

These are vital questions without an answer to which there can be no pretence of knowing the enemy. It is astonishing how little inquiry and reflection has so far been applied to its search. Even today many persons are content with excessively superficial expla-nations. In all seriousness people believe that a phenomenon like the welding together of the Nazi Party with all it implies—the de-struction of private life and the family, the ban on thought, the war against Christianity, humanity, and culture, and the institution of gang-morality—can be traced to such ephemeral things as certain clauses in the Treaty of Versailles, the redistribution of wealth as a result of inflation, or unemployment during the depression of 1929–33. These factors have indeed been exploited by Hitler for demagogical purposes and may have helped to enroll some of his casual adherents and voters—his occasional clients. But they can never explain the real "miracle," the decisive event that took place long before the "public" debut of the Party, namely, the rise of the Party: the fact that to the muddled, purely emotional appeal of one Hitler, a person as obscure as he was monstrous, literally hundreds of thousands responded with their body and soul as if all their life they had been waiting for him. What sort of people were they, and for what were they waiting?

They were essentially people belonging to the generation born in 1900–1910, who as children had experienced the Great War, as schoolboys the dismal failure of the Left revolution, and as youths the inflation of 1923. They had experienced the War not, let it be noted, as a reality like the soldiers at the front, but as the grandiose sporting event it was made out to be by German war propaganda for home consumption. They were never again able to envisage nations as anything but gigantic clubs for the purpose of promoting war sports. Never again would they be able to rid their minds of the belief that every other political conception denoted either hypocrisy or slackness. They were strengthened in their convictions by the collapse of the confused Left revolution of 1918–19, whose rather muddled slogans, with their strange mixture of belated Radical–Liberalism, Marxism, and Pacifism, seemed the only alternative to the War–Sport idea. Finally came the inflation, which for a mad carnival year put the reins in the hands of the young people and brought ridicule upon the life-long experience of the aged. This wild orgy, in which all bourgeois notions of order went up in flames like rotten tinder, gave the youth boundless self-confidence, recklessness, a passion for disorder, and a love of adventure. These were, so to speak, the positive qualities in which they excelled other generations. To this was added a pronounced "dynamism," a strong instinct for immediate and short-lived success, immense unsteadiness, and incalculability, and a complete indifference toward the morrow and the day after.

The following years, in which life in Germany temporarily tended to become normal, reveal what this generation lacked. It was not a little. They especially lacked any talent for private life and private happiness—a talent that, at the best of times, is less developed among Germans than other nations. Capacity for affection, reflection, quiet industry, a taste for the refinements of civilization, and the "small joys"—all these were non-existent. It was the generation who invented the "new matter-of-factness" in love, and whose artistic productivity was stone-dead. And they did not look upon this as a shortcoming—far from it. For they were lacking in values and in tradition. Their forbears themselves were a very uncertain generation and had been thrown completely off their balance by the War. They had largely deserted their own beliefs. Their eyes were turned to the "youth," with patient flattery and with longing to abdicate. This youth, untaught and unwilling to learn, rejected as ridiculous and valueless everything that it could not undertake, everything that occasioned effort and was too delicate for its senses accustomed only to coarse fare. The label of these rejected values was "bourgeois." Under the leading "bourgeois" fell in gay confusion—the list claims no completeness—love, family life, religion, sense of responsibility, modesty, individuality, art, business probity, good manners, Beethoven, Goethe, "all this education-blather," authority, tolerance, objectivity. The sole virtue of private life seemed to be insipid amusement; its insipidity was realized and private life correspondingly eschewed.

What was there to fill a satisfactory, "higher," "worthwhile" life? Along those powerful, unforgettable delights remembered from childhood and youth: the war game, disorder on a gigantic scale, car-driving, speed, "corporate unity," vast dashing collective ventures, sensations, revolution, assault and murder, and inch-high newspaper headlines. That is what these young people expected. A new "Great Age," an age of strong sensations provided free of cost by politics, "mad goings-on," new proofs that the impossible is possible, and new crushing blows at the despised "bourgeoisie" and all that it comprised in the terminology of these young people. For that they were ready joyfully to stake their lives that were becoming so tedious. If they did not have to stake them, so much the better. They were certainly ready to offer the lives of the "bourgeois."

And now we see and understand why Hitler and his Nazism fitted this generation like a glove, as if made for one another. We perceive at last the decisive points of contact and cease to wonder why the Nazis do not forsake Hitler when he leads Germany into barbarism, into inflation, into war, into decline. That is just what he had promised them, just what they expected from him! They had a very sharp ear for Hitler's speeches. They did not read them as foreign statesmen do, but heard them—and hence knew very precisely that "peace," "culture," and "anti–Bolshevism" were phrases for the dolts, the "bourgeois" and the foreigners; while for them, the initiates, what counted was the *tone,* in which so often there was more significance than in the words: the "give it to them," the "up and at them," the "we'll show them," and the "skin them.". . .

All the resentments and all the negations of Nazidom were already present in these young people. What a satisfaction at last to be able quite openly to set their foot on the neck of the strange, uncomprehended, and despised world of the spirit, of civilization, of the "bourgeoisie." The burning of the books, the assaults on the universities, on literature, the theater, the press, the law—that was all a grand joke, whatever the slogan under which they actually took place. As in 1923, one could again show the out-of-date old grumblers just what did and did not matter. Crude, good-natured, radiant-eyed vandalism, the gay destruction of all that was dear to the "bourgeois" (Nazis now like to call them "philistines" instead), and because it was dear to them—that was one of the few remaining, untasted joys of life. The strange secret of the "Nuremberg Laws," reserved for the initiated Nazis, was the declaration of war against lovers, particularly against true lovers who kept together in spite of the law and in spite of threats. Here was their revenge at last against unbusinesslike "bourgeois" love! The healthy fun of fetching the sentimental baggages out of bed, and a little prank or two before ordering them off to the concentration camp, the penitentiary, or the castration chamber!

The dissolution of family life, the degradation of the family to a mass-breeding establishment, the transference of the center of life from the family to the gang, to the SA, the SS, the Party, the Defense League, the Hitler Youth, or whatever it may happen to be, satisfies old desires. How this generation had enjoyed its freedom from the family during the War, with fathers on the battlefield and mothers at their jobs! How they had hated these "bourgeois institutions"! And the war against "parsons," that was gladly winked at and taken up with cheerful alacrity; not by any means for the sake of the new "German Faith"—that was naturally only twaddle; a smart boy believed no more in Wotan than in Jesus—but just for the satisfaction of "showing them." To say nothing of the Jews, who seemed to be created to be beaten, just because they were utterly unable to beat back. Shabby curs they were, with their spirituality, sentimentality, family life, prickly individualism, fine feelings, showily displayed culture, love of Art and—curse them!—of money. Indeed, Nazism had in stock many wonderful small gratifications for the 1900–1910 generation. The substitution of marching for thinking; the service motor cars in which one could rage through the streets (the "revolution" began with SA men raging through the streets in service motor cars); food restrictions that at last took the butter off the "philistine's" bread and robbed him of his cup of coffee after his afternoon nap; inflation that made the smug "bourgeois" tremble for his money; and the concentration camps that at last taught him respect. . . .

But it was not only small joys that Nazism brought to this expectant youth. It brought what it most needed to feel happy and content: the great game of war. At last there was meaning in life again, a simple clear life-content accessible to their intelligences: the German Sports Club, to which one belonged in order to enlarge its borders, and every year bring off a triumph or two. And how excellent that one simply belonged to the Sports Club by force of "race," of the fact that one had four baptized grandparents. A splendid idea! How stupid it would have been if one could only be admitted on the strength of some "bourgeois" eccentricity, such as embodying the "spirit of the nation" (what did that mean, anyhow?), or insisting that one should "earn to possess" (*Faust*). Here am I, Fritz Schulze, son and grandson of exclusively German and Aryan Schulzes, six foot, blond, blue-eyed, without corporal blemish, without soul, and thus belonging to the Chosen Race to which, thank God, everything is to be sacrificed—in other words, for which all ballast is to be thrown overboard. It is not to be denied that this simple substitute for religion brought happiness to many Nazi Schulzes, a cheap, readymade happiness such as they had never known before.

Let us immediately correct some misunderstandings that may have been created by this picture, painted as it is in bare outline and without detail.

Firstly, when we speak of the 1900–1910 generation, we naturally do not mean that everyone belonging to it is a Nazi; nor that there were no Nazis to be found in the older generation; but that the attitude of mind and soul inclined to Nazism is more widespread than in the preceding generation. It differs again—we shall soon see how—from the succeeding generation that has grown up under the Third Reich.

We have tried to visualize how Nazism affected the soul of a simple, average man of this period. Naturally, there were among them many who were, in their way, also men of intelligence. They complicate the picture, which consequently becomes unsuitable for brief treatment. The chief complication consists in the fact that with these intelligent Nazis the sacrifice, or perhaps more exactly the distortion and perversion, of intelligence became an added stimulus to

Nazism. For intelligence belonged to the values that this generation instinctively rejected; and since, where it exists, it is hard to destroy, it must at least be misused. Indeed stupidity can employ a great deal of intelligence to justify itself; and the role of devil's advocate is not without its charms. Among the Nazis it is not unusual to find men who play this stock part.

The qualities essential to Nazism—so widespread, alas, for the world, in a single German generation—were an urge for activity, craving for sensation, and lust for adventure on the one hand, combined with mental laziness, lack of imagination, and want of talent for life on the other. It is hard to say which is the positive and which the negative side. For, as far as we know, never before has a generation made such a virtue of necessity, and extracted such strength from weakness; from emptiness, "dynamic," and "activism"; from lack of character, mobility; from lack of thought, enthusiasm; from lack of feeling and knowledge, push; and from nihilism and cynicism, élan.

Psychologists of the distant future will not deny the curiosity of this phenomenon. The practical danger and strength of the Nazis varies with their spiritual baseness; almost every "dynamic" asset has against it a moral debit. Not only in the moral sense—that the abandonment of moral scruple can bring practical advantages is a banal truth that does not merit especial emphasis—but also in a literal and, as it were, medical sense. The Nazis are men who are psychically deficient, who, because they have played truant with life, are ignorant of its very elements, such as love, responsibility, and *joie de vivre*. Psychically undeveloped, backward, crippled, they are able to mold their very deficiency into a menacing power which fully developed men can only restrain with difficulty. That is the phenomenon of Nazism.

One more striking example to illustrate it.

The "cruelty" of the Nazis. Everyone knows that these men, inside and outside their concentration camps, have for years committed daily abominations that have not their like in European history for system, extent, and degree. I shall spare the reader details. The facts are well known. Anyone who is ignorant of them is referred to the British Government's White Book, with the assurance that it contains only an infinitesimal portion of the milder cases out of a vast body of established blood-curdling fact.

If one studies the subjective side in these cases, the doer of the deeds, a surprise awaits one. The doer does not fit the deeds. The enormity is committed by extraordinarily banal, weak, and insignificant men. They are psychologically, not morally, lacking altogether in the positive quality of cruelty. In the watery, expressionless eyes of these tall SS men there is nothing of the sensual, conscious cruelty perhaps familiar to the East and, in a different way, to Europe in the Middle Ages. They are merely men of unusually gross, dull, and stupid insensitiveness. They increase the agonies of their victims and daily think out fresh torture in order to drag out of themselves a little sadistic satisfaction, as an impotent man seeks to stimulate himself with every perversion. No different are their bureaucratic colleagues who sit in offices and torture their victims by methods less physical and palpable, but no less effective. Everywhere this sadism is pedantic and crude, and the agonies of the victims are thereby intensified to an unbearable pitch. The torturers must inflict a maximum of pain to evoke the slightest reaction in their poorly endowed nerves.

And this, the resurrection of sadism, for the prevention and suppression of which Christian Europe strove for two thousand years, is the solitary contribution of the Nazis to the History of Culture, with which they leave their mark on history! And even this springs from insufficiency, not from excess. They have the whole orchestra of sadism playing, but they cannot rise above the note of brutality. All the same, it helps to make them feel they are "terrific fellows," to impose mightily upon themselves. Here, as on all occasions, the Nazis, at least those of the first generation, must display an excess of activity in order to convince themselves afresh, "maddened by their own insignificance," that they matter. At the bottom of their feverish dynamic lies the fear of nothingness. And Nazism, reduced to its shortest formula, may perhaps be said to be nihilism in action, world-domination out of boredom—something new to history. Little wonder the world is reeling in the face of such a foe.

If people had taken the trouble to study the Nazis and inquire into their psychological possibilities and limitations, they would have soon known that Hitler's promises of peace *must* be false even if he sincerely meant them. With such followers as his there can be no peace, for the simple reason that peace bores them to death. The only way in which they can kill time is by preparation for war, by war itself, by destruction, and by further preparation for war. There are many who say that the German nation, like every other, consists of people who want nothing but to live in peace, work, love, rear children, and enjoy life. This is certainly untrue as far as it concerns that part of the German people now in the ascendant, those Germans upon whom rests Hitler's power.

The thought of a peaceful life, of its toils and joys, stimulates nothing but great yawns of disgust in real Nazis, in those spirits avowedly lured and wooed by Hitler to the deliberate exclusion of all other Germans, who endure just as great oppression as the Czechs and the Poles. He who marvels at their continual sacrifices to "Führer and Nation" overlooks the fact that everything that denotes sacrifice for the normal, fully developed man signifies for them liberation from discomfort and boredom. They find no pleasure in private life, the family, peaceful work, thinking their own thoughts, or leisure; on the contrary, all that terrifies them. And this terror they transform into hate and contempt so that they may be able to go on living. Isolated in a peaceful and happy community, a Nazi is quite naturally a very unhappy being, and Hitler is quite right when he says that he has helped many miserable people to find happiness and self-confidence. But what kind of people! Here it is that the immensely powerful sense of forming a "clan" or "gang" has its roots among the Nazis. Only an environment of entirely similar beings, alike unfit for life, alike bent on war, disorder, and destruction as life's entire content, can rescue the Nazi from the dim consciousness of his own misbegotten self. Here originates the compulsive urge toward continual assault, the need for continual crushing victories; for the Nazis need constant spectacular proof of their superiority over the despised "bourgeois," the men, that is, who have learned to live, or they could not quite believe it. Above all, they need continual, and continually more vigorous sensations and adventures to escape boredom; and these sensations can only be warlike and destructive, because peace, for them, is synonymous with boredom.

Even today Bernard Shaw asks whether Hitler would not become pacific after the abolition of the Treaty of Versailles, just as Bismarck became peaceful after the foundation of the German Reich. There is no need, in reply, to make use of such arguments as that Hitler has gone far beyond the destruction of the Treaty in his conquest of countries like Czechoslovakia and Poland which had never belonged to Germany. There is a far more vigorous and forceful answer: behind Hitler stand the Nazis. Bismarck had no Nazis behind him but quite another specimen. With the possible exception of some ambitious lieutenants, there was scarcely a man in the Prussia and Germany of Bismarck who would not have preferred the blessings of peace to life spent in endless warfare. Not so the Nazis. What in the world would the Nazis do in peacetime? Hitler himself would perhaps pass the time in designing vast edifices—but the millions of Nazis, would they be content to be masons? Anyone knowing them must laugh at the idea.

Nor is the destruction of conquered countries a lasting entertainment. The day comes when they are utterly and finally destroyed. Then something new must be destroyed, something bigger. Just as morphomaniacs must constantly increase their dose if it is to have a perceptible effect, similarly the Nazis must enlarge their undertakings; which is rendered possible by the increase in war-potentiality that every happily contrived enterprise brings with it. *In fact the Nazis are constitutionally incapable of keeping peace.* This is the simple and terrible fact that must be faced. All their pretexts for their wars—and they did not start in 1939—whether it be the seemingly plausible complaints about the Treaty of Versailles or the provocative lies that preceded the attacks on Austria, Czechoslovakia, and Poland, are nothing more than dust in the eyes of the "bourgeois," in Germany as well as abroad. The German "bourgeois" who have remained loyal, with some assistance on the part of the Gestapo, allow themselves to be blinded. Bernard Shaw's example shows that outside Germany there are people who allow their vision to be thus dimmed.

The Nazis were a human and cultural curiosity before they became a political phenomenon. They are even today more clearly defined as a group of men, a psychological specimen, than as a political organization. For, as we have already said, not every member of the Nazi Party is a Nazi. The creation of an "Order," that would have provided the genuine Nazis with a political organization of a pure and comprehensive form, has not succeeded. Two of Hitler's measures prevented it. The one he took during the "period of struggle," the period before the seizure of power, during which the all-important event took place when Nazis scattered all over Germany gathered together to form the Party, the political troop. We have seen that Hitler always framed his appeal so as to draw those natures he most needed, that is, Nazis. But one of his political weaknesses, which even in those early days let him down is his constant need of trashy effects which again and again leads him to distort, to sugar-coat his political conceptions. He could not forbear pouring over the appeal to an active nihilism a sweet sauce of sham patriotism, socialism, and heroism, thereby diluting and spoiling it. Most men, it is true, sniffed the meat through the sauce; but some avidly devoured the sauce. Thus, isolated among the oldest members of the Party are found individuals who are not really Nazis, but either patriots, socialists, romantics, or muddled idealists. They, unlike the real Nazis, took seriously some of the "Ideas" expounded by Hitler the demagogue; such as "Back to the Soil," or "Common profit before private profit." Many of them fell away before the seizure of power. Such a group of seceders is the "Black Front" which still today is a nuisance to the Nazis. These pseudo-Nazis, who entered the Party by mistake, provide today some of the best-informed critics of Nazism, like Strasser and Rauschnig. Others did not have their opportunity, for it is not easy to get out of the Party once in it, and they are only distinguishable when, in spite of their golden Party badge, one gets into conversation with them. The existence of these non–Nazis, several thousand in number, in the very midst of the Party's Old Guard, contributes to that incoherence and inner weakness at its very heart which this outwardly rigid organization unmistakably betrays to the attentive observer.

These defects have become far more marked owing to the decision carried out during the last few years to admit and even compel some millions of new members into the Party. It is known that Hitler and his advisers hesitated for a long time before they came to this decision, and that for some years their policy had been, on the contrary, one of maintaining the Party as an "Order" composed of the original genuine Nazis, to be reinforced from the ranks of the Hitler Youth. This was the only possible course if they wished to keep the real Nazis as an exclusive body of shock troops, and continue to apply Hitler's recipe for success, appealing to "dynamic" natures, while excluding all others and reducing them to subjection. However, it was given up, and the Party today contains more members enrolled, as a speculation or by compulsion, during the years 1937–38 than "true" Nazis dating back to before 1933. There is no doubt that in this way the Party as an instrument of force, conquest and domination has seriously suffered. It is now considerably increased in size, but its solidity has decreased. The present-day mammoth Party is less immune to schism than was the old, smaller but psychologically more homogeneous body of "born" Nazis.

However, we must beware of the mistake, common in the democratic countries, of concluding that the new "Party Comrades" might change the character of the Party from within, by the weight of their opinion and their votes, and finally liquidate the genuine Nazis. There is no chance of that. The NSDAP is not a "Party" in the democratic sense, but an organization even more authoritarian than the German Reich that it controls. The ordinary Party Comrade has only duties within the Party, no rights, though outside he may possess certain privileges and powers of intimidation. He has nothing to do but "hold his tongue and obey." He is even more strictly ruled and more rigidly controlled than the ordinary "citizen." He is obliged to devote the greater part of his spare time and money to the Party, and woe betide him more than anyone else if he shows any sign of disloyalty or of having ideas of his own. Quite apart from motives of money and prestige, the desire to keep a tighter hold on some millions of people—many of them belonging to the "higher" and more influential callings—may have played a part in this resolve to "open up" the Party. And there is no doubt that these people, who by seeking admission into the Party have already given proof of weak-mindedness, tend, once they are in the Party, to lose rapidly their former opinions and acquire Nazi convictions. For it is only possible for very strong natures to persevere in thinking and feeling differently to what they express in words and conduct. Once words and conduct are prescribed irrevocably, the thoughts and feelings of weaker natures tend gradually to coincide with them. And, as we said, the new Party Comrades are not exactly the strongest characters.

So far, so good—apparently. But only apparently. For there is, in the last analysis, a great difference between those who out of weakness or adaptability or speculation accept Nazi convictions, and a genuine Nazi. It is the difference between men who howl with the wolves, and wolves: or, better, who hum with the dynamos, and dynamos. The original Nazis are men who *must* be Nazis out of psychical insufficiency, because they can be nothing else; and behind their aggressiveness lies all the energy created by despair and lack of outlet. The new Party Comrades are literally mere hangers-on. The irrational appeal with which Hitler raised his original troop out of active nihilists was a stroke of genius; the method of combined compulsion and persuasion with which he today makes Nazis out of the weakest and most malleable natures is a political gamble. It is based on a deep-lying miscalculation that can only be demonstrated by exposing the Party to severe pressure and strain. If the moment comes for the supreme test of unscrupulousness, for which in the last resort the Party exists; if, without any moral support, it must rule with sheer terror over a refractory people, we shall see how much less fitted it is to do this today than even three years ago. Already we know of a number of Party Comrades, small functionaries and block-wardens, who secretly listen in to foreign wireless stations in the company of their neighbors, instead of denouncing them. That does not amount to much in itself, but it shows the lie of the land. In 1933 this would have been impossible.

At the moment the old and genuine Nazis hold the reins of power completely in their hand, while the pseudo and the new conform outwardly as far as possible, and the general impression is one of a homogeneous, vigorous political army. But the emergency has not arisen. If it does, and if, under extreme pressure and against great odds, all Nazis are put to the test, it will probably be found that a large proportion within the Party itself, particularly those belated members who are not genuine Nazis, will not survive it. But, under the circumstances, such a situation cannot be brought about by propaganda but only by pressure. Propaganda has to penetrate in other directions and affect other people. As to the new Party Comrades, we cannot influence them more vigorously or make them feel more uncomfortable in their shoes than by taking them at their word, treating them like the Nazis they pretend to be, and making relentless war on them. The more openly one seeks to cut off their retreat, the more will they instinctively strive to cover it. Unlike the Nazis, though perhaps as types no less repugnant, they wish to be at all costs "on the winning side," and allow fear and calculation to determine their behavior. They have been attracted by success and power; failure and weakness will scare them off.

And nothing else! It would be quite wrong to confound them with the "decent German people," with whom "we have no quarrel," and who are only in need of enlightenment and liberation. They have taken their stand in the enemy line. But they are the weakest position in this line against which the strongest assault must be launched.

It seems that higher Nazi circles are aware that the Party has been watered down and no longer represents an efficient shock-troop organization. And not only the Party; all the mass organizations into which large numbers of subjected non–Nazis have been crowded, such as the SA, Labor Front, and Food-growing Front, have, in the last few years, tended to disappear from the political front line and become a kind of reserve force. Two organizations, on the other hand, have become more influential, the Hitler Youth and the Gestapo. In the latter as well as the former, the second generation of Nazis is strongly represented, the youngsters who have grown up under Hitler and have practically no acquaintance with normal civilized life. Two of the most significant events of recent German history have been, firstly, the fact that the great Jewish pogrom of November 1938 was for the most part entrusted to the Hitler Youth, to boys, that is, between fourteen and eighteen years of age; and, secondly, that immediately after the outbreak of the present conflict, while the veterans of the World War without regard to Party membership were sent to the front, the Gestapo recruited its volunteers between the ages of seventeen and twenty-three. They both prove that the Nazi regime is beginning more and more to rely on its second generation.

Here Hitler and his lieutenants again show that sure instinct that rarely forsakes them when it comes to preserving their power. For while all their speeches about the unification and Nazification of the German nation as a whole are empty boasts, the Nazification of the growing generation has been to a high degree realized.

The rise of Nazism in Germany extends over three generations. It begins with the libertinism and cynicism of those born between 1870 and 1900, the first generation to grow up in the German Reich. In this generation begins what one may call the decadence of German spirituality: the great apostasy from that humanity and reverence for spiritual values which in the century between 1770 and 1870 had made Germany's greatness and won for her such a high place in European civilization, though without bringing about the "Reich." Its place was now taken by the worship of temporal success. Even before 1914 some essential elements of Nazism prevailed in Germany: boredom with civilization, cynicism, nihilism that paints its cheeks red and apes vitality, Pan–German aspirations, peace-weariness, and joyful anticipation of the war, which, when it comes, is greeted with a cry of rejoicing and redemption. Then a hiatus: the "War Generation," who really experienced war and bore its burdens, had enough and wants no more of it. But neither has it anything else, no positive aims, no spiritual traditions; it just fades out.

The following generation—the first Nazi generation—completes the open breakaway from the European values to which their fathers still paid lip-service, and asserts its wholehearted Nazism. All the same they still have a feeling of being "revolutionary," they still sense, in the beginning at least, the intoxication of disorder, the great adventure, anarchy. There still are among them picturesque conspirators and knights-at-arms, figures like Röhm, Rossbach, Ehrhardt. They still have a last perverse connection with the great European and German spiritual world, even if only that of resentment and hate. The brilliant reflection of that which they destroy still sheds its light on them. . . . The next generation grows up in an already dead, barren machine-world. It knows no better.

The second Nazi generation, roughly speaking, are those born after 1918. For the most part, it has never come into contact with the values, problems, and ideas that make up European civilization, not even in enmity. These young people know of all this only as a dark, superseded, hypocritical superstition of past ages and backward democracies. They have been reared in disrupted schools where they learned nothing. Many of them spring from Nazi families, and all have been brought up to mistrust their family in so far as it is not Nazi. All from the age of ten marched and trained. To all from childhood Nazism has been offered as their sole spiritual food, and upon all is indelibly imprinted the idea of the German Sports Club as members of which they are to pass their lives. Those among them who, from youthful disposition to contradict and criticize oppose these ideas, have not yet found anything else in which they believe and to which they can devote their lives. Their only choice is cynicism and a shrug of the shoulders. Those whose families preserve more civilized traditions live from their early days in two worlds and learn to lead a double life and play the hypocrite, so that often after a time they no longer know when they are being sincere and when hypocritical. The average, however, the mass, spend their days in training, beating drums, singing Nazi songs and, in preparation of future wars and victories, burn down synagogues (tomorrow it will be Catholic cathedrals), denounce their relatives, plunder Jewish shops, race in service cars through the streets and voluntarily offer themselves at seventeen to the Gestapo or the SS.

This generation of Nazis knows nothing of the saccharine coating of patriotic sentimentality that Hitler still loves so dearly. Speaking with these young people one might at first think they were hard-boiled partisans of the Opposition, so cynically contemptuous are they of the "official twaddle" concerning "Blubo," "Führer and Nation," "Strength through Joy," "Winter Relief," "the enslaved Sudeten Germans," and the rest. They are, in fact, such good Nazis that they no longer need all that. With them, Nazism has shed its gaudy relics from the temples of Wagner and Makart where Hitler worships, and has become streamlined. What inspires and excites them is the vision, already quite undisguised, of the vast, uniform establishment for work, procreation, and recreation to which they will shape the conquered world; the dream of the *tabula rasa*. The intelligent among them read Jüngers and Niekisch, and the saying of the Soviet Marshal Tuchachevsky that "The world must become naked again" draws forth a deep response from them.

These boys lack the paroxysmal manner with which the older Nazis are wont to intoxicate themselves. Their style is almost dry. To them murder, torture, and destruction are no more a voluptuous disorder but "the New Order." Life in the guard-rooms of the concentration camps is a gay unemotional one of comradeship. The apostle of this generation is not the somewhat tedious Führer, whom they are willing to leave alone for the moment, yet are apt to mock jokingly as they would a slightly ludicrous old teacher; but rather Himmler, the man of pedantic methodical extermination, the never excited, thin-lipped, smiling, quiet hangman with pince-nez on his nose. Rauschnig finds that the obvious aesthetic and personal short-comings embodied by the first generation of Nazis are not so conspicuous in the second. Well, that is a matter of taste. Personally, if I must choose, I find those hystericals, in spite of everything, not quite so utterly repulsive as these prize scholars of inhumanity.

One striking fact must not remain unmentioned: the overwhelming resemblance of the Nazi second generation to the Bolshevik second generation in Russia. It cannot be denied that the two first generations differ widely from each other. But both, remarkably enough, served the same cause, the abolition of freedom. The one began with the destruction of economic freedom and private property and went on later to tackle freedom of speech, conscience, and thought: the other proceeded in the opposite sequence. Both insulted one another unspeakably and tried to persuade their public that there was no deeper and more deadly contrast on earth than between their two different methods of doing the same thing; a spectacle which, in retrospect, does not lack humor. Be that as it may, human freedom, in all its expressions, has been destroyed in Russia as in Germany. In both countries, the dividing ideological husks have now fallen off or worn thin—even if in Germany Hitler and Göring have not yet been declared Trotskyists and liquidated— and in all its naked monstrosity stands the Robot: the man who has lost all connection with mankind and lives by plan, product of a breeding stud, cog in a machine for industry and war, spiritually fed with "Strength through Joy" or physical culture, emotionally satisfied by car rides or parachute leaps, raising the arm and emitting inarticulate sounds like an automaton, repeating sentences like a parrot, and ready to do everything that an unknown center shall command—man from whom conscience, mind, and soul have been extracted as by an operation.

In the first generation this was done with an ideological pretext; in the second the pretext has ceased to exist, and the question arises in all seriousness as to whether these beings are still to be called men. Physically, to all appearance, they are still men; spiritually, no more. But who knows in how few generations physical degeneration may overtake them.

But, at the moment, we are concerned neither with spirituality nor biology, but politics. And from our observations there arises a very clear political conclusion.

Many voluntary and involuntary propagandists for Hitler are trying at the moment to frighten the Western Powers into the notion that the only alternative to Nazism in Germany is Bolshevism, and that a conquered Germany would become Bolshevik out of spite. The truth is that this is not the *alternative* to Nazism, but its inevitable and predictable *consequence,* and that whatever may happen to a conquered Germany a victorious one must go that way. This follows not so much from the present Ribbentrop–Molotov pact which is a tactical maneuver and may turn out to be ephemeral, but from the inner developments in the two countries which grow increasingly parallel. Russia today is in many ways already Nazi, and the Nazi second generation already Bolshevik, bar, in both cases, the nomenclature. It is very possible that, in the moment of defeat, this second Nazi generation will try to save themselves as one does in chess by castling. They will change their labels and call themselves Bolsheviks, liquidate their former leaders like the Russians did in 1936–37 and—continue to rule as before. Such a change of name should not frighten anyone too much. "Bolshevik Germany" would mean that, christened anew, all would be the same as before; the same people would beat and be beaten, and Germany present the same danger to the world.

But we do not say the world must let this happen. The practical answer to the threat of a Soviet Germany consists in combating and destroying not only Nazism, but the Nazis. The danger of a Bolshevik Germany will vanish with these men.

The theoretical answer, however, is this: now that the Germans have challenged a superior coalition to war, it is no longer in their hands to threaten us with a Germany constructed to their will. The problem today to which the patriots among them must devote their thoughts is whether Germany can be preserved in any form whatever. Astonishingly enough, England and France have so far omitted to assure the Germans that the possibility exists of Germany's destruction, and that only they themselves by a positive effort can eliminate this risk. Such an announcement would be dynamite to the conceptions of international politics held by the loyal and patriotic Germans outside the Nazi Party. It would at last place before their eyes a responsibility of which, at present, they—believe it or not—know nothing.

4

The Loyal Population

It is very important that we should understand the difference between the Nazis and the loyal Germans. Not out of consideration for the latter, nor because great wrong would be done them to be placed in the same category as the Nazis whom they support; but because to distinguish between picked troops and untrained auxiliaries is just as important on the moral and psychological battlefield as on the military and strategic.

Certainly for the soldier in the field it makes no difference whether his counterpart shoots at him because he is a Nazi and feels an inherent joy in shooting; or because he is a loyal German and looks upon shooting as a hard but patriotic duty; or, finally, because he is forced to take up arms against his will and sees no choice but to grind his teeth and shoot so as not to be shot. But for the propagandist and politician, who may wish to facilitate and when possible shorten the soldier's task, it makes all the difference in the world. Against the first of these three men there is nothing to be done but to incapacitate him physically from fighting; against the second and third, however, there are perhaps psychological and political means which, if rightly applied, prevail upon him not to shoot, thus effecting as much from the military and, perhaps, even more from the political standpoint than if he were to be shot dead, wounded, or taken prisoner. But rightly to apply these means one must know exactly what kind of man one is dealing with and how he looks at things. There is no point in saying impatiently: "Caught with them, hanged with them." It is better to examine the motives of the doubtful adherent; then perhaps one can provide counter-motives that will prompt him to adhere no longer and so save one-self the trouble of catching and hanging him. But this is not to say that the counter-motives need consist exclusively of pats on the back and sweet words.

Let us look into these questions. Who constitute the loyal population in Germany? In what way do they differ from the Nazis? Why do they, nevertheless, tolerate and support them?

The loyal—that is to say whose who without being Nazis faithfully serve the Nazi regime—even today make up the largest single political section in Germany, about 40 percent of the whole; and when one speaks in general terms of "the Germans" or "the average German" one instinctively thinks of these people. It is at the same time that group in Germany which is historically most clearly on the wane. In the Kaiser's Reich and during the World War it comprised almost always 90 percent of the population; at certain peaks of national unity, such as August 1914, almost 100 percent. Their fundamental political doctrine was "Kaiser und Reich," and devoting to "Kaiser und Reich" a larger portion of their life, in time, money, work, and sentiments than most people are wont to sacrifice to the State. In return they expected the "Kaiser und Reich" to pursue a policy which would satisfy their rather sensitive self-esteem, that would make them feel "proud to be Germans" and for the rest would reserve for them a private zone, subject to the same loyalty, in which they could "just be human beings." In these preserves they were, in their way, charming and highly civilized. In the political sphere, in their capacity as subjects of the Kaiser and citizens of the Reich, they were even then a trifle strange.

For a time all went smoothly. But under the surface there were many changes. The Kaiser's Reich, firstly, had collapsed in a remarkable way—in a way which, to every honest observer, revealed a deep-lying fault of construction. Though the damage was to some extent patched up, and many Germans never fully realized what it actually meant, it gave some of them food for thought. Secondly, out of the large undifferentiated mass of the loyal population, the vandalistic and sub-human element, the enemies of civilization, had flocked together under the Nazi banner. And, thirdly, one day they seized power. This has not failed to have an effect on what remains of the original loyal population. For the new overlords, unlike the old, do not bother in the least about allocating to their subjects private zones of freedom, but frankly and coolly order them to place themselves "totally" at the disposal of the State; and they pursue a policy which compels every decent German to hide his head in shame. In effect, they have driven large numbers of the Kaiser's devoted subjects into disloyalty.

But the somewhat more numerous remainder try blindly and violently to preserve, under completely altered conditions, the old conceptions which ruled their life under the Kaiser, with the single difference that instead of *"Kaiser und Reich"* the catchword now is *"Führer und Volk."* These people still believe they are just making a few sacrifices in order to feel "proud to be Germans," and they are still, in private, quite unsuspectingly pleasant and highly civilized. In brief, the loyal population in Nazi Germany today still consists of the Conservatives and National Liberals of the Kaiser's era, who will not admit any essential change has since taken place.

This already shows that despite their large numbers they are the weakest and inwardly the most brittle section of the population. They are men who live in an unreal world, who zealously ignore the fundamental facts of their existence and, upheld by unceasing propaganda specially devoted to their benefit, feed on illusions and lies. This also accounts for the two great landslides into disloyalty, in 1934 and 1938, which occurred among them.

Once again, as with the Nazis, it is impossible to locate the loyal population in Germany, or to name definite organizations, ranks, regions, or ages in which they are gathered. Once again, they are to be distinguished only as a psychological type, not as an organized unity. They are, in fact, to be found everywhere, in every class, every district, and every level of culture. One can only give a few pointers. The strongholds of loyalty are the petty bourgeoisie and the provincial upper middle class, while the upper middle class of the large towns is, for the most part, disloyal. Loyalty to the Nazis is especially lacking, on the other hand, among the high aristocracy, among the orthodox Catholics, though not always among the orthodox Protestants, and among the middle-aged and elderly workers who were schooled by the former Socialist trade unions. Scarcely any more data can be supplied as to the degree of loyalty in the different social strata. Regionally, East Prussia, Pomerania, Silesia, and Saxony are more loyal than South and West Germany. But the political scene often changes in the most astonishing way from one town to the next. Thus Nüremberg is one of the most loyal, Würzburg one of the most disloyal cities.

The loyal population still holds certain positions in the internal organization of the State, which it could, if it wished and if it were not so loyal, strengthen into key positions. In the Civil Service the loyalists are still almost as numerous as the Nazis; in the legal profession they are still in the majority. They are well represented in universities and schools. And the joke is that the Press employs many more loyal, and even disloyal, non–Nazis than Nazis. I have heard one of the highest officials in the Reich Press Chamber say that he knew for certain that 75 percent of the editors were politically unreliable, but that he must put up with them as there were never enough suitable Nazi journalists. And put up with them he can, since the "unreliable" editors play their parts no worse than the best Nazis. Filled with dread, cynicism, and ambition, they cre-

ate the notorious Nazi Press, flouting both truth and their conscience. It was, above all, the Army that, till a short time ago, served
as a safe shelter for a conservative loyalty to the Reich which sometimes insisted on not being identified with Nazism. Since February
4, 1938, however, the Army has become increasingly nazified. The
younger officers, as a rule, are Nazis. The older ones are still mostly
loyalists, a fact on which one should not stake too much, but which
all the same should not be left entirely out of account. Circumstances can be imagined in which this might be of some consequence. Incidentally, the curious fact may be mentioned that there
are loyalists in the Government of the Reich itself: the Minister of
Finance, Count Schwerin-Krosigk, and the Labor Minister, Seldte,
and the Minister for Railways, Dorpmüller.

In what, then, consists the decisive difference between the loyalists and the Nazis? What gives us the right to draw a line between
them and discuss them in different chapters? For they both are in
full agreement on two decisive points, the preservation of the Hitler
regime and victory in the war, and behave so similarly in practice
that at the moment it matters little whether a post is occupied by
Nazis or by loyal Germans.

The difference is this: the Nazis, *because* they flourish, prosper,
and are happy; the loyal Germans *although* they suffer, groan, and
are unhappy, want to see the Hitler regime preserved. The Nazis
have fully realized the main principles and intentions of the regime
and maintain it on account of those very principles and intentions.
The loyal Germans deceive themselves deliberately as to these, and
maintain the regime in virtue of this sedulous daily deception. The
surrender of personality, religion, private life, and civilization the
Nazis regard as a release and deliverance, the loyal Germans as a
hard patriotic sacrifice. Because it is their war the Nazis want to
win it. The loyal Germans want to win it although it is not their
war, but because it is right and proper to want to win the wars of
the Fatherland. The Nazis are as self-confident, consistent, cheerful,
and calm as so many efficient engines. The loyal Germans are self-
contradictory, unsure, and at anguished conflict with themselves.
The Nazis lie to God and man, but are most cynically and shamelessly honest with themselves. The loyal Germans lie to themselves.
The Nazis know what they want. The loyal Germans know not
what they do.

That is the difference. Let me repeat that on the military battlefield it means nothing at all; but on the moral and psychological battlefield, where through pressure, threat, discussion, propaganda, ideas, words but also through deeds, the will to fight of the enemy is strengthened or broken, it means everything. It means the difference between an enemy whose mind is unalterable and one whose mind is extremely changeable. A difference, it seems to me, deserving some consideration.

But here we must beware of a fatal mental shortcut. If the loyal Germans are inwardly uncertain, if their psychological position is badly exposed and built on unsteady foundations, it does not mean that they are friendly, reasonable people to whom one has only to make a fair offer—such as that if they remove Hitler and give up Poland and Czechoslovakia, markets for raw materials will be given them in return and they will be helped out of their self-devised bankruptcy—in order to win them over at once to the side where obviously both their private and national advantage lie. It is not so simple. Far from being reasonable, these people are the most unreasonable in the world. Their mentality is not simple and clear but incredibly complex and confused; an astonishing mixture of lofty idealism and low cunning, mistrust and innocence, greed and readiness for sacrifice, cruelty and sentimentality, decency and infamy, astuteness and stupidity, obstinacy and inconstancy, sensitiveness and tactlessness, harmlessness and maliciousness, versatility and obtuseness—and all that possibly allotted to different compartments, neatly partitioned off from one another. We must not begrudge the trouble of undoing the knots and hooks in these brains if we want to find out how to influence them. Do not let us shrink from the effort. It is one that has its charms, like solving a difficult puzzle. And its solution wins a prize that is worth while.

It is indeed a puzzle—one of the greatest that contemporary Germany sets the world. On the one hand, are several million normal civilized Europeans, as private individuals often decent and sympathetic, frequently lovable, sometimes highly educated; on the other, are the unforgettable atrocities of our age crying out to heaven, atrocities committed in the names of these normal and civilized people, often with their connivance, generally with their consent, always without their expressed disapproval. Turning from one to the other of these phenomena, one cannot understand how they come about. It would be laughable, were it not so menacing, that this wonderment and lack of comprehension should continue through years and decades. I turn up the correspondence columns of an English newspaper and read consecutively in the same issue:

> Germany, a nation every bit as civilized as ourselves. . . . Hitler rose to power on the empty bellies and dissatisfaction that came of Versailles, the occupation of the Ruhr, reparations. . . .
> Germany is fundamentally predatory . . . has made five wars in seventy years . . . would continue to revere Hitler if he were able, as promised, to deliver their neighbour's goods. . . .

Therefore:

> . . . When this dreadful war is over, we shall be able to help our opponents to their feet again. . . .
> . . . "Smash Germany" should be the order of the day, utterly destroy them. . . .

So it goes on, day in and day out. As far as the considerable remnant of loyal Germans is concerned, both opinions fail to realize that they are both right; that these Germans are leading a double life like Dr. Jekyll and Mr. Hyde; that they are at one and the same time the nice, kind, hospitable, pleasant people of whom their English and American acquaintances simply cannot imagine evil, as well as the apologists, if not the culprits, of the crimes against the Belgians in 1914, the Jews in 1933–39, the Poles and the Czechs in 1939–40, of whom these same Englishmen and Americans read in their newspapers and shudder. It is difficult to understand. But it must be understood if one wants to make any progress. Based on illusions and half-facts, any words to these Germans will misfire, in war as in peace.

The English and Americans would be aided in understanding the loyal Germans if they turned their gaze to the champions and friends of the Nazis in their own countries. The political imagery of such people is often indistinguishable from that of the loyal Germans: no wonder they often gush forth mutual sympathy over a glass of hock. On both sides are found the same touching innocence as to the real essence and meaning of Nazism; the same somewhat shabby, weak ethical judgment that confounds immense crimes and atrocities with petty excesses and delinquencies; the same cheap political taste; the same predilection for gaudy show and phrases; the same ill-understood patriotism; the same national sports-club mentality; the same readiness to be deceived by others and themselves; the same feeble sense of reality. Even the propaganda is almost identical with which the Nazis net simpletons at home and abroad.

We shall begin our analysis of the loyal German population with a survey of this propaganda; not because we think that it is alone responsible for everything—far from it; but because every well-contrived propaganda provides indications as to the mentality of those for whom it is intended.

There is a peculiar quality about Nazi propaganda; it is not believed, yet it works. The close collaboration of Dr. Goebbels with the lie is just as widely known inside Germany as outside. Only the most stupid accept word for word the claims and pretensions of the Ministry of Propaganda. But even the cleverest are affected by it, as they are by commercial posters. No one, except the most fatuous, seriously believes that by using a certain toothpaste he will acquire teeth of gleaming whiteness; that one soap or another leads to a happy or an unhappy marriage; and malt or cocoa at bedtime to dismissal for incompetence or promotion for efficiency. But although he does not believe all this, he will, in many cases, buy the toothpaste that promises dazzling white teeth, the soap that promises connubial bliss, and the beverage that promises advancement, simply because the names impress themselves on his mind and are subconsciously coupled with pleasant sensations.

Similarly, Nazi propaganda aims not so much at being believed and at persuading, as at creating in our minds tenacious ideas and fantasies. Only very stupid Germans believed, for example, the atrocity stories that they were told in 1938 about the Czechs and in 1939 about the Poles. Most Germans with a knowing air said: "Goebbels." But though they may recognize every statement for a lie, an image finally takes shape in their heads that recurs every time the cue "Czech" or "Pole" is mentioned, recalling a snub-nosed, unpleasant, misbegotten, dwarfish half-ape brandishing a revolver, whip, or rubber truncheon at a number of barely clad women, children, and blond men bound to posts. *And this image cannot be corrected by reflection or reality.* It molds opinion and determines conduct just like the posters of pearly teeth and married contentment.

Hardly anyone seriously believed the fantastic lies about the moral offenses of monks and Catholic clergy which filled the German newspapers some time ago. But almost everyone then and for some time after had, when he met a Catholic priest, a subconscious mental picture of a moral criminal. And that was the object of the tales. Again, many people in Germany regard the Nazi theory of race as nonsense and detest anti–Semitism; but no one, confronted with a dark-haired man, can help silently asking himself: "Is he a Jew?" That is the effect intended by the propaganda. I do not know how many of the Germans at the moment seriously believe that Winston Churchill sank the *Athenia*: not many, I dare say. But I know for certain that an inevitable mental connection between Churchill and the *Athenia* has been established in every mind. "Churchill—that is the *Athenia* man." If they think seriously about it, which is rare, they often realize it is a most incredible story. All the same, Churchill remains "the *Athenia* man."

Just as propaganda creates imaginary pictures and mental associations that supplant reality, so it can make reality vanish—not by denial, but by silence. At bottom every German knows, and rules his conduct by the knowledge, that there are concentration camps where people are ill-treated. But as concentration camps scarcely ever appear in his newspaper he often forgets, in another section of his brain, that they exist. He visualizes no image of them; at most a vague picture of unshaven, beggarly, unpleasant figures, whom he would not like to meet, drawn up and watched over by tall blond youths. This picture dominates him when he entertains his foreign guests, when he smilingly refers, over a glass of hock, to the fairy tales about atrocities in Germany. It is only when he himself is in danger of incarceration that he breaks into a cold sweat at the knowledge that is really his. Strictly speaking, every German knows from observation what is done to the Jews in Germany. But the fact that he rarely reads anything about it, added to the dim feeling that it is not good to know too much about it, causes him often for long stretches of time to doubt his own eyes. And when the Führer just then opportunely remarks: "Not one hair of a Jew's head has been touched"—well, there you are! In this way many events that temporarily absorbed the Germans have subsequently, by calculated silence and distraction, been made to seem as if they had not occurred. Was there really a Reichstag fire? A Thirtieth of June? No one speaks of them now. Perhaps they never happened.

Outside Germany people often wonder at the palpable fraudulence of Nazi propaganda, the stupid, incredible exaggerations, the ludicrous reticences concerning what is generally known. Who can be convinced by it, they ask. The answer is that it is not meant to convince, but to impress. Believed or not, it must not be forgotten. Nazi propaganda disdains to appeal to reason: it addresses emotion and fantasy. Its manipulators know that Germans are not stupid from want of reason, but from surfeit of emotions; and they proceed to harangue these emotions.

Obviously, such propaganda can only be successful among people with a very slight sense of reality. Such, indeed, are the loyal Germans. It is the first thing one must learn about them. They have unusually limited powers of perception and discrimination, and little common sense—and that irrespective of their degree of education and intelligence. The housemaid and the university professor are equally inclined to trust a suggestively presented statement rather than their five senses and eagerly to ignore their own better judgment. With the housemaid this is called muddle-headedness, with the professor profundity, but it is the same thing. Germans— and especially those we are dealing with here—completely lack the gift of seeing simple things simply and of believing their eyes. This is a widespread talent, especially with the Latin nations, who cannot · conceive of its absence. It is impossible to convince an Italian or Frenchman that he is replete when he is hungry, or that he is making an advantageous deal when his purse is being filched. It is possible daily to convince many Germans of this. A vigorously painted picture that looks like something of which they once heard somewhere, convinces them far more than their own perception. That sounds like a jest but it is the sober truth.

Here is the proof. Every second German, in *complete good faith,* will tell anyone who will listen that in Germany under the Republic malnutrition, housing shortage, and want were prevalent, while now "everything has progressed," and "no one in Germany is hungry or cold." All in good faith! Perhaps he will even add that he is, on many points, opposed to Hitler, but we must admit that . . . however, the facts which he not only sees with his eyes but feels with his stomach, prove exactly the contrary. Under the Republic, whatever else could be said against it, there was food in abundance, low prices, high wages, plenty of house accommodation, and leisure; since then there has been less and dearer food, low wages, housing shortage, and overtime toil. But what the loyal German daily reads in the newspapers, hears at meetings, and sees on the propaganda films impresses him far more than hunger at dinner, quarrels with his wife over the household budget, vain hunting for a dwelling, or any such prosaic vexation.

The German always stands with one leg in this world; with the other he likes to plant himself in a world of fantasy—and this world of fantasy is now provided by Nazi propaganda. Somewhere, moreover, in a most secret corner of his mind, he knows this and turns it to account. His capacity for deceiving himself makes it possible for him to deceive others in an astoundingly convincing manner. The whining tales of lamentation about oppressed and outcast Germany were retailed with the most gusto and most profit, not by the Nazis, but by their honest, decent victims. They had been so moved by these fairy tales that they ended by believing them against their own better knowledge. How complicated! How German!

If one inquires *what* Nazi propaganda tells the loyal Germans and *what* it keeps from them, one sees that it constitutes a fair testimonial to the ethical standard of its audience. The Nazis supply two very contradictory kinds of propaganda. The one, intended to lure more Nazis, is found chiefly in camps and training centers, in the "lodges of the Order," and similar establishments. It is, in general, provided orally to closed circles, but frequently penetrates the Party Press, and thus reaches the public. It woos with brutality, ruthlessness, hardness, fanaticism, with outspoken plans for world subjection. In a word, it is cynical and honest.

The other is meant "for the people," more exactly for the loyal people, the disloyal being more or less written off. It is consistently perjured, but with perjury it offers the homage of vice to virtue. It issues from the Ministry of Propaganda. Its principal vehicle is the uniform Press. Its tale is full of righteous rage and humility. World Conquest? Only blockheads and defamers believe us, "us Germans," capable of such a thing. "We" love peace with the patience of lambs. We are prepared to contract pacts of non-aggression with every state. Has not the Führer said so in his repeated peace speeches? If we wage war it is only from the lofty motives of Lohengrin: for the rescue of oppressed innocence and persecuted helplessness. How gladly we would have spared Austria, Czechoslovakia, and Poland! It is only their incurable wickedness and cruelty that compelled us in the end to annex them. Terror? Mass executions? Torture in concentration camps? Of course, no. All fabrications of the Jewish Press. Talking of Jews, not a hair of a single Jew's head has ever been touched by us. At most we are protecting ourselves against the notorious Jewish world conspiracy to destroy the German nation. We want nothing from England, we have no quarrel with England, although she is the enemy of mankind and must be annihilated. But we have nothing against her. We want nothing from France, nothing from anyone except our stolen colonies. And living space. And those American Germans born to us. We threaten America? Ludicrous.

Almost too silly and disgusting. But all the same, it shows that the Nazis find it necessary to play a strange comedy before their loyal followers in Germany; and that they regard them as rather decent people, though perhaps not too intelligent. In particular, the Nazi taste for cruelty, persecution, and oppression does not seem to be shared by these loyal Germans. To make it palatable, the SS men must always appear to be the cruelly persecuted and oppressed, while the dangerous sadists are those behind barbed wire in the concentration camps. The Press is told over and over again to produce no pictures or news that could awaken compassion for any person or group. The Nazis have a frank dread of the loyal Germans' power of pity. Obviously they reckon with some sense of justice, and a certain measure of peaceableness. And if, on the one hand, they cautiously polemicize against these qualities from time to time and try paternally to talk the Germans out of them, they feel, on the other, obliged for the time being to pay regard to them in devising their propaganda.

The Nazis, in the eyes of the loyal Germans, are not the breakers and destroyers of the family, but its protectors and champions. ("Who has done more for the family than we have? Marriage loans. Raising of the birthrate.") Not the enemies but the saviors of Christianity and the Church. ("What do these quarrelsome parsons want? They have to thank us that they are allowed to preach unmolested; that their churches are not burnt down. We have never interfered with the cultivation of souls.") Not revolutionaries but armed guardians of the State. ("Germany an island of peace. The foundations of order totter all around us. From country to country spread the flames of revolution. The standard of living falls. Unemployment, wars, civil wars, governmental crises. We are spared all this! We celebrate the harvest festival in thankfulness and concord. The Führer watches over us.") Thus the Nazis have to persuade the majority of their countrymen to believe the opposite of almost everything that they are and want to do, in order to win and keep their loyalty. That they succeed to such a large extent speaks against the intelligence and political maturity of the Germans; but that they are obliged to make the attempt speaks for the essential morality and decency of the German people.

But there is an important reservation. The Nazis do not keep the two kinds of propaganda neatly separated and are by no means careful to see that "the people" do not know what is actually going on. Intentionally and with a certain subtlety, they make it difficult for them to believe the lies they tell them. Simultaneously, they declare that no Jew has ever been harmed and display *Der Stürmer* at every street corner. They work constantly in two directions. They vaunt their humanity and humility as well as their ruthlessness and severity. They talk, almost in the same speech, of Germany's boundless love of peace and of the "new division of the world." And they know that they can count on applause in both cases. Above all, they have a nonplussing way of letting the mask fall when the deed is done. They seem to know that they can afford to do this, that something inherent in their public is ready to be imposed upon; indeed, that it perhaps wants first to be deceived and then to be surprised by the result. Thus Hitler uninterruptedly from May to September 1938 gave out to the German people, who engaged in the Czech adventure most hesitatingly and reluctantly, that Germany wanted nothing from the Czechs; that the Czechs had only to cease oppressing the Sudeten Germans; that nothing more was wanted than autonomy for the persecuted minority. But ten days after Munich he declared, and amid loud applause, that he had, no later than May, given the "command to march into Czechoslovakia at the latest by October 2." If the Germans were just simply decent and ingenuous people they would have reacted with fury to this disclosure that their stupidity had been exploited and their decency abused, that they had been made to commit murder with their eyes bandaged. But their response was admiration and acclamation. So, perhaps, this was just what they wanted: to commit murder but not to know it; to have a bandage over their eyes during the deed, but afterward to get the victim's gold watch and purse; to enjoy the fruits of wrong-doing and to be cheated only of a bad conscience.

We meet here a characteristic of the loyal Germans that is no less difficult than necessary to understand; one of those complexities which to the Germans, and only to them, are natural and self-evident. It is the two-fold, or, to speak exactly, the three-fold morality to which they pay homage in the realm of politics—and used to pay homage even before the advent of the Nazis.

The German, in his personal life, is not more amoral than other Europeans. In his own opinion he is even more moral; but in this, too, he is no different from others. Of course, he sometimes behaves immorally, but he pays for it in the usual way, with a bad conscience; he recognizes, that is, the existence of a moral law above him even when he disregards it. Perhaps German morality is shaded differently from that of other nations. For example, Englishmen have sometimes observed that the average German, even in private life, does not fully come up to the English standard of fair play. That may be. Fairness, however, is a typical English virtue; with Germans its place is taken in the ethical scale by the more oriental, less distinct, but no less noble virtue of generosity. We shall not further pursue this point. Suffice it to say one would do the German injustice to deny that as a private individual and in time of peace he feels and acts morally.

But it is a fact, much noticed and marvelled at, that nothing remains of this morality and decency of "the German" when "the Germans" appear on the scene; that as a political mass they differ from other civilized nations—and not only since the coming of the Nazis—by virtue of their unusual lack of scruple, their untrustworthiness, bad faith, lying, and barbarity.

The incredible, comic thing is that the average German is unconscious of this. To him it does not appear that he is immoral in politics but that *politics* are immoral. Politics appear to him to be a sphere where it is the universal custom and rule to be unscrupulous, faithless, fraudulent barbarians. All other nations, he thinks, are the same; and to pretend, like the English, there is a moral law in politics appears to the German a perverse and repulsive hypocrisy, the authors of which merit immediate extermination.

We must, for the moment, postpone the question of how the Germans persuaded themselves that politics is a game of which treachery, malice, and bestiality are the rules. The fact is that they did. "Politics spoil the character," says a German proverb, and a diplomat, according to the average German, is a man who lies all day long; a successful diplomat one who lies better than his rivals. And the attempt to introduce laws of decency and morality into the political sphere provokes the German to the immense honest indignation that is aroused in every man by a gross and cunning foul against the declared rules of the game. For the average German there is a private and a political morality, political being the exact opposite of private. Treachery, extortion, theft, perjury, murder, rapine—these to the German mind are not crimes and excesses in political life as they are in private. On the contrary, he insists, politics *consist* of just these things. If anyone maintains anything different it is only to lull the stupid German, who is too good for this world, into a sense of security so that his foe may be less hampered in plotting his political downfall.

For the German is quite unaware that his conception of politics is a purely national peculiarity. He thinks it is forced upon him. He yearns to be good and peaceful, but the wicked world forces him to take an unwilling part in the evil game. Personally, he does not care at all for this game of politics. For this reason the decent, normal, moral German generally shrinks from political endeavor. No one is by nature as unpolitical—one could say anti-political—as the German. There is nothing to be said against this, especially when one recalls the great musical, poetical, and philosophical achievements—all of which Germany owes to this political self-effacement—so long as it is honestly accomplished. Even today the normal individual German prefers to have as little as possible to do with politics. "A nasty song—phew—a political song," he says. He prefers to leave politics to those who volunteer to look after them on his behalf, to Kaisers and Führers.

But here his moral judgment again takes the wrong turning. His leaders, who commit the crimes from which he recoils but which he secretly feels to be necessary and desirable, and who in benevolent deception take from him even the feeling of complicity—these men he adores as no other nation has ever adored its statesmen. And their successes, won in his name and in part dependent upon him, intoxicate him, although he would have flinched from employing the means by which these successes were achieved. That is the secret why these good-natured, easygoing, decent people always go down on their knees before unscrupulous, brutal, sadistic Führers. Their relation to the elect, their princes, leaders, and heroes, is like that of primitive people to the gods who protect them, give them victory and at the same time take upon themselves their guilt. Other nations have most confidence in those of their politicians in whom they recognize themselves, who conduct, on a vast scale, the affairs of State in the same way as their countrymen conduct their private affairs. But the Germans desire those rulers whose politics bear not the least resemblance to their private life; who are quite different, "great," "demonic," "geniuses," "inspired." The Germans do not want honest deputies and administrators; they want idols. If their idol fails them, if he loses their war as the Kaiser lost the War of 1914–18, he is sent into the wilderness laden with all the guilt, and the people face the world wide-eyed with innocence and limpid conscience, outraged if they are held in the least responsible for the actions of their idol or called upon to make good.

If, however, the idol obtains victory, their adulation knows no bounds. Consider the attitude of the Germans to Bismarck. It is not one that nations adopt toward a successful statesman and a notable personage who has sprung from their midst; it is one only to be expressed in theological terms. Bismarck has become the eternal tribal god of the Germans. His utterances have the final, oracular power possessed by biblical citations in the scholastic discussions of the Middle Ages. The popular anecdotes about him, chosen, significantly enough, with some bias and almost always depicting him in visible or invisible jack-boots, have the consolatory power of the legends of the divine and semi-divine. The thought of the future Iron Chancellor bullying his judge as a young briefless barrister or the delegation of the defeated enemy as a peace negotiator, induces in the most bashful German a feeling of exaltation and power as if he himself had just completed the conquest of the world. And the same German father who gravely reproaches his son for striking a weaker school fellow or falsely accusing someone, says to him on solemn occasions, with a quiver in his voice, "What a tremendously great man he was, to take upon himself the unique responsibility of revising the Ems telegram. He thereby unleashed a war to the death, overthrew an Emperor, and welded together with blood and iron the German Reich!" He would turn white with anger, were he to learn his son forged a doctor's certificate in order to skip a lesson; but in face of the greatest falsification in world history, he is numb with religious awe as before the crucifixion of Jesus.

Having seen the types of sentiment and mentality to which Hitler can appeal we shall have little difficulty in understanding that his untrustworthiness, his promptitude in breaking faith, and his greed for conquest, those qualities in fact which finally drove the world to lose patience with him, form the very pillars of his power in Germany—and that far beyond inner Nazi circles. Conquests seem to the German the natural aim of politics, untrustworthiness and bad faith their means; successful extortion or fraud is "diplomatic victory," and the indignation of foreign statesmen at Hitler's methods is the green-eyed jealousy and resentment felt by the less efficient toward their more gifted rivals. If Hitler had nothing more on his conscience than his foreign policy, the breaking of his word, his conquests, and his plundering of other nations he would have no need of a propaganda of lies to make himself acceptable to the Germans. The weak points of his rule are just those features which the world, perhaps not quite rightly, was, and still is, inclined to indulge and ignore as the "internal affairs of Germany": the war of annihilation against private life, private liberty, and private morality; the destruction of all the private amenities which under Bismarck and the Kaiser flourished peacefully in the shadow of a wicked policy; the intolerance and cruelty that make a hell of life in Germany; the progressive enslavement of every German and the swallowing of all private "living space"; the daily accumulation of atrocities which lure Nazis almost as inevitably as it scares away other Germans, and which must, therefore, be erased from the consciousness of the latter by continuous propaganda. All this, far more than Hitler's foreign policy, has driven so many Germans into disloyalty, and the loyal themselves to question their sentiments. For the loyal and disloyal are not two different Germanies as many people like to represent. They are essentially cast in the same mold, however much they hate one another today. The chief difference between them is that, with the disloyal, private conscience and private honor have been strong enough to overcome patriotism and loyalty, at least in their hearts; while the others only simmer in unfruitful conflict and self-torment. The Nazis hold too many trumps against them. Some of these have already been considered, but intentionally the highest has been left to the end. It demands exact examination. It is the appeal to patriotism.

When the loyal German most wavers in his loyalty; when some crass enormity in his immediate circle tears aside for the moment all veils of propaganda and makes any self-deception impossible as to what is going on; when one of Hitler's "culture" speeches and "culture" deeds make the educated man feel sick; when the small shopkeeper sees his "national-economically unproductive" shop closed down by order of the authorities and is himself carried off for compulsory labor on defense works and motor road construction; when the hundred and ninety-seventh questionnaire has to be filled up; when the National–Socialist Livestock Breeding Front or the National–Socialist Skat Association demands his membership, subscription, and attendance at the district muster; when the Dentists' Association puts the choice before him between separation from his non–Aryan wife and being "struck off the rolls"; when bitterness, despair, shame, and scorn threaten to overwhelm the most loyal, what restrains him is the thought—so moving at first sight—that he endures all that "for Germany."

Let us not deceive ourselves. Concerning many things the loyal Germans may be told lies by the Nazis, or they may tell themselves lies; to many they may shut their eyes, about many be honestly mistaken; many they may reluctantly endure or secretly wish to see altered; but there comes a point where they sincerely agree with the Nazis, where Nazism exactly coincides with their aspirations and ideas. This point is decisive. If somewhere this real harmony did not exist they would not be so willing to blind sacrifice, and deceive themselves. Only when they change their minds on this score can there be hope of separating these loyal followers from the Nazis.

This is the strange misconception of patriotism that has dominated Germany since the foundation of the Reich. The Nazis are the terrible consequence of opinions that, long before their day, in harmless and civilized times, were propagated and inculcated at German universities and schools. They are the terrible incarnation of the ideals of the bombastic ceremonial orator who flourished from 1870 to 1918, and after. Loyal cultured Germans, when inwardly trying to break away from the Nazis, feel disarmed by their own most sacred ideals. Are not the Nazis working exclusively "for Germany"? Have they not made Germany more powerful, more feared, more victorious than anyone before them? Does not everything they do, however frightful it may seem, serve to make Germany still more powerful, more feared, more victorious? And must one not put "Germany above all"? Must one not, therefore, make every sacrifice that the Nazis demand? And is not each of these sacrifices a trifle, an irrelevance beside the dazzling triumphs that the Nazis have won "for Germany"?

Now patriotism and readiness for sacrifice are certainly virtues. But every virtue, as we know, can turn to vice, and German patriotism is an example of this transformation, if ever there were one. It had degenerated long ago, long before the Nazis. It has lost all measure and meaning. It debases the "Fatherland" to an empty, hollow formula and, at the same time, exalts it to an Absolute. Analyzed to its core, it reveals the same feature that is inherent in Nazism: active nihilism or, reversed, destructive totality. It is the point of least resistance in pre–Nazi German thought through which the Nazi toxins forced an entry. And it is still the only point of real unity between the Nazis and many civilized non–Nazi Germans.

Patriotism is an emotion that, in a healthy condition, should be latent. It is nothing more than the natural reaction to an actual *threat* to the "Fatherland"—to soil, language, the customs of the people, the independence of the State and the rights of self-determination. Healthy patriotism is what the Belgians in 1914 or the Finns in 1939 have shown to the world. The patriot in peacetime appears a slightly comic, though perhaps pleasantly comic figure. It is normal and natural to love one's homeland and one's countrymen in peacetime, and secretly to prefer them to foreign lands and people. But the more secretly the better. Peacetime patriots, even the most innocent and likeable, remind one a little of men who kiss and caress their wives in public.

What have the Germans in the last hundred years made of this healthy, shy thing "patriotism"?

First of all, wherever they may be, they are conscious of their "Germanness." In time of profound peace they go about as if they

are in a national green-room, anxiously resolved, on the most trifling occasion, to think "in a German way," feel "in a German
way," love "in a German way," and eternally "remember that they
are German." What exactly this Germanness amounts to will soon
be scarcely recognizable. The "Germany" of which these unfortu-
nates have learned to be conscious from morning till night is a kind
of mystic Godhead. On what does this Godhead live? On sacrifice.

Every sacrifice must be made for "Germany"—that has been im-
pressed on German children for generations before the Nazis. And
so in fact for the last thirty years Germans have made sacrifices "for
Germany" with an alacrity and patience that would be touching
were they devoted to a better cause. In this present era they have
only once been normally fed under the Republic for a space of six
years. In the last year, in the first years after the war, under Brüning
and under Hitler, they have "for Germany" willingly and patiently
eaten "substitutes" to win the war, to "save Germany from Bolshevism," to prove they could pay no more reparations, to prepare for
the next war. By now German patriots are able to extract a kind of
spiritual satisfaction from eating bad food, such as the Flagellant
Brothers of the Middle Ages extracted from their weals and swell-
ings; a government that gave them enough to eat would even arouse
in them a suspicion that it was not patriotic enough and did not
do enough "for Germany." The Germans have twice allowed their
savings to be stolen from them "for Germany" with the helpless,
sad patience with which a poodle allows his bone to be taken out
of his mouth; to say nothing of the thousand senseless sacrifices of
leisure, cash, comfort, and minor pleasures that have been daily and
systematically imposed on them by Hitler. "For Germany I will
willingly give one night a box on the ears," says the German patriot
when he is commandeered by the SA for a night march. The finest
expression of this attitude I heard from a small bookseller, when
in 1936 the rubber bands, which were conveniently slipped round
parcels of books, were withdrawn (the rubber was needed by the
army for tires). He sighed a little and said: "But I shall gladly tie up
every parcel with string if it helps the Führer to preserve peace."

So far all this is rather pathetic, even if slightly crazy. But "Germany" not only demands sacrifices of comfort, goods, and chattels,
to say nothing of a man's life; she not only demands honorable sacrifices. "Germany" also demands sacrifices commonly considered

dishonorable: sacrifice of character, conscience, insight, morality. "For Germany" one must be parted from one's wife if she is not Aryan; one must lie, steal, and kill. Already the Kaiser, anticipating Hitler, had informed his soldiers that they must fire on their relatives if he ordered them to do so. And German patriotism swallowed it—with a certain exaltation. Here the business begins to be disgusting. The demoralizing, destructive character of the patriotic degeneracy that afflicted the German people begins to be manifest. But this is not yet the culmination. That is still to come.

As sacrifice "Germany" also demands—Germany. The national essence, culture, inherited character, institutions, and usages that make up the real Germany, the landscape, architecture of the towns, the country's well-being, good name, honor—all must be sacrificed to "Germany." This "Germany" to which men's sacrifices never cease is not the beautiful, fertile, old country between Alps and sea, with its towns and fields, factories and railways; with its inhabitants, customs, language, poetry, and music—all would exist as well and better without sacrifice, but all are the doomed victims of immolation. The "Germany" to whom one must sacrifice is a mysterious phantom, a ghost. But it has an earthly symbol: the "Reich."

The patriotism which Germans have learned since the foundation of the Reich is not love of the Fatherland, but fatherland-fixation. It is a feeling that partially paralyzes moral, intellectual, and aesthetic responsibilities. It is, so to speak, a blind spot in the spiritual eye.

The Nazis have not created this fatherland-fixation. On the contrary one might say that it has created the Nazis. At least the Nazis have found it readymade and have been able to work wonders with it.

It has not grown out of nothing. It has been reared and nourished by the historical legend of the German Reich. And this legend is the psychological basis of the German Reich itself; the Reich, the earthly incarnation of that "Germany" to which Germans for the last seventy-five years have blindly sacrificed everything, their personal and national individuality, their civilization, their national mission. In England people have always been inclined to regard this "German Reich," with which they are for the second time in twenty-five years engaged in a life-and-death struggle, very innocently, as the natural unification of forces tending to coalesce, as the final result of a healthy historical process, as the fitting political receptacle of German civilization. They favored the German Reich at its birth, helped to put it on its feet again after its first major catastrophe, and would, even perhaps today, wish nothing better than to live again in peace and concord with a German Reich "come to its senses." It is time, however, to ask whether the Reich *can* come to its senses; whether this political entity—into the tradition and legend of which the Nazis fit so uncannily; in the name of which they coerce into conformity with themselves so many resisting, so many better Germans; and from which have arisen almost all the great crises and wars of the last seventy-five years—may not perhaps be something most unnatural and dangerous; not the peak of healthy evolution but the start of a fatal disease that will annihilate Europe; not the fitting receptacle of German civilization but its destroyer; what Nietzsche, with his clear vision, dreaded as early as 1873, when he spoke of "the downfall, indeed the extermination, of the German spirit for the sake of the German Reich"?

We cannot here discuss this immense question with the thoroughness it deserves. But it must be broached and its main points outlined. For it would otherwise be impossible to understand what gave the Nazis their psychological chance in Germany, where they found a link with German tradition—indeed, *what made them possible in Germany.*

The German Reich of 1871 was not the result of a long and consistent process of historical growth, as were, for instance, the great powers of the West. Rather it was a sudden, surprising deviation of a history that for fifteen hundred years had striven for quite different forms and aims. Historically regarded, it appears somewhat curious and dubious, like the attempt of the contemporary Zionists to make the Jews, after two thousand years of unique history as a civilization and community without a state, again into a small Near-East State. It was very characteristic that, since attaining civilization, the Germans, unlike their Western neighbors, had never striven for national unity and cohesion, but always for universality. And when their attempt to revive the Holy Roman Empire in a practical form had failed they—rather like the Jews—laid the center of gravity of their national existence in the "extra-State," in the acquisition of a spiritual universality that, precisely because of its worldwide extent, unconsciously became a national characteristic. The political basis on which the spiritual world of the Germans was erected was a bundle of unambitious small states. Some of the smallest among them were, from the point of view of culture, the greatest; for example, the Saxe–Weimar of Karl August. And we must recall the unique serenity and deeper detachment of Goethe when he encountered Napoleon as one sovereign meets another, in order to understand the dignity and self-assurance that political renunciation, together with spiritual world-dominion, gave to the German. It was these powerless small states that fostered the vigorous achievements of the German spirit—from which today the barbarized, unspiritual, un–German, robber "Third Reich" derives its right to trample under foot all those highly civilized small countries.

The "yearning for the Reich" in the nineteenth century was nothing but a decline of confidence in Germany's unique position and source of national greatness. Strange to observe, this sudden irresolution and puzzlement, this unexpected false step, this jerky failure of instinct, and this forgetting of the very laws of life! Again and again it happens in the history of great nations. Sometimes it is a momentary dizziness that passes without a trace; sometimes a growing madness that drives a nation into blindness, convulsion, and delirium. The German "yearning for the Reich" had as its invisible motto the word *also*. The Germans wanted "also" to have their Reich, because the French and English had theirs; not because they needed it or were in any way spiritually equipped to manage and run a great Nation–State. This "also" mentality has ever since persisted in the history of the German Reich. It forms one of its primal urges. Thus, later, Germany must "also" have colonies, a great fleet, and interests in the Far East, not because they are vitally needed, but because other powers have them. Thus today Hitler's oppression of the Czechs and the Poles is justified in the eyes of his patriotic followers by the argument that England, under Warren Hastings, "also" employed methods of brutal coercion. Thus, even his wars of expansion are partly supported by the "also" theory. Has not France "also" grown by annexing and crowding out her neighbors—three hundred or five hundred years ago?

But the psychological motive of these wars is different. The "Reich," as we remember, was in the end not created by longing, but by Prussia swallowing all the German states—Prussia, that small robber state, its whole history a continual devouring, first of smaller, then of large, countries; its only glory, lacking independent civilized achievements, a constant aggrandizement, its state-ethic subjecting the lives of its people to its territorial greed. This political morality Prussia bequeathed to its successor, the German Reich. In its place the conquered small German states had nothing to offer, morally weakened by the betrayal of their spiritual mission and the irrepressible "also" doctrine. Prussia was the cancer of Germany. Its law was: grow, swallow, and destroy. Since Germany forgot and denied its own law and accepted Prussia's; in other words, since it became the "German Reich," it has become the cancer of Europe.

The German Reich arose by means of three of the most cynical and criminal wars known to history; the brutal overpowering of the small neighboring Denmark, the lightning war against the Germanic Confederation, resulting in the absorption of the small North German states, and the unjustified war against France, artificially provoked by the falsification of documents. The Reich was "welded together" by a joint plunderous expedition on the part of its future member-states. Now states, like individuals, if they are to "thrive and prosper," must, as Goethe says, "obey the law that gave them life."

Bismarck, who had an acute, but not a profound mind, probably did not know this. He may have been quite sincere when he announced that Germany, after 1871, was a "saturated" State, when he regarded the foundation of the Reich as the conclusion of German history and sought to introduce the new German Reich, as smoothly as possible, into the company of the old European Great Powers, as if its natural place had always been among them. In his day the Germans were so confused and bewildered by all that had happened between 1862 and 1871, by the humiliations and sufferings that had suddenly changed to happiness and triumph, that for the moment they were content. In fact, for twenty years the German Reich was a satiated and peaceful state. However, it was remarkable that Germany's spiritual tradition seemed suddenly to run dry; that cheap display and smugness supplanted austerity and constant self-criticism; and that Treitschke began to compose a new German historical legend from his university chair.

After Bismarck's downfall the giant plaything that had been pressed into the hands of the Germans began to reveal its demonic spirit. Now that they owned a great power machine, should they not do something with it? But what? Expansion, of course! Prussia became great by growing, so the great German Reich, its heir, had to grow even more vigorously and more rapidly. Of course it had to have all that the others possessed. But soon the Germans, with a parvenu's uncertainty, began to tremble in their new role. Where was the sovereign dignity and quiet self-assurance with which the Germans of the eighteenth century surveyed the quarrels of the world from their unconcerned small states as from high hills? They now spoke disparagingly of the "German small-state outlook," and were ashamed of their past as a nouveau riche is ashamed of the mean abode of his parents. They did not know how to wear their new clothes and, continually ill at ease, they felt maligned and above all envied.

Since the inauguration of the Reich the Germans have suffered from persecution-mania. They are convinced that all other nations want to take it from them and are lying in ambush to encircle and fall upon them. Morbid self-consciousness, resentment, mistrust, saber-rattling, and cowardly shirking of responsibility—all these completely new traits in their character are the neurotic consequences of betraying their very essence of which the Germans were guilty in destroying their spiritual past and trying to play the Great Power, without being in the least prepared for the role by history. Later came the fatherland-fixation, the convulsive worship of a single dubious ideal to which everything had been sacrificed and must, therefore, continue to be sacrificed.

> *On and on to prosper and thrive.*
> *Obey the law that gave thee life.*

The Reich could only pursue a war-and-victory policy, an "also" policy. Partly from persecution-mania, partly from urge for expansion, it had to arm, threaten, assault, make a disturbance, bully; the perverted Reich Germans had to do all that to be "able to carry their heads high as Germans." Formerly they had been able to carry them high without all that, although they were only Württembergers or Saxe–Weimarians. But they had been healthy men. Now they needed narcissism, self-dramatization, and self-praise in order to keep up appearances in their own eyes. For all that, those were times when the mind was still tolerated as a plaything and pastime for leisure hours, even if it were no longer taken seriously, as in the days of the "small state outlook." There was as yet no overt barbarism, no Jew–baiting, no concentration camps. There was only, one day, the inevitable great war.

The Reich was vanquished—but it survived. It had to surrender unconditionally, acknowledge its war guilt with its own lips and promise reparation; it had to give up some former booty and it had to disarm. But still it survived. And again its demon began to assert itself, impelled by the inescapable law of its being. Those in power might have been men of good will, they might have really wanted to pursue a policy of peaceful identification with Europe. But the Reich was stronger than they. This immensely powerful edifice built for war and expansion demanded from its rulers the policy for which it had been constructed. For a policy of peaceful adaptation no Reich was necessary. Then, as soon as it was noticed that the giant plaything had remained intact and essentially undamaged, the bad loser began his loathsome whining over the "shameful peace": the comedy of misery was played as the first act of the Drama of Revenge. . . . The kindly Weimar Republicans submitted, reluctantly; perhaps only to take the wind out of the sails of the Nationalists; but in the end they were to chase after them, always running a little more unsturdily and less vigorously than they, but in the same direction. They were already beaten when in their constitution they resumed the title "German Reich." Then the social Democratic Reich President Ebert in 1919 proceeded to declare the National Anthem to be *Deutschland über Alles*. They were finally obliged, unwillingly, to accept the German legend about the World War, and to talk of the "War guilt lie," of the "shameful peace," and "tributes." The last years of the Republic were suicide. Piecemeal the Republicans pulled down their own regime. They could not govern against the German Reich. This murderous monster continued to gravitate against their wills, in the direction it desired, toward new war and pillage. At last the Republicans would bear the responsibility no longer. They vacated the ruler's seat. And into it swung those who fitted it: the Nazis.

They really fitted it—that is the hideous fact that cannot be denied. How wonderfully the Nazis are suited to the idea of the Reich.

They were the first to take seriously the bloodthirsty ceremonial speeches. They serve the Reich "totally": its growing, its swallowing, its destroying. They have no regard for civilization, humanity, or morality. They tolerate no more private zones. They are consistent. They are whole-hoggers. And how well they know to play on the already attuned note of patriotism! How they importune German uncertainty, indulge German self-pity, cultivate the German manias of encirclement and persecution, appeal to the eager spirit of sacrifice of the *Deutschland über Alles* patriots, and offer the Germans the only thing that still comforts their perverted souls: the success of the cancer eating into a new organ; the drunken satisfaction of seeing Germany an ever larger spot on the map; the drunken satisfaction of triumphant resentment and the victorious propagation of their own misery; growing, swallowing, destroying. . . .

We have arrived now at the great question that covertly lies behind all the events of recent years, and which in Germany has been ten thousand times fruitlessly debated in loyal and patriotic circles: can the German Reich still part from the Nazis, or must it stand or fall with them?

The loyal Germans have no clear reply. Very many of them perhaps wish they could get rid of the Nazis and yet preserve the Reich. But they dimly sense the diabolic opposition that the Reich puts up to this desire. They feel that their patriotism to the Reich does not permit them to reproach the Nazis with barbarism, bestiality, and infamy, when humanity, civilization, and honor have previously been sacrificed to the Reich. *Deutschland über Alles.* It is only when some unmoral action threatens immediate political harm that it may perhaps remain unperformed. What is worrying is not that concentration camps exist, but that they "create ill-feeling"; not that the Czechs are tyrannized, but that it is dangerous to "take into the Reich" so many Czechs. One may argue against a policy not that it is criminal but that it may turn out wrong. If it turns out right, one is refuted. And so far it has almost always turned out right. Twice, when crime did not pay, or threatened not to, in 1934 and 1938, many of the loyal patriots turned traitor almost with relief. They dared again to turn against crime because crime menaced injury to the Reich! But on both occasions they had miscalculated. So now the patriots have become very cautious. They suffer under the Nazis, they groan, they would rather not watch what they are doing, they despair and hide their heads in shame, but all the same they do not want to see the Nazis fall. They have an overpowering feeling that the Reich would thereby lose its greatest chance of glory and world conquest. They feel that the Reich will never have a government that better suits it, that is better able to get out of it all it has to give; that has such tremendous success. Perhaps, they think, this time it will "do it." Perhaps this time it will win the World War.

But perhaps not, these loyalists agree. Since 1918 they cannot exorcise a secret dread that there is such a thing as victory to death; that the bow too tightly drawn may snap one day. But even against such an eventuality they feel a certain wanton security. Versailles, they think, proved the Reich to be indestructible. "If our enemies could have done it," they say, "they would have destroyed us then." The worst they expect is a second Versailles. And they have seen how the chains of Versailles can be thrown off.

Perhaps that is just where they are wrong. Perhaps the Nazis, in suiting the Reich supremely well, have opened the eyes of the world to the vastness of its peril, so that this time the Reich will not be given another chance. If the loyal Germans are plainly told that their Reich will not survive if they leave it any longer as a weapon in the hands of the Nazis; and if, at the same time, they are shown by deeds that victory is extremely doubtful, then and only then will they feel, again perhaps with some relief, that patriotism allows them to yield to conscience and to dismiss the Nazis. It would be the only way to influence the Army to bring about the much-debated and long-awaited monarchical coup d'état.

But is it to be desired? Would it be worth while to preserve the Reich in order in another twenty-five years to wage, not the War of 1939 but probably that of 1914? Is there no other hope? Apart from the loyalists, is there no other element in Germany with whom we could unite to overthrow the Nazis and bring about peace?

Having lashed the Reich and Reich patriotism to a climax, the Nazis have reduced them to an absurdity—even in the eyes of a large number of Germans.

Besides the shamefully large number of "normal" Germans who have tolerated the Nazis, let us not forget those, almost as numerous, who eagerly await an opportunity to prove their disloyalty.

5

The Disloyal Population

The disloyal Germans are today in danger of being forgotten; and that would be tragic for them and perhaps unfortunate for those who forgot them. For the most natural means of shortening the war and, at the same time, of finding a solid foundation and a reliable partner for the future peace consists today, as yesterday, in winning over and mobilizing those Germans who have the same enemy as France and England, namely, their present rulers. To be counted in millions, they are in fact scarcely less numerous than the loyal Germans. And their ruling political passion exactly coincides with the aim of the civilized powers; which is the overthrow and chastisement of Hitler and the Nazis at almost any price. Germany today is a country split from top to bottom, and split by the very question around which the war is being waged. This is, it seems to me, a piece of luck for England and France without parallel in history, an unusual piece of luck, even though we admit that the disloyal section of the German people at the moment is not only helpless under the heel of its ruthless oppressors, but unorganized, dispirited, and often in despair. It is, nevertheless, worth some mental effort to discover how to improve the situation, which is perhaps all the more possible since the Allies bear some responsibility for its development. For from 1933 to 1938 little was done by the Western Powers that did not contribute to the discouragement of anti–Nazi Germans. Though we speak without reproach, it would be well to remember this before dismissing a vast, temporarily paralyzed portion of the German nation with an impatient shrug of the shoulders. This danger threatens today.

It is a danger, for every mistaken estimate of the mass-psychological facts concerning the enemy is a danger. Just such an error was the constant expectation, especially in left circles, of a spontaneous revolution and Hitler's removal by disloyal Germans. Nothing justified this hope. People would be just as wrong if, today in their disappointment, they were to assert that there are no disloyal Germans at all, and that it would be better to act on the assumption that all Germans are Nazis or at least their loyal followers. That may sound "healthily pessimistic" and convincing, but it is altogether wrong. There are Germans who are wholeheartedly disloyal and hostile to

Hitler and the Nazis—vast masses of them. Between the two extremes of imminent revolt and loyal devotion there lies a wide field. It would be instructive to mark exactly the position—an uncomfortable and besieged entrenchment—occupied by some fifteen to twenty million disloyal Germans, who are the potential allies of England and France.

Anyone who has followed the author thus far will not suspect him of dispensing sedatives. He is not one of those who represent the Nazis as a superficial phenomenon with no hold on the German nation; nor does he pretend that the "true Germany" is a boundlessly pacific, humanitarian, liberal, anti–Nazi society that would never have put the rudder into Hitler's hands if only the Treaty of Versailles had been milder and claims to reparations waived sooner; nor that it would immediately overthrow him if only invited to do so with a few touching words. In no detail have I minimized or slurred over the magnitude of the Nazi danger and the firmness of their grip on the mass soul of Germany. Hence I may perhaps expect a little belief if I paint the other side of the picture. This is an undertaking that assumes a little credence on the part of the reader, for it is difficult to produce proofs. It is in the nature of things that this side of the picture is not overtly discussible in Germany. An adherent of the Nazis can freely and openly avow his sympathies; but an opponent does best to hold his tongue or maintain the contrary of his convictions. It is, therefore, not surprising that tourists and even official visitors from abroad scarcely notice the existence of disloyal Germany.

But anyone who has lived long in Hitler's Germany and is familiar with the people cannot fail to notice the uncanny twilight quality that life, political as well as private, has acquired through the existence—or rather dual existence—of these millions of disloyal people whose lives run against the stream. He must have noticed something of the hundred thousand little circles, anxiously kept airtight, from which Nazism and the Nazis are excluded and into which one steps as into a strange land, hardly ever without having first, so to speak, uttered a password. He must now and then have been appalled at the immense glowing mass of grief and hatred that smolders restlessly beneath the surface. If he is an attentive observer, he must have noticed one or another of the tiny but strangely numerous rifts in which the terrifying power machine abounds; the regular and dependable leakages of secret information; the remarkably frequent anonymous warnings that people receive before their arrest; the countless smuggling routes through and out of the country—for news, money, and men. He must have had one of those tiny but indescribably illuminating searchlight experiences: such, for instance, as hearing this remark from a conservative highly-placed officer: "The only thing that can save us is military defeat." (It must not be thought that all German officers are of this opinion.) In a word, he must have noticed that Germany at the moment is leading a double life; that, by the side of the excessively familiar, crudely placarded Germany of swastika flags, uniforms and marching columns, there is yet another, very different, secret Germany, a shadow Germany, intangible but omnipresent.

Germany today is like a palimpsest or a picture painted over; if one removes the visible surface patiently and cautiously—above all, cautiously—quite another writing, quite another picture appears beneath, damaged perhaps by the overlay and also perhaps by its removal, but in itself complete, coherent, and organic. This is a very new phenomenon when one thinks of the epoch before 1914 and remembers how deeply ingrained in the German mind was loyalty to the Reich; how Germans then almost completely forgot that they had once been something other than a predatory and an ostentatious parvenu Great Power. On the other hand, what now appears to be happening dates back to ancient, almost venerably ancient times; growing visible are the features of pre–Bismarckian and even pre–Napoleonic Germany. That Germany had willingly allowed itself to be absorbed, to its peril, by the Kaiser's Reich. Today that oldest and, I believe, most vital Germany is clearly breaking away from the Nazis by whom the Kaiser's Reich, in its turn, had allowed itself to be swallowed. It forms an immense resistant block. This is an historical development of the first magnitude, although it occurs as invisibly and provides as little "news" as the imperceptible separation and crystallization of the Nazi spirit under the Weimar Republic; which, in its way, also acted as a solvent like the Nazi Reich. Indeed, it is distressing that these vast processes of mass psychological chemistry are never recognized nowadays until it is too late.

However, there were some who perceived what was afoot. The Gestapo. As far back as 1937, Himmler declared in a confidential talk with high Reichswehr officers that, in the event of a war, he would have to occupy the "internal front," which would be just as dangerous as the external land, air, and sea fronts; and that the SS Black Guards would have to man this internal front, so that they would not be available as reinforcements on the external fronts. The number of trained soldiers that Himmler considered necessary for the home front at the time was 250,000. (To dot the *i* of this remarkable story, the stenographic report of these confessions that were uttered in the strictest confidence before a small group was three days later in the hands of an emigrant German committee in Prague.)

That was in the autumn of 1937, four years after the removal of the last remnants of organized political opposition in Germany. Since then the SS have been continually strengthened; the concentration camps increased in number and enlarged; the treatment of prisoners grown considerably worse, the arts of espionage and denunciation developed and refined, the watch over all "National Comrades" become closer (for example, by the introduction, since the beginning of 1938, of wardens of the Nazi Party to inspect every single house); the arrest of obscure private persons "on suspicion" become more frequent; in short there rages beneath the surface in Germany a noiseless and secret war, a war against a jack-in-the-box opponent who needs stronger measures of repression every day. In the grotesque and—even for their own adherents— exaggerated brutality of threatening the death penalty for ludicrously trifling offenses, in the increasing nerve-stricken raids and arrests we may trace a certain despair, the despair of people who have to deal with an unusually intangible, impregnable, invisible enemy—an enemy who stands up again and again just when one thinks he has been struck down.

This enemy is not the wretched, hunted remnant of the former communist, socialist, or democratic party cells. It must be a new, uncannily tenacious enemy, who is not on the decline, but on the increase. It is not the discredited, discomfited political groups of yesterday. Nor is it a definite, labelled, new political doctrine or movement; for such a thing is nowhere to be seen. It is the disloyal population. It is the spirit, quite new to Germany, of a silent, dangerous, malignant, snarling disloyalty toward the State and Authority; a deaf ear and utter indifference toward all "national" slogans, a menacing, waiting hatred which, denied in the face of the Nazi investigator, instantly reasserts itself behind his back; a hatred that is not yet clear as to its own foundations, that does not yet know whither it will lead, but that it is very much there; that is born anew every day and is strengthened and deepened by every new tightening of oppression's screw. This disloyalty and this hate have so far found shape in no political doctrine and organization. That is their weakness but also their strength. It makes them, for the time being, incapable of action, but also remarkably invulnerable. How can one convict a man of political untrustworthiness who has only just begun to notice, with a feeling of slight dizziness and startled terror, that he secretly rejoices at every military reverse of the Fatherland and is profoundly dejected at every news of victory. There are millions of such men. And, contrary to the precarious loyalty of the loyal who need eternal self-deluding and self-blinding, who are rent by conflict and in danger of suddenly turning disloyal, the disloyalty of the anti–Nazis tends to clarify, deepen, and solidify. With sufficient "healthy pessimism," we have reckoned that the mass of the loyal population today has still a small numerical majority over the disloyal; roughly 40 against 35 percent. But we have no doubts which is the growing and which the dwindling side.

The spirit of treason spreads through all ranks and classes, like evenly distributed seed, whose concentrations here and there cannot be located with great exactitude. However, it is obviously more thinly sown among the petty bourgeoisie than elsewhere. We must perhaps look for it chiefly among the people who, from the beginning, were anti–Nazi and who, as late as March 5, 1933, voted against the Nazis; that is, principally among the formerly organized workers, orthodox Catholics, and certain circles of the upper middle class in the large towns. But we must make three important qualifications, which alter the whole picture.

Firstly, the Nazis gathered their last great harvest—in 1933—from among those people whose ears till then had been securely plugged against Nazi propaganda by means of certain equally violent counter-doctrines; especially among the younger workers who had formerly been Communists or extreme Socialists, and who were more or less temperamentally akin to the Nazis. In fact, no anti–Nazi section of the population has been so successfully nazified in the Third Reich as the former Communists. This is no surprise, considering the deep affinity between the instincts attracted by Communism and Nazism. But Hitler found loyal adherents, if not new Nazis, also among the extensive ranks of patriotic and success-worshipping bourgeois who until the last moment "did not believe in the Nazis," but were won over during the years of their domination and triumph.

Secondly, however, during those years, many people became disloyal who, in March 1933, had voted either for the Nazis as their faithful hangers-on or as German–National sympathizers. They include countless disenchanted, deceived, and embittered people who were as much dupes of the Nazis as later many statesmen and intellectuals throughout the world, whose disappointment has made their hatred all the more intense. Indeed, many of these people have since subjected themselves to drastic self-inquiry and, having seen the consequences of their earlier convictions, have revised them. It is this exceedingly numerous group of people who most clearly reveal the function of Nazidom as a social solvent. In the Kaiser's empire, they were patriots and Reich nationalists. Later, they opposed the "sloppy" Republic. It was "not the thing," scarcely a faithful incarnation of the Imperial idea. But now the Nazis have shown them what "the right thing" looks like, what is the logical culmination of the inherent idea and law of the German Reich. And today these people, who between 1870 and 1918 would never have dreamed of being bad patriots or bad citizens, have often reached the stage of telling the whole German Reich, *Führer und Volk,* to go to the devil if only by that means a little decency, humanity, and culture might return to Germany. Of course, there are also others who, "in spite of everything," are still loyal and, with a sigh, consider that these virtues should be included among the sacrifices to "Germany." However, the number of those whom Hitler has driven to disloyalty is very considerable.

Thirdly—this is the most important reservation—it would be very mistaken to think that those who, from the beginning, have been and never ceased to be anti–Nazi, have maintained their political opinions and principles unchanged throughout these years. In the country today there are infinitesimally few Communists, Social Democrats, Democrats, German–Nationals, or members of the Catholic Center. Political doctrines in Germany have grown threadbare during the last decade as never before. Particularly those who have given proof of their unwavering hatred of the Nazis have often felt the necessity of throwing overboard in bulk their opinions, political philosophies, cherished phrases, and catchwords, if they did not wish to be spiritually disarmed by the Nazis. Many discovered later that they were opposed to the Nazis not because they were, for example, "no true Socialists" or "too extreme Socialist," but because of a deep instinctive yearning for decency, honor, civilization, and the true values of life.

Today, when one recalls political polemics in Germany before 1933—perhaps in reading the old newspaper leading articles—one is astonished at the superficiality of the objections with which the opponents of the Nazis contented themselves. The Nazis have meanwhile performed deeds before which the oracular dictums of the Marxists, the "realist" subtleties of the middle class parties, and the phrase making of the nationalists appear alike comical and meaningless. But it is these deeds, and the horror aroused by them, that have produced reactions from deeper sources than those which supplied all the logical and emotional objections to Nazism in the years 1930 to 1933. It is safe to say that today the disloyal Germans, in spite of their lack of a program, are in many ways more politically mature than they were seven years ago, and than their fathers and grandfathers had ever been. Foreigners are often surprised by the quiet disdain with which such Germans, in all their misery and oppression, look down on many political doctrines and opinions that are gravely and eagerly discussed by clever men in free countries. It is felt, perhaps, that such disdain ill becomes them. For all that, it is understandable. These men have been through purgatory. They know many things unknown to others, to happier men. They know what is consumed in purgatory and what withstands its flames. Once their vague feelings solidify to political convictions, they will be simpler than most of today's fashionable political doctrines; simpler and far more real.

Meanwhile, however, I owe the reader an answer to the question which all this time has undoubtedly been on the tip of his tongue: If there are so many disloyal Germans, why don't we see them? Why are they silent? Why is their presence not felt? How is it that terror runs its course unhindered and unchecked? Why do not these disloyal Germans prevent all that happens, perhaps against their will, yet in their name? Where are the acts of sabotage? Where is the revolution against the Nazi regime?

As long as this question is not satisfactorily answered, an inherent doubt will linger as to whether there are any disloyal Germans; or, if they really exist, whether anything can be done with them?

Without a doubt, the question is justified. The disloyal Germans have not yet cast their weight into the political scale. The regime meets with remarkably little open opposition; acts of sabotage do not take place on any considerable scale. When German emigrants talk of a revolution in Germany as of something immediately impending, they are confusing wishful thought with reality. Continual instances of individual martyrdom may be found in Germany (some like the cases of André and Niemoller are famous; many others take place almost daily in the darkness of the most complete anonymity); numerous but inconspicuous individual acts of minor sabotage; and a remarkably tenacious passive resistance in the private sphere, where people, often at great risk, try to defend and preserve their sense of decency against the totalitarian claims of the Nazi State. Thus, for example, during the great pogrom of November 1938, the newspapers reported instances of Jews being saved by their "Aryan" friends who concealed them in their cars and drove them around the streets all day, revealing the striking fact that many Jewish–"Aryan" friendships have been preserved intact. It is nevertheless true that there is at the moment no active revolutionary mass opposition to the Nazis.

There are three reasons for this. The first is purely a matter of power politics: the enormously powerful and apparently unassailable position of the regime. The second is psychological: the unrevolutionary mentality of the disloyal Germans. The third is a question of political ideas: the unfortunate ideological muddle that has reigned in Europe during the last seven years, and the lack of new, inspiring political slogans.

Each of these needs closer examination, which will help us at the same time to form a clearer picture of these disloyal Germans and tell us what can and must happen if they are to be used as an active political factor, which admittedly they are not at present.

Those few people who have concerned themselves with the question why widespread opposition has not yet produced a revolution in Germany, usually conclude with a pessimistic shrug of the shoulders and the hypothesis that the anti–Nazi Germans are presumably cowards. Typical of this view is the comment of the American journalist Villard, who toured Germany for a few weeks shortly after the outbreak of war. When half a dozen people had asked him, one after the other, "What can I do as a single individual?" he began, he writes, to ask himself whether personal courage and capacity for martyrdom were not more scarce in Germany than elsewhere. It is understandable that one should ask oneself this question, but it is not right to leave it unanswered. People would do well to remember that whatever may be said of the Germans, cowardice is not one of their prominent national faults. Another consideration occurs in this connection. The same soldiers who behave in a dastardly manner in a badly led, beaten, discouraged army, often a short time later fight like devils if they are given new leaders, new aims, and new self-confidence. Hitherto, no one has bothered about the disloyal Germans: and they need encouragement. They have a series of frightful blows behind them. More than once they have been deserted by their trusted leaders. And they have an immensely difficult and disheartening task before them, one that is often underestimated by the Western democracies.

It is very easy, from the high horse of assured and guaranteed civic rights, to reproach these Germans with cowardice when they do not lay their heads on the block for their political convictions with the same unconcern with which other people throw a piece of paper into the ballot box. It may be answered that the challenge to these political convictions, and to all human and moral instincts, is far stronger in Germany than in any free country. But always and everywhere martyrdom without any concrete prospect of success, only to salve one's conscience, is only to be expected from a few specially heroic individuals; and this martyrdom occurs daily in Germany, behind the closed doors of the special courts, in the execution yards of the prisons, and in the cellars of the concentration camps. To resist the oppressor at the risk of their lives, the *masses* can only be won over when there exist plan, method, and a reasonable prospect of success. It is hardly too much to say that hundreds of thousands in Germany daily rack their brains in the vain search for such a plan. The question "What can I do?" may in many cases have had a far more urgent ring than Mr. Villard heard in it.

Those who wonder at the delay in the coming of the revolution against the Nazis very often overlook the fact that the Nazi regime has discovered new means of oppression, to combat which new revolutionary methods must be found. One may say the Nazi regime is, to a large extent, a machine specially designed to render revolutions impossible. As far as the wielding and safeguarding of power are concerned, the Nazi leaders combine instinct with precision and science. They have carefully studied the methods of past revolutions and have cut off all known possibilities of danger.

Two kinds of states, in recent European history, have proved "apt for revolution": feudal monarchies without deep-rooted popularity, and democracies without reliable armies. Against the former were organized the so-called classical revolutions, the rising, of the masses under the slogan of liberty; those of 1789, 1830, 1848, in Russia in March 1917, and in Spain in 1931 among others. (The revolts of oppressed nationalities against foreign domination follow, with slight deviations, the same plan of action, because the oppression is also similar.) Against democracies without military support either the direct military coup is employed—the Spanish and South American method—or a semi-military political party is smuggled into the civil party system, with the ensuing march on the capital, and the Army as a benevolent neutral onlooker. This is the most modern revolutionary method. Its classical example is Mussolini's march on Rome in 1922. The Bolshevik revolution in November 1917, and the Nazi revolution of March 1933 are variations of this. Against the political systems that later grew out of these revolutions, no successful technique of revolutionary overthrow has yet been conceived: neither in Germany nor in Russia and Italy.

When asked how the Nazi system holds the resisting portion of the population in subjection one thinks first of the Gestapo. To do this, however, is to overlook the decisive point. The Metternich states and Tsarist Russia had first-class secret police systems that yielded nothing to the Gestapo. Nevertheless, the revolutions of 1848, 1905, and 1917 took place and were largely successful. It is not too much to say that with the Gestapo alone the Nazis would not have lasted four weeks—and no longer without the Gestapo. But the Gestapo is only the last line of defense. Essential to the regime is the combination of police oppression, carried to an extreme, together with certain distorted elements of democracy. It is wrong to regard the Nazi State as a pure despotism. *Its power lies in its mixture of despotism and anarchy.* Metternich *plus* Gymnastic Daddy Jahn; secret police *plus* demagogy; terror *plus* propaganda;

organization *plus* prescribed disorder; not compulsory obedience but compulsory complicity; not compulsory loyalty but compulsory enthusiasm; this is the diet of poison against which no antidote has yet been found.

Claiming the advanced positions in front of the Gestapo and the other armed organizations are the millions of real Nazis: a volunteer army of enthusiastic spies and controllers, who, moreover, are able at any moment to stage an outward spectacle of popularity. In front of them are the entrenchments, under cover of propaganda, of the mass of the loyal population.

The disloyal, already handicapped by the feeling of being in the minority, find themselves opposed by these three lines of defense. They are, in addition, disorganized and deprived of any possibility of collaboration with one another, and enclosed, moreover, in compulsory organizations together with the Nazis and the loyal.

The organizations of compulsion and control—every German in Germany who wishes to earn his living, or even pursue a hobby, must belong to two or three of them—might be called the system's outermost line of defense. But since 1938 yet another line has been set up even beyond. This is the system of the Nazi house wardens appointed to watch every single house. They periodically pay surprise visits to all the occupants, question them as to politics, and keep them under constant observation.

It is obvious that the classical revolutionary recipe will not serve in such a situation, against an enemy thus entrenched. It will not be a matter of storming the Bastille, of barricades, or the general strike. The first prerequisite of mass revolution—or, what amounts to almost the same thing, organized mass sabotage—is wanting; namely, the possibility of forming any kind of organization. Every individual is completely isolated and completely under observation. The only known revolutionary method that is not stopped at its source is that of the Spanish military *pronunciamento*. Millions of Germans have hoped for this. Many still hope against hope. But the Army is for the present in the thrall of the "Germany" slogan. It is loyal as a whole; the few disloyal groups in it barely count. Moreover, the German Army lacks any tradition or experience of the coup d'état. Apparently even Spain taught nothing.

The pressing, anxious, ever-recurrent question remains: "What can I, as a single individual, do?" The individual is left with the pos-

sibility of deliberate martyrdom, of irrepressible outbursts, of min-
iature revolutions against the block warden, cell warden, or the
works leader, which result in long years of imprisonment. These
occur day in and day out. Above all, there remains a tenacious
clinging to what is still just possible, to the last line of resistance in
private life, to the small anti–Nazi closed circle of friends. That,
too, is by no means without danger. It is very hard for foreigners to
understand that heroism, though of a quiet and unassuming kind,
is needed for certain trifling things which still happen in Germany
a million times every day, such as the avoidance of the Hitler salute;
helping Jewish friends; maintaining relations with the loyal clergy-
man; spreading "information"; sabotage in the tiny measure in
which it can be individually committed. It is senseless triumphantly
to herald, as certain emigrants are incorrigibly wont to do, the practical "results" that are attainable within this restricted framework
as portents of the storm of the approaching revolution. But it is just
as mistaken to overlook the immense mass preparedness and stored
energy that lies behind these apparently insignificant symptoms. It
is a passive readiness; it needs release. If the release does not come—
and it can only come from without—this force remains unused and
without effect. But if it comes, it may occasion some pleasant surprises.

There is still another factor to be mentioned that has fallen to
the lot of the Nazis, a gratuitous gift to their immensely powerful
machinery of oppression: the extent, for long insufficiently realized,
to which the development of modern technique favors the ruler
against the ruled. The more destructive and irresistible weapons become, the greater is the superiority of the armed over the unarmed.
The Bastille could not be stormed with success in the age of airplane
and tear gas. Rifle-armed citizen militia have no longer any chance
against motorized police troops; to build barricades is vain labor
against a government that commands tanks. And it is not only the
development of arms that favors those in power against revolution,
the State against the individual; the modern technical development
and the elaborate organization that it engenders, work in the same
direction. Transport has made countries small and easily super-
vised. How full they were a hundred years ago of hiding places!
How every power then found its natural limits! Today there is no
hole or corner for the rebel. Even the spirit, even thought that pene-

trates walls like the wind—since it is linked to the mass propagation of news, to radio, film, and Press—has become "manageable." How long will it be before every house has its built-in microphone, before every private word is audible as is every telephone conversation today? The Kingdom of the Ant is at hand. It is perhaps no accident that countries like Germany and Russia have exalted technique to the rank of state religion. On the contrary, it is this very development of modern technique that makes the preservation of political freedom a more momentous need for humanity than it has ever been before. But that takes us away from our present theme.

Enough has been said to prove that Nazi political power is strongly entrenched. Alone it explains the delay in active mass resistance, in spite of widespread hostility; and anyone who reproaches disloyal Germans with cowardice must first discover a revolutionary recipe that promises success under the circumstances. As things are, it seems sufficiently clear from the external division of power alone that the section of the nation inimical to the Nazis sees no possibility of overthrowing them from within, but are content to preserve for themselves, as far as possible, those standards of morality and civilization that Hitler wishes to destroy; and that they are more inclined to emigration than revolution.

However, it is not my task to write an apology on behalf of the anti–Nazi Germans, but to present a psychological picture of them. Therefore, accuracy and completeness exact the admission that certain traits in the mentality of the disloyal Germans contribute to their passive attitude no less than external circumstances. The existing balance of power—without outside interference—would certainly prevent a successful revolution, even if the internal German opponents of the Nazis were aglow with revolutionary ardor. But actually they are not thus afire. The revolution would perhaps not take place even if the regime had not taken such drastic precautions. There is no lack of hatred against the regime, or of desire to see it ousted. But, if I am not altogether mistaken, the Germans would rather *see* it overthrown than themselves overthrow it by means of a revolution. In order to contrive one, they would have to offer some slight violence to their innate temperament and deepest feelings; after all, they are very bad revolutionaries and saboteurs, and that, at least in my eyes, not solely out of discreditable motives.

I must here combat the theory which, though propagated in utter good faith by adherents of the German opposition parties and emigrants, is, nevertheless, mistaken; that there is "another Germany" that is democratic and revolutionary; a Germany of *liberté, fraternité, égalité:* a Germany that is ready to create and lead a democratic Great Power. For years I have searched for the germ cells of this Germany, and I venture to assert that none exists. There is, of course, "another Germany" than that of the Nazis; a Germany distinguished by human universality, untamed individualism, cleverness in small things, openmindedness on large issues, and a deep, unconquerable, distrustful aversion for politics and politicians. It is this Germany that has today become disloyal and hates the Nazis. It is this and, in my opinion, *only* this Germany which adds to the European concert a unique and dignified voice, and with which one can live at peace. It is this Germany that should be helped to return to itself and to the political form to which it is adapted. Alongside of this Germany there is the "Reich" of the Hohenzollerns and the Nazis; there is no third Germany. To wish to make a democratic Great Power out of Germany is to look for apples on a rosebush. There are none. There never will be.

Let him who doubts consider the history of the Weimar Republic. Though it had astounding successes during the short period of its existence, it was on the whole a failure. Though the economic situation under the Republic was far better than could be expected after a lost war; though the Germans step by step improved their international status; though they enjoyed liberties as never before, they secretly felt unhappy and badly governed. The opposition grew steadily and the republicans themselves yearned for abdication and release. We know today that the two most important "defenders of the Republic," Stresemann and Brüning, were secretly steering toward the restoration of the Monarchy—to forestall worse. And the end of the Republic, the resignation and disappearance, without struggle and almost with relief, of the legitimate Prussian government before Papen's coup d'état bears all the marks of suicide. Even today one of the trump cards of the Nazis is the idea very wisely conserved and put about that, after their fall and the lost war, there might be a new version of the Weimar Republic.

Let us next look at the so-called supporters of German democracy and republicanism, chiefly, that is, the workers and the bourgeois of the large towns. What was the character of the organizations they created when they were able to do so? Democratic? Jacobin? By no means. The old trade unions and the old Social Democratic Party—to say nothing of the Communist Party—were rigidly disciplined, authoritarian, organizations of almost bureaucrat-ridden nature. As to those "democratic" organizations of the left-wing bourgeoisie, from the Radical Union to the German State Party, they simply did not function. Their history is one of continual schism, dissolution, and reconstruction, and of a progressive decline of political influence. Those who believe in the creation of a revolutionary democracy should produce evidence of a single democratic germ cell in Germany. And if they think that it can come about without any such cell, they should explain how a republic is to function without republicans, a democracy without democrats, particularly in a country where the Nazi spirit may still survive underground.

We are here again faced with a situation, the recognition of which is absolutely indispensable to an elementary understanding of German realities and possibilities. The disloyal, anti–Nazi, "other" Germans are no less German than the loyal. They share jointly the whole of German history and the experience, sunk in the subconscious, that it has left behind. They have the same blood, the same temperament, the same spiritual foundations. It is nonsense to represent them as oppressed Englishmen or Frenchmen in Germany. They represent the superior potentialities of the German character, but of none other, let us emphasize, than the German character. Like all other Germans, they have neither talent nor inclination for revolution, democratic self-government, or politics in general. Like all other Germans, they tend to the belief that politics are unavoidably bad and make people bad. Like all other Germans, they desire freedom within the State, not freedom to oppose the State. Like all other Germans, their political ideal is not to govern themselves but to be well governed. What differentiaties them from other Germans is that this ideal with them has been kept pure—or has been purified by the horrible warning example of the Nazis; that they do not, or do no longer, confuse "being well governed" with "being brutally ordered about"; that when politics and amorality go together they would rather renounce politics than morality and, above all, are not, or are no longer, ready to sacrifice the super-political values of life that they share in common with other Europeans to imperialist ambition.

Here runs the thick dividing line between loyal and disloyal. The loyal still feel an obligation to sacrifice to the Reich Idea their personal comfort, their personal decency and—the mission and spirit of Germany; the disloyal place one or another of these values above the Imperial Idea; and, indeed, for the vast majority of them it is the second of these values, decency. Personal privations and discomforts such as bad food, high prices, covert inflation, or longer working hours provoke very few Germans to disloyalty. If workers in conversation mention these things, it is not because they would under no circumstances be personally prepared to work for ten or twelve hours a day; but rather out of a certain class-conscious esprit de corps that makes a point of honor of the eight-hour day and similar principles. Indeed, the personal capacity for sacrifice of the Germans, if they have really set their heart on some aim, is almost unlimited. If the Nazi regime had nothing to be said against it but hunger and privation, it might have the Germans behind it almost to a man. On the other hand, the realization of Germany's real mission has been overshadowed by a hundred years of "longing for the Reich" and propaganda for the Reich, so that only a few independent and advanced minds are at the present time anti–Nazi out of patriotism. Most anti–Nazis hate Hitler out of fidelity to one of the nonpolitical values against which he wages a war of annihilation, be it religion, justice, humanity, freedom of conscience, or culture; while many—and they are not the worst—are his enemies out of loyalty to someone near who is persecuted by the Nazis or even out of downright instinctive decency.

But they do not thereby become revolutionaries. On the contrary. To most disloyal Germans, whether they are aware of it or not, the idea of the Nazis being overthrown by a revolution from, so to speak, below, is slightly alarming. Does one revolt against criminals? Is it becoming to stage a spectacle in which the Nazis play the part of the defenders of order and their judges that of rioters and rebels. Does one need revolutionary tribunals and dubious courts martial to send thieves and murderers to their punishment? This rather deep rooted sentiment restrains most German enemies of the Nazis, just as it makes them shrink from the idea of punishing the Nazis with assassination. Hitler must not be murdered; he must be condemned and hanged as he merits—that is the feeling. And so with all the others. They must not be removed in one way or another. They must get their deserts. It is a remarkable fact that, despite all their brutalities, the Nazis are, in many cases, not re-garded by their victims as oppressors who must be shaken off, but as naughty boys run wild who must be restored to reason. They do not seem a sufficiently legitimate infliction to merit being disposed of by a revolution. Quite apart from the questionable legality of their seizure of power, they are obviously usurpers, obviously ille-gitimate holders of power. One cannot help waiting for the real au-thority whose role it is to return and administer justice. Such an authority—not a revolutionary court—would gratify the German sense of order. And then at last one could quietly go back to one's life and work. . . .

This is another reason why most Germans who are disloyal shrink from revolution. They want, once the Nazis have been got rid of, to get back as quickly as possible to their life and their work, so long interrupted by the Nazis. They feel they have been disturbed long enough. If, they fear, they were to have a revolution, they would never succeed in restoring the old order of things. Instead of that they would—and at this thought they have an uncomfortable feeling in the pit of the stomach—have to take over the German Reich and once again play at running a republic. For that they are not in the least prepared. That way would lead still deeper into the hated region of politics. What they want is to preserve against bet-ter days, and if possible intact, their conscience, their soul, and a handful of spiritual values. For these things, if directly attacked, they are ready to fight with some resolution. They are even ready to leave the country as beggars if this struggle can no longer be maintained. They are ready to join with enthusiasm the colors of any legitimate authority that promises to free them from the Nazis. But they are most hesitant when it comes to organizing revolution and taking their political fate into their own hands.

If we examine this attitude—an attitude without particular merit but certainly not cowardly and dishonorable—we find a striking parallel. Transferred from the individual to the political sphere, it is identical with the conduct of the small neutral states in this war. They also feel terrorized and threatened by the Nazis. They also fer-vently pray for their removal and their punishment. Yet they, too, do not want to undertake the task of removal and punishment themselves, and are reluctant to go to war to bring that about. They are prepared only to defend themselves against direct attack. They, too, want to conserve against better times, and as far as possible undamaged, the good things of civilization for which they stand. In a conflict in which their own fate is being decided, they, too, want to remain passive as long as possible. This, again, is not prompted by cowardice. It would be unjust and ridiculous to reproach states like Holland and Belgium with cowardice—just as it is unjust and ridiculous to reproach anti–Nazi Germans, who for conscience' sake are tortured in concentration camps, with cowardice. Common to both cases in the "small-state mentality": the feeling in both cases of not being able to assume, beyond one's own limited capacity, large-scale political responsibilities. Whether they know it or not (in most cases they may not), disloyal Germans show that they are chips off the block out of which the highly civilized European small states are hewn.

It is important to recognize this. Particularly all in Germany that is dignified, decent, and courageous, that has withstood the Nazi ordeal, is politically destined, so to speak, for the status of small state. And this fact acquires relief and full significance if one considers in contrast the incredibly childish irresponsibility that has been, and remains, the mark of that Great Power, the German Reich, throughout its eighty years of history, right up to its menacing, grotesque overreaching in Nazism. It is impossible to say that the Germans, in all these eighty years, have shown any capacity to conduct themselves as a responsible Great Power, whether during the authoritarian Kaiser's Reich, the democratic Republic, or the present anarchic despotism. In Europe, nothing but mischief, unrest, and misfortune were generated by the deplorable contraption that has clearly proved too much for its designers, so many of whose heads have been turned by it. As far as Germany is concerned, the German Reich has brought her nothing but spiritual degeneration and decay. The question of its continued existence is now ripe for discussion. There are reasons, perhaps, for giving it yet one more chance. They would have to be weighty.

Meanwhile, back to the disloyal. Their lack of talent and preparation for revolutionary initiative certainly does not signify that they are resolved to fold their hands and sit still while history wends its way. They would in certain circumstances fight bravely and bitterly for their liberation. But, like all Germans in similar cases, they wait for a leader. There must be someone who assumes responsibility, who "can do it," who commands. Nothing happens by itself in Germany.

And here begins the tragedy of these Germans, a real tragedy for which the world has shown neither interest nor understanding, although it touches it so closely. It is the tragedy of a fine body of men, abandoned again and again without leadership or a leader. At the decisive last moment, when there was still a chance of their effectively combating the Nazis, the anti–Nazi Germans have been betrayed and forsaken by their chosen and trusted leaders. Since then they have clutched at every straw, rushed in masses to every party that promised anything in the form of opposition to the Nazis, only to be disappointed each time, discouraged, and finally left in the lurch. They have turned their hopes to the outside world, striven again and again to begin a mass exodus, only to find the civilized nations give signs of terrified refusal. They would rather have Nazis than refugees. These Germans have waited for some sign of approaching relief from outside, for some new rallying cry, for a change of the tide that would put an end to the triumphs of their oppressors. It was their lot to experience nothing but a succession of inglorious capitulations and that policy of appeasement which they could only explain as secret collusion with the Nazis. They could not, and cannot, imagine that so deep a misunderstanding of the Nazi mentality could prevail among foreign politicians as, in fact, formed the basis of that well-meaning policy. They have always found themselves being driven by circumstances and urged by sympathizers to do the one thing of which they are incapable and which, moreover, is impossible: a spontaneous revolution from below. The history of the last seven years is for them an unbroken succession of defeats and disappointments; of disillusioned hope and trust. The war finds them exhausted, discouraged, and without faith—and still without an aim and without a watchword.

Let the history of the last seven years, German and European, as it looks to these Germans, pass quickly before your mind's eye. It is a heartrending spectacle.

In a dramatic election struggle in 1932 these Germans had elected Hindenburg on the clear understanding that he was to be dictator and not simply President, and with the explicit mandate to resist Hitler and keep him at bay. The old traitor fulfilled that vow by putting Hitler in power. Even under Hitler, on March 5, 1933, 48 percent of German electors voted for candidates whose public slogan was "War against Hitler" and a further eight percent for those tactical allies of Hitler who promised to keep him in check. All were betrayed. Not three weeks later the Reichstag, thus elected, decreed supreme and unlimited power to Hitler.

But these Germans were not only ready to combat Hitler with the ballot box. Hundreds of thousands of young trained Germans at that time belonged to organizations like the "Black-Red-Gold Reich Banner," the "Iron Front," the "Bavarian Defense Corps," and subjected themselves to military discipline in order, weapon in hand, to repel the Nazis. They found no opportunity. At the decisive moment their leaders absconded. No shots were exchanged. In February and March 1933 everyone awaited civil war with confidence. Half the people were prepared to shed blood rather than submit to a regime concerning which they had no illusions. Instead, they found themselves betrayed, taken by surprise, and disarmed. It was the same brutal blow in the neck at the highest pitch of exertion and preparedness that in September 1938 shattered the fighting morale of the Czech people. Events of this kind are a thousand times more demoralizing than defeat in open battle. It takes a long time to recover from the abyss of such defeatist discouragement.

Nevertheless, the disloyal Germans, in the succeeding years, neglected nothing in which they saw a chance of forming new combinations against the Nazis. They were no longer fastidious and no longer inquired much about aims and ideologies. In the spring and early summer of 1933 there occurred the sudden avalanche-like increase in numbers of the Hugenberg "Battle Echelons" and the Stahlhelm. No need to ask whence came this sudden mass accretion to the formerly not too popular German–Nationalist Party, the last to survive under the Nazis, how it came to pass, or why. It was not their fault that their new leaders, like the old, lost their nerve at the decisive moment and unresistingly accepted capitulation, dissolution, extinction.

Hope turned to the Army. It was known that the Reichswehr did not see eye to eye with the Nazis. Enchanted, men saw weapons glisten in the hands of people whom they credited with honor, decency, and culture, and who, they believed, *must* one day lose patience with the Nazis. In the years of secret rearmament it was particularly the opponents of the Nazis who thronged into the Army. The melancholy outcome of this erring speculation is known, though perhaps not yet in full detail. Notorious is Hitler's sneering remark: "All those who would like to fight us now serve us—in the Reichswehr." Perhaps there was here and there among the higher Reichswehr leaders a vague, not fully earnest, readiness for revolution, an attitude of mind somewhat like Schiller's Wallenstein. It certainly led to nothing in the end. Loyalty to the Reich was too strong. The misconception of patriotism on which the Nazis were able to gamble was too deeply ingrained. It is today still difficult to say what chiefly contributed to the failure of the Reichswehr in the internal German crisis of 1934—want of insight, want of determination, or that infamous "craft" which Blomberg has proclaimed as the chief virtue of the contemporary German officer. In any case, the Reichswehr and the Reichswehr spirit finally proved to be nothing more than one of the means by which the anti–Nazi forces were finally entrapped into the service of the Nazis.

The last, already hopeless, attempt to find leadership somewhere was the sudden mass growth of the protesting Protestant Church in the years 1936–37. However innocent and unpolitical the actual kernel of the Confessional Church Movement, however defensive in method and religious in purpose, there is no doubt that the *masses* in the first six months of 1937, at the peak of the movement, suddenly thronged the long-deserted churches and the spaces around them and sang Luther's hymn *"Ein feste Burg"* because they scented possibilities of struggle and resistance against the Nazis, and for no other reason. One realizes the misunderstanding under which they labored, more honorable at least than that of the Reichswehr. The leaders of the Confessional Church wanted no political struggle. They wanted the salvation of their souls and the martyr's crown, for which they had not long to wait. The crowds who rushed to them stayed out in the cold, waiting, forsaken as before.

Since then nothing has happened in Germany that could again set in motion these dumb, waiting masses.

But in any case this forgotten host, after the great betrayal of the spring of 1933, would perhaps not again have staked high hopes on new political and semi-political organizations inside Germany. Almost from the beginning they looked for rescue and liberation outside the borders of the Reich, and at first with a certain quiet confidence. It is typical of these Germans that it never occurs to them that the outbreak of barbarism in the heart of Europe would be regarded by European Powers as an "internal affair of the German Reich." In their attitude we see intact, suddenly resurrected, the collective European sentiment of pre–Reich Germany. They took for granted that the European Great Powers would watch over the basic values of European culture; they took even more for granted the assertion of the instinct of self-preservation in England and France toward a policy of rearmament and war that was scarcely disguised from the start. Finally, they took for granted— their most modest hope—the readiness of Europe to give them asylum from persecution, a place to think, teach, and build anew.

One knows how bitterly they have been disappointed for years in every single one of these hopes. Why repeat, in detail, the horrible history of these years, recall the obsequious bows to gangsters, the supine acceptance of new and outrageous affronts? October 13, 1933, July 25, 1934, March 16, 1935, March 7, 1936, May 30, 1937, March 11, 1938—every single date a slap in the face to Europe. Is it incomprehensible that German Europeans lost hope and confidence? They began to doubt their values. Superstitious fear, bewitchment, and a feeling that all the rules of life were abolished overcame them. Western civilization began to look senile, old, and decayed, while the barbarism of Central and Eastern Europe, irresistible and inevitable, seemed to claim the future. And, out of doubt rose despair, when in the autumn of 1938, to the complete bewilderment of all Germans, came Munich and, a little later, the world shut its doors in the face of the fugitive German Jews. Much more must happen than what has happened so far if the moral effect of these two events on Germany is to be undone.

In all the years up to 1939 there was no active opposition to Nazism from Western Europe. But spiritual resistance was also lacking, attempts at a reassessment of values, searches for a new alignment, a new inspiration. The world's problems and topics of discussion were dictated, without opposition, by Hitler. He decreed anti–Semitism, and the docile world discovered the "Jewish question." He attacked Austria, and there was an "Austrian question." Similarly there arose a Spanish, Czech, even a Danzig "question." To make a "question" of Hitler, the Nazis, the German Reich, occurred to no one. Opposition—unacceptable, of course—came only from one quarter, the Bolsheviks. In those years European–minded Germans experienced a physical and spiritual sense of being utterly forsaken and lost, such as no one can realize who has not felt it.

Alone on one occasion something like a breath of wind blew across this suffocating desert; in 1936, at the time of the Popular Front, when during the Spanish Civil War international camps were formed. It was a strange experience to feel the underground reverberations in the German catacombs; the sudden revival of discussion, of hope, even of activity and enterprise. There were at that time not only German Legionaries in Spain, but volunteers, fighting on the other side. And the enemy they wished to encounter was not Franco but Hitler. It would perhaps have turned into a real struggle against Hitler but for "nonintervention," which smothered everything.

Indeed, from a certain point of view the policy of nonintervention must today seem justified; not, however, from the point of view, represented at the time as its basis, that it prevented the war in Europe, for every disloyal German already knew this war was inevitable, and the lesser evil; but from the point of view that it prevented the European War from being waged under false slogans and on false fronts. The Popular Front and the Spanish Civil War represent what is probably the last attempt—its failure is historically justified—to solve the problems of the twentieth century with the formula of the nineteenth, with the formula of "right against left." This formula has lost its meaning. Most of the problems that divided right and left in the nineteenth century have been solved or regulated to mutual satisfaction. In return, right and left have, in the last twenty years, generated and activated new anti-cultural and anti-humanitarian forces which, still opposed to one another in the Europe of the Spanish crisis, in reality belong together and today are found together. The task of the day is to muster, in their turn, the civilizing forces of right and left, not by a temporary compromise but by working out those common basic values of civilization which alone matter today. The front that must be formed for defense against the new danger is not the People's Front but Civilization's Front.

But the political thinking required for this is still in its infancy. It is in danger in all countries of being overlooked in the preoccupation of war while the war itself is in peril of losing its meaning. Nowhere could thinking bring about more radical results than in Germany. The mental readiness for the formation of new fronts perhaps developed further during the years of suffering and brooding among the anti–Nazi section of the German people than anywhere else in Europe. But it has no prospect there of crystallizing into political opinion, into a creed, or a program.

The illegal remnants of the old German parties and the premature layers of a new opposition within Germany are at the moment a hindrance rather than a help in this process of crystallization. Can they be utilized in any way? Let us scrutinize them.

6

The Opposition

Let us, first of all, exclude every possibility of terminological misunderstanding. Under the term "Opposition" we do not include every emotional distaste and hostility, however strong, to the Nazi regime. Of course, one can also use the word in this wider sense and designate as such all the hatred and abhorrence for the Nazi regime stored up in Germany. In this sense the Nazi regime has the strongest, largest, and most irreconcilable opposition of any government in Europe. But when we speak here of the "Opposition" we mean only positive political counterforces with a concrete program of action and a concrete aim; political groups, however small, that contain, at least in the germ, a positive *alternative* to the present regime; people who can give a clear and reasonable answer to the question as to what they will do when the Nazis are overthrown and how they propose to overthrow them; people who have the will—not only the wish—to overthrow them. In this sense the opposition in Germany is dwindling, small, and unready. It cannot be said that they have made any visible advance during the seven years of the Nazi regime. As far as it is possible for man to judge, no practical result within a reasonable space of time can be expected from the Opposition—once more employing the word in its narrow and precise sense—in Germany.

It is impossible to live for a long time in the country without noticing the widespread disloyalty to the regime, the suffering, hatred, and rage, the individual resistance of millions. But it is indeed possible to live there for years without in the least perceiving the existence of the illegal Communists and Social–Democrats, the German Freedom Party, the Black Front, and the other even more microscopic illegal political organizations. All that is occasionally reported outside Germany as to the secret pamphlet propaganda of these bodies, their organization of local strikes and acts of sabotage, is highly exaggerated. Such things do happen, but their radius of influence is so minute that they may almost be ignored in a general survey. It cannot be suggested that these underground activities play an effective part in normal everyday life. Who wishes to find them must search for them, so to speak, with a lantern; and even then they may elude him.

It is necessary clearly to realize this two-sided state of affairs. One must not deduce, as is often done, from the existence of widespread disloyalty, the existence of strong political opposition to the Nazis, or from its nonexistence infer the nonexistence of disloyal mass opinion. Both deductions are wrong to the point of peril. The fact is that the present German Government is undermined as is no other government. All the hatred that has accumulated under it is an explosive material that can blow up the entire State like tinder the moment the spark of a political idea alights upon it. But this spark is wanting. The sparks in existence are so feeble that they are immediately extinguished on venturing into the open air. And let us not forget that while the regime is not too anxious to hinder the accumulation of new explosives, or even to clear away the old, it is all the more zealously on guard to prevent the birth of sparks; to which end it does everything to render political thought impossible and political activity dangerous.

With despair, almost with hopelessness, the regime wrestles with the universal, unorganized, one might almost say unpolitical disloyalty. On the other hand, the struggle of the Gestapo against political opposition already in existence has undeniably been successful. The remnants of what there was in 1933 of organized political forces besides the Nazis are on the defensive or have been driven into hiding and become ineffectual. Indeed, one can say, paradoxical as it sounds, that those political forces and ideas that have been deprived of their machinery of organization have not perhaps been so completely enfeebled as those that still survive in shadow organizations—doing nothing and being nothing but death traps for their members.

None of the former political parties was in any way prepared for illegal existence and for struggle under conditions of illegality; not even the Communists, though they always boasted of this capacity. Even in legal times these parties constituted far less practical political instruments than do parties in Western countries. They were parties with a "world conception"; their wont was far less to engage in practical politics than to give expression to a political philosophy, a general and vague idea of "how things should be." Scarcely any of them, with the possible exception of the Catholic Center, had any clear conceptions and attainable aims; not one— again with the same exception—was a school for politicians who would be ready at any time under given conditions to assume the reins of government. Rather each party (and in this the Nazis are the true heirs and guardians of the old German party spirit) was constituted so as one day to take power alone, in a state governed according to its own ideas and conceptions. As long as this day did not dawn (in secret they came to realize that it never would), they pursued politics with a kind of mental reservation, unwilling to take responsibility and always on the alert to resume as soon as possible the "vacation of opposition," as the German parliamentary expression had it. They were, in fact, less parties than temples, in which Bismarck, Rousseau, or Marx were severally preached.

Adapted to this was the strange German electoral system under which there was no straight fight between two or more candidates with concrete slogans, but, as it were, an empire-wide collecting and counting of party votes. The German voter did not elect a deputy whom he knew, from whom he expected a certain policy and with whom he kept in touch. He elected a "party list," often without so much as knowing the names of the candidates it bore. His choice was not so much a political act as a metaphysical affirmation of Monarchical, Conservative, Catholic, Liberal, Socialist, or Communist doctrine. At the next general election he expected from his party not so much an account of achievements during the preceding four years, but rather a confirmation of their devotion to their political ideas and ultimate aspirations. The political topic of the day was a thing which he preferred high-mindedly to overlook; and the parties themselves, with the word "temporary" in mind, took up the subject with negligence that easily turned to boredom.

Such organizations, if driven into illegality, must cease to be effective political factors. Illegal politics are a serious, fierce, bloody business. History teaches us that illegal political parties, from ancient Greece to modern Russia, know no other political method than terrorism, the "hit and run" of continual assassination, sabotage, and guerilla civil war. Only in this way do they remain effective and dangerous; only in this way do they oblige their oppressors to relax oppression and to legalize them again (of this the classical example is the formation of the Russian Duma after the assassinations of 1905–6); and only in this way do they manage to survive in the eyes of a world already losing interest in them, forgetting them and ceasing to reckon with them, as well as in the eyes of their own members and potential members who, as compensation for the continual mortal danger in which they live, must at least have the consciousness of being themselves also dangerous and able to hit back. To be executed one day solely for the crime of meeting together every Wednesday evening in a back room to read Marx and declaim revolutionary lyrics, is no alluring prospect. This, however, is all that the existing illegal German parties have to offer to their faithful adherents.

These parties labor under the delusion that they can, on a modest scale, play illegally the role they used to play legally; that they can become sects instead of religions. They try, in their illegal position, to "influence" a pathetically small radius with the same means as in the good old parliamentary days; with preaching, enlightenment, and propaganda. At the same time they must use the utmost caution in avoiding discovery and consequent liquidation: a difficult task in these days, for to spread propaganda is to attract attention, when self-preservation demands invisibility. In the seven years of their existence none of the illegal political factions has given signs of having found a way out of this vicious circle.

The case of the illegal parties bears a remarkable resemblance to that of the German armed raider on the high seas today, which, though chased by the superior English fleet, strives to inflict damage on English trade. On the one hand, the first element of self preservation for these ships is to keep out of sight; on the other, the least of those tasks for which they patrol the oceans is just such a sign of life betraying their whereabouts and perhaps delivering them to their superior pursuers. Even when such craft engages in normal warfare, which would correspond to a terrorist guerilla campaign in the case of the illegal parties, it is very hard to find a happy mean between indispensable caution and indispensable daring. The illegal parties, however, wage no such war. They do not act like ships, who at least stake their existence on the capture or sinking of enemy vessels, on the positive harm they can do to the foe. Rather they conduct themselves as if these ships were content, from their little radio stations, to disseminate messages which might perhaps reach a couple of hundred people and make an impression on two or three, but which, in return, reveals their position and seals their fate. In short, the methods of the illegal factions are so senseless and fatuous that even their outpouring of courage and martyrdom can awaken compassion but no admiration.

Those happenings in the backyards of German internal politics in the last seven years are a horrible and heartrending tragedy, but certainly no inspiring and exalting drama of revolution. The Communists, in particular, have paid a terrible blood toll in concentration camps, death cells, and execution yards; in less measure the Social Democrats and the members of the German Freedom Party and the Black Front. Into hundreds, perhaps already into thousands, runs the list of anonymous martyrs of whose life and death there is no mention save, for a single day, a blood-red "proclamation" on the Berlin hoardings: "Condemned to death on such and such a date for high treason by the People's Court of Justice, so-and-so was executed this morning."

What is behind these executions? Assassinations, conspiracy, rioting? By no means. No more than—it cannot be otherwise expressed—a bit of German club life. A couple of typewriters in a back room, a meeting of foremen, the formation of a district or a factory group, formulation of policy for the group wardens, committee meetings with beer and minutes: "Comrade Müller reported on the progress of the meeting of the Comintern in Moscow"; "The meeting thanked the comrade for his valuable information gathered at the risk of his life"; perhaps an issue of hectographed leaflets which have a run of four weeks; occasionally a great "action," such as the distribution of pamphlets urging men "to hold out" in a factory or a block of houses, sending copies of an "Appeal to the German People" to foreign press correspondents, removal of a bust of Hitler here and smashing of a shop window there—and then, one day, arrest, torture, warders, "trial" behind closed doors, judgment, and execution. It is frightful, but this is what active political opposition amounts to in Germany today. There may be variations, but the public hears little of them. The show piece of the illegal political struggle is the little shortwave transmitter which every evening sends out messages from the German Freedom Party and until now has managed to remain undiscovered, though not undisturbed. Few Germans, in fact, have been able to listen in to this transmitter because the "official" jamming is generally successful. But many have heard of it and felt a tiny satisfaction and hope. Nothing more. Hope, however, mostly shrinks when, by accident, the transmitter is actually heard: vague appeals, leading articles from foreign newspapers, a few "disclosures" about the private life of Goebbels or someone else. Can that achieve anything, one asks? Can that change things? Is that worth the lives of a score of brave people? One switches on to London or Strasbourg. . . .

One wonders why none of the illegal groups has chanced upon another, more effective method of combat. Is it want of imagination or instinct? Want of courage it cannot be, for their fruitless undertakings entail an immense foolhardy courage; participation implies almost certain death. The answer is that, under a despotism, there is for proscribed parties only one way of fighting: terrorism. But they all lack the tradition to wage such battle. The dogma of the Marxist parties excludes all forms of terrorism. In certain recognized commentaries on their sacred books it is laboriously proved that assassination is a mistaken, bourgeois-anarchistic method of struggle that leads to nothing; and that only the union of all the workers of the world, etc. Indeed, one searches in vain in the history of the last thirty years for any political murder committed by a Marxist. Against this conviction there is absolutely nothing to be done. The Communists, undoubtedly the most orthodox and dogmatic of political partisans in Europe today, must cease to be Communists before they can bring themselves to fight oppression by terrorism. (Terror from above after the seizure of power is, of course, another matter. That comes under the heading of DICTA-TORSHIP OF THE PROLETARIAT—and is dealt with in another part of the sacred commentaries.)

As to the Social Democrats, whose harsh dogma might be parleyed with, they offer temperamental resistance, as also do the innocuous bourgeois German Freedom Party. The people in Germany who incline to the Social Democratic or Liberal faith are almost always constituted in such a way as to shrink with horror from political murder. And those who tend toward such crime are almost always to be found among the Nazis. The others must first be driven into deeper unplumbed abysses of despair to discover in themselves the capacity for such conduct; a fact which obviously speaks in their favor.

This brings us to a matter that we have already discussed elsewhere in these pages, that political murder is not the appropriate weapon to use against the Nazis, that one should not, so to speak, snatch them from their lawful judges. During these last years despair has grown so great that some of their foes may already be planning assassination. But it is in these same last years that events have followed such a course that only a campaign of terror on a grand scale—for which both organization and training are lacking—would promise success. In 1934, or even 1935, Hitler's removal would have had far-reaching results: it is scarcely so today. Today, perhaps, it may even do harm, as we explained at the end of the first chapter. Such considerations are widespread and act as a check on such elements as the Black Front, who are perhaps temperamentally prone to terrorist methods. Under these conditions one can hardly hope for terrorist resistance against the Nazis, anyhow not on a large and organized scale. And thus the so-called illegal struggle in Germany becomes meaningless.

But the manufacture of martyrs goes on. Yet martyrdom is only a potent political weapon when it is an overt and visible act; when it imprints itself on men's minds and is transmuted into legend and myth. Martyrdom without publicity is martyrdom misspent and the Nazis see that it is kept out of the limelight. One Dimitroff was enough for them. There are no more political show trials in Germany. There are only the padded double doors of the People's Court of Justice, through which no sound filters. Bitter to say, the heroes of the illegal struggle in Germany have died in vain, even as they fought in vain.

We shall do well, then, quietly to write off real, vigorous, political opposition within Germany for the coming decisive years. To expect an overthrow of the regime or even a perceptible disturbance of its machinery is to yield to illusion.

Because of this, however, the Opposition is not without importance. If it has discovered no method of effectually fighting the regime or dislodging it, it may yet be able, under certain circumstances, to fulfill another more modest yet highly important function: maintaining and rallying political forces that will be in a condition, after the overthrow of the Nazis—which must of necessity be brought about from without—to take over the German State or States; by carrying on and keeping alive, secretly and half underground, political traditions that the Nazis have striven to destroy; by preparing, on a small scale, for the future; and by forming nuclei of the future political mass armies. Probably this is the real aim of the Communists and Social Democrats for which they continue their very unpromising illegal struggle, and for which they immolate hecatombs of their bravest and most trusty followers. However, we shall presently see that it is extremely doubtful whether theirs is the right way to attain such an end.

Illegal organizations live under permanent war conditions. They are perpetually hunted, perpetually in mortal danger. They must beware of every companion who is not fully tried and proved, lest he be a police spy. Internal crisis, lack of unity, splitting into two camps, may drive the disputing factions to mutual extermination. Under these circumstances the organization of illegal parties has to be as rigid, its code as hard and infallible as that of an army. The political creed to which it has sworn must remain perpetually sacred. There must be no room for differences of opinion. Self-criticism and debate are things that a party, once illegal, cannot permit itself.

But self-criticism and debate are alone the means whereby a political doctrine can reshape and re-equip itself for battle after a severe defeat—and all German political parties have a severe defeat behind them. Before it can hope, with any prospect of success, to challenge again the opponent who has just floored it, it must master the lessons to be learned from the lost fight and rid itself of all the faults and weaknesses that this disclosed; even if it leads to drastic reform, to the abandonment of its most important articles of faith, to a change of its very identity. No Counter–Reformation without a Council of Trent! This is what we meant when we said that those German parties who have for the moment given up their visible organization, are not perhaps so completely checkmated as those who have chosen the path of illegality.

Organizations can, as soon as their day dawns, reestablish themselves relatively quickly and easily; what is hard to reestablish is lost confidence and lost reputation. And there is no doubt that *all* German political parties, together with *all* their doctrines, have lost the confidence of their former adherents and their reputation in the eyes of Germany. This was, in the first place, due to their grotesque prostration in the spring of 1933, but also largely to earlier political mistakes which were not immediately retrieved to their full extent, but allowed to contribute to the coming internal collapse. It is one of the trump cards of the Nazis that all their former opponents and rivals are discredited in the eyes of the nation—whatever its attitude to the Nazis. For everyone in Germany who speculates on the possible successors of the Nazis, instinctively turns to find them among those nearest at hand, among the former political parties, the German Nationals, Center, Liberals, Social Democrats, or Communists, and from each he starts back with alacrity. They all, without exception, had their chance and bungled it. They all were false prophets and inept gamblers. All their strenuous endeavors ended with the resounding triumph of the Nazis. What, then, is the use of again relying on any of them?

This feeling is so fundamentally powerful and universal that it is quite hopeless to try to vanquish it with excuses and recriminations, with "ifs" and "ands," and the wonted sophistries of memoir-writing statesmen. The facts speak their inexorable language. If anyone thinks that on the day after the Nazis are ousted he can as much as entice a dog from the fire with the old German party slogans, he is mistaken. The old parties are not only suppressed and proscribed; they have collapsed internally, are compromised and become ridiculous. Today, for them, it is not a question of "holding out" and "fighting on," but of death and resurrection, or at least of such a fundamental "molting" that what one day emerges out of the process as new Conservatives, Liberals, or Socialists will no longer bear any resemblance to the former representatives of these doctrines. Nothing, not even the most sacred principles of the past, can claim permanent validity. Everything must be freshly examined, freshly thought out, put to the test and adjusted. The moment is come for new syntheses and antitheses, for new fronts. And it is, perhaps, not altogether too optimistic to maintain that such a mental process is already in being, within as well as without the borders of the Reich. But it is not taking place within those banned party organizations, which vehemently ignore defeat and fight on, or at least make the gesture of fighting on. It is true they spill their blood. But blood is cheap today: what is needed is brain power. Courage of martyrdom cannot supplant wisdom of experience, a virtue conspicuously lacking among the illegal parties.

We will now examine in detail what the German parties, apart from the Nazis, should have learned, and cautiously determine what perhaps they have learned. To put it in another way, we will inquire what positive political forces can be reckoned with in Germany once the Nazis are removed. It would be naïve to set down the old parties at their strength when banned in the early summer of 1933. It is impossible to ignore the internal collapse from which every one of them was suffering at the time, concealed mercifully by their outlawry. But it will be, nevertheless, an expedient method to use the estimates on that date as a point of departure, because it is the last occasion when one has firm ground under one's feet. If thence one proceeds to seek the reasons of their collapse, one will come to the point at which the paths began to stray and at which the new road must henceforth deviate. If one warily follows a part of the way, until perhaps the outlines of a new program and a new front come into sight, one will have done all that is possible at this juncture. For, at the moment, it is only possible to try to guess the alternative possibilities and impossibilities in Germany. What can be realized of the present possibilities depends on other factors than organization, which is at the moment extremely embryonic. It would be idle, therefore, to subject it to a close examination, quite apart from the fact that it would be extremely unwise in a book that will doubtless not be overlooked by the Gestapo.

Back then to March 1933. How, a moment before the iron curtain was rung down on it, did the German political stage appear?

Beside the Nazis, four parties still had a more or less compact mass following: from left to right the Communists, the Social Democrats (who roughly correspond to the British Labour Party but were theoretically considerably more radical and Marxist), the Center (a Catholic party, culturally conservative, socially progressive and, for the rest, more opportunist than the others), and the German Nationals (the heirs of the Prussian Conservatives, pro–Hohenzollern, monarchist, militarist, and reactionary). Against the advancing tide of Nazism these four parties employed different strategies. The first three were actively opposed to the Nazis, while the German Nationals were, for the most part, tactically allied to them—except from August 1932 to January 1933. Their respective forces can be judged from the five big electoral struggles of the years 1932–33. The Nazis fluctuated from 11 to 17 million (11–13–14–12–17); the Communists from 3.5 to 6 million (5–3.5–5–6–4); the Social Democrats from 7 to 8 million (8–7–7); the Center (including its Bavarian branch, the Bavarian People's Party) from 5 to 5.5 million (5.5–5–5); and the German Nationals from 2 to 3 million (2–3–3). It was a noteworthy fact that in the presidential election, when Social Democrats and Center together supported Hindenburg (against the Communists, German Nationals, and Nazis), 18 million voters in the first ballot and 19 million in the second elected Hindenburg, although the Center and Social Democrats together never commanded more than 13.5 million votes and the combined bourgeois "splinter" parties not more than one-and-a-half million.

Most conspicuous in this survey is a void. The party is lacking whose opinions were predominant everywhere in Europe, not to speak of Germany—the Liberals. Liberalism was represented in Germany from 1932–33 by two "splinter" parties, the German State Party and the German People's Party. Together they raised between half a million and a million votes—the number fell steadily. In March 1933 they still had two seats in the Reichstag. Yet both parties had a great past. In the Bismarckian era the National Liberals, precursors of the German People's Party, had been for a decade the strongest party in the Reichstag, while the Radicals, forebears of the German State Party, constituted an important section of the Opposition. Even in the twenties of this century, under the Weimar Republic, both parties had a considerable following, commanding jointly, for a time, over a hundred seats. In 1930 began their rapid collapse, the first of the great party collapses, the only one that took place even before the Nazis came to power and so in the full light of day. It is in some measure a model of a *débâcle* in which the typical characteristics of all the others can be studied.

What happened was that the Liberals ceased to vote Liberal without ceasing to be liberal. That is the important point. The five or six million people, who for twenty years had voted Liberal, had not suddenly become untrue to their fundamental convictions. But they had begun to doubt whether these convictions were being adequately championed by the parties which had inscribed them on their banners; and also whether the party program, in which these tenets had always hitherto found due expression, did not perhaps reveal some secret fault of construction. They suddenly seemed to feel that a disastrous fault had crept in during the translation of their conceptions into real politics. They did not become untrue to their ideals, but mistrustful—indeed with good reason—of nearly all the inferences and conclusions that their parties had drawn for their practical guidance from these ideals. They began to look upon matters that had formerly been regarded, without proof or test, to be homogeneous as no longer obviously homogeneous. And this is exactly what has since happened to all the parties. Nor was it an accident that it began with the Liberals, for, recruited as they were for the most part from the cultured upper middle class, they were naturally the speediest in comprehension and the most sensitive in reaction. The failure of their party in the years 1930–33 was only the beginning of a general political crisis which no party was to escape. That the Liberals were the first to be overwhelmed by this crisis in no way indicates that they will be the last to surmount it.

It is clear that at the heart of every political doctrine there lies not a policy but a philosophy—this is certainly true of Germany. What inwardly divides Liberals, Conservatives, and Socialists is a different vision of mankind. The different conceptions of the State are merely the outcome. The differences arise from the fact that each party wishes to construct the State in a way that shall approximate as closely as possible to their conception of mankind, that shall favor their human ideal. At a still later stage is shaped the concrete political program, according to which the State is to be constructed and safeguarded. With each of these successive steps mistakes are possible and, indeed, frequent. Often the concrete political program does not in fact serve the State for which it is intended, and, for its part, the State does not favor the type of man for whom it is created. If the former happens there is a party crisis, if the latter a doctrinal crisis. The quicker and the more thoroughly these crises are overcome, the sooner does the idea that lies at the basis of the collapsed party and the unhinged doctrine recover its political force. It is only when its super-political human values or synthesis of values are no longer valid that a political philosophy ceases to be. This has certainly not happened in Germany today, either to the Liberals, to the Conservatives, or to the Socialists. The only question is whether the crisis, with any one of them, has reached its height, and, in fact, at what pace it is developing.

The human ideal at the root of political Liberalism is free and universal man; its social expression is the world-conquering upper middle class; its means and weapons are science, trade, technique, industry; its ideal state is the state legally conceived, bound by law, controlled without resort to myth and, as far as possible, without force; its political program, in the internal sphere, includes government by the people's representatives, toleration, universal education, freedom of the press, freedom of thought and speech; in the external sphere, *rapprochement,* world federation, and the League of Nations.

A peculiarity of German Liberalism was its delight in the Idea of the Reich. The "yearning for the Reich" was a special feature of Liberalism, even though the Liberal attempt to found a Reich in 1848–49 was frustrated. It went together with the Liberal distaste for the conception of the State historically evolved, rooted in unreason and myth; and with the Liberal preference for the modern, "broad," rational, comfortable state form. What we termed the "also" frame of mind which was the basis of the German Reich was essentially a Liberal contribution. Reich patriotism, however, did not prevent the Liberals from casting a sympathetic eye upon still larger, broader, more modern, more rational, and more comfortable state organizations. Stresemann, who brought Germany into the League of Nations, was Germany's last great Liberal statesman. And it was essentially the Liberals among whom the League of Nations was popular in Germany and who fostered the Pan–Europa project. It is also the Liberals in Germany who instinctively acclaim the idea of international federation—or would acclaim, if only. . . .

If only the German Liberals had not become doubtful about almost all these points which, outside Germany, are still generally regarded as the essentials of Liberalism. Not that the basic idea of Liberalism had disappeared or faded. The picture of free, mobile, unfettered, world-conquering Man is an ideal that, consciously or unconsciously, still stirs millions of people in Germany as elsewhere. Millions still have faith in science, technique, and progress. The cosmopolitan upper middle class style of life still appears to millions as obviously the best and most desirable. In fact, Liberalism is as alive as it ever has been. To conclude that it is dead because a crisis overtook its adherents and its doctrines, as so many glib Nazi aristocrat journalists and pseudo-philosophers have done for the last seven years, is a most superficial analysis. The crisis both of doctrine and party arose because they no longer effectually served the Liberal ideal, and not because the ideal had been discarded by its adherents.

The faults in the dogmas of Liberalism made their appearance just when the onslaught of the Nazis on the Weimar Republic began. The Weimar Republic was, one may say, a model Liberal state; free, comfortable, rational, without mysticism, but weak. The Weimar Constitution was essentially the work of two Liberal minds, Preuss and Naumann. It had the most untrammelled parliamentary government, the fairest electoral system in the world, the longest list of fundamental rights, and the strongest control over the executive that has been exercised in any country. The State had no hard-and-fast content and significance, no unalterable myth. It was scarcely more than the neutral screen on which the "will of the people" could perform its drama, every day a new one. Every party, every "world conception" had the same chance; in the open market one enticed one's adherents at the same time as one purchased an entrance ticket to supreme power in the State. The Liberal program had been so thoroughly carried out that there remained scarcely anything for the Liberal parties to do. And all the fallow lying passion for freedom was applied to ridiculous uses, as, for example, the strenuous advocacy of "literature of the garbage heap and cesspool." (In sober truth the Liberal Press for six months in 1926–27 conducted a campaign against a bill to protect young people from smutty literature with such fervency and zeal as if it were at least a matter of overthrowing a Nazi regime.)

Then all of a sudden things became serious. Against this model state began the attack of a dangerous, formidable enemy of whom everyone knew that, were he victorious, he would annihilate without quarter not only the Liberal state but also the Liberal precepts of life. And it soon became manifest that a weak, detached, free—in short—a Liberal state was defenseless against such an assault, and that the highest values of Liberalism, which it was there to serve, were without protection. The political doctrines of the Liberals tied their hands on all sides. The dogma of the freedom of opinion compelled them to stomach agitation from press and platform that appealed consciously and systematically to criminal instincts, using them as "dynamic" forces in the service of creed. The dogma of proportional representation compelled them to accept its consequences. The parliamentary dogma compelled them to bow in their own declared hangmen and murderers to supreme power; while their conception of the State's neutrality obliged them to offer State machinery for the protection of Nazi meetings and organizations.

The Liberals recognized with horror the faults of construction in their state; and, for the sake of those fundamental Liberal values which were no longer safe in the keeping of their own state they began to forsake their own parties and vote Conservative or Socialist—or perhaps cease to vote at all. They noted suddenly that they needed a strong state, a state with a myth and a meaning, a state with other than sublime but purely formal values, even, possibly, an irrational and uncomfortable state; one, however, that was able to defend to the last itself and its fundamental values; one that was not condemned to press the sword into the hand of its "legal" murderers. Perhaps Liberalism is by nature more at home and more in a position to give of its best in opposition than in government. Perhaps it needs, in order to rule, that little dose of healthy and invigorating inconsequence that made long and brilliant government possible for the English Liberals, but which their German counterparts will never acquire. Perhaps Liberalism has no better role than that of a tempering, loyal opposition in a traditional, deeply rooted, strong Conservative state. In any case, it was this role that the Liberals, over the heads of their abandoned, declining parties, attempted to play in the perilous years 1930–33. They even sought a state in which later they could once more act as the Opposition that was wise enough to remain in opposition. They voted Center, they voted Social Democrat, they voted German National. If only these parties, for their part, had been healthier than the Liberals! Many Liberals, sensing the decay also of these doctrines, resigned and stopped voting altogether—as did many Conservatives. Only once did they emerge out of retirement in a body and elect Hindenburg. That Hindenburg was a traitor they did not know at the time. In him they thought they were electing a Conservative monarchy, tolerant of Liberal values, and a stern foe of Nazi anarchism.

If one wants to sum up the whole process with an epigram one might say Liberalism has become Conservative, which is an important event of far-reaching implications. The fate of the Weimar Republic has taught the Liberals that their old political doctrines had been reduced to absurdity. Their new creed—this much can be said already—will bring them closer to the Conservative outlook. Today, the German Liberals can visualize a political system in which the Conservative concept of the State will be partially included in the Liberal; irrationality will be accepted on grounds of reason, tradition and myth for the sake of the individual, and the status quo recognized as the basis of progress, all of which would have appeared fantastic twelve years ago.

The collapse of the constitutional dogmas of Liberalism was followed by a scarcely less severe crisis in its theories of foreign policy and the super-state, though not quite so apparent because it took place, for the most part, during the Nazi regime and thus underground. As to the ideal polity, until the last decade Liberalism believed in the unromantic, rational, and comfortable new giant edifices—such as the German Reich, Pan–Europa, and the League of Nations. Liberals loved such systems for irrational reasons of feeling and taste, out of sheer delight in progress, in style, in "breadth," and everything rationally constructed and scientifically deduced; but above all, they admired the largest and airiest super-state constructions because they were attracted by the great freedom of movement they afforded, the vast scope for the strong individual. Before their eyes was a vision of the princes of the spirit, of trade and technique, lordly, audacious, and comfortable, borne in the powerful lifts of these national and supernational skyscrapers conquering space and boundaries—Vikings of the Lift. They had an unpleasant sensation of narrowness and mustiness when they looked upon the small historically evolved state, the poky one family house, the stairs of which one had to clatter up and down on foot.

But the Liberals discovered that lifts have a way of stopping sometimes, and that one is better off, after all, with an inconvenient staircase than a lift that does not function. The last decade has brought practical proof that in the modern Europe of the mammoth state and super-state the individual is far more cramped and shackled than ever he was in the old Europe of the venerable, unpractical small and medium sized sovereign state. The hidden satanism of the German Reich has come to light; the League of Nations has proved to be a failure; the International Labor Office has not been able to prevent the enslavement of the German workers, nor the international cooperation of capital the enslavement of the German entrepreneur. All the systems that should contribute to the individual's greater well-being have, as if by witchcraft, turned into hindrances, man-traps, and instruments of torture. The first sign of resistance to slavery and tyranny, the old archenemies of Liberalism, has not come from the League of Nations which was founded with that very object, but from two rather conservative and small states: Poland and Finland. And the hope of saving Europe rests, as in old times, on the two traditional Western Great Powers who make no pretence of pan–European ideals. Without doubt the credit of the old, naturally developed, organic state is again mounting, particularly with the Liberals, the political individualists. The faith in a synthetic super-state has become weaker; and the slogans of "Federal Union" or a "reformed" League of Nations have no longer much power of attraction in Germany, even with those who are sympathetic to such ideas, to say nothing of those who, at the mere odor of this synthetic dish, begin to retch.

It seems clear that for Germany, as for Europe at large, a conservative epoch is "due" to follow the present crisis, such as succeeded the reign of Napoleon; a rehabilitation of the old and the oldest cultural values, a period of preservation, restoration, and healing. The German Liberals have sensed this. Have the Conservatives?

The tale of the German Conservatives is a complicated one. The most genuine Conservatives are to be found outside the political parties, owing to the fact that the whole party system in Germany was from its inception unconservative and liberal. A "Conservative Party" is in Germany, quite unlike a country with an aged parliamentary tradition like England, almost a contradiction in terms. It is no exaggeration to say that this inner contradiction has always been the Achilles' heel of all German Conservative Parties. For this reason, the collapse of the Conservative Parties disrupts Conservative forces less than the collapse of the Liberal Parties disrupts the Liberals. Genuine Conservatism in Germany is fairly proof against crisis. One finds it in the churches whose magnificent resistance can be beaten down but never broken. One finds it in the higher aristocracy, especially in the former ruling houses who have silently and inconspicuously preserved and guarded their fund of experience and tradition as rulers all through the adventures of the Kaiser's Reich, the Republic, and the Third Reich. They form one of the few intact political assets of Germany, perhaps one day to be called upon to save her. One finds it in the higher ranks of the bureaucracy, which, also very inconspicuously, has conducted the daily business of the State for the past sixty years in very orderly fashion and without essential changes. Here, to be sure, the Nazis have destroyed much, but what remains of administrative tradition can serve as the nucleus of a regeneration. All these are conservative forces that will be able to function again when they find scope for their functions. But the Conservative Parties are in quite a different case. A crisis has struck them no less vigorously than the Liberals.

Of the parties in existence in the spring of 1933, two can be called Conservative, though in both cases with reservations. The Center and the German Nationals. The Center administered the inheritance of the old South and West German Conservatives, the German Nationals that of the Prussian Conservatives.

The Center's is a simpler story. It was the only party that did not wholeheartedly welcome the Kaiser's Reich. Founded soon after 1871, it attracted all the leading Conservative elements in West and South Germany that found themselves somewhat unexpectedly swallowed up by the new German Reich. Its aim was the advocacy of definitely supernational and extranational values, and, above all, those of the Catholic faith: it was the only party of the day which did not look upon the Bismarckian creation as the unconditionally ideal political form for Germany, though it was resolved to accept it as a fact. However, Bismarck's repeated accusation against the Center, that it rallied behind it the "enemies of the Reich" did not coincide with reality. The Center was formed, not as a protest against the Reich, but as a compromise. It accepted the Reich, though only with a shrug of the shoulders, and worked loyally with it, though only under certain conditions. These conditions lay in the cultural sphere; here the Center was always intransigent.

In all other fields it could afford to be opportunist. Its very name denoted this. It could, without self-betrayal, work with the right as well as the left. It could cooperate in ruling the Kaiser's Reich as well as the Republic, always exercising a moderating influence and successfully protecting the Church and Christian education and culture. A noticeable feature was that every question that was regarded as fundamental by other parties assumed secondary importance in the Center's eyes. It included right and left politicians, Socialists and Liberals, Nationalists, and friends of the League of Nations, revenge-jingoes and Pacifists. The Chancellors of the Reich, Papen and Wirth, were both members of the Center. The hallmark of its members was the unconditional acceptance of Catholic religious and cultural values. The Center may thus perhaps serve as the prototype of the German political parties of the future, proving as it did how apparently contradictory principles can be, in practice, united in the name of a sacred common value. It has already set German political thought its task of the morrow.

It is probably true to say that the forces behind the Center are relatively intact. Doubtless they will again evolve a political organization, at very short notice, when the time comes. But such an organization will not be a new Center. The Center at the last moment. wrecked itself through that very quality which, for sixty years, had constituted its strength, through its opportunism. It just exceeded the narrow line that marks the difference between flexibility and lack of principle, between tactical sacrifice and suicide.

It is noteworthy that the Center, both under the Kaiser and the Republic, was summoned to lead and save the country in the hour of crisis. Both times it did not save but liquidated the regime, to neither of which, it must be admitted, it was any too warmly attached. On the first occasion it acted admirably and soon found itself playing the same role under the Republic that it had filled under the Monarchy. On the second, it inflicted upon itself mortal injury and, what is worse, ridicule.

Brüning and Papen, the last two Center Chancellors, both tried to play a tactical game with the Nazis, and thus displayed their lack of instinct. For with people who do not recognize its rules it is impossible to play a game without making a fool of oneself. It is a mistake in which many international statesmen have continued to copy the Center leaders. The world could have spared itself many disappointments and much bloodshed if it had taken the trouble to study more closely German internal politics during those years. They follow a course almost identical with that of European politics during the succeeding years. The Center used against the Nazis almost every method except the right one of naked force. It tried every kind of appeasement, stumbled from the trap of one broken promise to the next, and finally into the Hitler–Papen coalition of January 30, 1933, and its fall. The actual suicidal act, the incomprehensible ineptitude that also sealed the party's moral doom, was the grant of supreme powers to Hitler on March 23, 1933, *after* the Reichstag fire, *after* the falsification of the elections of March 5, *after* the institution of concentration camps, *after* a whole series of brazen perjuries and obvious breaches of the Constitution and solemn oaths—on the basis of bare guarantees from Hitler's lips! From that day onward the party's opportunism acquired that characterless and supine air that disillusioned its most faithful adherents and caused them to stray. It has probably rendered impossible a return to its former status.

It seems clear that, relatively speaking, the crisis of the Center has not penetrated deep. It only affects the party, its method and tactics and, perhaps more deeply, its conception of a "detached" internal policy; but scarcely as yet the doctrine of a Catholic policy with its center of gravity in cultural values, and certainly not the philosophy upon which they are founded. Political Catholicism in Germany had proportionately little to learn, and the unequivocal attitude of the Catholic Church gives rise to the hope that it has, in the main, already learned it.

Things are much worse with the Conservatives of the Prussian–Protestant genus. Their entanglements and associations with the Nazis, above all their inner resemblance, has more thoroughly compromised them than the Center. They have behind them not only a tactical failure, but a terrible inner degeneration and—there is no milder expression—vulgarization, dating back to their "German–National" period. They have never fully outgrown this period! A process of soul-searching is in progress; but it advances with tortuous slowness. It has never disavowed Nazism in unmistakable terms, and repeatedly just as one thought it was about to do so there have been relapses. The much boosted class it represents, the class that produces the famous Prussian officer, is very slow in political thinking, and scarcely what one calls abundantly endowed and quick in comprehension. Unless it vigorously exerts itself, its old Liberal opponents may well have to take it upon themselves to save their common world.

This world—in its original unperverted form—would be well worth saving. It would be a pity to regard it as definitely decadent. One easily forgets, amidst all the evil that has proceeded from it, that it traversed a very admirable period in its history; roughly speaking, during the first half of the nineteenth century. With Berlin the home of romantic literature and of a distinguished school of architecture, Prussia was, at that time, a land with an elaborate civilization of its own, the exponents of which were the Conservative Prussian aristocracy. Reading the letters and memoirs of those Prussian statesmen and officers, contemplating the portraits of Scharnhorst and Gneisenau, of Gerlach, Manteuffel, and Radowitz—what a far cry to the bull-necked, haughty, cold masks of the modern Prussian officers and politicians; to Ludendorff and Brauchitsch, Seldte and Hugenberg! For Prussian Conservatism the "fall of man" came with Bismarck. Its last noble and saintly figure was William I. The historian observes with interest the constant struggle of the simple, gentlemanly instincts of this Prussian Conservative of the old school against the successful unscrupulousness of his minister. Is it certain who, in the long run, will have shown the deeper wisdom? Suffice it to say Bismarck won in his day, and compelled the Prussian Conservatives, after initial resistance, to follow in his path, a path which, to be exact, was also the continuation of an old and dangerously vaunted Prussian tradition; the tradition of Frederick, of brutal, unscrupulous, cunning aggrandizement at any price.

The Prussian Conservative Party under the Kaisers, which for forty-seven years held absolute sway over Prussia, sharing its power in the Reich with the National Liberals and the Center, possessed an inscrutable, double-faced character. It still had features that were genuinely conservative, patriarchal, gentlemanly, pious, and humorous, those features that Theodor Fontane has preserved for us in his novels. But it could, even in those days, give proof of a crafty, calculating, ruthless nature that was in no way conservative, but already, consciously or unconsciously, nihilist. Already in the Conservative was hidden the German–National; already behind the protector and guardian of the sacred values of honor, faith, service, and chivalry was concealed the destroyer and betrayer of all those values in the name of a hollow sports-club ideal of national prestige and expansion. The Prussian officers' corps still had a strict and unspotted code of honor, but it was a Prussian officer, Schlieffen, who, in peace time, coldly and without a twinge of conscience, devised the dishonorable plan for the invasion of Belgium. No one incorporated this Jekyll and Hyde nature so thoroughly as the Chancellor von Bethmann–Hollweg, who, on August 4, 1914, coined the notorious expression, "a scrap of paper." He was personally an honorable man, and his words issued from the depths of a violent spiritual conflict. But the fact remains that he spoke the word that is an indelible blot on the annals of Germany.

The phase of deepest decline set in 1918. The Party threw over all its conservative ideals and declared itself by name to be the "German National People's Party." It openly professed a policy of purely reactionary resentment; in external policy against the recognition of defeat, in internal policy against the democratic Republic, from the advantages of which it readily profited. Exceedingly demagogic in method, with an appeal to resentment, self-pity, and brutality, that anticipated many Nazi methods, led by a magnate of the newspaper and film industries, and recruited essentially from the nationalist petty bourgeoisie, the German–National Party hardly betrayed a single feature of its aristocratic and conservative inheritance. Worse than its later tactical alliance with the Nazis was its early association with them. In 1930 this led to a palace revolution on the part of the more conservative-minded wing. It seceded and, for a short time, formed a "Young Conservative Group," which was later to be engulfed in the whirlpool of the internal political crisis. Meanwhile, the German–Nationals ran all the faster into the arms of the Nazis. In the eyes of the masses, they were merely "somewhat mild Nazis," and many of their adherents after 1930 went over to the Nazis out of a feeling that having reached so far they could go the whole length. Nor did the kick suffice that the German–Nationals received from the Nazis immediately after their "common" victory. All the bare-faced, horrible barbarism and vandalist fury of the triumphant Nazis was needed slowly to reawaken the conservative conscience of the German–Nationals.

To be sure, this awakening is now taking place. But slowly, ever so slowly. And in their "molting" the Conservatives are far behind the stage reached by the Liberals as early as 1933. They have hardly got beyond slight doubts, vague twinges of conscience, and superficial indignation at "excesses."

Hitherto, their most noteworthy example of self-scrutiny and self-criticism is Rauschning's world-famous book, *The Revolution of Destruction.* It would be wrong to regard Rauschning, because of his former membership of the Party, as a "converted Nazi." He was, and is, a typical German–National Conservative, drawn like many others by God knows what mixture of calculation and misunderstanding, to the Nazi Party. Far be it from me to belittle the great value of this deep analysis of Nazism or to call in question the evident intellectual and moral honesty of its author. And yet, how feeble it is as a criticism of Conservatism, how superficial the search of its conscience. Rauschning evidently still believes with a slight displacement of the center of gravity, with a return to monarchy and to Conservatism as it stands, all will be well. One would like to know his reasons for thinking so. Where today in Germany—outside certain South German Center circles and, perhaps, the Hanoverian Guelph Monarchy—is the organized Conservatism that is unstained by Nazist nihilism, or cleansed of the stain? What will be the nature of the Monarchy? Will it simply be the Nazi State with a Hohenzollern in Hitler's place? Or are the old German State dynasties to return? In that case what can justify Prussian domination and the Hohenzollern Kaiserdom? All the widespread talk of "restoration" of the Monarchy and the reinstatement of the Conservatives is premature and perilously superficial. There is no Conservatism as yet today. It has not yet cleansed itself of Nazism, to say nothing of its German–National degeneracy. A great task of self-criticism must be faced before it can be reckoned with again; and if the work proceeds at the present rate, it will occupy many a long year.

But what the Conservatives have so far accomplished in this respect is gigantic compared with what the Social Democrats have done. It is a real tragedy that the German Social Democrats, the most immediate victims and temperamentally bitterest enemies of the Nazis, have made such an anemic contribution to the creation of those new fronts that are indispensable for success against the Nazi regime. Their stubborn refusal to subject themselves and their dogmas to inquiry and criticism and to consider the causes of their failure, is one of the great weaknesses of the German opposition; all the more since the Social Democrats, from their impossible position, strive to continue their hopeless fight, which only serves to make the German Opposition look like a body of hopeless out-of-date cranks. Everything about them is unfortunate; not only the methods, about which we said all that there was to say at the beginning of this chapter, but the intellectual basis, the point of departure, the slogan, and the aim.

To begin with, they use the wrong name. The Social Democrats, in forming their front against the Nazis, call themselves "Anti–Fascists." The Nazis, however, are not Fascists. They have, with more or less luck, copied certain external forms and methods of Italian Fascism: the greeting with the uplifted arm, the colored shirt, the introduction of military modes into civil policy, the tendency to "stage" political events in an operatic manner and the like; they may also share certain inner essential features with the Fascists, but in other respects they are obviously distinct. A thorough comparative analysis, which we cannot undertake in these pages, would be necessary in order to decide whether one can describe the two phenomena as spiritually akin—even to the degree that is increasingly apparent between Nazism and Bolshevism. But it is clear at a glance that there can be no question of identity between them. And an attack on Nazism that concentrates its heaviest guns against Fascism, hoping thus to encounter Nazism somewhere in the neighborhood, must, from the outset, arouse little hope.

But these efforts must strike us as altogether hopeless when we see how the German "Anti–Fascists" classify and explain the "German version of Fascism," and see the image they have created of the enemy and the battlefield. In their opinion "Fascism" is the last phase of the class war, the attempt of dying capitalism (or the dying bourgeoisie) to prevent by brute force the complete triumph of the advancing proletariat, "an attempt," they are prone to add rhetorically, "that may delay but can never, never avert this triumph." Unfortunately this picture bears no relation to the facts. Neither is

Nazism a "last" effort of capitalism or of the bourgeoisie, nor is its aim the class war, nor was the proletariat before the advent to power of the Nazis in any way advancing or even dreaming of victory. Rather is Nazism a "first" (original and new) form of radical nihilism, that equally denies *all* values, capitalist and bourgeois as well as proletarian. It serves no "class" in the Marxist sense; on the contrary, it has undeniably come nearer to nationalization and the classless society than ever did the Social Democrats in their day. And as for the impending triumph of the advancing proletariat, the sad truth is rather that, when the Nazis came to power, the proletarian parties had completely given up the fight, and Marxist doctrines were clearly played out as a political force in Germany.

The most pressing task of the Social Democrats after their political bankruptcy is exactly the same as that of all the other parties: to recognize defeat and to begin to think afresh. The recognition of their defeat is, paradoxically enough, the most valuable spiritual possession of all the German parties today—far more valuable than their old doctrines. It provides the scale by which they can measure the faults of their old doctrines and methods. If, instead, the Social Democrats ignore their defeat and seek to explain the Nazis along Marxist lines, as a predetermined and, to some extent, necessary incident, it will be a fruitless undertaking; worse, it is mendacious.

In fact, a phenomenon like Nazism has no place in the Marxist system, and can be neither grasped nor combated by the Marxist dialectics, unless the phenomenon be consciously misinterpreted. To everyone who does not deliberately shut his eyes to the facts, the rise of Hitler and the Nazis has demonstrated with the cruellest tangibility the weakness of a creed which ignores all those very forces that have brought about their triumph; and which ingeniously but unnaturally tries to exalt what was once, for a second of world history during the industrial revolution, an urgent problem of the day to *the* eternal problem of world history. Games of speculative thought such as Marxism; philosophies of the universe artificially balanced on a basis of one-sided truth; incredibly painstaking and exhaustive attempts to explain the universe from a single point of vantage, are the darling occupations of the German spirit. Every German understands the temptation to make oneself at home in the maze of such a world-conception and never more to leave it. One is also familiar with the unworldly ecstatic type of youth in

Germany, with visible spectacles and invisible blinkers, which every such system produces: the disciples of Kant, Hegel, Schopenhauer, and many lesser philosophers, who, good and fortunate people, swear by the word of the Master and thenceforth know the answer to all the world's riddles. But it is a bad lookout for us when such men turn to politics; which is the case with the Marxists.

Nothing confuses political discussion in Germany, and in Europe, nothing stands in the way of a classification of fronts so much as the academic dispute that has raged for decades and long lost its actuality, around the catchwords "capitalism" and "socialism." Capitalism or socialism—Good God, that is as momentous today as the question crinoline or hobble skirt. Who will venture to decide whether the complicated economic system of our time with its combination of private enterprise, national and international trusts, trade union control, factory democracy and state directed social policy should rather be called, in the language of 1840, "capitalistic" or "socialistic." Who today, in view of the developments of the last hundred years, can read without a smile the Marxist theories of historical determinism, the parallel growth of wealth and poverty, the dictatorship of the proletariat, the expropriation of the expropriator by the expropriated, the creation of a classless society! Who today can visualize without a smile the administration of the means of production by the workers? And who, without shutting his eyes and ignoring the chief cause, can explain any of the great world-shaking crises of our century in terms of economics?

For example, the Nazis? The spokesmen of the German Social Democrats will cling with touching gratitude to the trivial fact that the Nazi Party was, for a short period, financed, among others, by Thyssen and some other magnates of the German heavy industry. From which one concludes that the Nazis were the "mercenaries of capitalism." It is a charming example of historical irony that the most important of the capitalist financiers of the Nazis, Fritz Thyssen, is today a fugitive from Nazi oppression. If some German capitalists wished to make use of the Nazis in the way expected of them by the Marxists, as their hireling soldiers, then clearly the dupes have been not the Nazis but the financiers; as well as those Marxists who looked upon this petty Nazi deceit—one out of such a multitude—as of the very essence of the movement. What kind of resolute will-to-blindness is it that overlooks the fact that the Nazis have since enslaved the businessman and robbed him of his rights just as much as they have the workers, and that capital and labor have been equally exploited by the Nazis? It may be very sad that the conventional idea of the exploiting capitalist and the exploited proletariat does not fit into the Nazi world, but it is nevertheless true. Capital and labor today are in the same boat in Germany, and that boat even bears a name: the "German Labor Front," the gigantic State prison in which the Nazis, not without sadistic humor, have locked up the former enemies together.

No, contemporary Germany cannot be explained along Marxist lines. It is just as necessary for the Social Democrats as for all the other parties to rally and reconstitute themselves a stage *behind* their last political creed, Marxism. That is harder for them than for the others, because they were much more orthodox and much more dogmatic. But it must be done. And it is certainly possible. For the Social Democrats, consciously or unconsciously, serve a human ideal no less than the Liberals and Conservatives; an eternally young human value that is shyly hidden behind their bleak materialism and economic obsessions; the ideal of justice and brotherhood. It was this, the passion for social justice, of "one for all and all for one," and the stern honesty, uprightness, and sobriety springing from it, that preserved the old trade unions and the old Social Democratic Party through years and decades of persecution; far more than their obscure materialist gospel that has little cohesive force.

It was faith in this ideal, inarticulate but always revered and lived by, that made possible the grand labor of mass education undertaken by these organizations, a labor the fruits of which may still be seen today in the comparative immunity of the older workers to Nazi propaganda. It was this ideal that gave to the "class conscious worker" in Germany his fine self-assurance and quiet dignity and made him such a pleasant type, in spite of the slight comicality of his half-understood and parrotlike imbibed political philosophy that was doomed to become more and more unreal. It is this ideal that even today provides the Social Democrats with a strong bulwark against the Nazis, and not their Marxism riddled as it is and vulnerable in a hundred places. And it is this ideal that enables us to forget the unexampled failures of the Social Democrats as a party during the last twenty-five years.

These failures are marked by three dates: August 4, 1914, December 24, 1918, July 20, 1932. August 4 was the day when the Social Democrats granted Germany war credits and degraded at one blow the sacred dogma of the international solidarity of the proletariat and the pacifist strength of this solidarity to the same sort of "scrap of paper" as that to which Chancellor Bethmann Hollweg, on the same day, had reduced Germany's obligations under international law. (Incidentally, it was by this act that the Social Democrats later forfeited their right to look upon their Republic as something different from the Kaiser's Reich, and not to be held responsible for its sins.) December 24, 1918, when, for the first time, the "People Representatives" of the Social Democratic Party sent the Free Corps against their own people, is the date that commemorates the lamentable bankruptcy of the Social Democratic "Revolution" of 1918; a revolution that soon was afraid if its own courage, called upon counterrevolutionaries to preserve "law and order," and, as quickly as possible, abdicated to the Center and the Liberals. And July 20, 1932, is the day on which the Social Democratic Prussian Government, backed by the Prussian police, 120,000 strong, well-armed and ready to fight, yielded without a struggle to the coup d'état of the Reich Chancellor, von Papen, who was supported by no more than a single Reichswehr regiment. It thereby delivered millions of defenseless workers, for whom it was responsible, to the caprice of a political gamble between Papen and Hitler.

These are disgraceful memories, and Social Democrats have every reason to purge themselves of shame and discredit by drastic self-criticism. It does not at all become them to continue to act the infallible and chatter about the imminent triumph of the advancing proletariat. Once they resolve, however, to confess their sins and make a new start, their chances as an opposition party are not too bad. For millions of the older workers still want nothing better than again to follow the Red Flag, on which they have all their lives set their hope and trust, and the sight of which makes their heart beat quicker with pride and love as the sight to an old soldier of his regimental colors—if the worker were but given a chance of forgetting the dishonor that has befallen his flag and learn once more to believe in it. If the Social Democrats finally realize how they can rehabilitate themselves, they will again be in the running. Even then they will scarcely win the next round. They are too far behind—they are still in 1933.

With the Communists we can be more brief. It is a moot point whether it is right to discuss them here among the German Opposition parties. For, surprising and incredible as it may still appear abroad, anyone who has attentively observed events in Germany from within knows that today the best chance for the Communists no longer lies in opposing the Nazis but in amalgamating with them. As an Opposition party, the Communists have lost their opportunity. At the end of the chapter dealing with the Nazis we have discussed the sole means by which today a Soviet Germany may come into existence—a change of labels on the part of the second-generation Nazis, to which they might be tempted if things go awry. They might try to save the Nazi regime from the consequences of defeat. Those of the German Communists who have not already been absorbed by the Nazis would rush to join them, the "Right" wing of the Nazi Party would be liquidated, certain slogans and certain inmates of the concentration camps would give place to others and—everything would remain the same.

That, as we have said, is a possibility, if the West is willing to be imposed upon. But that the German people, if ever they succeed in ridding themselves of the Nazis, would turn to the Communists as an alternative, has been for years out of the question. Communism and Nazism are not opponents but rather competitors. Their bitter enmity springs (or sprang) from rivalry, not from ideological hate; from their both wanting the same thing, not from each wanting the reverse of the other. Both travel with the same stream, both are borne up by the same mass psychological waves; by a weariness of civilization, by an eclipse of the ideals of tradition, freedom and justice, and by the itch for a festive orgy of destruction, by the charms of the new and the different. Indeed, both movements arose on parallel lines, both found the majority of their adherents in the same generation; who, moreover, often changed over experimentally from one party to the other, mostly to the Nazis, with whom, as the characteristic expression has it, "there was more afoot." Both were anticultural, anti-bourgeois, anti-individual. They were rival bands of adventurers and robbers who scuffled over a helpless prey.

In 1932 a book appeared by H. R. Knickerbocker, called *Germany—This Way or That?*, its dust cover showing a clenched fist with a hammer and sickle, and an outstretched arm with a swastika. The question and the picture were very topical at the time. People sensed with resignation the relentless advance of the rival movements. They sensed the defenselessness and insecurity of the forces of tradition. they told themselves, "it will certainly be one or the other."

Eagerly their rivalry was followed as men follow a race. The Nazis were clearly leading, but it seemed possible that the Communists would prove better stayers. They looked more tough. What the Nazis scored with élan they made up with resolve. When in 1933 power was pressed into the hands of the Nazis everyone stood tensely at the "eyes left" and waited for the counterblow from the Communists, who had always boasted that they were "armed for the illegal struggle." And when people began to realize what it meant to live under the Nazis there must have mingled in their anticipation a slight unreasonable hope that the Communists perhaps were not *quite* so bad. . . .

Meanwhile, the Communists have shown what came of their "illegal struggle." The race against the Nazis, once so decisively lost, will not be run a second time. The psychological situation has changed since 1932. The Nazis have seen to it that freedom, tradition, and civilization are again enchanting ideals, and that there is no longer any demand for the goods that the vying Nazis and Communists offer. Germany is like a man who, placed in a certain situation, is forced to let himself be pinioned by the right or left leg. He chooses the right; but at the first moment he feels the fetter lie heavily on his right leg, he thinks that a fetter on his left leg would not have been so burdensome. But it is a vain thought, and meanwhile the man bethinks himself that it is perhaps best of all to be altogether unfettered. And if some good fortune were to liberate his right leg he certainly would not clamor for his left to be secured.

There still are, of course, Communists in Germany; but they no longer arouse any response. The only question today that can move the masses is: Hitler or no Hitler? Those who are in favor of Hitler see no reason to exchange him for Stalin. And those against him want to see him replaced by something very different from a Russian dictator. The Communists have fallen between two stools. They seem to be the only German Opposition party to have dropped completely out of the running. Their last hope is fusion with their superior Nazi rivals. And the last mischief that they have perpetrated is to give Hitler's agents in Western Europe opportunities again and again to invoke the menacing specter of a Soviet Germany after the fall of Hitler.

Meanwhile slowly, very slowly, the intellectual elements of the new front are being formed, of the opposition that really has a chance of overthrowing the Nazis. It shapes itself with tantalizing slowness, and the nightmare continues that it may not be ready in time, that it may not be there at the decisive moment. One must say, in its defense, that even spiritual processes are not easily brought to completion today in Germany. Even pure thought needs a minimum of "living space," discussion, verbal crystallization, and contact with critical opinion, all of which is highly dangerous, if not impossible. Above all, however, thought is hindered by the daily flood of propaganda. It is like trying to compose a symphony while the same potpourri of marches roars in one's ears in a continual and compelling *fortissimo*.

But a large part of German political thought is active today outside Germany, in Paris, London, Zürich, and New York, everywhere where the German spirit feels more at home for the time being than in the German Reich. And our picture is incomplete without the Germany that has come into being outside the borders of the Reich, without the new Diaspora, the German émigrés.

7

The "Émigrés"

The German émigrés have been misunderstood. Theirs has been almost universally regarded as a movement of sheer flight; as nothing more than an ever-swelling stream of men, persecuted, seeking asylum, imploring protection, and appealing to Christian and humanitarian sympathy, to be greeted with a reception that varied according to their numbers. Their problem has been faced, with a sigh, as a new problem to add to all the others, the "Refugee Problem." The emigrants have been overlooked amidst the refugees.

It was not noticed that the German emigrants came for the most part not with empty hands, though with empty pockets; that they brought with them a political opportunity. The opportunity was missed. The fact escaped notice that emigration, at least in the early years of the Hitler regime, far from being an escape from the Nazis, presented the only real means of combating them. The effect on Germany would have been incalculable if, from the beginning, the mass exodus of the German intelligentsia had been encouraged instead of turned away. (Or, perhaps, at that time such an effect was not desired?) No importance was attached to the fact that for years all Germany anxiously watched to see whether the emigrants would succeed or fail, regarding it as a test case by which to judge the attitude of the world to the Nazis and to the barbarization of Germany.

No chance was given to the advance guard of the opposition. No opportunity was given them to set up an anti–Nazi stronghold beyond the reach of the Gestapo, to hoist a banner that would make it clear to every doubter that Hitler is not so incontrovertibly Germany as he makes out. No German university was founded, no academy, not even a settlement.

The émigrés have been reluctantly tolerated in the cafés so long as they could—God knows how—pay for their coffee, and the one question has been how to ship them off as soon as possible to the ends of the earth. Their warnings—valuable and enlightened warnings as has since become evident—have been ignored with a superior shrug as hysterical chatter of fugitives. In short, people have not understood, have not wanted to understand. And, finally, the torrent arrived, of the refugees, as the emigrants were wrongly called, of those whom people wanted to deter by their treatment of the emigrants. Morally, Germany regards the rejection of the German emigrants by the Western civilized powers as a defeat suffered by France and England, even before the declaration of war, and one that was easily avoidable.

Naturally, the Governments who failed to understand the German exodus have their reasons. It was rather a complex event. Under a single name, often in a single case, and by no means neatly partitioned, it includes at least four radically different processes.

Firstly, the more or less voluntary release of the section of German Jewry with Zionist sentiments, practically expressed in their migration to Palestine. This does not here concern us at all.

Secondly, the entirely involuntary flight of defenseless persecuted individuals and families whose only desire it is to be able to live "somewhere" peacefully and harmlessly, safe from the Nazis who were after their lives. This is largely the case of those German–Jews who fled before the pogroms, but also of many an "Aryan" German, of many Austrian Catholics and aristocrats, Bohemian–German anti–Nazis, and prominent Czechs who, without being politicians or professing political opinions, have, for some reason or other, been singled out on the Nazi blacklist for torture and murder. They first took to flight on a large scale in 1938–39 and are the only category of emigrants who have been understood—which, however, does not imply that they met with a favorable reception. Tens of thousands of private persons and private organizations with wonderful generosity have held out their rescuing hands. But they have only been able to save a small proportion out of hundreds of thousands.

To save them all the governments, or at least one of them, would have had to do something. They did nothing. Not one of them, even in the winter of 1938–39, hearing the cries of innocents tortured to death, were able to open their frontiers and receive a few hundred thousand industrious, capable, grateful new citizens. It was an impossible expectation and an insoluble problem. Be it noted, however, that such problems were by no means insoluble for the absolute princes of the past, under the conditions of undeveloped trade and international organization in the sixteenth, seventeenth, and eighteenth centuries. In those days place was quickly found and with success for the exiled Spanish Jews, French Huguenots, Flemish Protestants, and others, although in those days there was no continual outcry over the falling birthrate and no undignified exhortations to citizens to beget more children for the population statistics. But those, we repeat, were backward times.

From our point of view, these refugees, though perhaps the most numerous, are the least interesting. It is natural for men to flee the butcher's blade. It could happen anywhere under similar circumstances. It is no disgrace and no merit, and it tells us little about the present day German mentality. For us there is only one indirect consequence, and that is the deplorable impression made in Germany by the refusal of the civilized governments to give refuge to the victims of the Nazis. Knowing well what they were doing, the Nazis did not fail to give the widest publicity to the Conference of Evian and all that happened after. The orators of Evian hardly imagined what an impression their polite commiseration: "Certainly, certainly, but at the moment, unfortunately, impossible . . ."

must make on people who had relatives or friends in the concentration camps at Buchenwald and Dachau, or who themselves might any day have been arrested and taken there. If the Nazis have ever had a propagandist success in Germany even among their sworn enemies, it was their advertisement of this attitude of the Western Governments, who offered the suppliant fugitives nothing but vague prospects of being sent, later on, to New Guinea—of course, not at once—while they were being tortured to death in the concentration camps.

In Germany they find it no less impossible to understand an attitude like that of the Americans who, in protest against the pogrom, took the trouble of recalling their ambassador from Berlin, but never even thought, say, of tripling at the German immigration quota for the current year at the expense of the three coming years; so that there are people in Germany who, when they collapse in Buchenwald under the kicks of the Black Guards, at least die with the comforting assurance that they had the right, duly substantiated by documents, to enter the Land of Liberty in 1942 or 1943, if they had but managed to survive.

Human psychology works strangely, not always logically. Thus it would be right, under such circumstances, to allot at least 99 percent of anger to the murderers and at most one percent to the unmerciful priests and Levites who looked away. But anger knows no reckoning in percentages and the governments of the Western Powers, by their attitude of superior and measured inaction to the refugee question in 1938–39, have managed, in the eyes of the Germans, to put themselves on the same level as the murderous Nazi Government. That may be unjust, but it is the fact. A good deal of the indignation aroused even in Germany by the horrible events of November 1938 has in this way been deflected to the Western democracies. The Nazis have since found it more and not less easy to represent every outburst of wrath at their misdeeds as hypocrisy—to flaunt an air of honesty with, "Well, we savages are better men."

Apart from this important indirect consequence, the political significance is small of this mass flight of persecuted, harmless people. It is all the greater in the case of the third and fourth categories of German emigrants who have been woefully neglected and misunderstood: the countless representatives of the academic and cultural intelligentsia, whose departure was an act of protest and conscientious revolt, and the members of the former opposition parties, who constitute the focal centers and the fighting forces of the exiles.

In the case of the former, we have the very opposite of an escape from persecution. These men, for the most part, left Germany not because they were persecuted, but because they refused to take part in persecuting or even bear indirect responsibility for it. I shall consider two prominent examples to make myself clear. One is Hermann Rauschning. Well-to-do landowner, enjoying high authority in the Nazi Party, President of the Danzig Senate, he could doubtless have had a splendid career in Hitler's Germany. But he preferred to sacrifice material possessions, rank, and honors, and go into exile rather than, at Hitler's command, inaugurate the persecution of Jews and Christians in Danzig, falsify election results, proscribe political opponents, and continue to serve a party which had revealed its fundamentally destructive character.

The other example is on an even higher plane. Thomas Mann, the greatest living German, who, at the first act of barbarism, silently turned his back on the land of his birth and his fame. Flattering invitations to return to grace the "German Cultural Senate" he left unanswered. Sixty years old, an Olympian accustomed to celebrity, he chose the path of exile and homelessness rather than play the role of a cultural signboard of Nazi barbarism.

The cases of Rauschning and Thomas Mann were news; people treated them with respect, if not with fullest understanding. A Thomas Mann could scarcely be refused a visa into the Western countries. But few realized that these were two outstanding examples of a widespread phenomenon; that in 1933 and later the greater and better part of German literature, an eminent section of German science, and countless anonymous representatives of German culture had shaken off the dust of Germany from their feet; not because they were no longer tolerated, but because they wished to have nothing more to do with it; because they did not wish, by their silence, to seem to tolerate and encourage the Monster of Nazism; because they felt that in the totalitarian machine in which they were caught, everything, even the most harmless nonpolitical action, would somehow, in an indirect way, be made perhaps to serve the great collective crime.

Finally, also to be numbered among the émigrés are all those umimportant and unknown private persons of all classes who, during the years when the statesmen of the great democracies were dreaming of appeasement, saw with their umprompted eyes how Hitler was planning the new world war. They refused to fight Hitler's war: rather they refused to fight on Hitler's side. They therefore left Germany while there was yet time, forfeiting position, means, security, friendships, and tender attachments. They number, without doubt, several thousand. And there would have been tens, even hundreds of thousands if the countries where they sought hospitality had not barred their path with steely obstinacy. That these men could one day be more of a nuisance as German soldiers than as German emigrants—they did not think so far ahead.

It is to these men that Germans can point, when asked where was the "other Germany" during those seven years, what sign of life it gave, and on what it basis its claim to recognition; this unending stream of people who were resolved at all cost to forsake the Fatherland and "go into misery," as the old German expression for emigration has it.

Here and there one hears the objection that going away is not particularly helpful; that the emigrants would have done better to stay and fight against Nazism in Germany. This view is superficial. It comes, without exception, from people who have not taken the trouble to study the conditions of life and "struggle" within Germany. With regard to the internal German situation we must realize, firstly, that all possibilities of resistance, opposition, even of political thought, are cut off and prevented with ceaseless systematic care, so that all that rebels against the Nazis have to expect is martyrdom without publicity; and, secondly, that even the most harmless private activity benefits through some channel or other the whole Nazi system, so that one can do no work, dispense no charity, breed no child even, without incidentally serving the designs of the Nazis; whereas every act of sabotage would be self-sabotage, the conscious destruction of one's life and work. He who lives and works in Germany is today part of a machine which, with irresistible mechanical power, forces him to suit those in charge of it and not to suit him, and if he offers resistance, simply cuts him to pieces. It sounds rather like mockery to suggest that he ought to "fight against the Nazis inside Germany." The only effective form of protest and resistance that remains is for him to go away, which, however, is not as easy as it sounds.

If foreign governments were blind to the fact that the emigrants were a danger to the Nazis, the latter were by no means blind to it. Moreover, they have not relied solely on the obstacles imposed abroad in the path of the would-be exiles, but have built some of their own. Double bars hold firmer, they know. Since 1937 it had become very difficult, whether one was Jewish or "Aryan," to get a passport; since 1938 it has become practically impossible. The Nazis know, what is not so well known abroad, that emigration is an old and dangerous German method of political warfare.

In fact, this is their particular form of national resistance. It is in their blood, as a result of age-long historical experience, to emigrate when tormented, just as it is in the blood of Frenchmen, under similar circumstances, to start a revolution. In Germany a subconscious memory still prevails of the mass emigrations during the Counter-Reformation and the Wars of Religion; silent, resolute migrations from Catholic into Protestant German countries. And one still remembers not only the moral but the startling material effects of emigration; when states such as, for instance, the Archbishopric of Salzburg, were reduced to empty husks, deprived of riches and industries as well as of their population.

Similarly, it would have been a blow to the German Reich, not only morally but materially, if, instead of some hundred thousand, a couple of million of its best, most intelligent, and most educated citizens had emigrated. It would not only have been the most effective counter-propaganda; it would have been felt in terms of battalions. It would have caused the most dangerous reactions among those remaining behind, to know that they could at any time go away if things became too bad. A little more consideration would have had to be shown them. They would have been consulted before they were disposed of; a liberty or two might have been conceded—and the Nazis would have found themselves on a sloping path. The iron grip once relaxed, who knows what might have happened! The ceaseless suppression, liquefaction, remodelling and robotizing of the German nation were only possible when all outlets had been barred from within, and with what delighted rubbing of Nazi hands one may well guess, from without. Now, for the first time, the Germans were utterly in their power, and they could do with them what they liked. Now, for the first time, the world could be told with impunity that the German nation stood to a man behind Adolf Hitler. . . .

It may be asked, perhaps, where are the millions ready to emigrate? Well, I can affirm that they were there, and it is not their fault if they are still in Germany. Apart from the emigrants who managed to escape despite every hindrance in their way, behind the regular, incessant, little individual drops and trickles seeping through the German frontier, bolted and riveted as it is inside and out, there are continually pushing and squeezing against this wall those who may be called the "internal emigrants," countless people who seek nothing more precious than a rift in it through which they may slink away, but find none.

It is perhaps remarkable that the percentage of the internationally "prominent" figures among the emigrants is disproportionately large. Thus, certain professions such as those of authors, actors, doctors, and scientists, are powerfully represented, while those, for instance, of musicians, philosophers, and architects very weakly, and ordinary employees and workmen, generally speaking, not at all. This is not because in Germany it is only prominent people as well as actors and doctors who are anti–Nazi and want to emigrate, while musicians, workmen, and simple folk are enthusiastic Nazis and wish to stay at home. It is because of all those eager to escape the first to find an opportunity were the celebrities, and next those fortunate ones with vocations that could be pursued and were in demand everywhere; while the unlucky ones who could take with them no immediately adaptable qualifications had to stay at home.

Here we find once more the terrible lack of comprehension that all along prevented the West from regarding German emigration as the great political chance that it was; that made them look upon it as a peacetime matter of culture and philanthropy; that made them haughtily pluck the conspicuous raisins from the cake, and at the most accept a couple of specialists of whom they might make some use or other. They never realized the political advantages of Germans in vast masses turning their backs on Hitlerian Germany and entering countries threatened by the Nazis, even though these emigrants did, in God's name, temporarily "burden the labor market there." In war there is rejoicing every time an enemy deserts; and no one asks if he is "burdening the labor market." But to perceive the significance of defections en masse, that would perhaps have prevented war—that was beyond the intelligence of European statesmen. It is an eternal pity.

The fourth group, the political emigrants, met with almost the same unimaginative response. Typical of their aims was the resolve of the German Social Democrat Party to transfer its seat to Prague. Many similar measures were later taken by other political parties, more silently and less conspicuously; and they are today in almost all European capitals, not excepting Rome, German and Austrian political centers working for the Germany and Austria of the future.

These people came as the defeated; many having recently endured peril and persecution. It was not to be expected that they would be received as foreign heads of governments and ministers. But what they should be scornfully treated, as happened everywhere, ostentatiously ignored and made to feel their undesirability, was, to say the least, shortsighted. The vanquished and exiles of today are often the conquerors and rulers of tomorrow. That the leaders of the German Opposition parties and the claimants to the Nazi succession should come to Western Europe and seek protection and support there, is without historical precedent and opens up vistas of great importance. That people were so completely blind to these possibilities; that they could see nothing in such events, not even an opportunity to establish covert contacts and, with a very modest outlay—a little protection, a little aid, a little consideration and courtesy—ensure high profits in the shape of future cooperation—well, that is typical of the generation of European statesmen who in seven years squandered all the gains of the World War and the peace.

The emigration of the Opposition parties was not the success it might have been. The fault is not theirs. In itself the resolve to go abroad was basically sound. Naturally here, too, people at first spoke of cowardly flight and a lack of readiness to assume responsibility, and were kind enough to ask the German politicians to go back to Germany and there "fight against Hitler." They did not know what they were talking about. The illegal struggle in Germany, as I have tried to show, is condemned under existing circumstances to complete nullity, and is nothing more than a form of suicide. Whereas the efforts of the emigrant Opposition parties, even within the limited scope afforded them by their unresponsive hosts, have thoughout been fruitful and not without its effect on Germany. If these German political emigrants had produced nothing more than Heiden's biography of Hitler, Rauschning's *Revolution of Destruction,* and Thomas Mann's *Exchange of Letters with the Dean of Bonn University,* they would have justified their existence. And they have to their credit more successes of this kind, whilst the opposition within Germany naturally can have nothing comparable to boast of.

It would also be quite wrong to maintain that the opposition, by its emigration, has severed its connection with Germany. It has proved far easier to write and print books, brochures, and pamphlets abroad and smuggle them into Germany than to write and print them there. Moreover, political reflection was only possible abroad. This was what the German opposition, after its defeat in 1933, most needed. All such thinking has been done abroad under circumstances in no way ideal, but certainly ideal in comparison with conditions in Germany. It has been demonstrated in this connection that really important ideas are still able to traverse frontiers. Thomas Mann's correspondence with Bonn University, for instance, and Heiden's book on Hitler, have often been the whispered topic of the day in Germany, although they have not, to my knowledge, been smuggled into the country in great quantities. But every German travelling abroad on business or holiday bought these books at the first foreign bookstall and was able, from memory, to retail some of their contents at home. The hectographed illegal pamphlets occasionally slipped under his door at night, gave him no comparable material for reflection and argument.

The basic aims of the emigrant German opposition had already taken shape. They were two: firstly, to think anew before it began to work anew, to which end it must seek an abode where thought was not stifled; and, secondly, deprived of all power in Germany, it must seek the alliance of states which still counted as Great Powers, and inspired respect in the eyes of Germany. Hence they turned to the democracies. However much people may smile at the thought of this policy of "threatening with the big brother" it nevertheless remains legitimate and sensible tactics. Thus, during the French Revolution the Royal House and aristocracy of France turned as a matter of course to the Royal Houses and aristocracies of England,

Germany, and Austria, as to a stronger second front, and found there, as a matter of course, recognition, protection, and alliance. And, from this base, with strong backing, pursued the fight against the Revolution in France that remained something slightly contemptible, lacking solidity and inchoate, so long as this "other" France, irreconcilable and firmly allied with France's powerful neighbors, stood glaring from across the border.

How close is the parallel with the dethroned democracy of Germany! Indeed, with what expectancy all Germany in 1933 and still in 1934 observed the progress of the migrating German democrats, of their reception by the democratic Great Powers! *All* Germany—including the Nazis, who have such a sure instinct for power and would soon have realized that it would be better to go slow had they seen German democracy obtain support and aid from the great democracies. There was a certain amount of fear in the frantic campaign they let loose in 1933–34 against the emigrants; in the prominence they gave to their first decrees annulling rights of citizenship; in the violence with which they denounced the emigrants as cowards, bankrupts, criminals, and traitors fleeing from the wrath of the people. The Nazis breathed more freely again when they realized that the democratic governments had let down the emigrant democrats, treated them as unwanted, contemptible, poor relations, to be relegated to the cafés of Prague and Paris, but otherwise to be ignored. At the same time, the domestic opponents of the Nazis began to lose hope, despairing of solidarity between Europe and European-minded Germans, as well as increasingly despairing of the West, a mood which the Nazis did their best to foster. Thus, on September 26, 1938, three days before Munich, Hitler said: "These great democracies—we have learned the deepest contempt for them"; a mood which the Western Powers themselves had cultivated by their German policy during seven years, and which they sought in vain to exorcise in a couple of weeks with pamphlets and circulars.

What is the good of complaining today about neglected chances? Let us, instead, see what can still be saved. The German emigrants, in spite of all, are still there; torn, disorganized, impoverished, discouraged, somewhat displaced by the stream of fugitives that swelled their numbers in 1938–39 without contributing much new intellectual strength. Yet they are there, a piece of Germany saved from Hitler's grasp to combat Hitler; the one clear and real manifestation of the "other" Germany that is not to be explained away; as symbolic in its unmistakable identity as, on the other side, the person of Adolf Hitler himself; and withal happily distinct from the unrecognizable contents of the melting pot, "Germany," where everything is involved, suppressed, out of place, and undecipherable. And if this piece of Germany is limited in quantity, though not by its own fault, it is not inconsiderable in quality. It contains a good proportion of the best and most famous German minds. Can they be used in no way?

If there was any general basis for the attitude adopted by the Powers for the last seven years of discountenancing the German emigrants, it lies in the policy of "appeasement" that was pursued at the same time. As long as it was thought that Hitler might be led to more peaceful ways by overtures and compromises; as long as it was thought possible, despite everything, to come to terms of neighborly cooperation with Hitler's Germany; so long was it understandable that men should look away from a phenomenon the very nature of which constituted an offense to Hitler, and the mere presence of which furnished a source of friction with him. When healthy, flourishing, highly civilized states such as Austria and Czechoslovakia were sacrificed to "appeasement," it was only natural that a weak German anti–Nazi movement, in need of protection and support, should also be sacrificed. But now, since this policy has collapsed, since all the sacrifices offered to Hitler have proved vain, since the Western Powers are engaged in a struggle to the death with Hitler's Germany, what grounds are there for regarding the German emigrants as a "nuisance"? Should it not be obvious that this German anti–Hitlerian movement should be used to its fullest capacity and made to render every possible service in the fight against Hitler as well as in the necessary reconstruction of Germany—services that no one is more eager to offer than the emigrants themselves?

8

Possibilities

Most catchphrases are stupid, but one of the stupidest ever attributed to an intelligent people is the saying, not unpopular in England

and America at the present time: "A war settles nothing." What utter nonsense! One might as well say an operation settles nothing, or a lawsuit. On the contrary, there are political conditions that can only be settled by a war, just as there are diseases that can only be cured by an operation and legal cases that can only be adjusted by a lawsuit. Like an operation, a war is unpleasant; and wherever possible, a settlement by peaceful means should be concluded. But sometimes this is impossible and the peaceful method proves to be a cause of mischief. A cancer cannot be treated with medicaments and diet, but only with the knife, and quickly at that. With a perjured cheat, one cannot negotiate: must go to law. A regime like Nazi Germany cannot be pacified by concession and compromise after it has been allowed to grow so strong: it must be rendered innocuous by war.

But there lurks in the stupidest catchphrase a distorted and misrepresented atom of truth. Here the truth within the nonsense is that war alone cannot settle everything. A war, to kill the comparison, is not a precise and circumspect proceeding like an operation or a lawsuit. Inevitably, in destroying what must be destroyed, a great number of things that should be left intact are demolished: men's lives, cultural values, the good things of life, emotions. Besides its desirable result, a war confronts us with many extremely undesirable indirect effects, for every disturbance that it quells provokes an unlimited number of new disturbances, the suppression of which calls for new wars.

Does that mean that under no conditions a nation should wage war? By no means. When cancer is diagnosed it must at once be cut from the body, even at the risk of injuring important organs. But the maximum effort and application must be expended in order, firstly, to remove the cancer without its leaving a trace behind, so that the agony of the operation will not eventually prove vain; and, secondly, to injure the healthy organs as little as possible, so that superfluous new maladies may not arise. Thus, to return to the war, one must know precisely—and not approximately—against whom and what it is being waged; one must know exactly—and not more or less—what is to be the immediate result of the war; "victory" is no answer to this question, nor is "a future better world." One must also know exactly against what the war is *not* being waged; and upon what the future recovery and existence of Europe can be erected. And all this must be clearly expressed beyond misunderstanding, again and again. For the aims of modern war are also its most potent weapons.

The military significance of modern wars is merely secondary. It is disastrous to envisage them as similar—but on a magnified scale—to the European wars up to the last century. They are quite different. Past wars were largely waged over the heads of the people, with professional soldiers who served their commander according to the iron principles of a military code of honor, under all circumstances and whatever his aim in waging war. To address them, to spread propaganda among them, or to discuss with them the meaning and object of the war would have been ludicrous. The achievement of military victory was the sole objective. The art of war consisted of the rules and finesses of a chesslike game of strategy, where each side strove for success on the battlefield with a minimum of material loss to itself and a maximum to the foe. The war aims of the past began first to play their part when one side was beaten; or when, supposing both sides to be exhausted, an armistice had been declared and peace negotiations begun. Till then the one and only preoccupation was to win the campaign.

Today it is another matter. Today it is no professional host but the people who fight. They do not fight because they are there to fight irrespective of the cause; they have no inherent military code. They have to be persuaded to fight by the most diverse means; by emotional appeals to warlust, fear, and hope, and by rational appeals to their sense of justice, prospects, and profit. The pure appeal to the passions and to the joy of battle (although not altogether negligible among Germans) seldom survives in view of the fruitfulness and repulsiveness of modern mechanical warfare. In the long run only *that* people fights which is convinced of its cause; of its profits, prospects, and justice.

Apart from military strategy, there exists something at least as important for the outcome of the war and more important for the preparation of the peace. It might be termed a great discussion between the nations, for "propaganda" is a rather weak and shabby expression for it; a spiritual struggle waged with every weapon, in which each party seeks to convince the other that the enemy's cause is a bad one and that they fight in vain. It is true that the arguments used are not only words, but also military blows, which serve to emphasize the hopelessness of a cause. But it is just as important to demonstrate its injustice and futility, and this has to be done with other than military weapons. Above all, it is most important to point, not vaguely and obscurely, but with glaring clarity, the alternative to a cause; for even the worst cause is more attractive than surrender to the mercy or mercilessness of an opponent whose intentions are unknown. When the Germans capitulated in the last war, they must have felt, apart from spiritual and ideological defeat, the gravest doubt as to their cause; the growing conviction that they were fighting for nothing and that the opposite side was in the right. This completely crippled their will to fight and resist, and finally decided the war. But this by no means implies that the last war was a clear, coherent, and successful model of spiritual and psychological strategy.

The capacity to talk an opponent into defeat and disarm his spirit, plays in modern warfare exactly the same role as the surprise of sudden troop movements and ingenious strategy in yesterday's wars. It is the art of war of today, if, by that, we understand the art of winning a war in the shortest, least bloody, and most effective manner. The old strategy, we know, is dead. The mechanization and mass formation of modern armies have killed it. On the modern battlefield the engineer and the organizer play the part of the strategist of former days. What was once a brilliant game of chess full of movement and surprise is today a mutual siege; gigantic, methodical, and patiently planned. The intellect has by no means been banned from contemporary warfare; its scope has been altered. All the methods of the old strategy, surprise, encirclement, outflanking, and outmaneuvring, all are employed today when translated into terms of the psychological battlefield, or could find employment were psychological strategy developed to its fullest extent.

But it is not. That can be seen from the very name given to the subject: "propaganda." Propaganda is a very small word for a very big thing. Its meaning here must be artificially expanded to include everything that can bring about the psychological disarmament and overpowering of the adversary; and in this task what is usually called "propaganda," the issue of broadcasts and pamphlets, plays only a subordinate role. Rather I would call it "psychological warfare." On the psychological battlefield everything counts, everything that takes place on this and every other battlefield. Broadcasts and pamphlets here count as the smallest guns. Propaganda is the *tactic* of psychological war. Its *strategy* is something quite different. And no one should imagine that the wireless news in German and the dropping of pamphlets over German towns play a larger part in psychological warfare than the skirmishes and artillery duels, of which the war in the West had so long consisted, in military warfare. As purely technical vehicles of psychological warfare, radio and pamphlets are naturally important and indispensable. But in order to have decisive influence they must convey more than mere "propaganda." Much more powerful than propaganda are ministerial pronouncements, symbolical gestures such as the internment of German emigrants in France, and military events. It may be said, in passing, that tactical decisions that appear quite sound from the purely military standpoint, can react fatally on the psychological battlefield; just as, on the contrary, partial and temporary military successes can, under certain circumstances, produce psychological reactions of a decisive nature.

The trump card of psychological warfare is the war aims policy; the slogans under which the war is waged, the threats hurled at the opponent in the event of prolonged resistance, the prospects and promises held out in the event of surrender. These are the mental foundations of the war. These thoughts circulate in the mind of every single human being among the warring nations, react upon him, make him ponder and brood—quite differently to the "propaganda" that he occasionally hears on a foreign broadcast. What grips his imagination wins him. The side that expresses itself with vigor, audacity, and conviction has immeasurable advantage over the one that falters, sounds confused and unauthentic. If a country discovers a clear and simple formula to explain the war, an explanation so plausible that it even impresses the foe, that country has half won the war. And it has also provided the best preliminary basis for the peace.

For it is a paradox of every war that it is waged for the sake of the peace that shall follow. The result of every war, at least of every reasonable and sensible war, must be a better and more stable peace. But the indispensable military measures, by their very nature, do not lead toward peace, but away from it. They inevitably promote hatred, enmity, bitterness, and ill-will, the emotions that burden peace in advance. But the emotions that prepare the way for peace can only be evoked by psychological means; and most effectively by its greatest weapon, war aims. If a nation can succeed in making its own war aims acceptable to large sections of the enemy nation, then all the hatred and ill-will aroused by the latter's sufferings will no longer fall on the external enemy, but on its own government which is prolonging the war.

To achieve this, it is necessary to make, at the beginning of the war, the not inconsiderable mental effort hitherto exerted at its end; it is necessary to discover the points at which their own war aims coincide with the interests and wishes of the enemy nation, or at least with its peace-loving sections, and on this foundation strive for an agreement with them; which, as long as the war lasts, will be an alliance, and, after the war is won, will automatically constitute the peace. To put it in another way, from the start an attempt must be made to form an alliance with those forces among the enemy with which, later, peace will be concluded. One must be clear as to the identity of these forces. One must seek them out, negotiate and conclude with them, if possible before the war begins in earnest, an alliance that is to end in peace. In this way not only is an ally acquired behind the enemy's lines, but also a friendly partner in the subsequence peace, who has not been embittered by a war directed against him. In this way, moreover, the initiative is snatched from the enemy on the psychological battlefield. The theme, so to speak, of the *pourparlers,* is determined. The enemy becomes conscious of the other side's views. A concrete proposal is put to him: "You can have this government and this peace; if you accept, the war ends today. What do you say?" More interesting, more solid, more powerful material for reflection than any "propaganda."

This presupposes complete clarity as to the desired peace, and as to the elements in the opposing camp with which it can be concluded.

I should now like to point out possible conclusions to be drawn from the survey in the preceding chapters, of psychological and political conditions in Germany today; possibilities of the reconstruction of the future Germany, of future peace with Germany, and of psychological warfare against the Nazis. Anyone who has closely followed the preceding pages needs no additional proof that these things are intimately and inseparably linked together. Two further indications, however, will not be amiss.

Firstly, the platform from which I speak rests solely on an intimate familiarity with German conditions and German psychology. When in this chapter I speak of things that do not treat of purely internal German affairs, I do it from the point of view of their reaction on Germany. It seems to me important at the moment to consider the policy of England and other nations from this angle—and not without advantage for England herself. But I know, naturally, that it is not the only point of view to be considered. And if, for example, I were to criticize England's recent war aims policy from this point of view, I have no intention of pronouncing final judgment on it. I know that it has to take into account many other points of view than that from which I survey it, such as its effects on the English themselves, or their allies, or on the chief neutral powers, and that from these points of view there may be overwhelming reasons in its favor. What I am trying to put forward is no more than an argument, though a substantial one in my opinion.

Secondly, what I indicate are only possibilities; perhaps it would be more explicit to say chances. Which of them finally assumes material form depends largely on which of them is pursued, and with what resolution. I shall endeavor to elaborate each with all the clarity and logic at my command. But I am well aware that history seldom allows any particular one of all the potentialities inherent in a situation to be fully realized at the expense of the others. I hope I shall not appear to be a doctrinaire or a prophet if I speak of the moot future with an air of conviction. I know that this war will probably share the fate of all human planning and striving—a jumble of good, bad, and indifferent. Yet it seems to me useful to think clearly and hope for the best.

What possibilities, then, does Germany offer to the war? What possibilities does the war offer to Germany?

The great psychological opportunity of the Allies is the fact that Germany enters the war as a thoroughly disunited nation, and that large sections of her people fear victory more than defeat. The regime that has brought Germany into the war has behind it only the genuine Nazis; no more than a minority of the population, whose desperate unblenching determination, however, must not be underestimated. But immediately behind them begins vacillation, disruption, and potential treason. Those loyal Germans who in 1914 shouted hurrah with single-voiced rapture, utterly lack enthusiasm for this war, feel uncomfortable about it, and would gladly be out of it as soon as possible. Moreover, they would, for the most part, like to see the occasion used to set up a more decent government. This section of the nation all the same prefers victory to defeat, even though it would most welcome an early compromise peace. But a strong minority—those we have called "the disloyal population"—fears nothing so much as the war ending in victory, and wants to be free of their present rulers at almost any price. It fears even a compromise peace lest it should allow the Nazi regime to continue in some form or other. Though indeed one cannot say that a considerable proportion of the Germans longed for the war and greeted it with a sigh of relief for the sake of the defeat—that would be an exaggeration. They were, however, resigned to a lost war as the only hope of liberation and as the "end of the Terror," which is certainly preferable to the "Terror without end." But naturally these people do not want defeat for defeat's sake; that would be too much to expect of them. They have their own definite "war aims"; they want the Nazis ousted and punished; they want once more to have a decent government and be able to live as decent men.

That is a war aim that can easily be combined with those of the Allies. It cannot be said, however, that the Allies have hitherto taken advantage of this promising attitude on the part of numerous Germans.

Meanwhile, the nature of the war aims controversy that has been raging in England and France gives rise to deeper misgivings than the previous silence of their governments regarding this subject. Moreover, it has made a painful impression on the Germans. It is remarkable how even today important public discussions echo beyond a country's confines as if the very air bore thought and speech from land to land despite frontiers and other barriers.

The proposals that have been approved by public opinion in England differ from those that have found favor in France. In England, the fundamental error of the war aims discussions is that they do not adhere strictly to the point. So far most people in this country who have written and spoken on the subject seem to expect far too much from the war; they want no more and no less than a new and better world order. One often hears it said that if the war does not bring this about it would not have been worth all the sacrifice. Yet the dullest man can see that such an outcome cannot be expected from a war confined to England, France, Poland, and Norway on the one hand, and Germany on the other. There are several neutral countries which will hardly allow their fate to depend on the issue of a foreign war. In fact, there would be little sense even in inviting them to take part in the peace conference; they would first have to be asked to participate in the war.

No; whether or not a new world order be due, it is certainly not a subject of discussion pertinent to this war. This war is concerned with the German question, perhaps—more limited still—the Nazi question. Regarding this, most English spokesmen are noticeably vague, so that one often gains the impression that they have devoted little thought to the question and have not fully grasped its gravity. "Germany, after the war, will naturally become a member of a European federation," they say. Yes, if only it were as simple as all that! A federation between England and France is today a healthy and promising subject. Twice brothers-in-arms against the same enemy, twice in the same deadly peril, that provides them with a common tradition on which lasting cooperation can flourish in spite of many differences of national temperament. But Germany? Close collaboration on the basis of a mortal struggle on two occasions, the wounds of which still bleed? One is somewhat reminded of Schiller's ballad *Die Bürgschaft*. Moved by the mutual devotion of the two tyrannicides, Damon and Pythias, who intend to slay him, the tyrant Dionysius ingenuously begs to be included in the partnership.

> *Ich sei, gewährt mir die Bitte,*
> *In Eurem Bunde der Dritte.*

A delightful *ménage!*

Moreover, what sort of Germany will it be that is linked in a federation with England and France? Will it be a Nazified Germany? Opinions vary on this point. Some with a certain airy idealism take for granted the removal of the Nazis and their substitution by a misty noble dream–Germany. (But, indeed, the very problem is how to bring this about, and where to find the regime that will replace the Nazis.) There are others who, in all seriousness, still maintain that Germany must be allowed to choose a government after its own taste, and, if this should happen to be a Nazi government, we must resign ourselves to it. We may well ask why then do they wage a war against Nazi Germany? Why not openly accept Hitler's domination?

But even this peak of political ingenuousness is over-topped. There are people who gravely propose to reward Hitler's Germany after the war for its plunder raids. According to them, Germany should receive Austria and the border provinces of Bohemia as "reparation for the injustice of Versailles," a couple of colonies should be thrown in and, if a remnant of shame did not restrain them, Danzig and the Corridor would also be ceded to Hitler. Such are the war aims of these spiritual and material "primitive Christians," for which the youth of England, France, and Poland must sacrifice their lives.

Proposals of this kind, though they emanate from alarmingly high quarters, need not be taken seriously. There is little chance that they will actually constitute English policy. The worst of them is the extraordinarily perverse reactions they arouse in Germany. Strange as it may seem, they completely destroy confidence. It is not possible for Germans who have not lived long in England to believe the sincerity and earnestness of such effusions. They strike the average German, inevitably and through no fault of his own, as record exhibitions of English cant and hypocrisy, as the handiwork of political cardsharpers. They tend to discredit in advance every friendly and magnanimous offer of peace that might be made by England. They play, involuntarily but effectively, into the hands of Nazi propaganda, which naturally does its utmost to sow mistrust toward every voice that sounds from England.

However, the discussion of war aims in England does not always sink to this level. But even those proposals that can be taken seriously reveal an important miscalculation of German political psychology. Many think that the bitterness of defeat can and must be sweetened for the Germans by an inspiring ideal such as that of a European Union. They overlook the fact that these aims scarcely have a sugary flavor for German tongues. The concepts of a world order, the League of Nations and Pan–Europa awaken a certain response in England, but scarcely any in Germany, not even with "good," human, and civilized Germans. They do not believe in them. Even German Liberals rate them low, as we have already explained at some length. Besides, to sweeten defeat for Germans, equally for all of them, would be very difficult. One must probably be content to offer something to those of them with whom one wishes to conclude peace and upon whose support peace will eventually be erected. But whoever and whatever they may be, they will not find the idea of an international political mammoth concern very appetizing.

But apart from this disposition to misunderstand the German mentality, there lies at the root of all the many war aims enunciated by the English yet a second mistake—a sympathetic but dangerous one. (It is a strange sensation for me, as a German, to bring it to their attention.) From a chivalrous and, within limits, wise wish to reconcile the beaten foe and treat him justly, almost all of them rather forget the gravity of the peril embodied by this adversary, and the need of future security against such peril. They are eager where the Germans are loath to search for blame within themselves and to absolve the adversary. Thus numerous Englishmen attribute the rise of Nazism to the severity of the Treaty of Versailles, and are inclined to experiment this time with mildness. This is a course fraught with danger. The Versailles peace was certainly no masterpiece—otherwise the war that it should have ended would not, twenty years later again be raging—but it is very doubtful if its faults lay in its rigor. Many Frenchmen, on the contrary, maintain that it lay in its mildness. I should suggest that it lay in its vacillation between harshness and mildness.

As a treaty with the Germany that attacked Belgium, devastated Northern France, perpetrated the abominations of the U-boat campaign, strove to dominate the world by brute force and mocked at all offers of mediation so long as it remained undefeated in the battlefield, it was too mild. As a treaty with the Germany that repudiated all this, honestly forswore militarism and imperialism, remembered its great spiritual past and wanted to be a well-behaved member of the European family of nations, it was too harsh. The misfortune was that Weimar Germany did not make it clear which of the two Germanies it actually represented; probably it did not itself know. It was a democratic republic still calling itself the "German Empire"; disposed to conciliation but only after defeat; incensed against its militarist and imperialist seducers but refusing to surrender them; full of remorse but protesting against the "war guilt lie," pacifist while secretly rearming. With such a muddled state it was difficult to conclude a clearcut peace. But perhaps it was just the very task of the peace to create clearcut conditions in Germany. At any rate, such should be its task this time when men, wiser with experience, are confronted with the same problem.

The task has become easier, for the German people, then a compact indivisible block, is now separated into clearly marked divisions. One can now determine much more clearly that which must be destroyed in Germany—destroyed and not merely curbed—and that with which genuine peace can be made. And it is important to make use of this knowledge. A milder Versailles, as is desired by many Englishmen, and a harsher one, as is wanted by many Frenchmen, are both equally unpracticable. Fruitless is every conception that looks upon Germany and the German Reich as given postulates, and regards all Germans alike. To wish to content the Nazis by unlimited mildness would be lunatic. To discourage their opponents by irreconcilable severity would be no less mad. He judges well who distinguishes well.

In our analysis of the Germans, we have encountered seven groups of power and opinion: Hitler, the Nazi leaders, the Nazis, the loyal, the disloyal, the Opposition, and the émigrés. With which of these one must come to terms is yet to be decided. The peace, when it comes, will wear a different aspect according to the partner chosen. So, too, will the future Germany and the present strategy of psychological war. Let us survey the possibilities.

The possibility of peace with Hitler, his underlings and his followers will so naturally be excluded by anyone who knows Germany and is capable of political thought, that the very mention of it sounds like a cheap joke. Alas, such is not universally the case. There are doubtless certain Government declarations which, superficially considered, seem to rule out the possibility of a peace with the Nazis. But scrutinized more closely they will be found to leave every possiblity open. Certainly Mr. Chamberlain, on the day war was declared, said that he hoped to live to see the day when "Hitlerism" would be destroyed. But that is a very vague statement. Hitlerism is not Hitler—why should not Hitler, turncoat as he is, one day forswear Hitlerism?—and the hope to live to see a certain event counts far less than the resolve and the promise to bring it about. More precise was the indication implicit in the rejection of Hitler's "peace offensive" after the conquest of Poland. After all their disappointments, the Allies, it was said, would only conclude peace with a German Government "whose word can be trusted." But that, too, if carefully examined, is a very cautious statement, and, what is obvious, intentionally cautious. Perhaps it means that peace is not possible with a Hitler–Ribbentrop Government that has proved itself so utterly untrustworthy. Which is not to say that a Göring–Neurath Government might not later be found trustworthy. And perhaps, under certain circumstances, even the Hitler–Ribbentrop combination? Cannot we conceive of circumstances in which their word, perhaps because it coincided with their interests, might appear more trustworthy than it does today? Are we being excessively critical and suspicious? By no means. A couple of weeks later, Mr. Chamberlain himself unmistakably sanctioned this interpretation when, on the occasion of the attempt at mediation on the part of Belgium and Holland, he declared his readiness to examine every peace proposal of the German Government—that is to say, the present Hitler–Ribbentrop Government! Let us have no illusions. The possibility of concluding peace with the Nazis still exists. Nothing has been said that unequivocally rules it out. "There is no question of peace with a Nazi Government" are words as yet unspoken.

Still less has it ever been proclaimed that the removal of the Nazi Government and the punishment of the Nazis for their crimes are the first and most self-evident of the objects for which the war is being waged. And certain English leaders and writers complacently discuss the prospect of Hitler's personal "retirement" clearing the way for a compromise peace. What this compromise peace will be it is easy to imagine. Its model we know—the Munich settlement of 1939. Chancellor of the Reich Göring in the name of President of the Reich Hitler, will withdraw to the Munich line and in return the Munich agreement will be ratified. Perhaps a colony or two will be yielded to Germany. Göring would promise to disarm, and later protest he was doing so. The Allies would disarm.

After all that I have said about Hitler, the Nazi leaders, and the Nazis, I need not expatiate on the fact that peace with the Nazis under any circumstances whatever is a morbid and suicidal idea; although obvious attempts are being made here to keep open this possiblity, it is in fact an impossibility, as long as England and

France do not intend to sign their own death warrant. To conclude peace with Hitler, the Nazi leaders, and the Nazis, is completely insensate because they are incapable of thinking in terms other than those of war; and because every agreement intended by the Allies to be a treaty of peace must appear to the Nazis, by reason of their inborn and unalterable mental outlook, as a tactical measure of war. Every treaty with Hitler and the Nazis *must* share the fate of Hitler's settlement with the Bavarian Government in 1923 and with the German–Nationals in 1933; of the Anglo–German Naval Treaty, the Non-Intervention Agreement, the Anti–Comintern Pact and the Munich Settlement; because to Hitler and the Nazis, pacts and treaties signify no more than the stratagems of war. The very act of negotiating and concluding a treaty with Hitler and the Nazis means to fall into their trap and lose the game in advance, no less than does sitting down and gambling with a resolute cardsharper. This needs no elucidation. He is beyond help who has not grasped this, despite all the evidence of the role played by the Nazis in German politics from their rise until 1933 and in European politics from 1933 to 1940.

And I should like here to point out what, to my mind, has long merited universal recognition, the immense propagandist and psychological value of a declaration to this effect:

Firstly, a deal with a Nazi Government, however composed, is under no circumstances possible. *Secondly,* the preliminary condition of any peace negotiation or treaty with another German Government is the punishment, inflicted on the very culprits, of all crimes committed by the Nazis.

These two measures—the expulsion of the Nazi Government and the punishment of Nazi crimes—must figure among the results of this war if it is not to have been waged entirely in vain. As far as the first is concerned, there is, after all that has been said, no need to say more. But the second is almost as important; for so long as the Nazis are at large they constitute a peril—the German peril. Many clever farsighted people in England and France fully realize that this war will have been waged to no purpose unless it leads to a change of what is called "the German mentality." But they rack their brains in vain to discover how this apparently spiritual transformation can be brought about by external military means. Indeed, it is not a difficult problem, and here is the key to its solution.

That part of the "German mentality" which must be eradicated is personified by the Nazis. And we have alreayd pointed out how apt an opportunity it is that all the inhumanity, subhumanity, brutality, unscrupulousness, and aggressiveness formerly scattered, as it were, throughout the German bloodstream, are not localized to form the violent cancer of the Nazi Movement. The cancer must be excised, and promptly at that. It is a further stroke of luck, though inevitable from the nature of the case, that the Nazis have themselves twisted the rope by which they can be hanged, while sparing their hangmen the odium of intolerance and ideological persecution. This they owe to the immense number of crimes that they have committed in the course of the last seven years. There will be no need to punish anyone simply "because he is a Nazi." It will be necessary only to mete out legal punishment for all the crimes of murder, grievous assault, forcible detention, loot, theft, fraud, blackmail, extortion, arson, trespass, deprivation, insult, embezzlement, misdirection of justice, and perjury that have been perpetrated in Germany since January 30, 1933. After that, there will not be many Nazis left, and Germany will have undergone an astonishing change.

The suppression of the Nazi regime and the chastisement of the Nazis are necessary peace aims. But, meanwhile, it seems to have been completely overlooked that their proclamation as such is one of the strongest psychological weapons of the war.

Very many people in England and France are disappointed that hitherto there has been no visible sign of revolt on the part of the German masses who are disloyal and hostile to the Nazi regime. In view of their own war aims policy, this disappointment is surprising. If the Germans are to rebel—a much more difficult and dangerous undertaking than people in the West appear to realize—they must at least feel convinced that the West will resist the Nazis with iron determination, and that their apparent Allies will not let them down at the critical moment and come to a compromise with the Nazis behind their backs. This certainty will be lacking until, beyond misunderstanding, all bridges leading to the Nazis are burned and all back doors yet open to an understanding with them are bolted and barred. That, as we know, has by no means happened. And it is impossible altogether to blame the Germans that they are exigent on this point and wish to have it very clearly stated before they believe it.

For, firstly, and this is the only point about the war that interests them, in so far as they are not Nazis or pro–Nazi: it is unjust to expect anything from them, as long as the suppression and punishment of the Nazis is not solemnly promised and guaranteed to them as an ally is promised and guaranteed his share of the benefits of the treaty of alliance. Secondly: the experience of the last seven years has made them pessimistic. They are not so sure that the governments which went to Munich in September 1938 might not possibly end this war with another Munich. And they have been trained by their experiences to pay just as much attention to the loopholes in the declarations of these governments as to the declarations themselves; to attribute at least as much weight, say, to the phrases of cautious diplomatic reserve in the three official declarations of Mr. Chamberlain analyzed above as to the words of challenge they also contained. In 1933 or 1934 a hint would have been enough to unleash active resistance against the Nazis in Germany. Today, when pressure from without no less than discouragement within have continually increased during the last seven years, a more powerful dynamo is needed. So long as the two points previously mentioned are not proclaimed in the most formal manner to be the war aims of the Allies, we cannot count on a rising of anti–Nazi Germany. Such an announcement is the indispensable condition if the "other" Germany is to regain its confidence and self-confidence. As long as it is unspoken, in the hope of being able at some time or other to negotiate with the Nazis, so long is one of the greatest chances of quickly winning the war being sacrificed to a nonexistent possiblity of peace.

The declaration would have powerful and beneficial effects, not only among the opponents of the Nazis, but also among the credulous yet irresolute and easily alarmed public of Nazi propaganda, among those we have called "the loyal." These people, as we know, are daily informed by the Nazis that the true war aim of the Allies is the annihilation of the German nation. Hitherto, the answer of the propaganda of the Allies to this has been, to my mind, weak and ineffectual. It consists in mere denial, in a mere "no, we do not want to annihilate the German people. We have no quarrel with the German people." This explains nothing and provides no food for thought and imagination. It makes it easy for the Nazis to answer: "See! What hypocrisy! They wage war against Germany, yet they maintain they have no quarrel with Germany. This only proves that they must have the most sinister plans. Believe us, their true war aim *is* the annihilation of the German people."

A war is violent and destructive. If it needs excuse and justification, institutions or persons must be singled out that are to be destroyed and that deserve to be destroyed. Hence, merely to state that one does not wish to destroy is to state nothing and awakens distrust. To the cry of Nazi propaganda that the Allies want to annihilate the German people a much more vigorous answer than the mere "No, we don't want to do that at all," would be to say: "No, but we certainly do want to annihilate the Nazis." For that is illuminating and credible; it is a positive idea to be turned over in the mind; it leaves no mental gap for the foe to cram with his unlimited propaganda fancies. To reply to this, the Nazis must explain how it pays the Germans to fight and die in order to save them from annihilation. Which is to say, the Nazis would have to become their own apologists—always a very weak position in an argument.

And it would be all the weaker, because from that moment the Nazis would be compelled to plead their own cause. This declaration would accomplish more than merely counter the suspicion that, for lack of another declared enemy, the annihilation of the German people is in fact, though in secret, desired. The Nazis would be robbed of the very platform from which they speak to the German people. It is remarkable how greatly people are discredited when exposed to immediate and concrete danger. No sooner is it made clear that this war is a hanging matter for the Nazis, that their necks are forfeit, that if the Germans do not win all the Nazi murderers and thieves, headed by Hitler and Göring, will dangle with halters round their necks from a long row of gallows; than all that the Nazis say to rally the German people to continue the struggle will bear a strange and unmistakable stamp of improbability. From that moment, it becomes a matter of personal interest for the Nazis to find other reasons for the continuation of the war than that of saving their own skins; and they will be speaking too obviously on their own behalf for their words to bear full weight with those whom they are sending to their deaths.

They will have themselves become far too much the subject of the discussion to be able to take an unqualified part in it. It is a psychological device which the Nazis themselves have employed most successfully more than once; when, for instance, they discovered the "Jewish question" and the "Czech question," and thereby seemed to revoke the right of Jews and Czechs to join in the controversy over their own fate on the ground that they constituted the "question." And, moreover, the Nazis were obliged to fabricate everything that threw doubt upon the right of Jews and Czechs to live, whereas the crimes of the Nazis have only to be revealed and named for the most loyal Germans to realize that there is a "Nazi question." Why on earth should it sound strange and unfamiliar to talk of a "Nazi question," while the "Jewish question" is on every lip? Is there no Nazi problem? And if there is, why is there no expression for it? Why, even today, this shyness on the subject of the Nazis? Why this refusal to exploit the only opportunity that they offer: the fact that they are such utter criminals and scoundrels that they seem to be enemies created for extermination? As future partners in peace the Nazis must be ruled out; but, as lightning conductors, to attract all the loathing engendered everywhere by the war, they are most welcome. As such, they may perform, though not in the way they intend, the greatest services in the cause of future peace.

So much for the possibilities that the Nazis offer to psychological warfare and future peace. Let us now proceed to the next of the "Germanies" we have described. What possibilities are offered by that section of the population hitherto loyal to the Nazis? Can they be made disloyal? Can peace be concluded with them?

These questions are of the utmost urgency and gravity. For it is perhaps this section of the population that the Allied Governments at the moment regard as their future partners in framing the peace. They will probably not negotiate with the Nazis unless the worst comes to the worst—and it seems bad enough even then; but they would, it seems, be very glad to come to an agreement with these decent and honest Germans, who are neither criminals nor savages, though they are patriots and nationalists. Vague conceptions even exist as to how it might be brought about and what the ensuing peace would look like. Something, unless I am quite mistaken, to this effect:

The nationalists, though not the Nazis, still constitute the largest section of the nation. They not only have numerical weight but political power; to them still adhere several of the higher bureaucrats and, above all, the generals. To put them in power, no revolution from below would be needed, but only a coup d'état of the Army; a change of heads with subsequent reorganization of the Reich on conservative-monarchical lines. The disloyal section of the population would thankfully accept such a solution, for it would at least mean their liberation from the Nazis; and probably the "moderate" Nazis would also be agreeable, so that it might be assured of a tolerable degree of stability. For the large part of the Army, it certainly represents the ideal solution. Further, the generals have an interest in preventing Hitler from staking the Army in its present state, since they know that it is still "unready" and not capable of a prolonged and relentless struggle. Thus, if danger threatens, they will be tempted both to overthrow Hitler with the help of the Army and, with it still intact behind them, treat for a peace that allows the German Reich on the whole to issue from the whole affair unweakened and perhaps even with a small gain of prestige.

To this end golden bridges must be built for them. Hence, for example, we must not expect them immediately to surrender or execute Hitler, who was once their chief warlord. Nor must we lay down severe terms. They will naturally have to evacuate Poland and Czechoslovakia, or at least what was left of it after Munich. Austria—perhaps a plebiscite? And when, in return for a promise to disarm of a Government "whose word can be trusted," they are helped out of the bankruptcy into which Hitler has landed them, the prospect would really be enticing enough to make them and send their present, highly unpresentable, Government with gentle force into pensioned retirement. Thus the war would end in universal satisfaction; and the shortening of the struggle would be a gain in itself.

All that sounds very hopeful, but contains, to my mind, certain grave errors of judgment. The most serious is the doubly faulty psychological estimate of the generals and the Germans, loyal to the Nazis and patriotic to the Reich, whom they represent.

The "plan" as it is here sketched demands of these people two qualities without which it cannot function, quiet measured reason and resolute courage capable of independent action. Both these characteristics, however, are abnormally weakly developed in them. The political temperament of the Reich patriot, be he soldier or civilian, alternates between the summit of confidence and the depth of despair, now jubilant, now grieving unto death. They are always inclined to gamble, stake high against long odds, and, should the game go badly, abandon it quickly. "It will not be so bad," they murmur and hope. To stop fighting "prematurely" and for what is scanty compensation in their eyes, is not their wont, particularly as long as there is a sporting chance of winning and covering themselves with glory. Time enough, they say, to talk of reconciliation and compromise when they are beaten, as in 1918. And the "weak-kneed" readiness to compromise on the opposite side, far from encouraging them to conclude peace, confirms them in this attitude. Nor must it be forgotten that they are in full agreement with the foreign policy of the Nazis; that the expansion and "greatness" of the German Reich is as much their concern as it is the Nazis'. They differ from the latter solely on questions of peacetime morality, culture, and taste. But in pursuing national aggrandizement and world domination they are no different from the Nazis, for, as we made clear in an earlier chapter, this is the traditional, irreplaceable idea of the German Reich. As long as they see no immediate danger of the Reich exploding they are determined to inflate it indefinitely. They are devoid of the humdrum wisdom of preferring a bird in the hand to two in the bush.

So, too, with the courage to carry out a coup d'état, even when discretion counsels such a course. This kind of courage is very rare in Germany and never to be found among German soldiers. German officers have courage only on the battlefield; at home they are cowards. It is no accident that German history records no instance of the Army overturning the State despite the most alluring opportunities. German generals have often played with the idea of making history, and not military history alone. But from Wallenstein to Schleicher they have never got beyond irresolute trifling, and in the end these powerful warlords have usually allowed themselves to be struck down without resistance. Professional courage apart, the German officer knows only the courage of despair. Under extreme pressure of conscience in a strenuous conflict of loyalties he has on rare occasions found the courage of his convictions. Perhaps Yorck turning against Napoleon at Tauroggen in 1812, and some generals of the Rhenish Confederation during the campaign of 1813. But for the Prussian officer to be brought to that, he must be provided with something very different to bridges of gold.

If a coup d'état on the part of the German army were a desirable aim—followed by the restoration of the Hohenzollerns, termination of the war, peace roughly on the basis of the boundaries of (January, April, or October) 1938, mutual agreement to disarm and let bygones be bygones—life must be made so infernally hot for the German officers that they will acquire civic courage through sheer fright. They must be informed with the utmost gravity and clarity that the possibility of such a move is open to them only for a short period which would automatically end the moment the German offensive began. And if they reject the offer and prefer to risk losing the war, they must be confronted with an alternative which shatters their facile optimism. They must be told there was no more question of peace with them and their like, nor of the continued existence of the Reich. As the inevitable consequence of probable defeat, they would not only have to face the prospect of a new and worse Versailles; but on the territory of the Reich, at whose expense neighboring states would be duly rounded off and a number of League of Nations' mandates created, not so much as an air gun or toy helmet would be permitted, and alone the armed force of a permanent international police would parade. Then, yes then, the generals might possibly sense the necessity of once again reckoning up their chances exactly, though they do it unwillingly; and even of staging a coup d'état, bitter duty though it seem, in order to prevent the dangerous adventure. But not so long as the Nazis promise them the British Empire and the British erect golden bridges for them. So long as the possibility of victory seems great and the risk small, the German army will play its Hitler-imposed role with zest, and Reich-patriotic Germans with it. He little knows them who expects anything else.

Thus ther German army and the "German–Nationals" must be addressed in a different tone if peace, a speedy compromise peace, with them is desired.

However, the question arises as to whether such a peace is as desirable as it appears at first glance. It certainly has one or two obvious attractions. But it contains at least as many dangers and weaknesses. In my opinion, if I may anticipate, the dangers are so frightful and the weaknesses so fundamental that the realization of this solution would be a great calamity for Europe and Germany.

The first apparent advantage is that the partner of this peace, the German army, can rally behind it an overwhelming majority of the German people; and that the Allies would rather conclude peace with those who have the approval of their countrymen than with those who offer few guarantees that they will be able at home to enforce the peace terms they accept. But also this advantage diminishes on closer inspection. The following that the army could gather would be large but not particularly staunch or faithful. It would contain far too many differing motives of adhesion, to be either stable or lasting. Moreover, a good many Nazis would probably be found among them, who in this way would escape the consequences of their deeds. They would strive to reconstitute themselves at the first opportunity and begin their old game all over again. And if the Germany army were to guarantee that fourteen years later "the German people" or whoever then rules them will not declare the peace to be a "shameful peace" and tear it up as "a scrap of paper," who will guarantee that the army itself will not do this at a suitable opportunity—in even less than fourteen years?

The second advantage is the more spurious. It is the idea haunting many minds, that "a strong German Reich" must be preserved as a "bulwark against Bolshevism," or perhaps even as an ally against Bolshevism. Now I am the last person to ignore the gravity of the Bolshevik peril and the need of bulwarks against it. But to find such a bulwark in a "strong German Reich" which is traditionally disposed to ally itself with Russia against the West; which itself helps to bring about Bolshevism in Russia; which throughout the period of secret rearmament cooperated with her; which today at the crucial moment is again aided by her; and the internal evolution of which is logically impelled toward Bolshevism—means no less than setting a wolf to mind the sheep. Perhaps a weaker but healthy and civilized Germany, without the Reich and without a powerful army, may constitute a far better rampart against Bolshevism than a highly militarized, anticultural German Reich thirsting for aggrandizement. Even in the West the force of arms is nowadays overestimated, the power of the spirit underestimated. Armies are certainly not to be despised, but only one's own can be relied upon. Armies of other nations have a way, recently exemplified yet once again, of making a sudden and surprising appearance beside those against whom they should form a bulwark. The spirit has at least the merit of not being able to do this quite so easily. A thoroughly European Germany, as proud of its spirit, culture, and traditions, as, let us say, Finland, is, despite its weak armies, a far better bulwark against Bolshevism than the blustering, mighty German Reich of Ludendorff and Keitel with all their ranting against the Red menace.

It is evident, then, that all the advantages afforded by peace with the German army and the German Reich which it embodies, are either of small, tactical, momentary importance or entirely illusory. All the greater and more terrible are the dangers that lurk in such a peace.

The situation that it would restore would be, in a word, the status quo of before 1914. This simple and indubitable truth only needs expression for the significance of such a peace to be instantly apparent. It would mean, firstly, that two great wars have been waged for nothing; and, secondly, that a third great war inevitably impends. For one cannot imagine that the Reich and its army would draw from this result the moral that they must change their ways and become peace-loving. Why should they? The result would represent a complete success and a clear justification for their policy of aggression. After two wars against the whole "envious world" they would be all the more conscious of their might, strengthened in their inherent dogmas and convictions, and more than ever before a menace to their smaller neighbors. The West would have waged the War of 1939 in order to set up that against which they took the field in 1914! The German Reich could have no clearer proof that it was not seriously menaced.

Not that it will be healed of its resentments, its lack of confidence and its megalomaniac pugnacity. If only the statesmen of the West could for a mere moment probe the mentality of this Reich and its zealots. I myself can already hear them, the speeches and conversations in which the "foul" and "half" peace would be justified; those clever reflections that "it was all they could do at the moment"; that the Nazis "had raged wildly at it," that "one must know how to stop at the right moment." And I hear still further back the silencing: "Wait and see!"

The generals may be personally more sympathetic, more cultivated, and cleverer than the Nazis. That does not prevent them from serving the same cause. And it is no accident but historical necessity that, in spite of personal antipathies and constant friction, they have clung to the Nazis until today. Both serve *Deutschland über Alles*. Both serve the cause of expansion at any price, which the German Reich inherited from Frederick's Prussia; it is its one and only aim, which no ruler can long thwart and still retain the reins of power. Compared to this, everything that divides Nazis and warlords is of secondary importance.

To accept the Reich of the generals is to accept new threats, crises, and wars. Perhaps they will conduct their campaigns of conquest more decently and humanely than the Nazis. Perhaps, but perhaps not. Belgium's invasion in 1914 was scarcely a model of decency and humanity. And, it appears from the meager news from Poland, it was the army, and not—as in Austria and Czechoslovakia—the Gestapo to which it played willing usher and beadle, which excelled in plundering and hostage-shooting. Be that as it may, what distinguishes the Third Reich from the German Reich are nuances. For the world at large they are identical; the spirit of aggression, aggrandizement, and world domination, which constitute the means, soul, and demon of this State. And I should like to add more quietly that to Germany, too, they appear the same: utter contempt, neglect, and destruction of the German spirit and the German mission, which make the Reich—Third or not—a German malady.

That this malady has become more virulent in the Nazi State than ever before; that it has assumed forms that would never have been thought possible; that it has driven a large section of the German people to sheer lunacy, but as large a section back again to sanity—here are the chance and the hope that this time the disease may be cured. Merely to restore it to its former passive and latent condition would be a wretched recompense for so much strife and tribulation.

There is one more possibility: peace based on those Germans who look upon the Nazis as their enemies. That is not as easy to bring about as, with the correct psychological tactics, a makeshift peace with the army. On the other hand, it is worth while; whereas the other is not.

The difficulty of this task is obvious. It lies in the fact that today the vast mass of disloyal anti–Nazi Germans are altogether without political representation and program. The partner with whom we may strike a deal is lacking. The army of peace exists, but it is an army without a leader. Widespread and deep-rooted as is the unorganized hostility to the Nazis, actual political opposition to them is weak, scattered, unready, and unrepresentative. It is indeed no alluring prospect to raise the edifice of peace on the Opposition as it exists today. Indeed, the foundations of future peace with Germany cannot rest on the Opposition, but only on the disloyal section of the population. But in order to convert the disloyal, mute and immobile as they are at the moment, into a political factor, they must be provided with political representation. And this needs a new idea, the clear vision of an aim—and the road leading to it.

The reverse was the situation during the last war. On the one hand the chances of a genuine, fundamental upheaval were far less than they are today; even in the last years of the war, the Kaiser's Reich never encountered such a concentrated mass of unswerving disloyalty, reasoned repudiation and mortal enmity as the Nazi regime faces today. There was increasing war-weariness, grumbling, and doubt as to the prospects, and, gradually, as to the true worth of the German cause; but even in the very ranks of Socialist workers there was no real desire for a radical transformation of Germany or for a new political destiny, and certainly no widespread secret yearning for a defeat such as exists today, which can render such a change possible.

On the other hand there existed, at that time, an active political Opposition. There was a parliamentary coalition of Socialists, radical Liberals, and the Center, which from the summer of 1917 began to steer toward a compromise peace, strove for power and finally, in October 1918—before the "revolution"—assumed office. Historically, the German parliamentary Opposition in 1917–18 was a far more superficial and far less promising force than is constituted today by the passionate disloyalty of a vast proportion of the German people; yet, contrary to the latter, it was a palpable political reality. Technically, it was no more difficult to conclude peace with it than with the German–National generals today. But as the history of the subsequent years has shown, it was not very fruitful.

Today, moreover, it would be no more fruitful; but today it would be unrealistic as well, which it was not then. In investigating the possibilities of a real peace with the real "other" Germany—a peace which was neither a capitulation to the Nazis nor a mere armistice with the military expansionists—it is advisable to exclude beforehand the thought of a repetition of the unsuccessful experiment of 1919, the plan of an "improved" Treaty of Versailles with an "improved" Weimar Republic.

Let us leave aside the highly controversial question as to the nature of the improvements contemplated. This would be an idle enquiry, for the conception on which the peace of 1919 was based has been totally and fundamentally refuted by history. According to this conception, it was possible to convert the German Reich into a peaceful democracy, after the Western pattern, without a complete upheaval of its historical traditions and geographical and political structure, with its inborn idea, its indelible legend, and its ineradicable character; and to conclude with it terms of healthy coexistence and cooperation in spite of discriminatory military and economic measures of precaution which were necessary, since its historical tradition and geographical-political structure had been preserved. The history of the Weimar Republic has shown that this was impossible. It has shown that within the framework of the German Reich—a German Reich maddened to foaming resentment by "the chains of Versailles"—the Weimar coalition of Socialists, Liberals, and political-minded Catholics, even with the most numerous. following, had no chance against the Frederickian–Bismarckian tradition of this State; that it could only retain power so long as the stunning effects of the defeat endured; and that as soon as concessions were made to the so-called democratic Reich, forces were again called into being which suited the old tradition and legend of the Reich better than the "democrats." It has revealed something even worse: that the sudden introduction of democratic forms "off the peg" in a country accustomed to obedience and discipline does not in the long run favor the democrats, but the Nazis; and that the overthrow of the lords does not lead to liberty, equality, and fraternity, but, alas, to that horror of horrors, the dictatorship of lackeys.

If the parties of the Weimar coalition were then unable to hinder such results, when they constituted substantial political forces with powerful organizations, when they still had the wind of history in their sails and inspired the hope, faith, and zeal of millions of loyal adherents; how much more so today after all their discouragements, disappointments, and failures! Those of the German Opposition groups who have nothing else to propose than repetition of the Weimar experiment (with "improvements") can no longer claim political credit. They deceive themselves and others if they believe and pretend that they can once again win over the masses, as in 1919, with the old rallying cries of a "Republic of Workers, Peasants, and Soldiers," of "Freedom, Work, Bread," or of "Unity, Order, and Freedom." Even when they might have done this, their efforts were altogether in vain. Meanwhile, however, the masses have grown deaf and distrustful toward these slogans. Dust and mold covers the glittering hopes of 1919. The promise of that year has turned to a mockery. The most ardent democrat in Germany has learned by instinct that, so long as the German Reich remains what it is, the freedom-loving, the peaceable, and the tolerant must yield to the tyrants and the warriors. Though they are conscious of the fact, few can explain it. The Germans feel an inescapable doom hanging over them, a magic spell. Indeed is it not magical—the demonic relentlessness with which the historical tradition of the German Reich defends itself against its foes? Nevertheless, if a real peace is possible, the spell must be broken. Which means: *the German Reich must disappear, and the last seventy-five years of German history must be erased. The Germans must retrace their steps to the point where they took the wrong path—to the year 1866. No peace is conceivable with the Prussian Reich which was born at that time, and whose last logical expression is no other than Nazi Germany. And no vital "other" Germany is anywhere to be found but that which in that year was worsted by the caprice of war—without ever totally succumbing.*

It cannot be said that the possibilities here revealed have hitherto been acknowledged, or that they have played their due role in public discussions of the war and war aims. But in no way must they be confounded with the "partition" and "dismemberment" of Germany, threats of which often appear in the correspondence columns of the newspapers and in the speeches of some politicians of the extreme right. "Partition" and "Dismemberment" sound more like a battle cry of passionate pugnacity than a deliberate and reasoned political program. The advocates of this policy seem to plan the total extermination of an organism, the quartering of a live body, a carnage that will deprive the Germans of all forms of political existence in the future; in fact, not only no "other" Germany, but no Germany at all—a fate such as the Nazis plotted for Poland.

Let us grant that people can temporarily entertain such ideas in the heat and fury of battle. But soberly and seriously to exalt them to political aims would be a horrible tragedy not only for the Germans, but for the French and English. For it would signify for the latter, firstly, in the long run, that they must bury all hopes of a real peace, of a restoration of the "European Concert"; that they would perpetuate German resentment and the German peril, so that their only chance of security would lie in a constant, sleepless, armed supervision and suppression of an enemy perpetually scheming liberation and revenge (and we have seen how quickly they weary of thus keeping armed guard!); and, secondly, in the short run, that they would be obliged to abandon every chance of waging psychological warfare, write off every possibility of winning over large sections of the German people and rely for victory solely on the force of arms; for the sure prospect of lifelong political imprisonment after the lost war would be the most powerful psychological means of driving even his most recalcitrant compatriots into Hitler's arms. The Allies would thereby accomplish the feat which has hitherto proved beyond Hitler: unite all Germans in an iron resolve to win the war—Hitler or no—at any price! Let us have no illusions. A war, crudely and simply, of the peoples, a war of Frenchmen and Englishmen against Germans to end in the domination of the victors and the slavery of the vanquished—such is the very conception and explanation of the war that Hitler has sought from the beginning to hammer into the heads of the Germans (and of the world)—but until now without complete success. The moment the Allies accept and sanction this view and thereby submit to the enemy's thesis and basis of discussion, they have lost the psychological and ideological war, whatever may be its military outcome (which from that moment becomes very much more doubtful, because psychological defeats have the military result of a reinforcement of the enemy's unity and fighting morale). From this moment the "theme" of the war is just as much determined by Hitler as was the "theme" of the preceding peacetime European crises—the Austrian, Czech, and Danzig "question." Counter to this, the conception and explanation of the Allies—wholly sound and healthy, which, thank God, have not yet been officially disavowed—have rather been that this war is a world police drive against the Nazis, in which even the Germans have every interest to participate. In order to have its full, overwhelming effect, this idea must be much more concretely, vigorously, and precisely elaborated; it must, so to say, sprout teeth. Instead, to renounce it, effecting a skillful tactical retreat, and surrender the entire psychological battlefield to the enemy, would mean a political Trondheim on a gigantic scale, and one that would mean not only a lost campaign but a lost war. Heaven preserve us from such an irrevocable calamity!

No, what we here propose is not the dismemberment and destruction of Germany for the purpose of her suppression and enslavement, but a highly constructive and organic solution, which does not violate her historical traditions but pursues their path; which cannot be achieved *against* the Germans, but *with* them and *by* them; and which promises not only her neighbors but Germany herself a healthier and happier political future than the present Prussian–German Reich can offer. That such a possibility exists, apart from the Reich, seems to have struck nobody. Indeed, it presupposes the recognition that the Reich is not Germany's natural and proper political form, but something quite different; and that the "other" Germany, when it once again becomes an effective political reality, must regain and develop its natural and living political forms. This fact has been overlooked by Europe. In Germany, I believe, after the terrible experiences of the last decades and in the reaction against Nazism, it will be more easily recognized than in the West, where one looks at things from the outside and has seldom been obliged to devote much thought to them. Such thought, however, is just as essential for the Western powers threatened by Nazi Germany as for Germany herself, enslaved and ravaged as she is by the Nazis.

There is nowadays a rather inexplicable inclination to regard all nations alike, all fitting into the same political mold—the national unified State. This fundamentally erroneous conception takes such complete possession of men's minds that it is often difficult even to make them realize that it is, at least, a problem and a subject of debate. Yet it is scarcely a moot point, for the very reverse of this universal opinion is the truth. Like men, different nations prefer different conditions of living. Some are predestined to the existence of large or small national states: others to that of super-national states; others to that of the city states—ancient Athens, for example, and modern Hamburg; others to that of small and medium-sized agricultural states; and again, others, like the Jews, seem to find their ideal in complete statelessness. If a nation accepts an unsuitable political mold, which has either been externally foisted upon it or which from dearth of instinct merely apes that of another state (the German Reich is a mixture of the two), the consequences for the nation may be various. It may founder altogether; it may adjust itself at the cost of its national character; or, if it fails to adapt itself, it may fall victim to a pathological neurosis. This last has been the lot of the German Reich.

The contemporary vogue for large national states makes it difficult for many to grasp the fact that something better and more healthy can exist. A development from large to small may, under certain circumstances, represent an advance and a process of healing: the reverse, decadence and a symptom of disease. I shall, therefore, illustrate the case of Germany by an historical parallel: the fate of ancient Hellas.

The classical Greeks, though undoubtedly a single nation and very conscious of their national cohesion, found their ideal political form in small sovereign states of the size of provinces. So long as they lived under these favorable political conditions, their culture flourished, even their political culture. But as soon as they were half "unified" and half subjected by Macedonia—a warlike and semi-civilized Greek border state—and became a Great Power, their political culture decayed rapidly, to be followed by their spiritual culture. Macedonia–Greece conquered a vast empire, but could not digest it. But what it gave to the world was at best a reflection of the fading glories of Athens, Corinth, Sparta, and Thebes.

The parallel with modern Germany is glaring. Germany was rather like the Hellas of Europe, so long as it consisted—in spite of all the healthy unexaggerated national consciousness of that time—of a number of small and medium-sized states. Since it has been "unified" by Prussia, the modern Macedonia, it has ceased to be Germany as Greece in the fourth and third centuries B.C.E. ceased to be Hellas. One can say that German culture withstood this process of unification even less than Greek culture. There is only one difference. Prussia–Germany has so far not succeeded in its Alexandrine role of world conqueror. After every new unsuccessful attempt the old Germany impatiently announces itself and anxiously searches for something that it has lost and that is called freedom, culture, beauty of life in exalted language, and quiet, decency, comfort in homely phrase. But it will recover all that together with its old political form, the only one that it has mastered. What is decisive is whether the recognition of this truth that remained concealed after the last war, will this time reveal itself.

Those to whom the conceptions "Germany" and "German Reich" appear synonymous—and, therefore, according to temperament, either resignedly accept the perpetuation of the German peril or can only suggest Germany's dismemberment and destruction as a means of ending it—overlook the fact that there are, fettered by the Reich, organisms, vigorous, long-standing, deep-rooted in history, which, if released, will play their full role. They ignore the fact that the German states, which must replace the Reich as the political lifeform of the Germans, do exist, are realities, and only the will is wanting to make them actualities again. Finally, they disregard the fact that among the traditions and state myths of these states are contained all those precepts of civilization which German history can offer as alternatives and counterforces to the present all-powerful Frederickian–Bismarckian–Hitlerian ideal of national aggrandizement. The Reich has never succeeded in renouncing this fundamentally Nazi ideal and giving itself another state myth; its one attempt in this direction, called the Weimar Republic, was a failure. Why, we may ask, should the Reich seek another ideal and destiny than that by which it was born and throve? The German states, however, have other ideals and destinies, and, according to them, these have lived and flourished for centuries. *All that stands against Nazism in Germany today is nourished, consciously or unconsciously, by the tradition of those centuries*—the magnificent centuries of German spirituality, now become almost legendary. It will regain power with the resurrection of its natural political form.

Let us review these states. Some have still scarcely ceased to be political actualities; they still are, so to speak, to be seized by the hand, and no more than a legislative act is needed for their complete rehabilitation. Others are more deeply submerged and are in need of a fundamental recovery to rediscover their political mission, their integrating idea. But they are all still recognizable as entities, with their almost astonishingly clear geographic, ethnic, and often, political markings. None is a synthetic academic product. All have the reality of a historically evolved, organic creation.

The states are: 1. AUSTRIA. From the standpoint of practical politics, Austria presents the clearest example. She never formed part of Bismarck's German Reich. Her brutal annexation, which has scarcely become history and almost still constitutes topical politics, can hardly signify more than an army of occupation in time of war. There are the Austrian emigrants, an organized body. There is what amounts to an Austrian government in exile. And there is the Pretender to the throne, who symbolizes Austria's historic right to an independent political existence. In Austria itself national independence has today practically become the watchword of all anti–Nazis—and its lure, unlike elsewhere in Germany, is potent even in the very ranks of the Austrian Nazis. The instinctive knowledge that Austria does not belong to the Reich has not for a single moment been forgotten by the Austrians; even at the height of the Anschluss jubilations, no Austrian ever forgot to make an obvious distinction between himself and the "Reich–German." Today Austria is a more complete and tangible political reality than any other German state. Her political reconstruction is scarcely now a matter of political manipulation and psychological preparation, but almost solely a question of military and constitutional action.

Nevertheless, the case of Austria is by no means the least complicated among the German states. All that is simple and easily explicable is on the negative side—the absence of any historical link with the Prussianized German Reich. Austria's positive mission, the role she is to play in the future, the voice that she is to make heard in the deliberations of a rebuilt Europe, is less clearly defined than that of the other German states. We must not forget that the historical past of Austria—unlike that of almost every other German state—is *not* a small-state past and has not created a small-state mentality. Hers is a Great Power's past and an imperial tradition. Her transformation into a petty state in 1919 at once created complex problems. For Austria in that year found herself in the position in which Prussia will be placed after a lost war. She was the real loser of the war, the state which had the difficult task of discovering completely new foundations for its political life; whereas the "Succession States," which had formerly belonged to her, had not lost their war but hers, and emerged from the struggle liberated rather than vanquished (an advantage which, with the right psychological preparation, can be shared by all the German states not excluding Prussia). Austria could not solve this difficulty; the absence of such a solution, the absence of a "red-white-red" to replace a "black-yellow" ideal was what gave the unorganic solution provided by the Anschluss its opportunity and its popularity in Austria. The horrible Nazi episode should at least have produced the one good result of curing the Anschluss mania once for all. Yet this does not spare the Austrians even more difficult future problems which they must solve in order that their country be as internally consolidated, stable, and contented as many another German state that is politically less mature and less real.

Ideologically and psychologically, the problems presented by each state become immediately more simple, when we advance northward from Austria.

2. BAVARIA. As an actual political unit, Bavaria is only a shade less clearly distinguished than Austria. Indeed, it is not since 1938 but 1871 that she has belonged to the Reich, yet with how many mental reservations, how little enthusiasm, and how jealous an insistence on her own rights as a state. Neither the Kaiser's Reich nor the Republic ever succeeded in fully integrating the rugged and self-willed Bavarians, who have never learned to utter the name "Prussia" without the appendage of a certain unparliamentary prefix. The Bavarian People's Party, which is nationalist, particularist, and potentially separatist, has always been stronger than any other party in the land, including the Nazis at the peak of their strength. In the spring of 1933 Bavaria was within a hair's breadth of seceding from the Reich—the historic rumor goes that it was only prevented by the failure to agree about the magnitude of the Bavarian king's civil list; at all events, the Nazis had to carry out a military coup d'état to compel Bavaria to toe the line; a procedure not unlike the armed occupation of Austria.

The desire for independence is scarcely less strong and widespread in Bavaria than in Austria; but its handicap, compared with that of Austria, lies in the fact that the political leaders, unlike the Austrian Pretender, are not yet ready for action and in contact with the Allies outside Bavaria, but are within. It is a situation where the disadvantages far outweigh the advantages, and one which, so long as Hitler's iron hold on Germany is unshaken, renders them incapable of striking. This situation, however, can yet be remedied.

Be that as it may, there is no doubt that Bavaria, no less than Austria, is a complete and intact political entity which is prepared to resume its political existence the moment circumstances decide. And, in advantageous contrast to Austria, Bavaria is not saddled with an exhausted imperial tradition, nor does she constitute the rump of an empire of the past. As a political structure she has established her boundaries and her form long ago, and only desires to begin anew her old life. Racially and geographically compact, unburdened by irredentist resentments and historical dreams, a state that feels as healthy as any in the world, and in which, incidentally, the "longing for the Reich" was always weaker and had less chance of revival than elsewhere; a state with its gaze toward the south, over the Alps and beyond, constantly and profitably linked with the culture of Rome, the German interpreter of the spirit of the Renaissance, from olden times a center of all plastic and graphic arts, and embodying a synthesis alone possible here, of rugged parochialism and sensuous, artistic subtlety, of Catholic fervor and heathen joy of life, of northern humorous dourness and a southern classical charm. We need not be concerned for a moment whence Bavaria will be able to extract spiritual and mental nourishment once it has shaken off the Reich's clutches!

Less outstanding in their national traits, but no less conscious of their individuality, are the two smaller southwestern states which also desire to preserve the political forms in which they have existed independently until 1871 and in subjection ever since: 3. and 4. WÜRTTEMBERG AND BADEN. The prevalent mode of the mammoth state will frown upon the restoration of these two states; for, whereas Austria, Bavaria, and the other German states, which constitute independent political units within the Reich, are medium-sized states of, so to speak, normal European size with seven to sixteen million inhabitants, these two unmistakably small states respectively contain no more than three million and two and a half million inhabitants. However, it would be senseless, so long as an organic solution is lacking, to join them together or to "attach" them to another state, for history has shaped them as individual structures each with its specific ethnic character and socialpolitical form. The Swabians of Württemberg—they are, in fact, the "poets and philosophers" of the Germans—differ greatly from their Bavarian as well as their lively, forthright, Westernized, urbane neighbors of Baden. Besides, a factor that makes for the stability of these two states is their unwavering attachment to their dynasties, each of which embodies a healthy and successful ruling tradition rooted in the soil. This tradition is particularly remarkable in the case of Baden; for this little state, the "model statelet" of the former Germanic Confederation, is the home of German liberalism. A liberal constitutional life did not develop here, as almost everywhere else in Germany, in battle with the local dynasty, but in league with it. At the time of the creation of the Reich, the Grand Duke of Baden was one of the leading champions of an anti–Bismarckian, liberal Reich; and when in 1918 the Kaiser's Reich hoped to avert the threatening catastrophe by means of a democratic-liberal reform of the constitution, the man who attempted the task was Prince Max of Baden, the last Imperial Chancellor under the Kaiser. A Prince of Baden Chancellor of the Kaiser's Reich was a revolution in itself! Baden is the only state in Germany which has long and successfully been ruled according to parliamentary and democratic principles; the only state whose inhabitants in race and spirit are somewhat akin to the Swiss. With its old and famous universities of Heidelberg and Freiburg, it is a traditional center of German academic culture; and it is extraordinarily well equipped to be a spiritual center not only by its character, history, and scenery, but also by its situation at the crossroads: France is near, Bavaria is near, Switzerland is across the border, and the Rhine provides a natural link with the Burgundian states toward the north. This little grand duchy has every chance of becoming a "model statelet" not only of Germany, but of Europe.

Southern Germany, it is clear, offers no great difficulties. Its political forms exist almost intact, appropriated rather than disrupted by the German Reich and easily to be restored to life. In the north, Prussia apart, things are not so simple. For here the summary solution of 1866 had been preceded by a secular process of Brandenburg–Prussian infiltration and disintegration, interrupted at the beginning of the nineteenth century by Napoleon's generous but mechanical attempts at a solution which proved ephemeral. The little states which even today find themselves strewn like enclaves amid the large "must-be-Prussian" provinces of the Rhineland, Westphalia, and Hanover, are by no means structures with solid historical foundations, sound and healthy as the South German states. And the frontiers of these "provinces" do not in the last coincide with those of the states that lie buried in them. Here, unlike in the south, one cannot be content to sanction and reimpose solutions discovered by history. Here an act of history remains to be performed. Which does not mean that this is a land to be mechanically parcelled out. It will be necessary to recognize the aims toward which these regions were historically striving before the Prussian annexation. Those very aims today constitute the alternative to their present effacement within the Reich.

North Germany is divided into four political regions, of which each has a different character, a different tradition, a different destiny, and, so to speak, a different direction of gaze: the Rhineland, Lower Saxony, Saxony–Thuringia, and Prussia. The last two already possess political consciousness and shape, and all they now need is a rectification of frontiers, indeed a drastic one in the case of Prussia. On the other hand, the first two have more or less a sense of racial unity and a highly distinctive character. Lower Saxony has also the remains of a political point of view, though more local than national. The task of state-building, however, still remains to be done in both cases. There is nothing depressing about this task but something extremely inspiring, if one investigates the cultural and political prospects of these two states of the future.

5. THE RHINELAND. A medium-sized state of about sixteen million inhabitants, it comprises the so-named Saar district, the present-day Prussian "Rhine Province," Westphalia, Hesse, Hesse–Nassau, and Waldeck (whether one should include the Palatinate, which geographically belongs to it, but traditionally to Bavaria, is a special question which we shall not pursue in these pages). To name its big cities would perhaps give the clearest picture of this region, for it is the most urbanized of all German states, a highly industrialized, commercialized, and intellectual country like Holland and Belgium. Within its borders are found Düsseldorf, Cologne, Bonn, Aix-la-Chapelle, Coblence, Wiesbaden, Mainz, Darmstadt, Mannheim, Frankfurt, Cassel, Essen, Dortmund, Wuppertal, and Münster. It is the land of big cities, of heavy industry,

of great commercial concentrations; yet withal the land of wine, of cathedrals and imperial tombs, the very heart of the Holy Roman Empire of the German nation degraded today to a "province" of its former colony Prussia.

Europe would be incomplete without an independent and nationally-conscious Rhineland. To find in its place a Prussian province signifies a sad void in the entire continent. For the Rhineland occupies a special site, the ancient preordained meeting place of the Latin and Teutonic spirits, a thousand times consecrated by great art and great history. Here belongs no Prussian province (nor French, for that matter), but a land for itself, with its own political personality and mission, a land to serve as sluice between France and Germany, to reconcile the two and, in the role of middleman, acquire the virtues of both. For the link is now missing between Holland and Belgium in the north and Switzerland in the south, the chain of the Rhine states is sundered—of those bright, bland, urbane states which could be the most wealthy, versatile, and flourishing in Europe. This favored west-eastern land, which more than any is showered with light from all sides, ever appears on the stage of Europe's history as Regnum Lothari, as Upper Burgundy—and ever vanishes; and on each occasion a brilliant epoch vanishes with it. Europe would be the poorer without a Rhineland.

No region in Germany presents so much hope—and so many problems. To discover the soul of this land of the future is not difficult. But its body must first be created. The Rhineland, unlike the South German states, has no living historical form which has merely to be resuscitated. Its present sad lot is the result of a long process of historical disintegration. It has few supports for the construction of a state. There is no nucleus, such as a dynasty or long-standing political institutions. And such cannot be transplanted from outside, least of all by force of arms. Napoleon's "Kingdom of Westphalia" and Poincaré's "Rhenish Republic" were both failures, and that despite the existence then and now of a separatist movement. They were failures, however, from which we need not draw the moral of resignation, but of prudence. This of all states in Germany cannot be improvised. It must be carefully planned.

The seats of government and administration created in the course of the Rhineland's history, are the bishoprics and the towns. We must proceed from them to find the natural political structure of the country: a sort of aristocratic republic, in which ecclesiastical and academical as well as urban and industrial elements can play their part. We can perhaps visualize one of the three archbishops (of Cologne, Mainz, and Trier in rotation) as the symbolical Head of the State, and a Chamber representing the towns and an ecclesiastical-academic Upper House as the legislative bodies; the substructure could be formed by the workers' trade unions, miners' associations, and professional guilds on the one hand, and the administrations of the churches and universities on the other. The country must create a synthesis out of the streamlined practical organization of an industrial country and the hierarchical institutions of a state whose essential mission is not political, but spiritual—a great task for German liberalism now become conservative. Incidentally, it is more important than it may seem that the preliminaries of state building should, in this instance, be carried out in Paris rather than London.

However, in the case of the other large North-German state that is to be constructed anew, they should undoubtedly be executed in London. I speak of:

6. LOWER SAXONY. Just as the Rhineland directs her gaze toward France and may be said to interpret French culture to the Germans, so does Lower Saxony look upon England. The historical connection of Hanover with England is not quite a fortuitous accident: it is supported by ethnic and social affinities. The "Anglo–German counsinhood" is a speech-day phrase; the Anglo–Lower–Saxon cousinhood is a fact.

Lower Saxony is clearly distinct from its Western and Eastern German neighbors. In contrast to the Catholic, industrial, urban, and continental Rhineland, it is Protestant, agrarian, commercial, and seafaring. In contrast to the militarist, bureaucratic, restless Prussia with its cult of efficiency, it is peaceable, individualistic, static, and lethargic (even the activity of Hamburg is easygoing compared with the febrile exertion of Berlin). In character and temperament, it belongs just as much to the English–Scandinavian cultural sphere, as to the German (and this is the very mission of the German states—each, proceeding from a different direction, assimilates and cultivates every European cultural influence, and thus makes it possible to savor all the diverse qualities of the continent in German terms). It is a Nordic land with a deep instinct for individual independence, unflustered, stationary conservatism, pacific dignity, with a conception of civilization whose symbol is not a bottle of wine, but a cake of soap, reserved, sparing of words, its gaze silently averted from the continent to the ocean. Its deepest trait comes of its Viking blood. Lower Saxony is he only region where the popularity of the Kaiser's colonial and naval policy was not due to the "also" mentality, but to the region's nature and instinct. German seafarers and colonial pioneers always came almost exclusively of Lower Saxon stock; and the country will probably continue to turn out sailors and colonizers. It would, perhaps, not be impossible to give to Lower Saxony a chance of colonization which healthy prudence forbids us to offer the Reich; for Lower Saxony is naturally endowed in this respect, whereas the Reich's colonial policy would be a mere "also" policy with ulterior motives of war and domination.

Lower Saxony consists of the Hanseatic city republics of Bremen, Hamburg, and Lübeck, the Kingdom of Hanover and the Grand Duchies of Oldenburg, Lippe, Brunswick, Mecklenburg, and Schleswig–Holstein, a vast region with a population of about 10 million. It would probably be wisest to preserve its historical structure and link the states in a loose union. For this profoundly conservative and profoundly nonpolitical land is no place for newfangled conceptions and experiments. It is a land where things stir slowly and endure long. Here seventy years of Reich history scarcely count for more than an episode, whose passing the Saxon will register with a calm nod. He will outlive all that now exists. The sense of political separateness is as universal and self-evident in the three Hanseatic cities as only perhaps in Bavaria. The Reich is good enough for an excursion, but little else. When the Nazi "Reich governor" disappears, the Senate and the Citizen's Council will continue to rule the land with rather less disturbance—that is all. Edifices almost blameless of history, the idyllic agrarian Grand Duchies—in which politics are amiably conducted behind the scenes, and are of no more account in the life of the inhabitants than the weather—represent the inherited and traditional expressions of their ethnic and linguistic diversities. The Mecklenburger is of another stock and speaks a Low German rather different to that of the Schleswig–Holsteiner; no reason here to alter frontiers and political institutions. Their erstwhile Serene Highnesses can move into their castles once again, as a sign that the political carnival is over and normal life to be resumed.

A graver political problem is that of Hanover, one of the largest and most important states in this region. Unlike the South German states, the Hanseatic cities and even Mecklenburg and Brunswick, Hanover was not mildly and considerately allowed to preserve her identity as a state nor cajoled with blandishments into the Reich; instead, her king was driven from his throne and her territory brutally annexed and reduced to the rank of colony by Prussia in 1866, just as Austria was subjugated by the Reich in 1938. Hanover has never forgiven this. Through two generations of Kaisers, she elected her own Hanoverian deputies to the Reichstag, who, barely interested in imperial politics, thick-skinned and insensitive to the jeers at their hopelessly outmoded ideas, intoned their monotonous *ceterum censeo;* they wanted their state and king back! They sat in the Reichstag beside the "minorities" of the Kaiser's Reich— Hanoverians with Alsatians, Poles, and Danes! And this mentality is not yet dead in the third generation. Even in the parliamentary elections of 1932, when the question of he restoration of Hanover or its dynasty seemed ludicrously inopportune, when Germany was split over the question "Hitler or no," 75,000 voters in Hanover announced their indifference about the latter and, in effect, declared: let him rule the Reich who will; they wanted back their Hanover and their Hanoverian monarch and, accordingly, were electing their one Hanoverian deputy. One may smile, but the deep, all-enduring, tenacious nature of this state tradition is obvious. It must be exploited. Incidentally, the Pretender to the Hanoverian throne is also an English duke—an historical coincidence which happily symbolizes the great affinities to England not only of Hanover, but of all Lower Saxony.

7. SAXONY-THURINGIA. Here again we find an already evolved, racially unified land with a sense of cohesion intact: the Kingdom of Saxony. Expanded to embrace Saxony, arbitrarily snatched from it to form a Prussian province, and the kindred little state of Anhalt, it constitutes an industrial country of nearly 9 million inhabitants. Its people, despite the similarity of name, differ so fundamentally from the people of Lower Saxony in nature, temperament, and endowments, that one can almost speak of two races. Temperamentally, the Lower Saxons are the most conservative of Germans, the

Saxons the most flexible and enterprising; the Lower Saxons are the most exclusive and aloof, the Saxons the most sociable and argumentative; the Lower Saxons the most insular and quiet, the Saxons the most travel mad and rowdy. Beneath the present superficial unification of Germany, the border between the two Saxonies is no less clearly perceptible than any other racial frontier; language, morals, architecture, food, drink, mode of life, all differ. Nor is Saxony any less distinct from all other German ethnic groups. It is a clear, closed unit.

It is difficult to prophesy what spiritual role Saxony will play in the Europe to come; but it is most probable that it will very rapidly find one, one which is adapted to the basic conception of the new continent with almost exaggerated perfection. For it is a peculiarity of this strange people that it seizes a situation and adjusts itself to it almost too speedily; not from lack of character, but from excess of mental agility and love of experiment. Saxony is almost a caricature of Germany in this; to grasp an idea there means to appropriate and execute it with extreme thoroughness; and the "bright" Saxons grasp very quickly. They were the most devoted and convinced German adherents of Napoleon—and the first to desert when he erred in his calculations. They fought fiercely against the Prussians in 1866, and in the following years were the first to accept and celebrate the foundation of the Prussian Reich. In the days of the republic they formed the "reddest" region of Germany—and today the most loyal to the Nazis. They have "grasped" Nazism more quickly than other Germans; and they will also grasp more quickly a superior conception opposed to Nazism. They are not, as one might think, born traitors. Their devotion to a cause, every moment it lasts, is wholly honest and ardent. But they change loyalties every moment. They are the victims of their excessive "brightness," of their over-enterprising intelligence. They are weather-cocks whirled by the wind of every vigorous historical idea. It is doubtless true that the Saxons have entered the Reich more willingly than any other non–Prussian people. But this must not delude us. If particularism becomes the historical mode again, the Saxons will excel all others in their 100 percent gusto for it. Not to say that they are a contemptible race; nimble intellects, whatever their shady traits, have their advantages. They have equipped Saxony in the past—

and will do so in the future—to make a success of almost each of its many incarnations.

Thuringia, adjacent and akin, stands politically by the side of Saxony and seems destined to form with her—if with any state—a larger political unit. She has, as a state, her own individual and unique potentialities and traditions, which deserve to fulfil themselves yet anew: her small ducal and grand ducal courts, patrons, outstanding and unsurpassed in Germany, of the noblest German culture. These duchies and grand duchies, too small to pursue politics, have for long pursued—civilization. Thus Saxony–Weimar nurtures a great tradition of poetry and intellect, and Saxony–Meiningen of the theater. To destroy these minute but infinitely cultured states, with their innate traditions and values, for the sake of forming a larger and more "practical" administrative unit, would be crass folly, of which not only the Nazis have been guilty, but also their Republican predecessors.

Strangely enough, the republic which selected Weimar as the birthplace of its constitution, abolished it simultaneously for the sake of that larger but meaningless structure, Thuringia! Thuringia, on a microscopic scale, symbolizes the problem of the Reich: that unification and centralization becomes often a senseless act of destruction; that the new and larger organism thus created has infinitely less character, feeling, and soul than the smaller ones it has devoured. Weimar and Gera, Gotha and Meiningen were interesting, so long as they were seats of their small patriarchal Muse-ruled courts; they lost all significance the moment they became Thuringian provincial towns with fiscal or administrative offices instead of a prince's palace. It is my firm conviction that the Thuringian "miniature-courts" must be restored, just because they are "constitutional curiosities," just because they represent something that is not to be found elsewhere: courts of the Muses, cultural centers, patriarchal idylls run by the state and endowed by its rulers.

It would, of course, be scarcely advisable for each court to have its own Foreign Office, its own envoys abroad, and its own customs organization. In all such matters the Thuringian duchies and grand duchies must be linked with the kingdom of Saxony, though not at the cost of their independence. Thus coordinated in external matters, the larger unit of Saxony–Thuringia would embrace some 11 million souls.

8. PRUSSIA. The real Prussia, excluding its "must-be-Prussian" German conquests, consists of Berlin and its hinterland of four agricultural provinces, Brandenburg, Pomerania, East Prussia, and Silesia. It is a country of about 16 million inhabitants, of whom more than a fourth live in the metropolis.

If the German states are reconstituted, Prussia will face a similar problem to that which confronted Austria in 1919; with an imperial past ending in tragedy and collapse it must be resolved to turn over a new leaf and formulate new precepts of life. That is obviously a more arduous task than that engaging the attention of the other states, who have merely to equip themselves again for their original destiny. Thus it must be expected that in Prussia—after the liquidation of the Nazis, which here, as everywhere, must be the unpleasant but indispensable immediate duty of the new state—the urge to resume the policy of Frederick and Bismarck would die harder than elsewhere. However, this does not justify—rather, it militates against—deliberately making a scapegoat of Prussia after the war and, by means of penalties, rendering its political future more precarious than that of the other states. The Austrian tragedy has clearly revealed the consequences of such a policy. Political wisdom demands that the new and more modest existence of such shrunken states be made as bearable and attractive as possible and that they be helped to salve their wounds. The contrary would be foolish, and also wrongful. As a political idea, "Prussia" may historically have been an important cause of the present catastrophe. As a state, Prussia is no more guilty than any other. Neither are the Prussians, the present occupants of the country, more guilty than any other Germans (Berlin is, in fact, one of the cities with the highest percentage of disloyal and anti–Nazi Germans). The guilty are the Nazis, and they are today a German, not a specifically Prussian, phenomenon. In order that the conscience of the world may be appeased and international morality rehabilitated, it is they who must pay the inexorable penalty, whether they are Bavarians, Prussians, or Saxons, and not the people of any particularly selected German state.

The problem is not how Prussia can be most effectively punished, but how she can be helped to new obligations and conceptions as a state. But such fundamental attributes cannot be imposed from outside. They must have their roots in the history and spirit of the land. Perhaps Prussia's lot in this respect is not so hopeless as it may appear at first sight.

In our analysis of Prussian Conservatism we briefly touched upon the fact that, apart from Frederickian expansionism, there is a second, very different Prussian tradition, which, for half a century, between Napoleon and Bismarck, seemed to rule supreme. Briefly expressed, it was based on an attempt to turn inward, away from military expansion toward cultural intensification. For fifty long years, the inherent and ineradicable Prussian virtues of industry and efficiency served the pacific ideals of civilization, and Prussia strove not for the propagation of her own stylelessness, but for the elaboration of her own style; and not, one must admit, without some success. It is not altogether an idle reflection that the three principle Prussian qualities; energy, precision, and thrift, have aesthetic value. They are morally colorless and, harnessed to an unmoral policy, can create havoc. But they are the virtues of an artist and can bear fruit if they help to promote, instead of the will to power, a cultural ideal, a specifically Prussian ideal that peaceably vies with the ideals of other German and European countries. So it was once for half a century, and that half-century has left behind an enduring product—Berlin.

Every traveler will have remarked the strange fact that this cosmopolitan, peaceable, skeptical, and intelligent city bears no resemblance to the gray, soldierly, stoic Prussian State, whose spiritual capital is Potsdam. Berlin has always felt rather detached and fundamentally disinterested about Potsdamized Prussia. Only once did Berlin become the heart of the country, in the years 1810 to 1860, when Prussia managed to Berlinize itself, to become pacific, intellectual, literary, and liberal. Berlin was not Prussian, as Vienna is Austrian, Munich Bavarian, and Cologne a Rhineland city; it was not even German, as Paris is French and London English. Berlin was Berlinized—it cannot be otherwise expressed—and cosmopolitan. It was, let us say it with Prussian precision, the very essence of an international metropolis. It had, so to speak, roots in the air. It extracted its life force not from the native soil of the surrounding country (out of whose inhabitants it was yet able to make good Berliners with amazing speed), but from all the great cities of the world. It is Europe's greatest cultural market. It did not work up Prussian raw materials, but it assimilated, criticized, and bartered the manufactured products of the cultures of London and Paris, Vienna and Prague, New York and Rome. Without itself being musically productive, it was for decades the world's unrivalled musical capital; and it was always striving to be the world's literary and theatrical center. In Berlin, the strange, unproductive but universal and untiring industry of Prussia had turned to spiritual energy, and had thereby lost its dangerous vandal character. Potsdam instinctively yearned to make of the world a military conquest; Berlin to make an intellectual conquest; to know, compare, criticize, experiment. The temperamental impulse is the same, but, whereas Prussianism destroys, Berlinism affords reason, gaiety, and profit. The future Prussia must be christened—Berlin.

This brief and sketchy survey lays no claim to finality; it makes no attempt to provide a complete and detailed program, but only traces the theme and basis of fertile discussions in the future. It should, however, suffice to prove one thing: the division of Germany into states can be a natural and organic process, and advance the security of Europe, as well as the special gifts and mission of Germany. A German loses the best part of his character when he concentrates on his "Germanness" and becomes nationalist; for to be German means, on the very contrary, to be universal and Catholic. A Germany dragooned and immured within the Reich loses significance and soul; it ceases to be German; it falls ill, despairs, and ends in Nazism, a political werewolf. What today makes the German Reich the scourge of Europe, no less afflicts, as a scourge, the life of every German. This is the essence of the present tragedy; its recognition will provide the germ cell of future peace. That same "Never again!" which daily sounds more loudly as the clarion call of France and England, can and must become the watchword of Germany. The reconstruction of the German states as the pillars of Germany's real destiny can become the common aim in war and peace both of the Allies and anti–Nazi Germans. And thus will it not only determine the issue of the war, but provide the basis of a lasting peace, unburdened by hate and desire for revenge.

Three things, however, must be clearly realized: (1) Peace with these states must be a real peace; that is, it must be the beginning of cooperation and friendship and not a measure of penalization and repression.

We must fully understand that we cannot both get rid of the German Reich and, identifying its "Succession States" with it at the same time, punish them for its sins. It must be the one or the other! If we treat the "Succession States" as we would the conquered Reich, it will have the natural result of their continuing to feel like the vanquished Reich—and rallying again to the Reich at the first favorable opportunity in order to seek vengeance. If we want the new states to take root and endure, and the Reich mentality to die—of which there is every possibility after the catastrophe of Nazism—we must give them a fair chance. Foreign armies of occupation, levy of reparations, moral discrimination, and one-sided limitations of sovereign rights would not constitute such a chance. The Treaty of Versailles erred in "punishing" the Reich and yet letting it survive. The right course would be to put an end to the Reich; and thus the need of political "punishment" would not arise. Let us realize that the idea of punishing a *state* is senseless. Men can be punished; and indeed the punishment of the Nazis for their crimes in peace and war is an essential condition of a lasting peace. As to the states, they can be abolished and replaced by others; and this is what should be done to the German Reich. Thus both sin would be expiated and peace ensured. To found states in order that they may live and prosper, and then to imperil their existence with penalties, would be to destroy the entire conception upon which the future peace of Europe must rest.

(2) Germany can only be rebuilt within the framework of an economically and politically reconstructed Europe.

It must be clearly realized that none of the German states is an independent, self-sufficient economic unit. This is an advantage on the one hand, for it precludes any attempt at an unnatural policy of economic autarchy. On the other, an effective international economy is needed in order that these states may find work and ensure the means of subsistence. The problem of its organization must be tackled today; the vast international projects to forestall the economic dislocation at the end of the war, must be devised today: to improvise them at the moment of crisis would be too late. They must form part of the peace treaty. And the roles of the future German states in the economic resurrection of Europe must be severally allocated in advance, to each according to its economic capacities and potentialities. Each must have its appointed task. The Germans are one of the most business-minded and industrious races. There is nothing more dangerous than unemployed Germans. Nothing more horrifying for Germans than the prospect of idle hands and no work.

A second consideration: seventy years of a conjoint economy cannot be ended by a stroke of the pen. Many economic bonds exist between the German states, which cannot be sundered without causing grave damage. On the other hand it would be dangerous to continue to use them to link the "Succession States" of the Reich in isolation from the rest of the world; for they could easily become the nuclei of a new Reich. The right policy would be to extend these economic links beyond Germany. Thus, for example, it would be unwise to divide the German railways into eight state railway systems; but cannot they be absorbed in a European system? Again, Germany today represents a single customs unit. Eight customs organizations in place of one would scarcely constitute economic progress. But, would not the end of the war signal, at long last, the moment for a European or at least a Central European customs union?

These questions demand a book for themselves. We do not intend here to do more than register their existence, their urgency, and the crude outline of the measures necessary for their solution.

Similar problems exist in the sphere of international political organization. The very removal of the menacing German Reich and the peril that it incarnates, clears the way for the restoration of the "European Concert," that is, of the stabilized, secure, and organized coexistence of the European nations. And this road must, in fact, be pursued. The experience of the past twenty years has shown that such matters cannot be left to the future. New organizations of international security and cooperation must be created when things are still fluid; which means immediately after the war, and not long after when they are again crystallizing.

The composition of the new "European Concert" would differ from that of the nineteenth century. The old was a quartet or sextet of Great Powers. The new will be an orchestra of small and middle-sized states. An orchestra demands different and more disciplined methods of work and organization than a chamber music band. Small states have greater need of security than Great Powers. It will, therefore, be esssential at once to devise and elaborate the international and supernational organizations which will form the basis of the new European polity. It is only within the framework of such a European system that the new plan for Germany can be consummated.

(3) The success of the whole operation depends largely on how and by whom it is undertaken. A state never frees itself from the grip of the law that determined its birth; the history of the German Reich proves this. It would be an irrevocable misfortune if German states could only boast of being reborn of the dismemberment of the German Reich.

They would then probably be no more than limbs of the German Reich, which, alive but invisible in the background, would one favorable day reappear in all its palpable reality. If the German states with which we are in future to live in lasting peace are to be fit for life, they must be resurrected in a natural manner; that is to say, their future rulers and administrators must be their founders. And it would be a good thing if, for as many of them as possible, their birth were not the outcome of defeat; if they could be helped to a portion of their new history, to the beginnings of their state myth—to something, for instance, like the annals of the Czech and Polish Legions during the World War. This can be achieved, and must be immediately tackled—with the aid of the German emigrants.

The first practical step in a positive and constructive policy toward Germany must consist in a positive and constructive policy toward the German émigrés. Let us at last grasp the great opportunity presented by the offer of cooperation of large numbers of the German political intelligentsia now living outside Germany and of a large mass of men who, mortal foes of the Nazis, are numerous enough to form at least a symbolic kernel of a German army to fight by the side of the Allies. It is not enough to treat the emigrants with mere humanity: political use must be made of them. It is not enough to leave them at large: they must be harnessed to the common cause. It is not enough to sigh and resign oneself to the presence of seventy to eighty thousand "enemy aliens" in England, not to mention the whispering campaign against them.

Above all, we must today set up organizations and perform the preliminary work in order tomorrow to found and govern the new German states. They can begin modestly, in the form of enquiry committees for Austria, Bavaria, the Rhineland, and the others, for the purpose of gathering and collating facts, discussing questions of propaganda, and elaborating plans for the future constitutional and administrative systems. The more they acquire the bone and body of organization, the more they find means of threading contact with the internal opposition within their own states, the more will they automatically assume the menacing authority of governments in exile. The decisive hour for which they must work will strike when the war has been carried on to German soil. A new state government must be ready to seize power in any such region, to conclude a separate peace, institute courts to punish the Nazis for their crimes, liquidate the Nazi administration, replace it with new institutions, and mobilize the land in the task of liberating Germany. Such action in any given region can have undreamed-of consequences throughout Germany, very different from the effects of a military occupation of a German frontier district. Such will be the first moment to count on internal revolts against the iron might of the Nazi regime. But this moment must be carefully contrived.

It seems time to begin to plan it; although it needs quick and hard thinking and lessons in new political formulas. When the sacrifice of his life is daily demanded of the ordinary man on the battlefield, it is not too much to ask of the politicians, whether they be Englishmen, Frenchmen, or emigrant Germans, that they should not spare their energies. Imagination, resolve, courage—these, in war, are the indispensable virtues no less of the politician than of the officer at the front. Allied statesmen and Germany's exiled leaders are on their mettle.

It is the role of the German opposition parties to realize that every attempt to save Germany from self-destruction while preserving the German Reich is no more rational than to try to wash without wetting oneself. From this knowledge they must draw their conclusions.

It is the role of the Western powers to realize that peace with the reinstated German states will serve them better than a temporary subjugation of Germany. And, accordingly, they must act.

It is the role of both to realize that they are allies, and lead their joint forces into battle.

Both sides are far removed from such knowledge. The fate of Europe depends on acquiring it with lightning speed. For it alone provides the great and inspiring opportunity of this war; the only opportunity of spiritual conquest as well as military victory; the only opportunity of loosening the German knot without hacking it; the only opportunity of rescuing Europe from Germany as well as Germany from herself.

The one is impossible without the other.

Translated by Wilfrid David

Titles Available in
The German Library

All titles available at your bookstore or
from Continuum International
15 East 26 Street, New York, NY 10010
www.continuumbooks.com

Beginnings to 1750

Volume 1
GERMAN EPIC POETRY: THE
NIEBELUNGENLIED, THE OLDER
LAY OF HILDEBRAND, AND
OTHER WORKS

Volume 2
Wolfram von Eschenbach
PARZIVAL

Volume 3
Gottfried von Strassburg
TRISTAN AND ISOLDE

Volume 4
Hartmann von Aue, Konrad
von Würzburg, Gartenaere, and
Others
GERMAN MEDIEVAL TALES

Volume 5
Hildegard of Bingen, Meister
Eckhart, Jacob Böhme,
Heinrich Seuse, Johannes
Tauler, and Angelus Silesius
GERMAN MYSTICAL WRITINGS

Volume 6
Erasmus, Luther, Müntzer,
Johann von Tepl, Sebastian
Brant, Conrad Celtis, Sebastian
Lotzer, Rubianus, von Hutten
GERMAN HUMANISM AND
REFORMATION

Volume 7
Grimmelshausen, Leibniz,
Opitz, Weise and Others
SEVENTEENTH CENTURY
GERMAN PROSE

Titles Available in The German Library

Titles Available in The German Library

Titles Available in The German Library

Titles Available in The German Library

Titles Available in The German Library